Praise for Nanovation

Nanovation not only captures the ... ome true; it shows us that what is good for business can and should be good for the world. The promise of the Tata Nano is saving and enriching lives while growing a business. We call it "Performance with Purpose." If you're interested in stoking the fires of innovation and making a profit while making a difference, *Nanovation* is a must read.

— **Indra K. Nooyi**
chairman and CEO, PepsiCo

Vibrant and energetic, the passion of the authors of *Nanovation* reflects that of the innovators it chronicles. The book not only recounts the revolutionary tale of the Nano but presents a practical guide for creating a radical culture of innovation. In an insightful manner, Kevin, Jackie, and Dain have challenged the new generation of entrepreneurs, executives, and business leaders to think and dream big.

— **N. R. Narayana Murthy**
founder-chairman and chief mentor,
Infosys Ltd.

Nanovation is a compelling look into what it takes to knock down the doors of business-as-usual. It reminds us that innovation is the lifeblood of any company. At Southwest, we are constantly looking for new ways to unleash the imagination and ingenuity of our people. The Freiberg's deep dive into a company that transformed an entire industry is loaded with hands-on advice—and a warning not to downsize your dreams!

— **Gary Kelly**
chairman, president and CEO,
Southwest Airlines

In a world where many business leaders focus only on short-term stock ticks, the great companies take a longer view. This is the story of a company that's been around for more than a century and continues to lead in innovation. Learn what you can build when you focus intently on the needs of customers. *Nanovation* is for leaders who want to leave a lasting legacy in the world.

— **Chris Connor**
chairman and CEO, Sherwin-Williams Company

I am a big fan of Kevin and Jackie Freiberg. They seek out business good news stories that teach and inspire. This time they found a beauty in India with Tata Motors. Read *Nanovation* and learn what you can do to create an innovative culture in your organization.

— **Ken Blanchard**
coauthor *One Minute Manager, Full Steam Ahead,* and *Lead with LUV*

Nanovation is a must read for any leader. It shows how an innovative idea, and a passion to make that idea a reality, can truly be a major life changer for the consumer and the company. Every organization should be focused on executing the next best idea to wow customers and win them for life. This book will get you thinking precisely that!

— **Eric Danziger**
CEO, Wyndham Hotel Group

In baseball we are always looking for new ways to gain competitive advantage. Sometimes that means stepping out of the comfort zone and doing what others think is crazy. *Nanovation* has strengthened my resolve to question the unquestionable. This book is for leaders who want to shake it up. And watch out! If Ratan Tata ever becomes a manager in the Major Leagues we all have a lot to be worried about!

— **Bruce Bochy**
manager, 2010 World Champion San Francisco Giants

Nanovation is a compelling book about the power of a dream and the people who made it come true. This is a well-told story of an aspiration that drove design innovation and the winning spirit that culminated in the production of the Nano. The Nano stands for true innovation for the emerging markets, a sterling example of a bottom of the pyramid product, which will redefine the global automobile market in the coming years.

— **V. K. Kamath**
non-executive chairman, ICICI Bank
and chairman, Infosys

Nanovation makes thrilling reading. Nothing in the recent period captures the promise of India better than the invention of the Nano. The Tatas have demonstrated that the seemingly impossible is possible through frugal engineering and a can-do spirit. This book is a must read for anyone wanting to start something big by thinking small.

— **Deepak S. Parekh**
chairman, HDFC Ltd.

Nanovation is the story of a movement that's sweeping the world, a movement filled with purpose, a movement led by people who want to make a better life available to everyone. Consumers around the world are not going to spend their money with any company that's not in the business of improving lives, and that's what *Nanovation* is all about. If you're a leader who's on fire to make a difference, you have to read this book.

— **Roy Spence**
chairman GSD&M Advertising and
CEO of The Purpose Institute

Once again, the Freibergs take you on an exhilarating journey to achieving elegant solutions that move an organization from the impossible to the possible. It all comes down to people: depending on, deferring to, and trusting the right people within your organization; and listening to, respecting and treating the consumer with dignity. A great book if you want to be the best you can be.

— **Mike Murphy**
president and CEO, Sharp HealthCare

Quite simply the most practical book about innovation I've ever read.

— **Vijay Govindarajan**
professor at Tuck at Dartmouth;
professor in residence and chief
innovation consultant at *General Electric*

True innovation, or *Nanovation* as the authors call it, happens when a firm strives for the triple bottom line—social and environmental performance that go hand in hand with financial performance. This must-read book tells you how a visionary chairman and a committed top management team can together unleash the creative energies of younger employees within a company. It is by far the most lucid and comprehensive narrative that I have read about the Tata Nano.

— **Bala Chakravarthy**
Shell chair professor of sustainable
business growth, IMD, Switzerland

A great read! A bold look at innovation, which will be the "differentiator" for sustained growth in this decade! Practical, applicable, memorable, and entertaining.

— **Jeff Simmons**
president, Elanco Animal Health

If you want to learn from a world-class example of real-world innovation, the Freibergs and Dunston have captured it in *Nanovation*. This story not only motivates and inspires; it offers a blueprint for success. If you want to expand your capacity to innovate and develop leaders who will step out and do it, this book will show you what it takes.

— **Chad Linebaugh**
general manager, Sundance Resort

Nanovation is more than just a story about a car. It's about leaders who color outside the lines, inspire others to reach new heights, and foster groundbreaking innovation. Read it and you'll learn how to achieve what most people think is impossible!

— **Hugh Gouldthorpe**
senior vice president, "Head
Cheerleader," Owens & Minor

This book provides fascinating insight into how world-leading design, manufacture, and production teams are brought together to develop and build one of the most innovative cars ever conceived. It demonstrates how the bold vision of Ratan Tata and his team was realized not only by outstanding engineering skills, but also by their determination to build a car that would enrich the lives of millions of people.

— **Professor A.J. Kinloch**
head of department of mechanical
engineering and professor of
adhesion, Imperial College London

Noticing a pressing popular need, unrealizable without the creation of a magical mix of affordable design, process innovation, and product development is the foundation of this compelling story. Technology is fundamental but it is never enough; social sensibility, managerial expertise, and ambitious goals for social and economic transformation are all part of this life changing narrative.

— **Professor Dame Sandra Dawson**
University of Cambridge

Nanovation is a unique example of cutting edge innovation and leadership excellence. It shows you how Tata Motors created a culture of innovation and made an impossible dream reality. This is a wonderful story about how technology driven enterprises can play a role in improving the quality of life for a large segment of consumers. If you want to create a competitive mind-set that achieves breakthroughs in businesses, this book answers the call.

— **Dr. Hischam El Agamy**
executive director, International
Institute of Management
Development—IMD, Lausanne
Switzerland

nanovation

nanovation

nanovation

How a Little Car Can Teach the World
to Think Big and Act Bold

By the coauthors of the international best seller
NUTS! Southwest Airlines' Crazy Recipe
for Business and Personal Success

Kevin & Jackie Freiberg
and Dain Dunston

THOMAS NELSON
Since 1798

NASHVILLE   DALLAS   MEXICO CITY   RIO DE JANEIRO

Published in Nashville, Tennessee, by Thomas Nelson. Thomas Nelson is a registered trademark of Thomas Nelson, Inc.

Thomas Nelson, Inc., titles may be purchased in bulk for educational, business, fund-raising, or sales promotional use. For information, please e-mail SpecialMarkets@ThomasNelson.com.

ISBN 978-1-59555-525-0 (TP)

Library of Congress Cataloging-in-Publication Data

Freiberg, Kevin, 1958-
  Nanovation : how a little car can teach the world to think big / Kevin & Jackie Freiberg, and Dain Dunston.
    p. cm.
  ISBN 978-1-59555-442-0
  1. Tata Motors. 2. Automobile industry and trade--India. 3. Nano automobile.
I. Freiberg, Jackie, 1963- II. Dunston, Dain. III. Title.
  HD9710.I44T384 2011
  338.4'76292220954--dc22   2011010641

Printed in the United States of America

12 13 14 15 16 QG 1 9 8 7 6 5 4 3 2

To Prakash Idnani, who swung the doors of
India wide open, enthusiastically welcomed
us with open arms, filled our pipeline with one
brilliant idea after another, and disrupted our
lives forever.

If you want to stand at the crossroads of where
indefatigable meets sheer optimism and five-
star hospitality, have a cup of tea with Prakash.

Autocar India

Contents

Prologue

We began with a cup of tea in Mumbai.

In February 2007 Kevin was invited to India to lead a three-day leadership program for the senior executives of Tata Motors. He was so impressed with the Tata Motors executive team that when he headed back to India in 2008 for another event, he stopped in for tea with Ravi Kant, then Tata Motors' managing director, at Bombay House, the Tata Group headquarters in Mumbai. This book is the result of what Ravi Kant and Kevin saw in those tea leaves.

Their conversation quickly focused on what had become the most exciting automotive news in the world, the January 2008 unveiling ceremony for the Tata Nano at the ninth Auto Expo in New Delhi. The more Ravi Kant talked about the Nano story, the global reception of the car, and the history behind it, the more fascinated and intrigued we became. Kevin left India with a burning desire to write the Nano story. Soon after, we proposed doing a case study and writing a book on the incredible journey of innovation behind the Nano.

We are drawn to stories about companies we'd love to work in, cultures we think are cool, leaders we would follow, and innovations we wished we had created.

When we proposed writing a detailed account of the Nano story, we knew it would require extensive research, so we requested unlimited access to the players—the design team, Ratan Tata, other Tata executives, dealers, vendors, and Nano owners. They kindly accepted, and thus began our journey to get to know the inner workings of who, how, and what led to the development of the least expensive—and arguably most significant—car in the world, the Nano.

Why is the Nano so significant? Because it represents the leading edge of a revolution in business thinking and design we believe will have a profound effect on everything that comes after it, not just in the automotive industry, not just in India, but in every industry around the world.

WE CALL IT NANOVATION

Nanovation is the story of how a little car is teaching the world to think big and just as important, act bold. It's the story of an incredible team of engineers, designers, and businesspeople who set out to develop a safe, affordable, all-weather form of transportation for a vast and growing market—Indian families emerging into the middle class—and solve a problem that was holding them back: how to get around.

Funny how much that last sentence sounds like Southwest Airlines, whose story we told in our international best seller, *NUTS! Southwest Airlines' Crazy Recipe for Business and Personal Success*. Like Southwest Airlines, the Tata Nano is also

- A PRODUCT BUILT AROUND AN EGALITARIAN CAUSE. Southwest was founded based on a dream to democratize the skies. The Nano was founded based on a dream to democratize the roads.

- A STORY FILLED WITH LESSONS OF LEADERSHIP, VISION, PERSEVERANCE, DETERMINATION, AND AN EGALITARIAN WORK ETHIC. Like everything else, it's not a story of a car, but a story about the heights to which the human spirit can rise—a story about the people behind the car.

- A DAVID AND GOLIATH STORY. Tata Motors, the underdog in the industry, fought to bring safety, value, and status to millions, against impossible odds. And while the company was doing it, Tata Motors emerged on the global stage to buy the legendary brands Jaguar and Land Rover. Three major carriers—Braniff, Continental, and Texas International—did everything they could to stop Southwest from flying, but they only made the company what it has become. For both companies, opposition made the teams even more determined to get it right.

- AN IMPOSSIBLE DREAM. Building a car for only Rs. 100,000 (the 1 lakh car) was an achievement that many naysayers said couldn't be done. People said Southwest would never survive by offering original fares of $15 or less.

- LOVED BY THE PEOPLE. The Nano has created a cultlike following. Like the customers of MINI, the VW Bug, and Southwest Airlines, people want to be a part of the community the Nano is creating.

- DRIVEN BY YOUNG VISIONARIES OF ALL AGES. Southwest Airlines was created by a young-at-heart team of people (many from outside the airline industry) who saw a market in opening up air travel to average people. The Nano was created by a young-at-heart team who was not bogged down and stalled by conventional, old-school industry rules. Instead team members brought a fresh, whatever-it-takes, collaborative spirit to the vision.

- CREATING CURIOSITY AND LEARNING. People interested in innovation, culture, and leadership will want to know how the team at Tata did it, just as they were fascinated by the Southwest story.

- A STORY OF MAJOR SETBACKS. Many hardships threatened to derail the product. A state-of-the-art production plant was shut down when it was near completion, launch dates were a moving target, yet the chairman, the team, and eager buyers held on to the dream of having the People's Car and democratizing the roads. From nasty competitors to the terrorist attack on 9/11, Southwest has had to overcome many crises that threatened its survival.

- A STORY OF LEADERSHIP AND CULTURE. Southwest has one of the most famous cultures in the world. Known for its irreverent, fun-loving spirit, it has one of the most creative and productive workforces in the world. At Tata, we discovered a story that starts in the 1800s, an incredible, against-the-odds saga of a fanatical focus on doing the right thing.

- A STORY OF A MAN WITH A MISSION. Ratan Tata, the chairman of the Tata Group, is a leader with some very similar characteristics to Herb Kelleher: an industry iconoclast, holding tight to a huge "impossible" dream; a thought leader with tremendous confidence, yet striking humility; a major catalyst for driving the vision; entrepreneurial to the bone; trusting deeply in the intelligence and character of his people; a service-over-self-interest leader who teaches, gets involved, and shows a contagious spirit of perseverance.

- A GREAT BUSINESS SUCCESS STORY. The people of Southwest Airlines changed the industry, the nation, and the world. The team behind the Nano is changing the industry, India, and the world.

- A STORY OF INSPIRATION. Southwest Airlines inspired a movement. People in the airline industry and beyond have borrowed from Southwest's unconventional approaches and transformed work environments everywhere. Nanovation is about inspiring a movement that can transform not just the process of radical innovation, but the lives of people, businesses, industries, and even nations.

Nanovation is the authorized story of an amazing car and the company that created it. The entire Tata organization graciously opened its doors to us and gave us unprecedented access to the innovators of Team Nano. The more we learned of Tata Motors and the vision, leadership, and legendary culture behind the design of the world's least expensive car, the more we are convinced it's a story with lessons for leaders at all levels and businesses in any industry anywhere.

DON'T WORRY IF YOU'RE NOT A CAR NUT

Nanovation isn't a book about cars; it's a book about people. It's about people thinking big, being brave, acting bold, and accomplishing the impossible. We believe it can inspire you to do the same. This book asks questions because you have the answers:

- Does your company consistently deliver products, services, and results that competitors say are impossible?
- Is your company a game changer that consistently redefines value chains, disrupts the industry, and delights customers?
- Is your company loaded with leaders who set the tone for innovation—leaders whom people love to follow?
- Is your company a career destination and a magnet for talent?
- Do big, bold, audacious ideas motivate everyone in your company to stretch and innovate? Are diverse opinions expected and revered? Is unconventional thinking valued?

- Do you reward and celebrate intelligent failure?
- Do your people see limitations as invitations to innovation and opportunities to differentiate, or excuses for why it can't be done?
- In a surplus society, a sea of sameness, are your products and services absolutely unforgettable? If your company were gone tomorrow, would it be missed—really?
- How bold and daring is your organization with regard to choosing the problems it takes on?
- How many projects under way in your company would score an eight or higher (on a scale of one to ten) on the game-changer scale?
- What if you got so caught up in a project that work became your calling—the cause for which you fight?
- Is yours the most respected company in your industry?
- Beyond all that, do you make a difference in the world?

Think back to a time when you were alive, inspired, fulfilled, and energized by the work you do. This isn't nirvana—it's a reality! Such work environments are real; they do exist. How can we be so sure? Because for more than twenty years we've been researching, writing, and speaking about leaders and companies that bring these practices to life.

Back in 1996 we wrote *NUTS!* as an in-depth, behind-the-scenes look at the greatest success story in the history of commercial aviation. Back then, people were searching for meaning in their work, ways to make work more fun, and ways to make a profit while making a difference. All of this hasn't changed. The search has only intensified.

Today, it doesn't matter where we are in the world, our clients are still asking, "How can we create a culture where impassioned people show up to work every day firing on all cylinders, where people are inspired to do their best work? How can we embrace opportunity-led change instead of being forced into crisis-led change? How do we make innovation a core capability and an essential part of everyone's job? How do we protect the environment by making our products more sustainable? How do we equip our people to take personal ownership for the success of the business? And how do we give back to the communities in which we do business?"

When you add the current economic, financial, and environmental concerns, the personal and business challenges we face today are even more daunting.

Clearly people are still hungry for success stories and still interested in learning and borrowing from our in-depth look at the unconventional leadership and culture behind Southwest Airlines.

If you are one of these people and you became a fan of *NUTS!*, we think you'll love this story, too.

WE CALLED IN THE CAVALRY!

Doing a case study of a great company is a long and arduous journey, and the time came when we realized we needed help on a story this big. That's why we invited Dain Dunston to coauthor *Nanovation* with us. His long experience working inside literally dozens of the world's innovative giants—particularly in the auto industry—helped steer us around many potholes and propelled us down the road with this story.

And along the way, we came upon an amazing insight: in the 1960s, we went to the moon to find innovation. Now, we're going to India.

Dr. Kevin Freiberg
Dr. Jackie Freiberg
Dain Dunston

NANOLINK

Want to see a video clip of the dreamer behind the dream? Catch Ratan Tata describing his vision for the Nano at www.freibergs.com/nanolink.

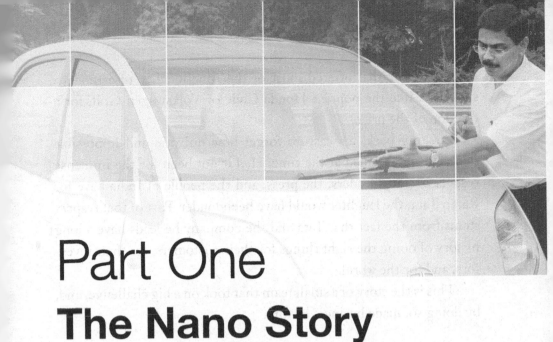

Part One
The Nano Story

I think that's when the whole thing started in my mind, looking at what is now a pretty familiar sight in India, an entire family traveling on a scooter with three or four family members.

RATAN TATA, CEO, TATA GROUP

T he story of the Tata Nano is one of radical innovation in the service of a cause. The cause was to reach out to those emerging from the bottom of the pyramid and offer them a safe and dignified alternative to the current, death-defying practice of putting an entire family on a scooter. The radical innovation was to take up to 50 percent of the cost out of manufacturing a small family car;

(Tata archives)

1

to make a car that offered most of the functionality of a modern small car, like the popular Honda Civic or Volkswagen Golf, for a fraction of the price.

Looking back, it's easy to forget how quixotic and impossible the challenge seemed at the time. Had it not been for the immense respect business leaders, the press, and the people of India have for Ratan Tata, the laughter would have been louder. Part of that respect stems from the fact that Tata and the company he leads have a long history of doing the right things for their customers, for their investors, and for the world.

This is the story of a small team that took on a big challenge, and, by doing so, made business history.

ONE
Nanovation Begins with Noticing

Apparently, there is nothing that cannot happen today.

MARK TWAIN

L et's set the scene with a look at life (and death) on the roads of India. If you want the ultimate definition of *pandemonium*, you'll find it in the words *Indian traffic*. Traveling in India is not for the faint of heart. No wimps, no whiners.

Particularly in the cities, traffic can be more than heavy—it can be nuts! Signs over the streets beg drivers to stay in their lanes (Lane Driving Is Sane Driving!), but no one pays attention. Pedestrians and bicycles are everywhere.

Open-sided autorickshaws—three-wheel scooters that serve either as taxis or as delivery trucks—belch smoke and fumes as they inch forward like a sea of black-and-yellow beetles clawing for forward progress. Two-wheel scooters weave through the traffic carrying

families or delivering lunch or anything else you can imagine. A camel pulls a flatbed wagon. A sacred white Brahma bull stops in the middle of an intersection to take it all in.

Amid the chaos, horns blare. Honking is acceptable and encour-

Indians have mastered the art of turning a two-lane street into five lanes of snarling traffic. Traveling in India is not for the faint of heart.

aged. In fact, many overloaded trucks paint "horn please" on the back of their vehicles because they cannot see you passing on either side. It's one near miss after another in a dangerous sea of coordinated disorder that generally follows the laws of hydrodynamics. And in many places, all of this happens with toddlers and young children playing—literally—just inches away from all the mayhem.

India has been working hard to build its infrastructure, strangled by decades of neglect, yet most roads are in rough shape. To say that they are congested is a major understatement. Traffic in the cities frequently comes to a standstill, and traffic on the highways often slows to fifteen or twenty miles per hour. And fortunately they're not going any faster.

(Paul Prescott/Dreamstime)

Crazy? Unstoppable? Or both? You decide. An overloaded truck in the agricultural region of Rajasthan.

India's minister of Road Transport and Highways, Kamal Nath, recognizes the severity of this problem. In his keynote address at the annual convention of the Society of Indian Automobile Manufacturers in 2009 he said, "We had the decade of IT in India. We must make this the decade of infrastructure. You build the vehicles; I will build the roads."

In the present decade, India will make a quantum leap from building one to ten miles of new roads per day using the best technology and latest methods from around the globe.

Against this backdrop, imagine riding a scooter in the rain. In India, when the rains hit, all the oil and grease accumulated from the dry season is flushed to the surface of the road, making driving conditions treacherous. It's not a good time to be driving, and it's an even worse time to be on a scooter or motorbike. It's uncomfortable. Undignified. And dangerous.

And that's where our story begins.

THE FAMILY ON A SCOOTER

In Bangalore during the monsoons of 2002, it has been raining all day, making it hard to get on with your life. The rain subsides for the moment; you stick your head out the window and ask yourself, *Can we make it?* You decide to go for it, so you push the family scooter to the street and climb on—mother and father, with one child clutched between the two of you, and one child standing between your legs.

(Dana Ward/Shutterstock)

Counting heads reveals a typical family of four on a scooter.

These people are not crazy. They're just unstoppable.

Like most of your friends, you are among millions of young, educated Indian families making do with what you can afford. You are doing better than any generation of Indians before you, working hard to give your children a better life. As you pull into traffic, everybody hangs on. Since most of the traffic in India is open vehicles—two-wheel and three-wheel scooters—people tend to wait for a rainstorm to end if they can. Frequently that just isn't possible. So you ride next to many who have obviously been drenched by the rain. They are wet, their passengers are wet, it's hard to see, the streets are congested, and the traffic is loud. It's no fun to ride a scooter in pouring rain. And it's not much more fun to ride it right after the rain, when cars and trucks splash through puddles and the spray from their tires hits you in the face.

YOUR WORST NIGHTMARE IS NO DREAM

You approach an intersection where you need to make a turn. You see up ahead that traffic has opened and people are increasing their speed. If you can just thread the needle and get by the Mercedes immediately in front of you, this narrow window might allow you to make it to your meeting before the rain starts again.

Suddenly your back wheel slides. Panic strikes, and a surge of adrenaline floods your veins. Your worst nightmare is unfolding right before your eyes.

You lose control, and the scooter goes down. No helmets. No leather. No protection.

You've seen this happen before but never thought it would happen to you. This time no one is seriously injured. As you collect your shaken family, you are incredibly thankful, yet ever more hopeful. The incident has intensified your dream of owning a safe, more dignified form of transportation, one that will get your family out of the rain.

This is not a hypothetical family. They are very real and so was their crash.

Now, consider the story through the eyes of Ratan Naval Tata, the chairman of the Tata Group. On this

Someone had to ask, "What if?"

same dark and dreary afternoon, Ratan steps into his car, knowing how dangerous the roads will be. But he has no way of knowing the magnitude of what is about to unfold.

"Please drive carefully," he tells the driver. "The roads will be slippery." The driver nods as he pulls away from the curb. A few minutes later, as Mr. Tata's car approaches an intersection, the family on the scooter passes it.

"I think that's when the whole thing started in my mind," Ratan told us, "looking at what is now a pretty familiar sight in India, an entire family traveling on a scooter with three or four family members." He points them out to his driver. "Watch those people. In this rain, they could slip."

His driver responds.

"Be careful; slow down," Mr. Tata says again as they enter an intersection behind the scooter.

And then it happens. "I had no sooner said the words when he lost control and went slipping down on the pavement, the scooter sliding one way and the family members tumbling in all directions."

As he steps from his car to help, Mr. Tata knows it could have been much worse: "If we had been going faster, there would have been no way to keep from running over them. The family was all over the road and could have been under the car. I thought, *This is really bad.* And I thought, *Now add nighttime to this. Add a little speed. Add a little bit of lack of control, and you have a really dangerous mode of transport.*"

They offered what help they could and then got back in the car and drove on. As they did, Ratan Tata knew he'd just been given a wake-up call that something had to be done.

Someone had to ask, "What if?"

A DREAM BORN OF COMPASSION

"Where observation is concerned, chance favors only the prepared mind."

Louis Pasteur

Most people would leave the scene of the accident feeling sad and sorry, but few would be in a position to take meaningful action. As Louis Pasteur said, speaking of his ability to recognize patterns and connections that other scientists missed, when, by long thought and study, your mind is prepared to see opportunity, you're more likely to have a breakthrough.

And this was not the first time Ratan Tata had thought about how to get Indian families off scooters and into something safer. In fact, he'd mentioned it in speeches and talked about it with his peers. As chairman of the Tata Group, which owns and manages Tata Motors, he had a car company at his command. He had the means and opportunity to act, and now, his heart pumping from the excitement, he had a motive.

Immediately his mind went to work. He couldn't shut the idea down; it played again and again in his head.

What if we could give these people something safer that they could afford? he asked himself. *What if we made a four-wheel scooter that was more stable? That could be enclosed? That could offer protection from the rain and from accidents?*

"Action speaks louder than words, but not nearly as often."
Mark Twain

Ratan Tata was raised from an early age to consider the needs of others. He'd spent a great deal of time throughout his career thinking about how he and the companies he leads could improve the lives of employees, customers, and India's poor. In addition to his responsibilities as chairman of the Tata Group, he is the chairman of two major charitable organizations. So on that rainy evening, his mind was prepared to see opportunities and to connect seemingly unrelated bits of information into the beginning of an idea.

On that rainy afternoon, Ratan Tata conceived a big dream in the service of a noble cause: he would find a way to put safe transportation within the reach of India's emerging millions. But while the Nano was conceived in that moment, it was a long way from taking shape. It would take nearly seven years before the keys to the first Nano were handed over to the first thrilled customer.

> **Innovation is often the result of connecting seemingly disconnected ideas to create a solution.**

PROBLEMS ARE INVITATIONS TO NANOVATION

Every creative insight, every burst of ingenuity begins with seeing or, more powerfully, experiencing a problem or opportunity that is meaningful to someone else. The pilot light of Nanovation was lit when Ratan Tata saw an invitation to make the world a better place, to build a business by serving others, and he responded.

There's a lesson here for would-be Nanovators. Pick up any newspaper, watch any news program, or just look around and you will see how many significant problems are out there calling for a creative solution. Nanovators are astute observers of people's wants and needs. They pay attention to how trends affect people and shape their lives.

WHAT IF?

What are the top ten problems facing your customers today?

What if you were faster at identifying these problems?

What if you were better at solving them than anyone in the industry?

Nanovation Begins with Noticing

As he drove away from the scene of the accident, Mr. Tata began to think about the enormity of the problem.

Each year in India, more than ten million people are injured in road accidents, and more than 125,000 die. India has a mortality rate approaching one hundred road deaths per million, nearly twice the rate in Europe. There is a number of reasons for this disparity, but the most important is that so many more people travel on scooters and other non-enclosed vehicles. In 2008, forty-five million two-wheel motor vehicles were registered on the road in India. There were six million cars. Can you see the potential for serious injuries and fatalities here?

As Ratan Tata saw, accidents don't just wreck vehicles; they wreck families. They hurt the nation.

"For six and seven months, whenever I got bored in meetings, I doodled, trying to figure out how we could make a scooter a safer form of transport. I thought about structural members going over the passengers so that if it fell, the people could stay in. I looked at perhaps having two wheels next to each other in the back that could give it some stability." But Ratan Tata's thoughts gravitated toward this question: Can we do a really basic car?

There were several reasons for this.

First, in India, as in all countries, you're safer inside a car than you are on two wheels. Two-wheelers, while lots of fun to ride, are inherently less stable. A motorcycle or scooter is more likely to get into an accident than a car or truck. In a million vehicle miles the number of motorcycle accidents is 7.7, compared to 4.2 accidents in passenger cars. So two-wheelers are nearly twice as likely to be in an accident as four-wheelers. As motorcycle riders will tell you, there are only two types of riders: those who have crashed their bikes and those who are going to crash.

The social cost of road accidents is 3 percent of India's GDP.

If you ride a **two-wheeler,** you're more than **five times** more likely to be **hurt.**

(Paul Prescott/Canstockphoto)

Scooters outnumber cars in India by nearly eight to one. This parking lot, choked with congestion, on Chandni Chowk in the city of Old Delhi is symbolic of the number of two-wheelers in India.

Second, a person involved in a motorcycle accident is much more likely to be injured or killed than a passenger in an automobile. Again, the statistics bear this out: per million miles, there are 6.3 injuries on two-wheelers versus 1.2 in cars. If you ride a two-wheeler, you're more than five times more likely to be hurt. Now put a family of four or five on wheels designed for two people, and the injuries—and deaths—multiply quickly.

Third, Mr. Tata realized there was a question of dignity. Tata Motors had already seen this in its investigation of the needs of rural farm and business owners, who told designers they would choose a four-wheel truck over a three-wheeler because it would increase their status in the village. In many countries, people ride a motorcycle or a scooter for fun. It's a leisure activity. It's a lifestyle statement. In India and many other countries in Asia and Africa, it's a lifestyle statement, too. It denotes being at the bottom of the pyramid. Riding a two-wheeler tells the world you can't afford anything better.

So even if you found a way—with a roll cage, for instance—to make a two-wheeler safer, you're still faced with the question of dignity.

And fourth, there's the matter of comfort. It's hard to have much dignity when you're riding a scooter in a rainstorm. When your hair is dripping down your face and your clothes are soaking wet—or worse, mud-splattered and ruined—it's hard to feel pride. Can you imagine trying to concentrate at work? And you can forget about that job interview you were heading to.

Dignity matters.

Dignity matters, and Ratan Tata knew that. As he doodled, he came to the conclusion that whatever they built had to be a real car that would bring safety, protection from the elements, and dignity to India's emerging middle class. And it had to cost about the price of a scooter.

It had to be a *real* car. Not an apology car.

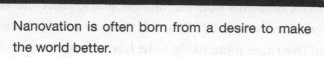

TWO
Leading Nanovation

It's not that I'm so smart. It's that I stay with problems longer.

ALBERT EINSTEIN

S o what does the chairman of a $71 billion industrial group know about the dignity of the poor? Why would he care? The short answer is, it's in his DNA. And it's in the DNA of the companies the Tatas built. Ratan Tata learned through example, from more than one hundred years and three generations of

Ratan Tata, chairman, Tata Group

Tata leaders who have modeled noticing, serving, and responding to the needs of India and its people. For more than 140 years the leadership tradition of "good thoughts, good words, good deeds" has become deeply rooted in the cultural DNA of Tata companies and Tata leaders.

Most of us arrive at our beliefs about leading people, building companies, creating corporate cultures, and serving customers through the individuals and events that have shaped our lives. So let us unpack the story of this remarkable man a little more thoroughly. Our purpose is to give you a glimpse of who and what have influenced the gutsy, global leader behind the People's Car, the man *Time* magazine named to its 2009 list of the one hundred most influential people in the world.

Of all the companies in India, none has a bigger footprint than the Tatas. As India's largest conglomerate, the Tata Group owns about one hundred different companies in more than eighty countries, with more than 350,000 employees. In 2009, revenues were nearly $71 billion, with 65 percent of that coming from operations outside of India.

If you live in one of the major metropolitan areas of India, you can drink Tata tea brought to you in Tata trucks made with Tata steel. You can build an IT infrastructure loaded with a wide array of Tata enterprise and business process solutions, assisted by Tata consultants. You can talk on a Tata mobile phone network and check your e-mail on Tata broadband on a computer driven by Tata power. You can sleep in a Tata hotel, watch Tata Sky TV, shop in a Tata retail store, put Tata salt on your *dosa*, and finish it off with Tata coffee.

If you live outside India—and particularly outside the Tatas' current sphere of influence in Asia, the Middle East, and Africa—you may know them only from the story of the Nano and their acquisition, in 2008, of Jaguar and Land Rover. But in coming years, you'll be hearing more of them. You'll be buying more Jaguars and Land Rovers. You'll be buying Nanos. And don't be surprised if your company sends you to the Tata Management Training Center to study their Business Excellence Model.

A LEGACY OF MAKING LIFE WORTH LIVING

The Tatas have proved to be adventurous spirits with compassionate hearts and undaunted wills. Since the 1860s, they've dared to accomplish things for the sake of the country and not just for the bottom line. Jamsetji Tata, the legendary founder of the company, set the tone in the early years. He was determined to leverage his wealth to help Indians become self-sufficient at a time when the nation was still laboring under the yoke of British colonial rule. Most business experts and historians agree that Jamsetji Tata and his heirs led India's first steps toward industrialization.

"We do not claim to be more unselfish, more generous, or more philanthropic than other people," Jamsetji said in 1895. "But we think we started on sound and straightforward business principles, considering the interests of the shareholder, our own, and the health and welfare of the employees, the sure foundation of our prosperity."

The founder's egalitarian spirit, passion for nation building, and concern for the disadvantaged became an integral part of the way he and those who came after him have done business. As you will see, the Tatas don't just build companies; they build communities. They are highly engaged in raising the standard of living and improving the quality of life for people wherever they go.

WHAT IF?

The Tatas were engaged in corporate social responsibility (CSR) long before it became a fad or buzzword.

What if your company had a reputation for giving back, for community and nation building?

What if your CEO and founders resided at the top of the "Most Ethical Leaders" list?

What if your customers were absolutely convinced that your business does well for itself by doing good for others?

A humble pedigree

(Tata archives)

Jamsetji Tata, the founder of the Tata Group, stands at center with his daughter-in-law, Navajbai, Ratan Tata's adoptive grandmother.

In spite of his last name, Ratan Tata did not inherit his position. Although he is distantly related to Jamsetji Tata, the founder of the Tata empire, his family branch was not originally part of the business. His grandfather died young, leaving Mr. Tata's father, Naval Tata, in near poverty. In fact, young Naval was a student in an orphanage when a wealthy relative decided to adopt him. That relative was Lady Navajbai Tata, the wife of Jamsetji's second son, Sir Ratan Tata. Since she was childless, she was encouraged by relatives to think of adopting a child, and the suggestion was made that young Naval was a good choice.

For Naval Tata, it was as if a fairy godmother had popped out of thin air and spirited him away to a new world.

With permanent residences in London and Bombay, Sir Ratan and Lady Navajbai were worldly and well traveled. They opened young Naval to a wider world than most people ever know. Sir Ratan was a man of fabulous wealth, who spent more time on philanthropic works than he did on the business of Tata Sons, the family's business holding company, which he left largely in the hands of his brother, Sir Dorab Tata. Instead he founded a trust to build hospitals in India and funded a chair of social science at the London School of Economics to study the causes of poverty. They were early supporters of Gandhi's efforts in South Africa. They traveled to Europe and Asia regularly and dined with famous people. But even though it was a life of privilege, Sir Ratan and his brother lived in relative modesty, using the best part of their inheritances to create a pair of charitable trusts that today hold 66 percent ownership in the Tata companies.

A history of entrepreneurial philanthropy

Many of the pioneering educational institutions in India—including the prestigious Indian Institute of Science, the first institute for social sciences, the first cancer hospital and research center, and the first institute for basic research in mathematics and physics—were established over the years by the Tatas and the Tata Trusts. Today, the trusts alone distribute approximately $90 million a year. The combined development-related spending of the trusts and the companies amounts to approximately 4 to 6 percent of the net profits of all the Tata companies.

> As a CEO, Ratan Tata is in charge of making a great deal of money. He's also responsible for spending it on good works.

Think about that: for more than one hundred years, much of the profits of one of the world's largest industrial groups has gone to charity. And Ratan Tata, as chairman of the Tata Group, manages a charitable empire with assets totaling as much as $50 billion. So while, like most CEOs, he is in charge of making a great deal of money, he's also responsible for spending it on good works, leading two of the world's largest charitable organizations, focused on reducing global poverty.

(Tata archives)

That's a young Ratan Tata with his legendary predecessor J. R. D. Tata, who led the organization from 1922 until 1991.

No Sense of Entitlement—He Earned His Way Up

It's true that Ratan Tata grew up inside the Tata business—his father became a director and was an active leader—but no one could say he was groomed to take over. In fact, he started off going in the opposite direction.

Ratan Tata was born in 1937. His parents separated when he was seven, and he was raised mostly by his grandmother. He traveled to Europe and the U.K. as a child and was quiet and artistic. He headed off to America for his education when he was just fifteen years old and, in the 1950s, studied architecture and structural engineering at Cornell. He had an early passion for flying and washed planes at the local airfield to pay for lessons. He most likely would have stayed in the U.S.—he had a job offer from IBM—had not family members encouraged him to return to Mumbai. His grandmother offered a simple and compelling argument: she was ill and wanted him to be near her.

Ratan Tata worked his way up inside the Tata organization for nearly twenty years and was given charge of an ailing electronics company belonging to the Group, which he led to profitability. Then in 1981, he was asked to lead a little-known and somewhat dysfunctional organization inside the Group, called Tata Industries. Tata Industries was intended as a think tank and incubator of new ideas in new industries. It was a mess, and his job was to clean it up.

He was only months into the job when his mother fell ill. Torn between his new responsibilities and his family duties, he decided that since he had only one mother, he'd better go with her to New York's Sloan-Kettering Hospital. Maybe distance from the business was a good thing because, as he sat there for weeks with little to occupy his mind, he began to formulate a strategic plan.

An Ability to See over the Horizon

He decided he would take Tata Industries in the direction of high-tech electronics, computer systems, and biotechnology. He bet on a future that was, at that very moment, just being hatched in garage operations in places like Silicon Valley and Redmond, Washington. Cisco, Oracle, and Microsoft got their starts that year. Apple was just a couple of years older. Although Ratan Tata was by then in his forties, he shared the same ahead-of-their-time vision of the twenty-five-year-olds on the West Coast: a world of wired (and soon wireless) technology that would bring computer access to everyone and change the face of business. Others in his position—including the then leaders at IBM—couldn't see it coming.

They laughed at the idea.

So when people laughed at the idea of a People's Car that cost about the same as a scooter, it wasn't the first time. "Question the unquestionable," Ratan Tata likes to say. And then do something about it.

In 1981, he was asking all the right questions. His strategy in the 1980s paid off for Tata Industries, and when, in 1991, J. R. D. Tata decided to retire, he asked Ratan Tata to take over. Succession was a huge decision, one that would impact the Tata Group, its employees and shareholders, and India for a long, long time.

What did J. R. D. see in Ratan? We suspect he saw a visionary, much like himself, who had the capacity to think big and the courage to act bold. J. R. D. saw someone who would honor the values that drive the Tata empire, yet one who was unwilling to accept the status quo and gutsy enough to be unafraid to shake things up.

At the time, Tata Sons had a small stake in some three hundred companies. He sold equity and restructured some of the companies and used the capital as well as revenue from Tata Consultancy Services, India's largest IT firm, to gain control of the companies that were left. All in all, Ratan reduced the number of Tata companies to fewer than a hundred, making the Group more manageable. As you can imagine, these broad and sweeping changes were dramatic. Seasoned company leaders within the Tata companies might have expected Ratan Tata to leave them alone to run their own fiefdoms, as his predecessor did. Instead, Ratan did the unexpected. He retired them.

The year 1991 was also the year the Indian government began the massive task of liberalizing its economy, returning production to public companies, encouraging entrepreneurship, and opening India's doors to the world economy. It was as if, all of a sudden, the world's most populous country suddenly realized two fundamental truths: first, globalization wasn't the same as colonialism, and India could play and win in the global game; and second, the hundreds of millions of impoverished Indians were an asset, not a problem. In a world competing on brainpower, hundreds of millions of educated Indians with a tradition of speaking English could be a very powerful competitive advantage.

In this tumultuous power shift, India and the Tata Group could not have had a better person at the helm to guide them through those changes than Ratan Tata.

Listen to his words and you quickly get a sense of Ratan Tata's forward thinking: "The vision I have for India in the next decade [the 2010s] is of a nation with vastly improved connectivity in communications providing education, personal interaction, e-commerce, and telephony contact for the overwhelming mass of its people. I see our country being connected through major highway networks, thus shrinking the time required to move goods to the marketplace. I see our consumers exercising an unprecedented degree of choice, with the Indian marketplace becoming a vibrantly competitive arena, fully integrated with the world. Equally, I foresee that the ambitions of the Indian entrepreneur will not be confined to domestic boundaries and our immensely valuable human capital will leave its mark on the global marketplace."

In 1991, the people of India realized they could play and win in the global game.

A Globally Respected Group of Companies

Today, the Tata Group is one of the most respected companies in the world. But don't take our word for it. In 2009, the Reputation Institute ranked the Tata Group as number eleven among the most reputable companies across the globe. In 2007, the Tata Group was awarded the Carnegie Medal of Philanthropy in recognition of the group's long history of philanthropic activities.

"I would hope my successors would never compromise," Ratan told us when we brought up Tata's reputation, "and never allow the Tata Group to join the growing number of companies which have shed their values, forgotten about their integrity, and closed their eyes on maintaining ethical standards. I hope the future generations in Tatas will recognize these traditions as being critical to the fabric and the fundamentals on which our group was built and grew so successfully for over a century."

A Generative Spirit

Generativity is the care and concern for future generations. It's about inspiring people to participate in creating a better world than the one they inherited. In our book *NUTS!* we defined *generativity* as "raising individuals, organizations, and communities to higher levels of moral development—the obligations, responsibilities, and rights associated with bettering the human condition in a just and civil society. It means using the collective wisdom, knowledge, and experience of leaders and collaborators to further the welfare of others."

A generative leader asks, "Are the people who are touched by my power and influence flourishing? Do they have more freedom? Have I spent enough time in the trenches to genuinely understand their wants and needs, hopes and dreams? Do our products, services, and business practices reflect this

Suddenly, they saw that hundreds of millions of impoverished people were an asset, not a problem.

understanding? Is the business a better business, and are the communities in which we operate better places as a result of both the process and the end result of my leadership?" Given the legacy that was handed to him, these questions come naturally to Ratan Tata.

They are also questions that keep him up at night.

Why? As we said, it's in his DNA and in the culture of his company. His personality, his focus on the larger picture, and the idea that leaders do well by doing good—these characteristics are not simply the idiosyncrasies of a powerful man. They are among the primary reasons that he was chosen for the job of chairman of the Tata Group. He was selected for these qualities because they have always been among the characteristics of leadership in the company. And for these characteristics, he's respected the way Warren Buffett is in the States or Richard Branson is in Britain.

GUTSY LEADERSHIP

It takes guts to move an organization in bold, new directions, and it takes guts to get out on the seemingly lunatic fringe where new ideas are given birth and new innovations are fueled.

Leading Nanovation is not for the faint at heart, because there will always be opposition; naysayers will ridicule you and tell you why you are crazy. Whether it is breaking a union strike in Pune, buying steel giant Corus Group, or pulling out of Singur to protect embattled employees, Ratan Tata has demonstrated the guts to stand upon his convictions and live his values out loud. He has also had the guts to lead the Tata Group to places that few would have the courage to go.

We like what the editors of Britain's *Car* magazine said when they named him one of their 10 Men of the Year in 2008:

Word of advice: don't get into a bragging contest with Ratan Tata about who achieved the most in 2008. Not unless you can beat purchasing Land Rover and Jaguar from Ford, launching the world's cheapest car, building a city car powered by thin air, exporting electric trucks to America and brazenly announcing your plan to buy a chunk of Ferrari. And perhaps also standing with dignity outside your gutted Mumbai hotel and announcing that terrorists will not defeat you.

An Authentic and Quiet Man with a Streak of Thrill Seeker

Although he's one of India's most powerful and most respected leaders, Ratan Tata lives alone in a modest apartment in Mumbai with his two dogs. His favorite getaways include a bungalow across the bay from Mumbai and the Lake House at Tata Motors' Pune plant.

Ratan Tata has three passions in his very private life: cars, aircraft, and German shepherds. Being the chairman of India's second largest automobile manufacturer notwithstanding, Ratan is a car guy with an eye for design and a penchant for speed. He has an interest in Ferrari on many levels—Tata Consultancy sponsors Ferrari's Formula 1 motor racing team—and could possibly own a stake in the company in the future. Engage him in a discussion about cars and you quickly realize that you are talking with an aficionado—who by the way is genuinely and graciously interested in your opinion.

Ratan has also been an avid aviator for most of his life and flies the company's Falcon 2000 business jet whenever time permits. He even copiloted the Boeing F-18 and Lockheed F-16 fighter jets at the Aero India air show in 2007.

There is a story about him that paints a picture of a world leader who has a concern for the little things. Whenever he boards the company plane, he is greeted by a small, brown dog. The story goes that the dog is a stray that showed up one day and Ratan asked his staff to care for it.

Apocryphal or not, the story is consistent with our experience. On any one of our six visits to Bombay House (Tata headquarters) in Mumbai, we found ourselves stepping over a couple of stray dogs that sleep on the beautiful marble floors of the entryway, where it is cool.

Why are they there? Because Mr. Tata makes sure they are watered and well fed.

Unlike many business tycoons, Ratan Tata has no entourage, and avoids displays of wealth or privilege. He's a private man who lives a private life. He likes to listen to music. He has close friendships with symphony conductor Zubin Mehta and Amar Bose, the founder of Bose Audio. He enjoys driving whenever he can, and he is often seen driving a Tata Indica around Mumbai.

Leaders do well by doing good. Good thoughts, good words, good deeds.

As we talked with him on various visits, both in India and in the United States, it was very apparent that Ratan Tata hasn't forgotten where he came from. Perhaps it is the sensitivities one acquires in a difficult childhood or what one learns from a grandmother who modeled servant leadership and treated everyone with dignity. Maybe it is the weight one feels from the responsibility of upholding 140 years' worth of legacy and deeply embedded values. Or possibly it is the respect one gains from walking in the shadows of iconic figures such as Jamsetji and J. R. D. Tata.

Whatever it is, we recognized that Ratan Tata shares two things in common with every great leader we've met: humility and a lack of pretentiousness. He has neither the self-congratulation of an entrepreneur who made billions nor the arrogance of a corporate infighter who clawed his way to the top. He *does* have the work ethic of one who shoveled limestone in the steel mill and the sophistication of one who has traveled the globe. He is quite comfortable with lawyers, investment bankers, and world leaders, yet he is very down to earth, self-effacing, and approachable with his blue-collar employees. In our experience he is as *interested* as he is *interesting*.

There's one more story about him that we find endearing. Once, as the story goes, while he was driving along Marine Drive in Mumbai, his car broke down. Stepping from it, he was recognized by a taxi driver, who stopped to assist and offer him a lift. Embarrassed, India's most influential man had to admit that he'd left home with no cash. The driver laughed and gave him a ride for free, just so he could tell the story.

After all Ratan Tata has done for India, it seemed the least he could do.

NANOBITE

Be generative—focus on the needs of a widely defined public.
In your care and concern for future generations you will find the impetus for innovation.

Hang on to deeply held values and legacy, but be willing to change strategy on a dime.

Dream big without losing the humility to remember where you came from.

Find the courage of your convictions. You'll need it to face those who can't see over the horizon.

THREE

A Culture of Thinking Big

*Whatever can be done will be done. The only
question is, will it be done by you or to you?*

THOMAS FRIEDMAN

I n early 2003, Ratan Tata met with leaders at Tata Motors, which
had a 55 percent market share in commercial trucks in India (plus
other business around the world) and was already making well-
received passenger cars. He asked them to put together an exploratory
team of young engineers to pursue the idea of a small car for the
masses. And then he flew to the Geneva Motor Show.

Geneva is the queen mother of all car shows. Begun in 1905, it's
still the premier world automobile event, the place where the CEOs
of every car company walk the aisles and make deals. And it's the
place where car companies introduce their new ideas.

It was at Geneva, in March 2003, that Ratan Tata first spoke
publicly of the Nano in an interview with reporter John Griffiths

from London's *Financial Times*. As he sat with Griffiths, he was very specific about the vision.

"It will look like a real car and have proper seating—stretched canvas seats would not, for example, be acceptable." Not that it would be a luxury car, he continued, "It would be all right for the car to be a bit more noisy than an ordinary car but it has to be both simple and safe."

Many say that a goal without a timeline is just a daydream. And Mr. Tata had a clear deadline in mind. "It is my dream," he said, "to make the car a reality within . . . five years."

Although he was clear that the car had to be affordable to the millions of people who presently could afford scooters, he wasn't ready to give a firm price target at the time, so when Griffiths asked what the car would cost, Mr. Tata said, "Around 1 lakh rupees." (*Lakh* is Hindi for one hundred thousand.)

The next day, March 10, 2003, the *Financial Times* ran the headline "Tatas Plan Rs 1 Lakh Car."

"I had two choices," he told us with a chuckle. "One was to refute it or, two, just take that as our task." And so it was official. Tata Motors was going to make a car that could sell for 1 lakh: Rs. 100,000. About US $2,100 at the time.

"I then had to pass that goal on to our people," Mr. Tata went on.

You can imagine the reaction of the designers back in India. Has the chairman lost his mind?

"First they ignore you; then they laugh at you; then they fight you; then you win."
Mahatma Gandhi

If there is anything we've learned in the course of getting to know Ratan Tata, it is that he does not lack big ideas and he never shies away from acting on one he believes in deeply. As we mentioned, the ability to think big and act bold has driven the culture of the Tata Group for 140 years, especially under Ratan's leadership. He is a man who studies those who excel in areas where he knows Tata Group and India can benefit and get better. This includes learning from other countries.

Ratan admires China for thinking globally, and he knows that the government of Beijing does not take small steps with regard to its own development. Rather, it gets big things done quickly. Tata concluded that whether it's building a port or highway, the scale with which China approaches its expansion often blows people's minds. If the Tata Group is going to remain a towering example of entrepreneurship and business innovation, he believes it must take a lesson from China: stop taking baby steps and start thinking big.

"I have always referred to China as an opportunity because it has shown us, and we have not yet learned, what can be done. I think China gave our country a wake-up call," he said.

When it comes to conjuring up big ideas and making the impossible possible, we draw our strength and inspiration from those who have done it.

> **Who do you admire for thinking big?**
>
> Take inventory of the people and companies that really have a propensity to think big. Perhaps some of these people lead departments or business units within your organization. Let this audit fuel your fire to think big. Let it inspire you to step up where others are holding back.

IS THERE A MARKET FOR SUCH A CAR?

The other question one had to ask was the business question, is there a market for such a car?

Which takes us back to that statistic—forty-five million registered two-wheelers—and a critical question: Why would you put your family of four or five on a scooter and head out into the gonzo world of Indian traffic?

Answer: Because you have no other viable options. You do what you have to do.

India may be the world's most optimistic country, but transportation issues are holding it back. Indians living in rural areas—nearly 70 percent of the population—have the fewest options. Although there are lots of roads in the rural network, many are unpaved. Forty percent of India's villages aren't served by all-weather roads. When the monsoons come, they may be cut off for the season. There are railways and buses, if people can get to them from the village, but they, too, face capacity problems. And in return, they offer little comfort. Little convenience. And little dignity.

That's why there's been so much growth in vehicle ownership—15 percent per year in the past decade. In India, people need wheels. And wheels cost money.

The Indian middle class is one of the largest and fastest growing in the world. While it's hard to pin down definite numbers, it's probably safe to say that it's nearly the size of the population of the United States. And the number of middle-class Indians has risend by more than one hundred million people in just the last generation.

In 1985, 93 percent of India's population fell under the category described by the World Bank as "deprived." In 2005, that percentage had dropped to 54 percent. And today it's poised to drop to less than 50 percent. A huge population of Indians has emerged from poverty and is marching toward what experts see as one of the world's brightest economic futures.

Marching, because most of them can't afford to buy a scooter, let alone a car.

The bottom third of that three hundred million middle class are some distance away from personal mobility. They're no longer deprived.

They've gone beyond that class. They no longer worry about their survival, but they're not running out to buy a scooter. They're probably still saving for a refrigerator.

By 2015, most of them will be there. Things are changing that fast. They'll need a way to get around. And they'll need to be safe. Suppose one-third of today's scooter owners are potential Nano buyers. Conservatively that's a market of almost fifteen million eager customers.

"Look at what India needs now," Mr. Tata told his colleagues in 2003. "We have millions of people emerging from poverty. They need low-cost products. So it is our duty to create those products and since we happen to be in the automobile business, one of the products we should create is a car that people can afford."

CERTIFIABLY NUTS OR SETTING THE BAR? YOU DECIDE

A few years ago, travelers passing through airports were treated to a billboard for a consulting company with a message that read: "A great idea is a job half done." But anyone who's ever seen an idea from inception through to implementation knows that statement is nonsense. A great idea is nothing without implementation. Implementation takes a lot of work. And the work begins with a leader who isn't afraid to set the bar extremely high because he deeply believes in the capabilities of his team.

With a 55 percent market share in commercial trucks in India, Tata Motors had a lot of momentum. Tata Motors was also responsible for bringing the Indica, the very first indigenously Indian-made car, to the market, and it had been very well received. Ratan Tata was making a bet and setting the bar based on experience, based on previous wins, not some pie-in-the-sky idea that had no merit.

As Ratan doodled with ideas, he went from the idea of a safer kind of scooter to a rudimentary car. "The first concepts of the Nano that I had were sort of an Erector Set kind of thing," he told us. "We would have members that could be shipped flat and could be assembled somewhere else."

Hold that idea, because it's a big one—a *huge* one—and we'll come back and unpack it later.

"We could have made something that did not have doors, that had plastic curtains and was a very rudimentary car but a car that provided shelter from the weather." But it soon became clear that customers were not going to accept half a car that always put them in a category that was neither car nor scooter.

Like we said, dignity matters.

Taking on an impossible challenge points out an important cultural peculiarity at Tata. They are culturally conditioned to think big. They have learned that just because you don't think something can be done doesn't mean it won't be.

If it ever will be done, it will be done by people who are able to get beyond *can't*. To quote Thomas Friedman, a keen observer of what the Indian business world has made possible, "Whatever can be done will be done. The only question is, will it be done *by* you or *to* you?"

"America has tossed its cap over the wall of space."
John F. Kennedy

The story of John F. Kennedy's challenge to put a man on the moon has long resonated with Ratan Tata.

"I was in college at that time he made that proclamation. My first job was in Los Angeles, working for a subcontractor to NASA. So I was aware of the kinds of things that were happening in the early Mercury and Apollo programs," he explained.

"I saw things being done that hitherto were considered impossible. Every day we went to work, new ground was being covered. No one had ever done it before, and so history was being made every few months. But before it happened, people said it could not happen."

Ratan Tata saw the same dynamics with the Nano. It looked impossible, but it needed to be done.

"The idea of the Nano did not come as an idea to make money or to gain great visibility," he told us. "It was really driven by an urge to provide a safer transport. Honestly, had I not continued to see entire families on a scooter, there might not have been a Nano." That doesn't mean that there wouldn't have been a people's car in India. As Friedman says, "Whatever can be done will be done."

Ratan Tata has a powerful vision of what India can accomplish. In the 1990s, before any company in India had produced a car from the design up, he gave a speech to the leaders of the automotive industry in India and suggested they work together to produce the first all-Indian car.

"I asked them, why should we not, in India, design and produce an Indian car? And I got scoffed at, in writing, by people who asked why I didn't focus on improving the quality of what we already made before I talked about building a car? And so we did it ourselves." That was the birth of the Indica, "the Big Small Car" that became the first car to be developed in India and that remains the biggest-selling car in its segment.

And then he tried to get the car manufacturers and the scooter makers together to build a low-cost car, a precursor to his thoughts about the Nano. He explained, "I thought we could take the large volumes that scooter manufacturers had and build a car out of scooter parts, which would be a low-cost car. There are about eight million two-wheelers produced in India each year and about half a million cars. So if you wanted scale from parts, then if all the scooter manufacturers and the car manufacturers could get together, you could produce a low-cost car."

What he was really asking what this: How can we make a scooter safer?

"If the scooter manufacturers had been willing to discuss this with us and work to make a safer form of transport, maybe the Nano would never have happened."

They weren't willing, and the idea was forgotten.

"It was forgotten until I saw four people riding on a scooter and kept seeing them. Seeing the dangers of that, and thinking, *Why couldn't we provide safe transportation at an affordable price?* is what brought us to the idea of the Nano," he stated.

YOU'LL NEVER PULL THIS OFF

There's no one like an expert to tell you something can't be done and why. And immediately the press and the online world were awash with expert opinions on why it was not now, nor never would be, possible to produce a car so cheaply.

No one was more outspoken than the chairman of Suzuki Motors, Osamu Suzuki. Suzuki was the first to bring an "affordable" car to India with the Maruti 800, a car created in 1983 in a joint venture with the Indian government. The car was a revelation to the Indian market—the first modern car available in India. The only other choices were the outdated Ambassador and Padmini, cars based on 1950s Austin and Fiat models.

Before long, Suzuki's Maruti was mobilizing Indians on the road and soon had more than 50 percent market share in passenger cars. In addition, Suzuki was exporting Marutis around the world. Even by the new century, as Tata, Renault, and others took positions in the market, more than 40 percent of the cars sold in India were made by Maruti, and almost a quarter of Suzuki's global production was made in India.

So nobody knew more about producing inexpensive small cars than Osamu Suzuki. And in 2003, he knew for a fact it was not possible to produce a less-expensive competitor to the 800.

He never said so directly. He just asked reporters to consider questions. Will it be an autorickshaw? Will it meet quality standards? Will it meet even the most basic standards? Will it clog the roads and pollute the air? When they say it will cost only 1 lakh, do they mean the cost of the parts, the cost to the manufacturer, or the cost to the customer?

"An expert is someone who tells you why you can't do something."

Alec Issigonis, designer of the original MINI

He was an expert, and experts know what is not possible. They sometimes know it so well, they miss what *is* possible. It was clear. There was no end of voices saying, "It can't be done. You'll never succeed. You can't do it."

Perhaps he should have taken a lesson here from Shunryu Suzuki, the Zen master who cautioned, "In the beginner's mind, there are many possibilities, but in the expert's mind there are few."

In every critical mass of unbelievers, there is one expert who does get it. One person who did not scoff at Tata's bold and audacious dream was Carlos Ghosn, CEO of not one, but two of the world's biggest car makers: Renault of France and Nissan of Japan. Of course, Ghosn understands doing the impossible and standing up to doubters. He's the business leader who resurrected Nissan from the brink of bankruptcy a year earlier than anyone thought he could. From the very beginning he believed that the 1 lakh car was possible—but only in India.

It wasn't the first time a Tata heard those words.

Tata's entire history is based on proving naysayers wrong. Here's a good rule: never tell a Tata he can't succeed. In the following months Ratan Tata made the point again and again: If we can put a man on the moon in eight years, is it really *impossible* to build a 1 lakh car?

The answer was no. It wasn't impossible. It just took people willing to think beyond the conventional wisdom, people willing to think big.

QUESTIONS

- People rally around boldness and specificity. Is your vision specific? Does it have a timeline (e.g., "We will put a man on the moon by the end of this decade")?
- Do you cultivate a culture of thinking big? Big doesn't just happen. It because stories are told, and people are publicly applauded for bold moves—even when they don't work out.
- Who are the heroes and heroines thinking big in your company? Industry?
- What have they done that inspires you? What can you learn from them?
- How can you draw strength from their bold attempts to move the needle as you envision a new project?

FOUR
The Nanovation Team

Noble life demands a noble architecture for noble uses of noble men. Lack of culture means what it has always meant: ignoble civilization and therefore imminent downfall.

FRANK LLOYD WRIGHT

O n a winter day in early 2003, a small group of engineers were called into a meeting at Tata Motors' Engineering Research Center (ERC) in Pune. Among those engineers were Jay Bolar, senior manager for development at ERC, who would later become the chief coordinator on the Nano project; Narendra Kumar Jain, who was responsible for the engine and was something of a legend around the Pune plant as an engine design pioneer; Ravi Rajhans, body systems expert who had been in charge of the body and interiors of the Indica, Tata's best-selling large car; and Nikhil Jadhav, who was in charge of exterior design.

"Please start brainstorming on a small car," they were told. "It can be a small package. You decide. The chairman will want to speak with you about it. Tomorrow."

That was a shock. When you work for a group of companies with hundreds of thousands of employees around the world, an opportunity to meet and present your very raw ideas to the chairman on a new concept doesn't happen every day.

"He wants to discuss ideas for a new small car for the bottom of the pyramid. Have some ideas ready."

The team spent the day brainstorming ideas and concepts, collecting data from studies that had already been done, but by their own admission, their thinking at that point in the process was conventional. They were still waiting for direction, although they'd already had some.

They'd seen the headlines from the interview in Geneva: "Tata to Build 1 Lakh Car."

"Obviously the first reaction was fear," remembered Ravi Rajhans regarding the idea of trying to design a car that could sell for so little. "We were really, really scared. We were sure it was a big project, and we were not sure where to start, where to draw the first line, even. At the time, the cheapest car in India was available at Rs. 200,000—almost twice the price."

Knowing they were heading for a meeting with the chairman, they tried to organize their thoughts as quickly as they could and decided to produce a document for the meeting, something he would be able to look at in advance. It was a sixty-slide PowerPoint presentation on the varieties of inexpensive transportation options currently available around the world.

The next morning, when they walked into the chairman's office at Bombay House in Mumbai, they saw a hard copy of the sixty-page document on the table in front of Mr. Tata.

"On every page of the hard copy there was something flagged with comment," Rajhans told us. "He had gone through it very carefully. So what were we supposed to present?"

They needn't have worried. Ratan Tata had been doing a lot of thinking about a people's car, but this was the first time he'd had the chance to sit down with other engineers and share his ideas.

His enthusiasm was evident to everyone as he talked about where the idea came from, the concept of affordability, and the challenges they faced: "The most expensive two-wheelers cost 100,000 rupees or more, and that's where this car has to compete. The second thing is, obviously, if you want to issue a challenge, the challenge has to be very difficult. Rather than just start off looking for a 10 percent improvement, you should start with a very tough challenge."

> "Rather than just start off looking for a 10 percent improvement, you should start with a very tough challenge."

From the beginning, Team Nano had a very clear objective. They weren't hoping to build a cheaper car or even the *cheapest* car. They were going to do something impossible: make a car for the cost of a motorcycle.

Because one leader believed it could be done.

An idea that dwells in the mind of one person is just a day-dream. But an idea that comes to life and is shared by an entire team soon becomes a cause. Sure, there were doubts. To some, it was the Chairman's Folly. To others, it was a design exercise in proving something was possible.

But most important, it was a start.

MISSION IMPOSSIBLE? NOT IN PUNE

As the Nano team members drove back to Pune from their first meeting with Ratan Tata, they were very well aware of the social and business responsibilities associated with this project. Let us remind you, accomplishing the impossible is deeply rooted in the company's DNA.

They knew the Nano, if successful, would not only offer safer mobility to hundreds of millions of Indian families; it would also offer business opportunities to millions. Even at that first meeting, they'd discussed the idea of an alternative manufacturing channel—a shade-tree industry assembling Nanos in local workshops. Along with a mass production facility, they talked about designing the Nano to be shipped in modules for assembly at small rural facilities.

"What if," they asked themselves, "a group of entrepreneurs could get funding to build a regional assembly facility? We could ship component and body assemblies, which could be bolted together quickly and with good quality. We could build a grassroots auto industry like nothing the world had ever seen."

From the start, they were thinking of the dignity of the family driving a real car and the dignity of a new breed of Nanopreneurs growing local economies across India.

"At our first meeting," Ravi Rajhans remembered, "we were not talking just about the individual product but about the universal impact. The need to conserve resources is a problem all over the globe. The need to empower local industries is a problem throughout the developing world. We saw that India could take a lead in creating innovations to serve these needs."

Narendra Kumar Jain nodded vigorously. "You see, this Nano is not the only project in which the Tata Group looks at the whole picture. We believe that what we get from society should go back to society. We are part of society, so if we do not act to make our society healthy, we are acting to make ourselves unhealthy."

That philosophy is deep-rooted in Tata. It's not just talk. All in the Tata Group say they're not working for profits only.

"What we're working for is sustaining the industry," Jain continued. "Unless we sustain the society of which that industry is a part, then how we can sustain our industry? If we cannot sustain our industry, we cannot sustain our profits, and we cannot sustain our company. The purpose is to sustain the business and make the society grow and remain calm."

They were excited, but they also bore a heavy weight. They were embarking on a project that was to consume years of their lives, a project so secret that they would not be able to tell their wives or families for years. While the challenge had been broadcast, the details of how they would achieve it would remain a closely guarded secret for another five years.

It wasn't going to be easy, but the assignment was clear. There was nothing left to do but go to their departments and begin the process we call Nanovation.

When the initial Nano team returned to Pune, they were coming home to the perfect place to nurture an idea with broad social impact. What Tata has built in Pune is so much more than a factory. It is a culture that has learned, through long experience, that great things can come from small seeds if you have the patience to let them grow.

At Pune's Engineering Research Center, they had already done the impossible. They'd built an Indian automotive industry. And then they'd gone on, time and again, to solve engineering problems that others said couldn't be done.

The Tata Group moved into transportation at the end of World War II and went big right from the start—making locomotives. Originally called Telco—Tata Engineering and Locomotive Company—the new company began by making locomotive boilers in a run-down workshop of the East Indian Railway in Jamshedpur.

Soon, they moved from boilers to designing and building entire locomotives—one hundred a year at their peak—with 98 percent of the parts made in India, either by Tata or by suppliers. They were building a network of opportunity not just for themselves but for entrepreneurs and small businesses that flocked to Jamshedpur to serve Telco and its growing roster of employees. It was good business, but it was limited. India's national railways were their only customer, and the government fixed the prices. They needed to export, or they needed to diversify.

The opportunity came in 1954 when they learned that Daimler-Benz was looking for a partner to assemble Mercedes trucks in India. Imitating Mercedes' standards and practices was the perfect way to learn to build an innovative car company. The Indians had learned everything the British had to teach about law and administration. They used the same intellectual discipline to learn everything the Germans had to teach about automotive engineering.

(Tata Archives)

The first Tata Mercedes truck, 1954.

When the contract with Daimler-Benz ended, they exchanged the Mercedes three-pointed star for the Tata *T* and continued to build great trucks. In fact, demand for Tata trucks so far outstripped supply that for many years they could have sold for a premium over the manufacturer's suggested retail price, something the company refused to do. By the time the Nano story starts, they had the dominant market share in trucks in India and a rapidly growing share of the automobile market as well.

In 1964, the company decided to invest more deeply into the automotive industry by building a plant that could manufacture not only trucks and truck parts but also the increasingly high-tech tools and machinery needed for the manufacturing process. They were no longer just building trucks. They were building an industry.

And so the Pune plant was born and, with it, Tata's Engineering Research Center, where the Nano team went to work. Once again, they were being asked to do the impossible.

To make a car for half the price. A real car people would be proud to own and drive.

Share your passion and conviction. There has to be something so alive in you that it awakens "aliveness" in others.

Nanovation starts with showing up and asking, "How can we make this work?" instead of saying, "Let us show you why it won't work."

Create an open, collaborative environment conducive to innovation.

If you are going to learn, learn from one of the best—think Mercedes-Benz—in the world.

- "How do our products and services empower customers, suppliers, and partners?" is a very different question from "How do our products and services make money?" Both are important, but money usually follows empowerment.

FIVE
The Search for Nanovation

I've always been told that the egg is something that can't be improved upon. Giving it some thought, I agree.

WILLIAM KRISEL, MODERNIST ARCHITECT

The average car has about eighteen hundred individual parts, but that's if you count assemblies, like the engine and transmission, as parts. Inside those assemblies, there are thousands more parts. Obviously a brand-new Bentley will have far more parts than a thirty-year-old econobox. So when you count up all the little bits—all the *parts* of parts—you're probably talking ten thousand parts.

The good news is that each and every one of those thousands of parts is an opportunity to apply your skills of elegant design and cost reduction. The bad news is that each and every one of those parts has already been through generations—maybe one hundred years—of analysis by the best minds in the business of automotive design.

So, if you want to overturn the price-to-performance paradigm in product design, where do you start?

The Nano team started with a basic assumption, that the unnamed new car would be what they called a "rural car." It would be incredibly simple, plainly functional, maybe even a new way of thinking about personal transportation.

Although Ratan Tata had already described the Nano to the press as something that would look like a real car, the cost imperative drove the design team to keep looking for solutions coming out of the world of scooters.

"You know you have achieved perfection in design, not when you have nothing more to add, but when you have nothing more to take away."

Antoine de Saint-Exupéry

Wasn't there a way to make a three-wheeler safer? Because if there was, they might be able to get a double cost advantage: cutting out one wheel and sourcing parts from the vast market of existing scooter parts. No idea was off the table. All ideas were considered worthy of discussion.

The team surveyed all the city cars currently on the road, like the Smart. They were mostly two-seaters aimed at special needs in the European market and not adaptable to the purpose in India. And the Smart, though small, was essentially a highly engineered luxury car far outside the cost parameters.

More interesting conceptually were vehicles like Ford's short-lived Think Neighbor and Chrysler's still-in-production GEM, which are classified in the U.S. as NEVs, or Neighborhood Electric Vehicles, and can be registered for limited road use. They're cheap, they're clean, they seat four, and they incorporate an external exposed frame.

The idea of building a small car with an exposed frame was

intriguing to the design team. "This was our starting point," designer Nikhil Jadhav told us. "It was unusual, and we thought, *Why not try an unconventional method of making a car, particularly if we can make it cost-effective?*"

The problem is that these look more like golf carts than cars, and fitting a small gasoline or diesel engine won't help with that issue. So from that starting point, the team kept moving in the direction of adding skins to the frame and got closer to a real car.

Initially they had safety bars across the sides to keep people from falling out and to provide at least some side impact protection. From there, they graduated to soft shutters to keep the rain out. As they progressed, they realized that the car needed to have proper doors.

And so it went. The final cost was set in stone, of course. But also safety: they decided early on that the as-then-unnamed Nano had to not just meet regulatory requirements, but surpass them.

That was the problem with some of the golf cart ideas. Yes, the vehicles could have a lower level of emission and safety norms, but that's not how Tata does it. Tata has never been in the business of offering customers embarrassing, unsafe options for which the company has to apologize.

That meant the little car would need to have the performance of a real car, not a golf cart. They knew customers wouldn't accept a car that was slower than a scooter. Who wants to have to drive along on the shoulder, waving people on motorbikes past you?

The other consideration was size.

"We started from the decision that it had to seat four people comfortably," recalled Ravi Rajhans. "So, given that, what was the smallest footprint we could put on the road? Because ultimately we were looking for fundamental changes in the way we think of a car. How can we minimize the materials to give us the cost reduction we needed? Are there new materials? New structural ideas? New methods of manufacturing?"

"I really thought we would have a totally new material for the car,"

Ratan Tata told us. He'd discussed his ideas with Jeffrey Immelt, the CEO of General Electric, and both of them thought this would be a great chance to produce the world's first mass-produced plastic car.

So one of the first discussions was about plastic versus metal.

DON'T SHUT THE DOOR ON NEW IDEAS

Intuitively it makes perfect sense. Plastic is inexpensive and light and can be very, very strong. There's already an industry making plastic parts for body cladding. That should not only help get the body cheaper; it should also mean better performance from smaller engines and thus better mileage and fewer emissions.

In addition, as the Nano team members pursued the idea, it looked as if plastic might be ideal for modular construction of body panels because they can be joined with high tensile adhesives (think superpowerful glue). Another benefit is that the plastic molded part is the same color all the way through, so the cars don't have to be painted. Imagine a group of well-trained young workers in a distant village gluing new Nano bodies together and you can see the appeal.

"Everybody was very enthusiastic about this discussion," said Rajhans. "Some felt that plastic was the better choice; others felt sheet metal would be better in the end. Various people were giving presentations to Mr. Tata and we had a lot of debate—I will not say argument—but a lot of spirited debate where the feeling was that plastic is the cheapest because of its specific gravity and low weight. So we were trying to move in that direction."

On paper, the figures indicated that sheet metal would be cheaper. For months, a great deal of work went into this single topic because until the construction material was decided, only the most conceptual design work could be done.

It seemed obvious that plastic would be cheaper than metal. It wasn't.

"We had almost a session a week probably for three or four months and probably six or seven meetings alone with Mr. Tata on this subject, and almost every time we went there, he had more material than us. We had to accept that we did not have sufficient material to really say that this is the way we should go," continued Rajhans.

"I think more important was, he wanted to really check whether the decision that we are taking is right because if you go for sheet metal or plastic, the entire body philosophy is dependent on that. It is an irreversible change."

A totally plastic-bodied car would be revolutionary, indeed. In the late 1990s, Chrysler experimented with a concept car called the CCV, which was designed with recyclable, injection-molded body panels. The car was made with the same PET plastic used in water bottles and styled to resemble the old Citroën 2CV, and Chrysler hoped to sell it in China for as little as $6,000.

This is one of the earliest sketches from Team Nano, showing the exterior frame and molded plastic panels, easily removable at the front and rear for access to service. Note that even at the beginning, four doors were considered a must on the Nano.

The CCV mirrored many of the innovative ideas that Tata was exploring. The body was to be constructed of four large panels, joined with adhesives in just six or seven hours, a third of the time it takes to make a normal auto body. It was expected to cut the costs of manufacturing by 80 percent.

So why didn't it work?

According to press reports, problems with the molding process itself shut it down. Chrysler officials reported panels sagged slightly, creating "duck ponds" in surfaces that were supposed to be flat or convex. By 2002, they'd given up the idea, although the techniques they developed in their studies were later used for smaller parts of cars.

Molded plastic parts are common on cars as front and rear bumpers, wheel housings, and mirror casings. But just because it hasn't worked yet for full bodies doesn't mean it won't work. The Nano team was tenacious and tried hard to be the first to put it into production.

Immelt sent engineers from the GE Plastics Technology Center in Bangalore with samples. But even with their partner having a base inside India, there were still problems.

First, the kind of plastic that was needed was not manufactured in India. The grades of plastic on which they were basing their cost estimates were imported. Build with imported plastics and you blow the budget.

The second challenge was curing the panels. It required putting them in an autoclave—a kind of giant pressure cooker—and that took a lot of time. Forget that there wasn't an autoclave large enough in India. The process took so much time that it didn't lend itself to mass production in the kinds of numbers Tata knew they would be producing the car.

So if you can't buy the plastic in India and you can't make the panels in India, your options narrow. Either you build the industry to produce plastics in a way no one in the world had yet perfected—something the Tata Group had certainly done before—or you build the car with steel.

Throughout 2003 and 2004, Nano team members explored every option and innovation. They looked at exterior panels made of paper honeycomb and interior panels of soya and woven bamboo. And the more they studied, the more they came to believe that these were all great, worthy technologies and that someday cars would be built with them. Maybe even Nanos.

But at that point, they couldn't build a 1 lakh car with those experimental technologies, for all their interesting benefits. They were not scalable, at least not yet. When you have a budget target like that, big, systemic, game-changing ideas quickly hit the ceiling.

But even if you could make the numbers work, there was another reason not to make a plastic car: customer acceptance.

Nikhil Jadhav explained, "There is a certain amount of refinement that has gone into two-wheelers over the last four to five years in India, and we were very aware of the kind of quality finishes that you get on the vehicles. So if that customer is going to move up the value chain when he buys a car, there is no way he is going to compromise on his expectations for a car."

In other words, don't give me a plastic, "toy car" with less perceived build quality than my scooter. Give me a real car made of steel.

> Chrysler showed the **PLASTIC-BODIED** car to the Chinese government, and the Chinese were **offended** by it . . . They wanted **proper cars,** not this plastic **thing.**

Interestingly Chrysler ran into the same reaction with its plastic-bodied CCV, which was targeted at the emerging Chinese middle class.

"It had a two-piece, blow-molded body with a seam along the roof and you couldn't paint it," former Chrysler CEO Bob Lutz told a reporter at the *Daily Telegraph*. "We showed it to the Chinese government and they were offended by it. They hated it. They wanted proper cars, not this plastic thing."

Plastic injection molding. Paper honeycomb. Soya. Bamboo. Can you imagine a car made from these materials? Off the wall? Yes, but that's Nanovation. It requires a lot of blue-sky thinking, and it leverages the power of what-if to push the edge of the envelope.

As discussions continued, the team quickly expanded, bringing in people from other plants and research centers, like Lucknow and Jamshedpur. They also invited teams from Tata AutoComp (TACO), a sister company that partners with many of the world's biggest auto parts suppliers to design and manufacture parts in India for export and for the growing Indian auto industry. We're talking about joint ventures with companies like Bosch, Johnson Controls, Toyo Radiator, Visteon, and Ficosa. TACO establishes individual research and design centers with each joint venture, so plenty of innovative talent was eager to join the team.

Collaborating and bringing in ideas from the outside are other parts of the Tata culture. "In today's world," insisted Ravi Kant, Tata Motors vice chairman, "you have to realize that you cannot do everything and you cannot control everything and therefore you need to have a collaborative workplace. For a project of this kind to succeed, you need to have everyone collaborating, which is easier said than done. Leading collaboration is a gigantic task in any organization.

"We had to make sure that right from the beginning our people had the ability to network and to get around to people to get things done, whether they were senior people, sideways people, lower people, or outside people. A leader must know how to create the linkages and how to spin these linkages into a nice web of activities. It is very crucial."

Of course, that meant creating access for the chairman to be part of the team and to do it in a way that encouraged creativity and expression instead of shutting them down.

"Leading collaboration is a gigantic task in any organization."

Nanovation brings a wide array of opinions to bear as early as possible in the process, so you don't end up with a small team defending its pet idea against all reason, even if the pet idea is the chairman's. And you don't end up with a chairman who won't let go of ideas that don't work.

Great design moves fastest when it's open to new ideas and when there's diversity in the people offering the ideas. When it comes to great design, Nanovation says the more, the merrier.

That means opening the design process to a broad and diverse group of people. Not just engineers and designers, and not just a design team. Going into the project, the Nano team members knew there wasn't just one true way. Though they didn't know what the right way was yet, they knew they'd find it. They knew they couldn't approach this car in the ordinary way, so they found a new way to design an automobile.

They hadn't found it yet, but they were searching for Nanovation.

NANOBITE

Challenge conventional design, open the door to new ideas—the crazier the better—and encourage people to consider the absurd.

Learn from ideas that won't work. Don't take your eye off a future molded plastic Nano.

Ask, "How far outside the box can we go with a product and still gain customer acceptance?"

When it comes to collaboration, cast a very wide net.

- What could you take away from your products, processes, or service to make them more elegant?
- How could you embrace simplicity to cut costs, reduce cycle time and increase speed, or improve service?
- What off-the-wall materials could you use in new or existing products to cut costs or increase sustainability?

SIX

Shell Shock

"For every failure, there's an alternative course
of action. You just have to find it. When you
come to a roadblock, take a detour."

MARY KAY ASH

The meetings, brainstorming sessions, arguments, and sleepless nights that began in 2003 dragged on through 2004 and 2005. What seemed like just an impossible challenge when the chairman announced it to the world was becoming an unbearable weight.

Many on the team began to wonder secretly if the 1 lakh car was unreachable, a shimmering mirage that moved farther away with each new step. It wasn't until April 2005 that a working mule—a hand-built rough prototype designed to test ideas about the package and the dynamics—was rolled out on the test lot at Pune. And that was an experience almost everyone who was there would like to forget.

So what went wrong? *Shell shock.*

"Delay is the deadliest form of denial."
C. Northcote Parkinson

When people are faced with an impossible task, apoplexy and paralysis are not unusual responses. (Ask us what it feels like to face the blank page at the start of a new book or even the start of a chapter.) This phase—often comical to observers—usually doesn't last long and is often followed by a phase we call "wheel spinning," the process of trying anything that feels like action, hoping you'll get traction somewhere along the line.

Mountain climbers planning an ascent of Everest will tell you of the overwhelming urge to continue planning, organizing supplies, and repacking. Anything to put off the awful—and yet wonderful—day when they actually have to leave base camp and begin the ascent. Daunting, gutsy challenges inspire daunting, world-class procrastination and meaningless distraction.

Different team members grasped for different ideas. Some went back to investigating the idea of safer scooters. They experimented with three-wheelers, open vehicles with soft weather protection, and scooter-based concepts. Some focused on materials—like the plastic versus metal debate—hoping they might discover a magic elixir for low-cost innovative design through a green, sustainable, low-impact material that would revolutionize industrial design. Others got focused on subsystems and iterative design concepts, as if trying to micromanage the solution into being.

And some just gave up.

"We hit the first roadblock," Ratan Tata remembered, "which was our people saying it could not be done. And we lost a lot of time."

Much of the understanding of what happened to the team comes now with the benefit of hindsight and also in the glow of success. But in the early years, success seemed increasingly ephemeral, and there was little clarity about where they were.

(Chris Mayne)

One problem with a three-wheel solution was the association with autorickshaws.

Resistance comes from people who have been doing something one way and do not believe that there is another way to do it. And in the early days of the process, the Nano team members encountered an unwillingness to look at things in different ways. They encountered it from suppliers, from their bosses, and most damaging, from themselves.

"I think if the older segments of our company had run this project," Ratan told us, "it probably would never have happened. The Nano project team was made up of engineers whose average age must have been twenty-five to twenty-six years old. They were willing to believe anything was possible. But the project leader needed to believe that it could be done, too."

We used the term *chairman's folly* earlier. We got it from Ratan Tata himself, who said, "There was a general undercurrent that this was the chairman's folly, that it cannot be done, that people have tried it before and it didn't work. And so the progress was rather slow, and I remember on review meetings I used to get quite upset.

"I found myself in meetings where we got bogged down with what we were going to do. So you sit back and say, 'Why don't we do this?' and then there is usually dead silence in the room and then there is someone who says, 'We could, but, but, but, but . . . ,' and someone else who says, 'We need to look at that.'

"There are two things you have to have. You have to have what-ifers who will explore innovative new paths, and you have to have people who will tell the truth: 'That is not an elegant solution.' Because there were solutions that were inelegant and they would have been put into production unless someone said, 'We are not going to put this on the car. Go back and try again.'

"I think that kind of forced discipline on what we did played a role in making sure the Nano did not just melt into some sort of jelly bean."

Of course, it takes a certain courage to stand up in a meeting and say to the chairman, "This is not an elegant solution." What kind of company allows that to happen?

Mr. Tata is aware of the leadership challenges: "I think I spent more time with the design people on the Nano than any other project in the company. Pretty soon, you get to be on the first-name basis with them and they do open up and sometime they open up and get put down also. Not because of the fact that they opened up but because what they are saying is not going over well."

Working with creative people is one thing many leaders find difficult. It helps that Mr. Tata is also an architect by training.

He explained, "They are all creative. If you can sit with them on a drawing board or at a workstation, and if you can help them along, and if you can excite them with your solution, and if your solutions are not absurd, they will work on them. If you ask, 'What if?' and maybe have the humility to say, 'This is a silly question, but why could you not do this?' you will have most of the people working with you on the same page."

But how do young designers interact with the head of the company without being intimidated? Ravi Kant was running the Commercial Vehicle Division at the time and saw the process close up on many projects. "It has to be an open discussion," he said. "There has to be a good chemistry, and people should be able to talk very freely on both sides. Mr. Tata should be able to talk. If he does not like something, he says so bluntly, and it is taken in the right spirit by the team. At the same time, the team stands on its own ground and fights for their ideas, too. And after discussion, they make a decision together."

"Argument is meant to reveal the truth, not create it."
Edward de Bono

When people criticize what they have not even seen, how do you push through that?

Think about your workplace. How many potentially great ideas get launched and then sink with the weight of doubt as no one steps up to own the project? How many times has your CEO or president launched a slate of supposedly mission-critical imperatives to turn the company around, only to wonder why nobody—but nobody!—got engaged in making it happen? How many "flavor of the month" consultant projects have come and gone, all promising a breakthrough in your performance?

What happened?

Was it that leadership didn't follow up, or did everyone just stonewall the effort? How many times have you been part of the stonewalling, just assuming people would get tired of ramming new ideas down your throat so you could go back to doing your job as usual? How many times have you been charged with leading change in your organization, only to find you were completely on your own?

What do you do when you discover everyone's hoping you and your big idea will go away? Do you keep pushing them gently forward? Or do you give up and go in search of other, more receptive teams?

It's not that people don't care. It's that we become hardened to change and incapable of believing in the possibility that something great is on the other side of the door, were we only to open it. We come to believe so firmly that nothing will change for the better that we stop believing it can. Even worse, we stop hoping it will.

Ratan Tata, after a couple of years, could understandably have decided that the Nano was not going to happen. That it was too hard a challenge and he was not short of challenges. But he didn't give up. He stayed with it and encouraged people to press on.

In our experience, big projects fail because the leadership fails to do four things:

1. Make the desired results crystal clear. You hear a lot of talk about goal setting, but what you don't hear is what getting to the goal is supposed to accomplish for the company, for the customers, and for the community—the altruistic results. Talking about the altruistic value in realizing a goal gives people something more meaningful to work for than just numbers or targets.

2. Get involved with the work. Leaders can't send out a memo—or even the best-thought-out strategic plan—and expect it to accomplish anything meaningful. They have to follow up and be part of the process. They have to identify with their employees, feeling and experiencing their frustrations. That means working with and understanding the people who will make it happen, understanding the customers, understanding what can change and what must never change, and then showing people that they really will support them in getting the results.

3. Identify believers. A leader can't champion an idea without believers because a leader can't be everywhere, can't know

everything, and can't do everything. Believers aren't yes-men. They'll push back and help you refine your thinking because they believe in the results, not the process. And they'll put a shoulder to the wheel with you to get those results as long as they believe you're involved. Get enough believers, and what do you know? The impossible becomes achievable!

"We spent much of our time disbelieving," Ratan told us. "Getting over the disbelief was the hard part. The soft option was to move away from the target. But when they realized I was not going to budge and we made the appropriate leadership changes, we finally started to make some progress."

4. Understand there is no quick fix. Leaders often have good instincts; they know what to do, why they should be doing it, and in many cases, how to get a project done. In a world that increasingly expects instant gratification, the challenge is slugging through the pain and sacrifice required to make a big dream a reality. It's not easy. It takes intensity, tenacity, and the discipline to say no to short-term distractions. Many aren't up to the task. As David Maister points out in his brilliant book *Strategy and the Fat Smoker*, most fat smokers already know they should change. They also know why; and having access to plenty of proven strategies, they know how. So why don't they change? Many lack the willpower to go through the pain and hard work it takes to get there. Many people simply can't or choose not to weather the ups and downs, trial and error, of doing something really difficult. Just because the way is clear and the answers are obvious doesn't make it easy. Many business leaders and would-be innovators are up against the same challenges.

One important lesson of Nanovation is this: on the road to the impossible dream, one can't expect a speedy trip. There will be roadblocks, detours, potholes, and traffic.

You can't succeed without first failing.

On the day the Nano was first revealed to the public—to international acclaim—everyone on the Nano team told us this was more a story of failures than a parade of successes. Most great advances are. Getting there took six years of grinding experimentation, failure, and starting over. This is why the bigger and more daunting the project, the more a leader must become a dispenser of hope and encouragement.

DON'T SETTLE
FOR THE SECOND-BEST IDEA

In one sense, Ratan Tata himself slowed down the process with what designers and engineers on the Nano team describe as his "no compromise" approach. He urged them not to settle on a concept too early, not to narrow down their options, not to limit their creativity.

"Creativity is a great motivator because it makes people interested in what they are doing. Creativity gives the possibility of some sort of achievement to everyone. Creativity makes life more fun and more interesting."
Edward de Bono

He even encouraged the reinvestigation of three-wheelers and other scooter-based options. Although he already made it clear in the *Financial Times* interview that this new little vehicle would be a real car, it was reasonable to allow others to follow that thread. If a scooter-based option could get them to the desired results, it had to be looked at.

Call it two years of research and team building, not wasted time. Two years of asking some of the most fundamental questions and reaching conclusions based on hard work. Two years of trudging through fear, doubt, and frustration, putting one foot in front of the other, holding on to a thread of hope that it could be done. From this point on, most of the design work would be iterative—looking at how to improve individual design items, how to take costs out of them, and how to innovate an entirely new class of car. The work of deciding what kind of car it would be was done.

It would be a four-seat, four-wheel car. It would have four doors. It would be made of sheet metal.

And it would have its engine in the rear.

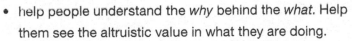

NANOBITE

If the innovation is truly disruptive and game changing . . .

- help people understand the *why* behind the *what*. Help them see the altruistic value in what they are doing.
- get senior leaders to roll up their sleeves and get involved so they can feel the team's frustration and celebrate its small wins.
- build a critical mass of champions and believers whose enthusiasm for the project is contagious.
- realize there's no quick fix. Expect fear, doubt, and frustration to show up disguised as procrastination, resistance, and shell shock. Then prepare for how you are going to deal with it.

QUESTIONS

- Do your senior executives make it comfortable for junior people to talk freely? To disagree with them?

- Do you have what-ifers on your team—people who ask, "What if?" and aren't afraid to look for answers in seemingly crazy places?

- Do you have truth tellers on your team—people who stand up in a meeting and say, "That is not an elegant solution; let's go back to the drawing board"?

- What if your company refused to be "seduced" by its own success?

- What if more than half your profits came from products and services developed in the last two years?

SEVEN

Have an Ace in the Hole

There is a caste system surrounding science, where scientists are isolated from economics while the wider population waits hopefully for scientific solutions. The result is two castes, those who do science and those who have science done to them.

KUMAR BHATTACHARYYA, BARON
BHATTACHARYYA OF MOSELEY

Y ou don't just wake up one day and build a car that blows the doors off the world's expectations in a brilliant display of Nanovation. And the Nano isn't the first time Tata Motors decided to build a radically innovative vehicle that brought dignity and mobility to the bottom of the pyramid. They did it just a few years before—to incredible success—with a small utility truck called the Ace.

The Ace was designed as a global alternative to the three-wheel utility scooters used for city deliveries, rural transport, and farm work. It's small enough to negotiate ancient alleys and narrow farm tracks, but it's big enough to carry a significant amount of materials, like a couple of full-sized refrigerators, a load of car engines, or three-quarters of a ton of animal feed. Priced about twice the cost of a Nano, it instantly created a new, unfilled niche in the market, not just in India but throughout the world. And best of all, it's a real truck with a real, enclosed cab and four wheels.

A real truck, with dignity.

(Tata Motors)

This is the Ace. It's a real truck.

Okay, so big deal. They built a little truck. But that's not the whole story. It's much bigger than that.

Nanovators start with the conviction that new ideas are about dignity for both employees and customers. For customers, it's something that makes their world better—a better design, a better life, a better world. For employees, it's the dignity of being part of something great.

Think of it this way. You come into work every morning and sit down at your desk. If your mission for the year is to increase the uptake of unit CKR3995-AB3R (and also AB3R-W if you can convince your customers it's really not the *worst* thing your company ever made) by double digits, we think you might need a bigger cup of coffee to awaken your interest. We can't think of anything less interesting than just pushing mediocre products out the door.

But if you sit at that desk know-ing that the product you're pushing is going to uplift the lives of 250,000 farm families by the end of next year, you'll sit up and take notice. If you know it won't just make a little difference but will provide them new opportunities by an order of magnitude, you start to get engaged. And if you're in a great country that's working to take its place at the table with the rest of the world's great countries, and making this new product is part of the wave of can-do spirit that's going to get your country there, now you're excited. You want to get involved in that. Your friends and

(Chris Mayne)

How are you going to lift yourself out of poverty if this is how you get your product to market?

family want to hear about your exciting project. And if you're frustrated by the numbers of your fellow citizens who live in poverty, out of reach of opportunity—if you see that getting them in the game is good for everyone—you'll get passionate about your product and your job.

If you see that they are passionately waiting for you to finish your coffee and start pushing that product out the door, you'll become a believer, a fanatic. People love to push cool products, especially if they have an emotional connection and deep understanding of what their work is creating.

To understand the story of the Nano, you have to understand the Ace. And you can't understand the Ace unless you go back to a day in May 2000 when Tata Motors posted the first red ink in the company's history.

"It was corporate India's biggest loss ever," Ravi Kant told Robyn

Meredith of *Forbes* magazine. The Indian economy had hit a recession in 1999, causing sales of Tata trucks to drop 40 percent. In fiscal 2000, the company lost $110 million. "The crisis changed us. We told ourselves, 'Never again.'"

Stunned, the leadership turned to the Warwick Manufacturing Group, a British consulting organization founded by the Indian-born engineer Kumar Bhattacharyya. Bhattacharyya, affiliated with Warwick University, had done so much to revive British engineering and innovation in the last few decades that he was honored with a lifetime peerage. The man with the impish smile is now known as Baron Bhattacharyya of Moseley and sits in the House of Lords. Bhattacharyya already had a relationship with Tata, coming in once or twice a year to offer advice. Ravi Kant, then running the Commercial Vehicle Division, was at the meeting when the team made a presentation on their plans for cost reduction.

(The authors)
Former managing director of Tata Motors, Ravi Kant, the man the press called "Mr. Impossible."

Baron Bhattacharyya offered up the unpleasant truth: "You have to cut more."

"We were talking about less than a 1 percent cost reduction at the time," Kant remembered, "and it was very hard to see how we were going to get more than that. But Lord Bhattacharyya just laughed at us."

Bhattacharyya told them, "What are you talking about, a 1 percent reduction? One percent is a rounding error. You should talk about a 10 percent reduction in costs."

"We were stunned. Everyone went, 'What? Ten percent? How

is that possible?' At the time, the margin of profitability in the automobile industry was 5, 6, maybe 7 percent. How does one talk of a 10 percent cost reduction?"

Shaken, Ravi Kant emerged from that meeting and immediately called together a task force to work on the problem. The leaders of the car division did the same.

A small group of engineers and managers gathered the next morning at the Lake House, a beautiful retreat and meeting center across from the Pune plant, looking out over a lake the company had built to supply the plant with water. Most of them were under thirty years old, and among them were two people who were to play a big part in the story of the Nano.

(Sanjit Kundu, *BusinessWorld*)

Girish Wagh was just one of many talented young engineers at Tata.

One was an engineer named Girish Wagh, just twenty-nine years old. People thought of him as a bright young man to watch. They were right.

The other was Prakash M. Telang. At the time, he worked in light commercial vehicle manufacturing at the Pune plant. Today, he runs all of Tata Motors, succeeding Ravi Kant as managing director after the delivery of the first Nanos to the public.

Ravi Kant got right to the point: "We have a problem. We're bleeding money."

He explained the 10 percent cost reduction target. The young engineers looked at each other. It was not in their boss's nature to be a kidder, but what else could this be? It had to be a joke. They knew that costs had increased every year since the company was formed. Take 10 percent out of the cost of the entire company? It was absurd.

(Tata Motors)

Prakash Telang was president of Light and Small Commercial Vehicles when he led the cost-cutting charge. He now runs Tata Motors. Here he is talking with former General Motors CEO Rick Wagoner and other auto executives.

Nevertheless, they had their task. Ravi asked Telang to chair the meeting: "Please work up a basic plan. I want to present it to the executive committee at 3:00 p.m."

Sure. And tomorrow we'll walk to the top of Mount Everest for a group snap.

Shock, however, soon turned into a focused and heated brainstorming session on where they could radically trim costs. Because the company had always grown, costs had always been regarded as a number that followed the rising top line. Keep the ratio in a reasonable and responsible relationship to revenue, everyone figured, and costs would take care of themselves. Now they had to rethink everything their company had done since 1945.

"It wasn't easy," Ravi remembered. "People here were very proud, even a bit arrogant, which happens with successful organizations. The big loss dented our pride; it punched a hole in the arrogance and complacency. The company could have sunk under the weight of the loss, or it could have pulled up its socks and rejuvenated itself. We chose to do the latter."

Again, you can see the resolve and conviction that are so much a part of the Tata culture. The humility to say, "We've become arrogant," and the courage to say, "We will fight our way out," make up the very spirit that moves a company from crisis-led change to opportunity-led change.

By midafternoon of that day, the young engineers presented a plan to their bosses. They had come up with ways to cut costs by

The Lake House at the Pune plant, the conference center where Tata executives hold strategy meetings and where Ravi Kant told Girish Wagh, Prakash Telang, and the team to find a way to cut 10 percent of Tata Motors' operating costs in just six hours.

6.5 percent. Watching their presentation, Ravi Kant was astonished. "It was an amazing breakthrough," he remembered thinking, but it wasn't enough. "We told them to go back and keep trying. We needed 10 percent, not 6.5 percent."

In just three weeks, they had a plan that took them all the way to 10 percent and were well on their way to getting there. They instituted online purchasing from Internet auctions, then began holding their own reverse auctions, inviting suppliers to compete for the right to supply them for less. They identified six thousand redundant positions and offered voluntary early retirement instead of mass layoffs. They began benchmarking processes to see where they could take time, people, power, or other costs out of everything they did. And very quickly, it all began to work.

In two years, they went from a loss of $110 million to a profit of the same amount.

When Girish Wagh talks about those days, there's still a hint of astonishment in his voice at what they pulled off: "While we were working on the commercial vehicle business, the passenger car people were working in parallel, and whatever worked, we shared with both sides." At the time, the Indica had just been launched, and the development costs of that car were still weighing heavily.

"Tremendous work was done on cost reduction on the Indica, and that helped the Indica break even pretty fast. We took their processes and made them work, and that's how we went from the biggest loss in business history in India to the biggest turnaround in the country's history."

The press called Ravi Kant "Mr. Impossible." He shakes that off with humility. "See," he explained, "one of the key strengths of Tata Motors is we are steeped in technical knowledge and a passion for doing something that is impossible."

> What kind of culture do you work in? What kind of culture do you tend to inspire? A "what if" or a "yeah, but" culture?

He offered as an example the story of how the Indian government once decided to stop the inflow of all technology into the country: "The year was 1969 and we had to stand on our own. That is when the ability to rely on ourselves began to develop. Over time, that turned into a deep-rooted expertise and competence in solving problems. Given a strong challenge, the company responds extremely well."

A culture of doing the impossible makes a big difference to companies that try to do . . . well . . . the impossible!

How many times have you pitched an off-the-wall idea and had it shot down by your teammates, only to see someone else in another company bring it to life? How often have you been the one doing the shooting, the one who said, "That's not the way it works"?

Tata has created a culture where people at all levels are inspired and free to "what if" the impossible to life. Unfortunately there are far too many companies that allow a "yeah, but" culture to put potential Nanovations to death.

As we said earlier, a great idea is nothing without the ability to execute. And that takes a culture with excellent skill sets in getting things done. A culture of competence. A culture that isn't afraid to put that competence to work in the service of something that seems far out of reach to ordinary people.

But that's the Tatas and that's their culture. When the British told Jamsetji Tata that India couldn't be a steel-producing power, that India couldn't produce the right kind of coal for steel mills, that India couldn't produce hydroelectric power or produce the quality of steel needed for railroads, he did it anyway, recruiting the technical help he needed from the United States and Japan.

But it didn't stop with him. When J. R. D. Tata decided to start an airline, he was told he could never compete with the European, American, and Japanese airlines. So he started Air India and proved he could.

And then there's Ratan Tata, whose technical competence is exceeded only by his vision. If he can imagine something, there are very few people left who would dare tell him it couldn't be done—not after all the times he's been able to do what he said he would do.

Virtually every corporate leader we spoke to in India, from Dr. Brijmohan Lal Munjal of Hero Honda and Jamshyd Godrej of Godrej & Boyce to Anup Banerji of the State Bank of India, said the same thing: "If Ratan says he is going to do it, he will do it."

So, delivering radical cost cuts that no one thought was possible? Not easy, but for Tata, doable!

That's an understatement, as Kant, Telang, and Wagh were about to prove again.

In December 2000 just six months after that fateful meeting at the Lake House, Ravi Kant called Girish Wagh to his office. He told him that they needed to think about protecting their market share, which was then 55 percent of the commercial vehicle market.

"Any new player coming in will nibble away on the market share and start growing. A nimble company can get very close to the customer and bring them something a big company like ours will not even think of.

"So let's be nimble. Let's think first."

At the time, Ravi Kant was drawing up a strategic plan for the market, driven both by rapid demographic growth and by the accompanying, come-from-behind efforts of India to provide the highway infrastructure needed as the economy expanded. That meant there would be huge growth in the long-distance hauler, 18-wheeler market to transport goods between cities and into rural areas, and in the small trucks needed to go the last mile for deliveries.

"Given a strong challenge, the company responds extremely well."

And Tata Motors was short in both markets.

Girish looked at his boss and groaned inwardly. *Please*, he thought, *pick someone else!* He was in the middle of a complicated and critical rollout of Balanced Scorecard throughout the division, something he felt he should see to completion.

But Ravi was persistent and shared his vision and strategic thinking with Girish, explaining that he had formed four cross-functional teams of young engineers to go into the marketplace to see what was missing. Where was there a market opportunity that no one was seeing?

As Ravi talked about what was at stake for both the company and its customers, Girish began to get excited. He remembered a recent meeting where a grinning Bhattacharyya sat with a group of young engineers and told them they should take a close look at developing something for the bottom of the commercial vehicle market, a "down and dirty" truck for the little guy, as he colorfully described it. An entry-level truck that could wean drivers off three-wheelers and even bring new entrepreneurs into the short haul and delivery business.

And now here was Ravi Kant, reaching for the same thing. Reaching for the Ace in the hole.

NANOBITE

Crisis usually precedes change—buck the trend.

A wake-up call can produce either ideas for rejuvenation or excuses. It's your choice.

You are most vulnerable to arrogance, complacency, and indifference when you are successful.

If success has gotten the best of you, have the humility to ask, "Where have we become arrogant?" and have the courage to ask, "How will we change?"

QUESTIONS

- Is your corporate culture characterized by "yeah, but" or "what if?"
- When outsiders walk through your door with far-flung ideas, do you give them serious consideration or write them off as "not invented here"?
- Does your organization have a history of attempting big things that are far out of reach or a history of going for the guaranteed win?

EIGHT
People Ignore Design
That Ignores People

Unless we're in touch with our customers, our model
of the world can diverge from reality. There's no
substitute for innovation, of course, but innovation
is no substitute for being in touch, either.

STEVE BALLMER

What both Ravi Kant and Baron Bhattacharyya knew was that, because the Indian economy was expanding so quickly, there were service vacuums throughout the infrastructure. One of the most pressing demands was for people who could provide efficient and reliable delivery services when the trains, planes, and big trucks rolled into town. In 2000, only two vehicles in the lower end could fill that need. One was the three-wheel autorickshaw, which was selling from Rs. 90,000 to 160,000 (about $2,000 to $3,000). The next product available in that market was the pickup, which was selling at Rs. 300,000 to 350,000, about twice the cost of the autorickshaw. And there was nothing in between.

"We had a pickup in those days, but it was not doing so well," Girish admitted. "It cost too much to own and too much to run for a small delivery business. The economics didn't support it. And that was all we had to offer."

You have to admire the spirit of someone who refuses to be stopped by practicality, reality, or embarrassment. This may be the most coconuts ever loaded onto an autorickshaw. No information on how far it got. Now do you see why we say India is unstoppable?

Without a market alternative, the number of smoke-belching three-wheelers was exploding. And since they were already clogging city streets and country lanes, no one but the autorickshaw makers was happy with the situation.

India needed something better, and so did Tata. But how do you fight against a competitor—even the hated smoky autorickshaws—when they sell for half the cost of a truck?

Girish and his fellow team members went out to see what people needed. And our wording is very exact: they didn't go to find out what people thought of them or their products, and they didn't hold focus groups to see if people liked their ideas. They went to see what people *needed*. They went to the bazaars and the small factories. They went to the villages. They talked to farmers, truckers, builders, and small entrepreneurs.They asked endless questions, and they listened to the answers, just as they've done since the 1800s.

In their search, they found a revelation.

"We started meeting customers," Girish Wagh remembered, "and I mean, you can use all those phrases, 'wow effect' or 'moments of truth,' but it was really fascinating meeting the customers. It really opened our eyes.

"We discovered a sweet spot in the market that no one was serving. There was a clear indication from customers on both sides that they would move to the middle of that spot if we offered something.

"The three-wheeler owners wanted a four-wheeler with a larger payload and were willing to pay more and sacrifice fuel economy to get it. The pickup owners were ready to compromise on payload and speed for something less costly."

They spent a lot of time with potential customers, watching how they worked, how they used their pickups and rickshaws, trying to understand what they needed in a new kind of truck and how it would change their lives. What he found was not much different from what Ratan Tata and the Nano team saw when they looked into why people wanted to get off scooters and into real cars. They wanted reliable mobility. They wanted it to make sense economically. And they wanted dignity.

That word again.

In Tamil Nadu, in southern India, Girish spent several days meeting villagers, farmers, and small business owners. India's most urbanized state, Tamil Nadu has the highest concentration of business enterprises in the country. People there are industrious, interested in expanding trade, and even in the villages, focused on growth.

They are hungry for change, hungry to succeed, and limited only by the reach of their pocketbooks. But give them a chance to make a rupee, and they will make five. Give them the chance to make money with a truck, and they will turn it into an unstoppable business proposition.

(Chris Mayne)

Villagers make money by selling pottery, spices, and furniture, among other items— only if they have a way to take those goods to market.

In one small village, Girish spent an entire day with one young entrepreneur. The man was as yet unmarried and, without a family, put most of his energy into his business, which he conducted from an auto-rickshaw. He made deliveries and carried loads back and forth from the nearest town.

"Yes," he said, "I would very much like to have a four-wheel truck if I could afford it."

He gave Girish several reasons. First, a four-wheeler was more stable, and he could carry larger loads. Larger loads meant the chance to make more money per trip. Second, the roads to the villages were often rough and sometimes muddy. Three-wheelers were unable to traverse these roads or had to do so very slowly. So a small four-wheel truck would go faster from village to village, with a bigger payload. The increased payoff would allow him to expand.

Yes, but what else? As they rode together on the man's rounds during the day, Girish kept asking, "What else?"

"A four-wheel truck is safer."

"What else?"

"A four-wheel truck wouldn't have to work so hard. It would last longer."

"What else?"

"A four-wheel truck with a proper cab would be more comfortable. I could carry a helper more easily."

"What else?"

The young man kept listing all the benefits of a truck, and Girish kept asking. He felt there was more somehow, another element that was beyond the functional attributes the man was listing.

Finally, at the end of the day, they got down to it. As the sun was setting, the man told him what else was in his head.

"With a truck like you are talking," he confided in Girish, "I will get better marriage proposals in the village."

Now, there's a cause worth fighting for! And when Girish Wagh headed back to Pune, he knew he had the team he needed to win the battle.

Real men don't drive
RICKSHAWS.

The truth Girish learned that evening in a Tamil Nadu village was that while there are good economic and practical reasons to justify the expense of a truck over a rickshaw, the real reasons were aspirational: personal pride, status in the community, and bragging rights. Four wheels are better than three for many reasons, but the best is that they make you feel better about yourself.

Real men don't drive rickshaws.

"That was his way of expressing the latent desire of graduating to a four-wheeler," Girish remembered. "Customers who were driving three-wheelers told us that society looks down on them because they drive these vehicles.

Girish continued, "If they could get a four-wheeler near the price of three-wheelers, meeting all the regulations and norms, with better payload, a safe, stable, good-looking vehicle, they would jump on it."

But not just three-wheeler drivers. They also talked to lots of customers who already drove good, strong trucks, like the Tata 407, which had been around since the mid-1980s and was a major success for the company, much more popular than similar trucks from Toyota, Mazda, and Nissan. It was a terrific vehicle, popularly called "the Champion" by customers around India.

"One day I was with a customer in Gujarat, and we were traveling in his 407. I was sitting beside him, and I asked, 'Why are you not happy with your business?' He said they were not happy because they were competing with three-wheelers, and the three-wheelers could charge less. They were taking away their business, but he did not want to go for a three-wheeler because he felt it was lowering his prestige. He said, 'You reduce the 407 to half of its size, half of its price, and double the fuel efficiency and give it to us. We will buy that.'"

So the sweet spot in the small truck market was defined by customers below the niche who aspired to more and by customers above the niche who needed to cut costs while maintaining their pride.

(Tata Motors)

This big boy—the 407—was one of many bruising, hardworking trucks that gave Tata a 55 percent market share in India.

Discovering what people *need*. Isn't this one key to all blockbuster products? The essence of great design is being there. Being where the customers will be when they use the product. Experiencing what the customers experience. Letting the customers feel your presence in the product and think, *Someone identifies with my life and work.*

WHAT IF?

What if everyone on your design team was required to spend one week each year shadowing and working with customers and experiencing their experiences?

Girish Wagh demonstrated something we see in all great Nanovators. He was unwilling to stop at the first answer or the second or even the tenth. He kept digging. Like an ethnographer, he genuinely wanted to understand the rational and emotional needs of the customer at a deeper level. And he refused to give up until that understanding was realized.

Like the Nano team a few years later, the Ace team found themselves with a mission to bring dignity and improvement to life in the villages and towns and give increased mobility to the lowest rung of emerging businesspeople and farmers.

Returning to Pune and the ERC, the small truck team went to work assembling their data and using it to translate customer requirements into product specifications and performance targets. Ravi Kant arranged for external market research, and it verified what Girish Wagh and the team had reported from the field.

There was resistance inside the company from people who felt the little truck was somehow "beneath" them, but Ravi Kant continually supported the team. "He didn't look at it from the point of view of whether Tata should or shouldn't do something," Girish remembered.

"He looked at the opportunity in the market and pushed us to do something."

They produced a mule, which was shown to Ratan Tata, who was extremely encouraging. "This is a good opportunity," Mr. Tata told the team. "We should explore it."

And explore they did.

Remember, the organization was still in the middle of a massive cost-cutting discipline, and the Ace project became a test case for best practices on how to drive a project through to completion and how to take costs out of both the product development process and the production process. They learned to design costs out of the product itself and the production process, right from the beginning, instead of presenting the production team a set of blueprints and letting them try to figure out how to save money. They took what they'd learned from the development of the Indica, which was the first car developed entirely in India. And they took direction from outside consultants brought in to help them transform their game.

"Finally," remembered Wagh, "we were an engineering company, and the product was an engineered product. So, from the company's perspective, we had a leap in learning on the engineering front as well as on the business front."

In the case of the Indica, the first models to hit the road were not as good as they needed to be, and everyone at Tata saw that. Wagh said, "But the people were very fast to react and to come out with a refined product. It was a big learning, and that engineering learning percolated into the Ace when we began to develop it."

They were learning how to engineer products and processes.

They were learning how to drive more efficient production.

They were learning how to take costs out.

"It was all a fantastic learning experience for us," Girish Wagh says now of the 350-member team that developed the Ace. "How a suspension should be designed so that it gives comfort to the passenger is some very, very core engineering. It's not about management or process. It is core engineering. We got that learning from Indica, and we put it to work on the Ace."

They were leveraging their strengths and everything they were learning.

They learned to give more value per rupee than anyone in the market. The lowest operating economics, the lowest operating cost, higher fuel efficiency: they began to build these key drivers of success into all their processes internally and into all the products they offered the public. Girish Wagh was named project manager of the new truck, now called the Ace, and they took everything they'd been learning and put it to work.

In May 2005, the new Ace was launched, and the company sold one hundred thousand trucks in the first twenty months, all manufactured at the plant in Pune.

(Flickr/Scratanut)

This Ace owner is unstoppable. What a change!

Priced about Rs. 225,000 (about $4,000 at the time), the truck hit right in the sweet spot. It was easy for a rickshaw owner to justify the 50 percent premium over a three-wheeler and easy for a bigger truck owner to justify downsizing to a more efficient-to-run small truck.

The Ace has already had a powerful effect on Indian rural life.

"It's like the cell phone," explained Ravi Kant. "When cell phones hit the villages, suddenly people were able to communicate across distances. Forget long distance; I mean just being able to ring up someone in the next village. Once upon a time, you would have had to walk, maybe several hours, just to deliver a message. Just to say hello. Now you can ring them up.

"It's the same with the Ace. As we connect the villages with motorable roads, people begin to make trips. What once was a half-day trip on foot paths, now you drive an Ace to the market and back in thirty minutes. It was a trip one might make once a month. But now you might go three or four times a week. Suddenly getting from the village to the town is a reality. It's an explosive thing. He takes his entire family of six. There is a beauty parlor, a library, or a picture show. There is shopping.

"So one trip a month becomes twenty or thirty *human* trips. The Ace helped fuel an explosive need to travel and an explosive increase in the reach of goods and services."

The success of the Ace did not go unnoticed around the world. In 2008, Chrysler signed an agreement to import electric-powered Ace vans into the United States for the U.S. Post Office.

And it didn't go unnoticed inside Tata, either.

By 2005, Girish was participating on some cross-functional teams helping the Nano team look at ways to take costs out of the car. He had also been making presentations on the Tata Business Excellence Model to other companies. One of these presentations was to a board on which Ratan Tata sat. Impressed with what he saw, Ratan invited Girish to his office at Bombay House.

Entering the chairman's fourth-floor office for the first time ever, Girish was understandably nervous: "I mean, he was so kind and I almost went weak in the knees. He took me around his office, showed me everything, and asked me lots of questions." The chairman talked to him at length about the Ace and what they had learned from the experience.

"I think the first thing we learned," Girish told the chairman, "was that you have to create a balance between cost, quality, and time. Out of balance, one will suffer. Out of balance, you send an inconsistent message to the team. Too much push on cost, and either quality or time will suffer. Rush too much to get a low-cost solution, and that's all you get, low cost. We wanted more. We wanted a great low-cost solution that would be a landmark, not a passing bump in the road.

"Second, we learned how important it is to set stretch goals for the entire project team. You energize the team, but you also have to support them in difficult times. Stretch goals challenge your talent and your beliefs about yourself. There is a time when you wonder if you are good enough to make this happen. But stretch targets force you into innovative thinking because nothing but real innovation will help you. And when you find yourself suddenly having break-through thoughts—and putting those thoughts in action—it really increases the confidence of each member of the team. You think, *Okay, we did that. What can we do next?*"

They talked about the Nano, too. "He said, 'One of these days, I would like you to get more involved with the small car project, maybe even lead it." It was a flattering thing to hear, but Girish didn't pay too much attention. He had enough on his plate ensuring the production of the Ace continued to keep customers happy.

The meeting ran so long that Ratan had to push back his next meeting. But his focus has always been on identifying and encouraging young leaders in the company. Girish had led a team of 350 engineers, designers, and manufacturing experts on the Ace project, and they delivered something that was changing the game.

And in 2005, that was just the kind of leadership the Nano team needed.

NANOBITE

People ignore design that ignores people.

Be an ethnographer—dig deep to understand your customers.

Innovation starts with experiencing your customers' experiences.

Customers may not be able to tell you exactly what they want, but spend enough time with them and they will show you what they need.

Stretch goals challenge what you believe about yourself and expand your capacity to innovate.

QUESTIONS

- When was the last time someone in your firm spent enough time with customers to watch how they work and how they use your products and to really understand their needs anew?
- When people use your products and services, do they think, *Someone identifies with my life and work*?
- Stretch goals help you identify talent. Is there someone on a project team today who shines and could lead a new innovation project tomorrow?

NINE
From Silos to Seamless

I think tolerating a certain degree of failure—not because it's good for you but because it's a necessary part of growth—is a very important part of the message the leadership can give.

HOWARD GARDNER

As happens in many companies, the Tata Group had its share of silos and people acting territorial. And one of the learnings from the events of 2000 was the importance of tearing down those walls. As chairman, Ratan Tata pushed hard to make the companies more seamless—not just within individual companies but across the entire Group. If Tata Motors perfects a new product introduction process, Tata Steel and Tata Teleservices need to explore how to adopt it to their uses immediately. And if they improve it, the improvements need to flow back. Immediately.

Ravi Kant was just as passionate about increasing seamlessness and cross-functional sharing. The experience of cutting costs and turning the company around, along with the lessons of the Ace development, proved to be valuable lessons for everyone in Tata.

And whenever they encountered a challenge, he picked up a team of bright people from all parts of the organization, put them under the guidance of a senior leader like Prakash Telang, and got them thinking, talking, and sharing.

"It's hard to believe," Girish Wagh told us, "but there were people who had worked for twenty-four years in the organization in Pune or Jamshedpur, but they had never visited the other plant. Ravi completely broke that isolation. He started alternating monthly reviews between the two plants, so one month we would have the review in Jamshedpur and all of us from Pune would go there.

"People used to complain, 'What is this? I mean, thirty people flying from Pune to Jamshedpur, what is the cost? Hotels, guest houses, what is the cost?' But he had a clear objective. Just like, unless we go to the customer, we do not understand what the customer wants. So, unless we go and empathize with somebody, unless we try to be in his or her shoes, we will not understand the problem. It took a lot of effort, but he broke these seams."

THE TRUE TEST OF LEADERSHIP IS INFLUENCE WITHOUT AUTHORITY

As an extreme test of seamlessness, when Girish took charge of the Ace project, he had direct authority over a team of only five or six people. That meant he was accountable for a landmark project in the company but needed to depend on department heads of other groups to support him, some of whom were several levels his senior.

"I must say, it was a painful process," he recalled. "It is not easy. You are the head of a big department, a general manager, a very senior level, and I was very junior. Yet I am coming to you and asking you to do things. There were some initial reservations—'Why is he coming and asking me things?'—but I took the approach of being humble but forceful: 'Sir, this is something we need your help on. Please. Now.' And once we had his support, his people were glad to help us."

Ratan Tata made sure the same interaction was happening over on the Nano team, and one morning in April 2005, everyone on the Nano team gathered in Pune to test-drive the first mule, the first drivable "lab" for ideas. On hand were the four members of the initial team that met with the chairman back in 2003, along with engineers from all over the company who had been part of discussions during the past two years. Also on hand were several top leaders in charge of the plant, engineering, and the passenger car business. Ravi Kant was there from the Commercial Vehicle Division, along with Girish Wagh. And of course, Ratan was there.

A mule is the first chance for designers and engineers to see their ideas in three dimensions and to test them against the realities of gravity, friction, and space. Have they allowed enough room for occupants? Are the overall dimensions pleasing? Does the engine provide enough power?

On this first mule, the frame and body were hand-tooled sheet metal on a borrowed suspension. There were four seats but no doors. The engine was a 20 horsepower, single-cylinder marine engine made by another division of Tata. "We wanted to see," said Narendra Kumar Jain, the head of the engine team, "if an engine like that would work."

It didn't.

Ratan Tata got in the prototype and drove it around on the test track at the plant. When he got out, he wasn't impressed and everyone knew it.

"I think I should not have driven this," Mr. Tata said to the assembled engineers. Clearly 20 horsepower was not enough.

Listen, Learn, and Move On

How do you keep the team motivated when you fail? When you've worked for more than two years, only to have the chairman drive the test bed and say, "This is not it; it's not even close," you have to have a culture that inspires resilience. That means "listen, learn, let go, and move on." You have to have a culture that fervently believes tomorrow will be a better day.

As they stood around the mule that day, few lightbulbs were going off. And really, no one expected anything different. They knew they weren't there yet. The decision was clear. They were going back to the start on virtually every idea but the basic layout of the car.

"Keep trying," Ratan Tata told the team as they stood there that day. "We can do better."

Learning what doesn't work is as important as learning what does, and no one knows that better than Ratan Tata. He pushed the team to meet stretch targets, but there was no blame for ideas that didn't work.

That first mule proved they didn't have enough power, and so they set a new stretch goal of at least matching the road performance of what was then the least expensive car on the road in India, the Maruti 800. It wasn't a power target but a performance target: there are many ways to get a car with a smaller engine to match the performance of a more powerful car. You can reduce weight, change gearing, or increase torque. What mattered to the Nano team was that the car could keep up with traffic both in town and on the highway, that it would feel and drive like larger and more expensive cars, and that no one in an autorickshaw would honk for the car's driver to get out of the way.

It's not pleasant to show an idea to a crowd of your peers and have it disappoint, and it's critical that no one plays the blame game. So your idea doesn't work, big deal; okay, so now we know. And your idea helps us cross more options off our list so we can begin to narrow in on the ideas that *do* work. A lot was learned from that first mule, and everyone who was there went off knowing two things: they weren't there yet, and there were going to be no easy answers on this project.

In July 2005, Ratan asked Ravi Kant to move up to managing director of Tata Motors. In August, Girish Wagh came over from the Commercial Vehicle side to run a one-day cost-reduction workshop on the Nano. While they were brainstorming, Girish got a call on his cell. It was from Ravi Kant, so he put the phone to his ear and quietly said hello.

"I know you are in the workshop," Ravi told him, "so just listen to what I'm saying and don't respond. I'm moving you onto the small car team. I want you to run it like you did the Ace project."

Girish's answer? "What can I say? You told me not to respond!"

And that was that. Of course, Girish wanted to work on what everyone thought might be the most exciting project for years. Everyone in the company was aching for it to succeed. And with Ravi and Girish on board, things would begin to move quickly.

The Ace posse was in town and ready to ride.

NANOBITE

Nanovation requires a lot of prototyping.

Prototyping requires resilience—listen, learn, let go, and move on.

Resilience requires optimism. Believe that tomorrow will be better.

Optimism requires a leader who believes in you but won't let you off the hook.

Have no shame in ideas that don't work. Learning what doesn't work is as important as learning what *does*.

QUESTIONS

- Is your culture seamless and cross-functional?
- Do you routinely get diverse people together to share ideas and learn from each other?
- If you didn't have a title, would anyone follow you?
- Does your culture reward people for trying new things, even when they don't work out?

Part Two
Defining Nanovation

Dream no small dreams for they have no
power to move the hearts of men.

JOHANN WOLFGANG VON GOETHE

N anovation doesn't just happen at random. In our experience, it occurs when seven critical ideas and actions are present throughout the process. And the first, and most important, is this: Nanovation is an impossible dream in the service of a cause.

In the following section, we'll follow the leadership and design paths of Team Nano from the impossible dream of the 1 lakh car to get families off motor scooters, through the building of a movement and the process of revolutionary, elegant, more-with-less design, through the return on innovation.

Fasten your seat belts. It's going to be quite a ride.

Part Two
Defining Nanovation

TEN

An Impossible Dream in the Service of a Cause

> The human mind, once stretched by a new idea, never regains its original shape.

OLIVER WENDELL HOLMES

Nanovation is inflamed by the daring pursuit of a big, big challenge, a dream that seems, literally, impossible. Inflamed because it lights a fire that won't die down, an itch that won't go away. Daring because it invites scorn, obstruction, and very public failure. Impossible because if it were easy, someone else would have done it.

The doors of Nanovation blow open when we choose to challenge the *known* and venture off the map into the *unknown*. Unless you are willing to tackle seemingly impossible problems that scare others to death, you'll never develop the capacity for Nanovation.

Think big. Act bold. Give history a shove. Nanovation takes guts. On the tails of a gigantic, game-changing success, Nanovators look like geniuses. But going into it, they look like the lunatic fringe.

If the problem is big enough, you feel that you are in over your head. A sense of desperation comes with trying to solve it. This is healthy. Call it enlightened humility, but when you are desperate, you clearly recognize how needy you are. This creates an openness that wouldn't exist if the problem were not overwhelming. It motivates you to look to anyone, anywhere, at any time for an idea that might lead to a solution. While others remain stuck in their own shortsightedness, a wicked big problem forces you to ask, "What if . . . ?" and "Why not?"

"You see things and say, 'Why?' but I dream things and say, 'Why not?'"
George Bernard Shaw

The Nano was a big dream, but the fact that it rose from the Tata Group shouldn't be surprising given its history. Undeterred by lack of precedent or experience, the Tatas have a reputation for choosing bold and daring problems to solve. For more than a century, from Jamsetji to J. R. D. to Ratan, the Tatas' propensity to ask, "What if . . . ?" and "Why not?" has dramatically contributed to the development of India.

"Do you want to spend the rest of your life selling sugared water, or do you want a chance to change the world?"
Steve Jobs to John Sculley, on inviting him to become a short-lived CEO of Apple

Nanovation isn't about finding a double-digit increase in market share. It's not about maximizing short-term profits or raising the stock price or any of the usual business metrics most people look for. Those things are great, but they don't lead to Nanovation. Nanovation comes from doing something you believe will change the world.

(JFK Library Archives)

JFK asked the world to think beyond the boundaries of what we thought was possible. Do you have a dream you think you can't reach?

We mentioned the Apollo space program earlier. Let's go back and look at the parallels to the Nano project. On May 25, 1961, President John F. Kennedy announced before a special joint session of Congress the dramatic and ambitious goal of putting an

American on the moon and bringing him home safely before the end of the decade.

The dream was bold and audacious, but it galvanized a nation and launched a movement. That one simple, yet extraordinary declaration ignited the entire U.S. scientific community along with an army of government officials and private sector entrepreneurs. Thousands of people from thousands of places worked insanely long hours making personal and professional sacrifices to bring thousands of puzzle pieces together. It was a herculean effort—one of the greatest mobilizations of resources and manpower in history!

Kennedy was under no illusion about the magnitude and difficulty of this undertaking. He told Congress, "No single space project in this period will be more impressive to mankind, or more important for the long-range exploration of space; and none will be so difficult or expensive to accomplish."

What was so compelling about Kennedy's vision? Why were the people involved so committed? It appealed to our spirit of adventure. Space revolutionaries were determined to give history a shove by doing what no one had ever done before. It appealed to our sense of pride.

For Americans, our reputation was at stake. The thought of the Soviets beating us to the moon was unbearable, and no one wanted to let our country down. It appealed to our fight for freedom. For the rest of the world, it was the thrill of opening new doors. Not only would a successful moon landing open up a new frontier for humankind, but it would inevitably spawn new innovations. Computers, Teflon, freeze-dried foods, and a raft of other new technologies came from the program. Universities were filled with students inspired to study science and expand their knowledge of physics and engineering.

And though JFK couldn't have known it when he made the challenge, the journey to the moon became symbolic of his vision. After his assassination, as America went through the turmoil of the

Vietnam War, the civil rights movement, and more assassinations, the Apollo program seemed to symbolize the America we wanted to be.

Despite skeptics who said it couldn't be done, astronauts Neil Armstrong, Buzz Aldrin, and Mike Collins left the earth's atmosphere and traveled a quarter of a million miles to an unknown world. On July 20, 1969, more than a half billion people from around the world watched as Neil Armstrong took a small step for himself and a giant step for humanity. It was a stunning achievement that showcased the best of human ingenuity and boosted American confidence and prestige at home and abroad.

Victor Hugo said, "There is nothing like a dream to create the future." An audacious dream is the first step to Nanovation. The Apollo 11 moon landing illustrates what can happen when people are bound together by a common aspiration. Experts estimate that we only knew approximately 15 percent of what we needed to know to accomplish this goal when Kennedy made the commitment. Yet somehow a critical mass of innovators and technologists opened their minds, tapped into the intellectual capital of the nation, and rose to the occasion.

Consider this: Apollo 11 occurred only one hundred years after the first transcontinental railway was completed in the U.S., a feat similar in scale and audacity to the moon shot. And the Nano was revealed one hundred years after the Model T, the car that put America and most of the world on wheels. In terms of real dollars, the Nano cost just one-tenth the price of the Model T when it was launched. Imagine if we could go to the moon for one-tenth the cost of the transcontinental railway.

No company and no nation can outperform its aspirations. We are limited only by what we believe is possible. The heights to which we rise depend on the weightiness of our dreams. Legendary mountaineer Todd Skinner affirmed this: "We cannot lower the mountain; therefore we must elevate ourselves." A pioneer in his own right—creating strategies for summiting Mount Everest never before achieved—Skinner said, "Always adjust the mind to what's possible; do not adjust what is possible to the mind."

NO LAKH OF DARING

Like President Kennedy, Ratan Tata demonstrated no lack (or should we say lakh?) of daring when he ratified the *Financial Times* headline "Tatas Plan Rs 1 Lakh Car" over the story by reporter John Griffiths. Taking the headline as the goal, Tata launched a project as seemingly impossible as the moon shot.

How do you build a car for 1 lakh (US$2,100 at the time) without compromising aesthetics, functionality, comfort to the customer, or safety and environmental regulations? How do you build a 1 lakh car that will not require an apology? Essentially it meant wiping the slate clean and throwing out everything the auto industry believed to be true about cost structures, design and development, and distribution. In doing so, Team Nano learned that the passion to solve a huge, complex problem sets the stage for extraordinary innovation.

How do you determine that a dream is audacious? Your first clue might lie in how people react to it. Is it stunning, frighteningly cool, and unforgettable? Does it go *way beyond*, make you *gasp*, and create *buzz*? Is it a *ladle dropper*—as in so unimaginable and astounding that you drop your ladle in the soup? Is it enviable and soul stirring?

> Is your dream big enough? Five years from now will anyone remember or care about what you are doing today?

When a dream is this far-reaching, you know it addresses a problem that is consequential and momentous. When the dream is this inspiring, it has the potential to truly differentiate your business in a sea of sameness. When a dream is this profound, people come out of the woodwork with fire in the belly to play a role in fulfilling it. When a dream is this big, it has the power to unleash a tidal wave of imagination, creativity, and ingenuity.

THE DREAM MUST SERVE A HIGHER CAUSE

Big, audacious dreams are magnificent, but the energy and excitement they generate are even more powerful and enduring if the dream serves a higher cause. The Nano project was the result of a weighty, awe-inspiring idea, but it was also grounded in a moral imperative. The purpose of the Nano was to raise the dignity, status, comfort, and safety of a people.

A moral imperative often rises out of indignity. Call it leadership by outrage, a genuine sense of empathy and compassion, a purpose driving actions, or capitalism with a conscience, the Nano grew out of one man's desire to make life better for others.

On that rainy afternoon in Bangalore, where others might have felt sadness, resignation, or even irritation, Ratan Tata felt fury.

He was furious at himself.

For years, he'd been talking about the problem of having whole families on scooters. For years, he'd been suggesting that others should do something about it. But he, with all his resources, had done nothing.

In his incredible humility it was almost as if Tata felt a bit of shame: "Why aren't our company, our country, and the world addressing this problem?" It wasn't the result of a management retreat with high-paid consultants. It wasn't some newfangled management technique that Ratan Tata or Ravi Kant drummed up to make Tata Motors' employees more productive. It came from the heart of Ratan Tata.

As a moral imperative, the Nano was created to serve a larger cause, to be the means to a greater end, not the end itself.

These are the questions from which legends and legacies are made. They are also the basis for true Nanovation. Most people don't lay down their lives for a job, but they will for an inspiring cause that is noble and heroic. People don't give their all to make budget or quarterly numbers, but they will for a higher purpose. The Nano is a tiny car that elicited big ideas and big contributions. Why did members of Team Nano make so many personal sacrifices to accomplish the impossible? They did it for the same reasons that the Apollo 11 team did. The cause was noble. It was worthy of giving everything they had.

Team Nano understood that this project wasn't just

about building another competitive product designed to gain market share and make money. They saw the Nano as a way to satisfy their deepest desires to do something meaningful and significant, to engage in work that matters. They knew the Nano could have an explosive impact on people's lives. Just as Americans viewed the moon landing, they saw the Nano as an opportunity to raise the self-esteem of a nation and contribute to building a better country.

A Qualifier

Now, let us be very clear here, because we don't want you to get the wrong impression. There is nothing wrong with making money, raising status, and expanding influence. These things can become powerful tools for positive change in the world.

What **MADE** the cause served by Nano **NOBLE** and **HEROIC?**

Ravi Kant made it very clear to us that the Nano project was about making a profit as well as making a difference. He said, "We are not a charity. We are a business house. We are a company responsible to our board of directors and to our shareholders. Yes, it's a magnificent dream, but it's going to make money for the company."

For 140 years the Tatas have been devoted to building profitable enterprises and creating wealth—but always as a means to a greater end, not the end in and of itself; always as a tool to serve a larger cause, not the cause itself. The entire Tata empire was built on one impossible dream after another, each in service to something greater.

If you think the idea of a higher calling in business is a little far-fetched, think again. This is what made the cause soul stirring:

Saving Lives

It sounds rather sensational to say that the product you are creating will save people's lives, but this one will. If for a little more than

What if you could cut those fatalities by just 10 percent? That's 120,000 lives! the price of a motorcycle, Team Nano could take a family of five and put them in a car, how many lives would it save? Multiply this by every developing country around the world and you have a huge opportunity to be a positive force for change.

Today, emerging countries account for 90 percent of the world's annual 1.2 million road fatalities. India is a country of 1.1 billion people. Less than 5 percent of that billion who use the roads in India ride in cars. The rest are on foot, motorbikes, scooters, autorickshaws (three-wheel taxis), or bicycle-pulled carts. It is estimated that nearly 350 people die each day in road accidents—that's 125,000 people a year! Sixty-seven percent of Thailand's annual traffic deaths, 40 percent of Indonesia's traffic deaths, 33 percent of Sri Lanka's, and an even higher percentage of Vietnam's traffic fatalities are drivers or child passengers on small scooters and motorbikes.

What if by making the transition from a less safe form of transportation to the Nano, you could cut those fatalities by just 10 percent? That's 120,000 lives! What if just 10 percent of the people in India who would get injured in road accidents don't? That's another million people. Add to this the people out of work, jobs lost, the cost of caring for the disabled, and the impact is huge. Team Nano would tell you that this is what they are fighting for.

Now You Can

The Nano was born out of a dream grounded in an egalitarian spirit—a spirit determined to discover a solution that would put a car within reach of everyone, not just the elite. With more than two hundred thousand advance orders (of which one hundred thousand were accepted in a lottery), fifty million hits on the company's Web site, and a tidal wave of media attention from every corner of the world, the Nano became one of the most eagerly awaited products ever. While the Nano team never could have imagined this level of enthusiasm, they knew they were addressing the aspirations of people who dreamed about owning a car but realistically figured it would never happen.

Today, less than 10 in 1,000 people own a car in India. By comparison, it's 765 in the U.S., and 600 in Australia. India is a very status-conscious nation with a burgeoning middle class and a median age of twenty-five. Within ten years, 50 percent of India's billion people will be between the ages of fifteen and fifty. These people dream of a higher standard of living and a better quality of life. They want to rise with the rising economy of India. Moving up the ladder from a moped, motorcycle, or electric rickshaw to owning a real car is a big deal. In fact, the market for cars in India is expected to reach four million a year by 2015.

(Agencia Brasil, from Wikipedia)

Dr. A. P. J. Abdul Kalam, former president of India, is a visionary who actively supports open source software and action to develop India into a knowledge superpower. A scientist and aeronautical engineer by training, he is affectionately known as *the People's President.*

Imagine a man sitting barefoot and cross-legged in front of his tiny shack along the road while he repairs shoes. That's forty-two-year-old Maruti Jaywant Bhandare, who makes his living as a cobbler in the Mulund District of northeast Mumbai. For seven years, he saved Rs. 50 a day (about $1) to buy a Rs. 60,000 motorcycle. But when Ratan Tata confirmed the 1 lakh price, Bhandare decided to wait two more years and save for a Nano instead.

Bhandare has to stitch a lot of frayed sandals to achieve his goal. So you can imagine the commitment he made when he paid 95 percent of the cost of the car up front in cash to reserve a Nano. You can also imagine how disappointed he was to learn that he was not selected as one of the first one hundred thousand people in India to get the car.

Team Nano was driven to create a product at a price point that says to Bhandare, "Now you can." Now you can fit a car into your budget. Now you can change the way you travel. Now you can comfortably put your family in a safe, reliable, all-weather form of transportation. Now you can drive one of the most fuel-efficient cars in the world. Now you can go places and do things you couldn't before.

The Nano is not just the dream of Ratan Tata and his team. It's the dream of millions of Indians. This is why the little car has endearingly earned the reputation as the People's Car.

National Pride

Perhaps they weren't totally conscious of it, but Team Nano sensed that if they could pull it off, this tiny car could become a badge of honor, a huge symbol of national pride.

From an automotive design and manufacturing point of view, cynics around the world used to wonder, *Can anything good come out of India?* Team Nano knew that they had a unique opportunity to answer this question. With the world watching, this project became more than a source of personal pride. India, of all nations, would have achieved something that had never been done before and something that few people thought it was capable of. The Nano would contribute to solidifying the emerging nation's place on the world stage.

Team Nano members also knew that they were working on a

project that could be another "first" on a long list of breakthroughs that the Tata companies have brought to India. Thanks to the Tata Group, India had its first cotton mill, its first steel mill, its first hydraulic power plant, its first college, its first luxury hotel, and its first indigenously designed passenger car (the Indica). If the Nano were successful, they would be doing their part to uphold the Tata legacy of restoring India's wealth and contributing to the rise of a nation.

 "Dream is not what you see in sleep. Dream is the thing which does not let you sleep."

A. P. J. Abdul Kalam, former president of India

NANOVATION IS ABOUT CREATING A LIFE THAT MATTERS

It makes sense, doesn't it? All people want to know that they are important, that the world takes them seriously. Who doesn't want to live a life that matters? Yet how can we build lives that matter if we aren't engaged in work that matters?

In a business where work is nothing more than just a job, people derive meaning from the money they make, the status they have, and the power they can wield. The more they have, the more they want because the law of diminishing return takes hold. Money, status, and power will never overcome the emptiness that comes with a mundane job—at least not over the long haul. This is why even the smallest annual raises and bonuses or the least bit of authority become so important to people.

Where money, status, and power are temporary motivators at best, we go outside our jobs to find meaning. Then work becomes something we tolerate and endure for the sake of something bigger elsewhere. But this is hardly a recipe for cultivating Nanovation. How do you create breakthrough innovation with a company of dead people working—people who are psychologically and emotionally checked out? Where do you find the creativity to radically change the rules of the game with a workforce that shows up every morning DOA—dead on arrival?

MEANING AND SIGNIFICANCE IN RETURN FOR DEVOTION

There's a lesson here for innovators. Everyone craves meaning. The human need for significance is colossal. The opportunity to give history a shove and leave a mark on the world is the ultimate source of motivation and the impetus for innovation. Doing something meaningful and significant drives scientists and researchers to find a cure for disease. It drives doctors like world-famous surgeon Michael DeBakey to invent one medical breakthrough after another. It drives rock stars like Bono to leverage his platform in the fight to eliminate extreme poverty in Africa. It drives entrepreneurs like Nandan Nilekani, the cofounder of Infosys, to lead India's infrastructure revolution. And it drove the people of Tata Motors to build a car that will change the world.

These innovators make work a cause. Their ingenuity is the result of a deep-seated need to solve a problem that could change history. Pursuing the dream and finding the solution become part of a noble, heroic cause that turns into something bigger than any one person can handle. But it's a cause that would not gain momentum if it weren't for the audacity of the dreamers.

Now, the cynic or realist in you might say, "Okay, but what about the factory worker in India living at the bottom of Maslow's hierarchy, struggling to barely support his family? Is he or she motivated by a noble, heroic cause?" Of course. What could be more heroic than the survival and future prosperity of your family? What could be more heroic than to create a legacy within a company that opens the door of opportunity for your children and your children's children?

Is it not noble to say, "If I'm a part of building a product that changes the world—and incidentally helps people like me own a car—then I contribute to the long-term success of my company. I'm also building an excellent personal reputation inside Tata Motors as a worker who makes a difference."

Given the loyalty Tata has to its employees and its notoriety for being an extremely ethical company, your personal brand will create more opportunity for you and for future generations of your family. What are you fighting for? A chance to raise your family's standard of living in a country where you see the middle class growing explosively. You want to be a part of that. The Nano's success is your success.

The struggling factory worker might not define her dream or her cause the same way Ratan Tata defines his, but we would argue that their dreams are inextricably linked and *no less important*. Even when your primary concern is meeting your most basic needs, there is still a sense of pride and dignity that comes with doing good for yourself while doing well for others.

When your life and work become a cause, others will notice. Others will follow. Others will help you make your impossible dream possible. When that happens, what follows is a movement.

"For too long we have been dreaming a dream from which we are now waking up: the dream that if we just improve the socio-economic situation of people, everything will be okay, people will become happy. The truth is that as the struggle for survival subsides, the question emerges: Survival for what? Ever more people today have the means to live, but no meaning to live for."

Viktor Frankl

NANOBITE

When the business becomes a cause . . .

- people find meaning and significance and bring more of themselves to work.
- people find the courage to think big and act bold.
- the focus is on making a difference while making a profit.
- superstars who thrive on solving big problems opt in.
- ideas become more important than titles, job descriptions, and tenure.
- people are bonded by a common sense of outrage and/or hope for a better tomorrow.

QUESTIONS

- How bold and daring is your organization with regard to choosing the problems it takes on?
- Is your company or your project defined in terms of a cause? Does the cause for which you fight liberate the world from some limiting condition?
- Would your cause be compelling enough for Ratan Tata?
- What if your people were so passionate about this cause that they remained focused on it despite everything else that competes for their attention?

ELEVEN

A Cause Becomes a Movement

An idea that is developed and put into action is more important than an idea that exists only as an idea.

EDWARD DE BONO

NANOVATION CREATES A MOVEMENT THAT CAN CHANGE THE WORLD

When the process of Nanovation identifies a cause that is worthy of creative minds, it can't help but create a movement. When you define the project as a noble, heroic cause, something very exciting happens. No one has to ask, "Does my work matter?" Suddenly people connect personally with the cause because they have a direct line of sight that links their individual contributions to something bigger, something deeply meaningful. Instead of just doing a job, they know they are making a difference. Knowing this becomes a powerful motivator. They give more discretionary effort; ask better, more provocative questions; become more resourceful; and do things they didn't know they were capable of doing. Now, rally a critical mass of people who think and act like this, and you have a movement in the making.

So ask yourself: Am I part of a business, or am I engaged in a movement? The people with whom I work—are they just doing a job, or do they bring the maniacal focus and missionary zeal of a crusader to the game? These aren't just philosophical questions; they are foundational to creating a culture that is fertile for Nanovation. Here are some of the reasons why:

NANOVATION UNLEASHES ENERGY AND CREATIVITY

Team Nano is a band of impassioned people who show up to work every day fully awake, fully engaged, and firing on all cylinders. Talk to almost any one of them about the car and the significant problem it solves, and you quickly get the sense that they are serving a cause that serves them in return. It's as though they have tapped into a source of power that makes them bigger, better, and more capable than they would be without the cause.

Are you part of a **business,** or are you engaged in a **MOVEMENT?**

This is what a big dream that serves a great cause can do. It captures our attention, draws us in, and enlists and elevates us. If the cause is truly heroic, it will touch people at a visceral level. Something in it will resonate with our deep-seated values and sense of idealism—our better selves.

By capturing some of our deepest aspirations, a noble cause floods our veins with adrenaline and unleashes our creativity. The cause brings energy, vitality, and life to the organization, just as breathing pure oxygen after a rigorous climb brings energy to a mountaineer. It creates a buzz. Our hearts are aroused, and our minds are stimulated. Limitations fuel creativity and become opportunities instead of constraints.

Imaginations run at full bore. New ideas abound. We are more willing to take risks and be accountable for decisions that support the cause. Policies and practices that aren't aligned with the cause are challenged. Petty preoccupations submerge in the wake of a bigger, more exciting *yes*! Language intensifies, confidence goes up, and our convictions become stronger. Now, what part of that isn't critical to game-changing innovation?

NANOVATION AWAKENS THE WARRIOR SPIRIT

The quality of a true warrior lies in serving a purpose greater than oneself. A warrior is hardwired into all of us. Perhaps it is more dominant and visible in men, but don't be misled: women are warriors, too. If you doubt it, try doing something deceitful, distrusting, or harmful to a child, and watch the fury of a mother descend upon you. We've seen this in our family on many occasions.

A noble, heroic cause awakens the warrior within us, and this is a good thing because impossible dreams could not be realized without it. Warriors act. They intervene. If the need or problem is worth fighting for, if the opportunity is big enough, they bravely rise to the occasion, step into the breach, and face the danger to make a difference. Nothing seems impossible. There is no room for passivity in their vocabulary.

In many ways this is the story of the Nano. Ratan Tata had finally had enough. It's as if he recognized a problem, woke up one day, and said, "This can't go on. As Indians, we are smarter and more capable than this. We've got to do something." He wasn't intimidated by a seemingly impossible challenge. Listen to his own words: "Again and again here in India, I see families riding a single scooter. And each time I think, *Oh, God, can't we do something to help these families travel more safely?*"

Warriors learn—often through trial and error—not to yield their hearts to anything. Despite the fact that few global carmakers believed it was possible, Ratan Tata listened to his heart—a heart that had empathy for the underprivileged. He was unwilling to compromise the dream because the cause was so great.

There's a lot of discussion and debate among leadership theorists about whether great leadership requires charisma. If having charisma means being flamboyant, extroverted, and gregarious, we don't think so. We've met too many great leaders engaged in Nanovation who are introverts. But if having charisma means having a presence, being magnetic and influential, and arousing devotion through your contagious passion for something that matters, the answer is yes.

The business press has characterized Ratan Tata as "shy, reticent, and almost reclusive." Apparently in our interviews with Ratan, a different person showed up. He was charming, charismatic, and loaded with strong conviction. Perhaps that was because the majority of time we spent getting to know him focused upon things that deeply matter to him.

Ratan is an incredibly humble and gracious man, somewhat of a tentative, even nervous public speaker, a man disdainful of pretense, and a person who certainly does not like to draw attention. But competitors and opponents who underestimate his warrior spirit do so at their own risk. The man has an inner resolve and an unyielding heart characteristic of a warrior.

B. Muthuraman, Tata Steel's managing director, said that Ratan Tata will never back down from a fight. When a strike occurred at Tata Motors' Pune plant in 1989, militant unionists assaulted Tata managers and took over a section of the city. Ratan said, "If you put a gun to my head, you had better pull the trigger or take the gun away, because I won't move my head."

Tata broke the strike by signing an agreement with a rival union after police confronted the militants. Muthuraman cautioned not to be fooled by Mr. Tata's poise and dapper style. He said, "He's one of the toughest people I've ever known."

When a controversy in Singur (one we will unpack later in more detail) heated up over the location of the new Nano plant, many people in West Bengal assumed that Tata Motors was too deeply invested to move. After all, the company had already sunk $350 million into the facility. The warrior spirit of a seventy-one-year-old revolutionary roared, "If people say that that we will protect our investments irrespective of anything, then they are wrong. I will not bring my employees to Singur if there is threat of them being beaten up. Tata will do whatever necessary to protect its employees." As the world saw, it was no idle or empty threat, and Ratan acted decisively to back up his statement.

It was the same warrior spirit that made him take up the cause in the first place, the cause of defending India's emerging middle class against unsafe, undignified transport. It was a warrior spirit that caused him to take up the seemingly impossible task of building the Nano, even though the competition mocked him. And it was the warrior spirit that led the team to stay the course until they had truly delivered their Nanovation.

NANOVATION VALUES COMMITMENT OVER COMPLIANCE

Game-changing innovation doesn't come from compliance. It comes from 100 percent, full-blown commitment. It's not enough to dream with great boldness. At some point you have to wake up and bust your butt to make that dream a reality. Fulfilling an audacious dream means that people must be as bold and daring about *realizing* the dream as they are about the dream itself.

Compliance is about buy-in. Buy-in happens when senior executives decide: *This is what we are going to do. Now how do we get the people who have to execute on it to buy into it?*

Commitment is about opt-in. Opt-in happens when people are inspired by the bigness of the dream and the nobility of the cause it serves. Their response is more often: *Break me off a piece of that! How can I play? I want in!* People do not need to be convinced; they can see themselves in the cause. People do not need to be motivated;

they motivate themselves. People do not need to be micro-managed; they set their own rigorous targets. People do not need to be told to collaborate; they willingly reach across boundaries because their passion for fulfilling the dream is bigger than their need to control information, turf, or other people.

There is nothing wrong with compliance unless you are trying to create a culture that fosters Nanovation. It is true that the dream for the Nano emanated from the chairman, but you can't do the impossible when people feel it is their duty or obligation to buy in just because the top dog wants it done. Creativity and ingenuity just don't flow as freely under such a command-and-control approach.

People who are committed bring special energy, passion, and excitement to the game that compliant people can't fake. They might not have cast the dream, but they become dreamers in the process because they identify with the cause and want the dream as badly as the originators do. People who comply may willingly accept the cause as worthy, but it's not *their* cause. They may see value in accomplishing the dream, but it's not *their* dream.

Commitment is about discretionary effort. It's about going above and beyond the call of duty for a chance to make a difference. Compliance is about taking orders. Compliant people play, but only because there is something else at stake. Compliance comes out of a contractual, nine-to-five mentality that says, "You give me a paycheck, benefits, and a promotion, and I will give you a fair day's labor."

Commitment fosters a covenantal mentality that says, "We share a common purpose that I deeply believe in. Because of this, I will subordinate self-interest to the common good, lock arms with you, and do *whatever it takes* to fulfill that purpose."

Opt-in happens when people are inspired by the bigness of the dream.

Commitment shouts, **"I'm in!"**

People who are compliant tend to be rules oriented and title conscious. That is, they hide behind rules and regulations as an excuse for not attempting the things that lead to breakthrough innovation. People who are committed are often irreverent. They assume ownership for the outcome of the game, but they don't feel compelled to play by the rules of the game. If the rules are stupid, cumbersome, or disabling, they create new rules. If the person with a title has a bad idea, they challenge it. They work around things that stand in the way of achieving the dream.

People become genuinely committed because they have been recruited by the cause. The core members of Team Nano were invited to participate by the chairman, and for most of them, that was certainly an honor. But think of the daily frustration and fear that come with doing what has never been done before. Think of the perseverance needed to press on in the face of less-than-elegant solutions to big, gnarly problems. Or think of what happens when you have no solutions at all. Something more was going on with this project. A raw sense of commitment and discipline kept them going when things got really difficult.

Put yourself in the shoes of a young designer or engineer. You've been invited to participate in something that is unprecedented, transformational, and dangerous. How cool would it be for you to take on a project that could be defined in these terms? Think about the adventure of being engaged in an expedition that will push the envelope of innovation to a place that could turn the automotive industry on its head. Would you jump at a chance to do that? To blow the doors off business as usual and build something new? How inspiring would it be to pursue this audacious dream working side by side with a visionary like Ratan Tata?

You can legislate compliance, but there is little or nothing *you* can do to *command* commitment. You might think you can, but your best efforts to get people on board will most likely yield a superficial agreement. And then you're back to compliance. Besides, your brightest people can smell manipulation from a mile away.

This is why the dream must be wicked big and massively bold, and why the cause must be noble and heroic. As we've said, people want to belong to something bigger that gives meaning and identity to their lives. So great is this need that when we find it, our complacency is challenged, our comfort is shaken, our passion to reimagine what's possible is awakened, and our resolve is made stronger. Then and only then will we give the totality of who we are to it. What kind of cause would be worthy of this commitment in your organization?

NANOVATION FUELS THE FIRES OF COURAGE AND PERSEVERANCE

Big dreams that serve a noble, heroic cause have staying power because they touch something deep inside us. They give us something to do that matters. If the dream is truly about making a difference as well as making a profit, it has a chance to survive. Big dreams, whether motivated by service or self-interest, are about doing the impossible.

By its very definition, doing the impossible is about confronting unprecedented challenges in uncharted territory. Where do you find the stick-to-itiveness to hang in there when darkness sets in, the terrain gets rough, and the way is uncertain? You find it in a movement that has so much meaning to you that you would fight for it even if it brought you no fame, fortune, or power. You find it in a movement that makes you feel alive even at the cost of great personal sacrifice.

Many great, innovative ideas meet opposition, and cynics and naysayers often laugh at visionaries like Ratan Tata. As we noted, most of the automotive industry scoffed at the idea of making a car for the price of a scooter, saying it would take a miracle to make it happen. Even after the Nano had been unveiled and people could see it was a bona fide, real car, critics complained that it would pollute the air, congest traffic, and impair safety.

There is a lesson here. If your dream falls into the category of big, bold, and audacious, there will always be people who will tell you why it can't be done. And the more radical the dream is, the more resistance you will face. The creative genius Albert Einstein said, "Great spirits have always encountered violent opposition from mediocre minds." Nanovators would do well to follow the lead of

Team Nano members in the design center. They worked incredibly long hours against the odds to make something that captured the attention of the entire world.

Ratan Tata, Ravi Kant, and the rest of Team Nano, who apparently subscribed to the Chinese proverb: "Those who say it can't be done should get out of the way of those doing it."

Nanovation is not for the faint at heart. While many people choose the path of least resistance, Nanovation is about taking the "road less traveled." Navigating it is a game of risking more and failing faster that requires tremendous perseverance and the ability to bounce back—again and again.

Where does this resilience come from when you are going through the birth pains of a new innovation? It comes from a sense of destiny. It comes from a dream that you believe must be fulfilled. You press on and push through the turbulence because you believe that what you are doing is meaningful and significant to the world. Victor Frankl, the great psychotherapist and Holocaust survivor, said that the people most likely to survive the horrors of the concentration camps were those who had a reason to live, those who had something significant yet to do with their lives.

The road to Nano was punctuated with many potholes—trials and setbacks that threatened to distract, disempower, and derail its dreamers. Yet members of Team Nano were unwilling to let the naysayers tell them why it couldn't be done. They let the rightness of their dream strengthen their resolve. Had they just been seeking fame, fortune, or power, had it been only about giving the shareholder a return, they might have caved in.

Find courage in the cause.

When materials costs skyrocketed by as much as 40 percent, yet the goal remained a 1 lakh car, they found courage in the cause. When the decision was made to move Nano's brand-new manufacturing facility (80 percent complete) from West Bengal to Gujarat due to unforeseen political protests and violence, Team Nano found courage in the cause. How do you shut down one plant, immediately start construction on another plant in another state, ramp up production on a car, and source parts from all over the world—and do all of that simultaneously? When it came to answering this question, the team found courage in the cause.

Ratan Tata had lots of opportunities to cave in. In many respects, Ratan is no different from the rest of us. He's human, subject to the same fear of failure and fear of rejection that haunt us. Harassed by the same self-doubt that beleaguers us and is periodically tempted to ask: Do I have what it takes? Who likes to be chastised, ridiculed, or thought foolish for chasing a dream that you believe has monumental importance? What do you do when respected friends and colleagues beg you to distance yourself from a project because it's too exotic? How do you handle it when those same friends and colleagues begin to distance themselves from *you*?

When he couldn't get the motorcycle and car manufacturers in India to engage in a dialogue about building a safe, reliable, alternative form of transportation for the masses, Ratan could have retreated, but he didn't. When the *Financial Times* headline trumpeted the 1 lakh People's Car, Tata could have hedged. When the automotive industry said it couldn't be done, Tata could have ducked and run in embarrassment.

But he didn't.

"Risk more than others think is safe,
Care more than others think is wise,
Dream more than others think is practical,
Expect more than others think is possible."
Anonymous

That's not the Tata way. That's not the corporate culture that Ratan Tata had been handed. That's not the legacy that he had been called upon to protect. His strength came from a passion to help

Indians fulfill their dreams and become who and what they want to be. His resolve came from a deep-seated belief in what his dream could accomplish for India. He, too, found courage in the cause.

Sometimes it takes the light of a burning bridge to show the way ahead. In accepting the 1 lakh target, Ratan Tata essentially burned the bridge. When he did, Team Nano had no retreat. When they accepted the fact that the only way out was forward, they found the courage to innovate.

NANOVATION GIVES PEOPLE SOMETHING WORTH CHANGING FOR

Perpetual innovation throws the organization into a constant state of creative tension and ongoing change. It often requires that people expand their capabilities, acquire more knowledge, and reach across boundaries to collaborate with people they don't even know. A lot has been written about change, but in the final analysis it comes down to our will and actually *doing* what we know is good for us. This is why personal change usually precedes organizational change.

No one needs to convince us that smoking is bad for us; that we ought to buckle up in a car or wear a helmet when we ride a motorcycle. No one needs to inform us that exercising and watching our weight are healthy. No one needs to tell us that we ought to create a culture where employees are engaged and customers get best-in-class service. It usually comes down to this: Do I have something or someone worth changing for? Is there a larger, more compelling reason to ensure that I do what I already know I should do—particularly when the changes aren't easy?

People who are part of a movement rise to the occasion when it comes to making difficult changes because their passion for the cause is bigger than the discomfort or fear that comes with doing things differently. Equipping themselves to make the greatest contribution possible, to be valuable players who advance the movement drives their desire to learn something new—even when it's scary. If you are constantly navigating uncharted waters as Team Nano did, you are constantly being challenged to learn, stretch, and grow. If you are going where no one has ever gone before, you are more in touch with your need to tap into the intellectual capital of anyone who might light the way with a fresh idea. So, you collaborate. It was common for the members of Team Nano to reach out to their colleagues in the commercial truck division as well as those in other Tata companies to seek answers. Anyone with an idea was welcome in the game. Compare this with many companies where people get caught in the "If it wasn't invented here, it isn't any good" syndrome.

As a project like Nano ebbs and flows, team members are required to look for the voids, step into the breach, and play any number of different roles. When you are caught up in a movement, you will do whatever it takes; you will be true to the cause no matter what your role. The chance to transform the economics of an entire industry becomes more important than your insecurities and fears. Protecting families, giving them a safe, affordable form of transportation, and bringing momentum to the movement are worth changing for.

Nanovation, then, begins with a big dream in the service of a great cause, and out of that cause comes a movement that invites us to unleash the best of who we are. In the service of a cause, we will choose to change our behaviors and our beliefs about what's possible. We will choose to opt in instead of checking out. We will fight like warriors to reach the goal. And we'll reach out to anyone who wants to join.

We've seen the future. We have a movement. Now it's time to start the revolution.

NANOBITE

Consider these characteristics of a movement:

A movement is driven by a deep-seated desire to change the world for the better.

A movement is born from intolerance and an intense dissatisfaction with the status quo.

It demands self-sacrifice and single-hearted allegiance.

Members of the movement didn't know they couldn't do it.

People are sustained by a fervent hope for the future.

People gain a sense of purpose, confidence, and belonging by identifying with the movement.

A movement gives people something worth changing for.

It inspires commitment instead of compliance.

- When was the last time you invited your employees to participate in something that was unprecedented, transformational, and dangerous?
- Do your employees have a direct line of sight to the cause? Do they see how their individual contributions support the cause?
- Have your people been recruited by a compelling, noble, and heroic cause? Do they opt in, or are you trying to figure out how to get them to buy in?
- Are your employees just doing a job, or are they caught up in a movement? Are you breeding commitment or compliance?
- Do your people bring the maniacal focus and missionary zeal of a crusader to the game?

TWELVE

Nanovation Starts a Revolution

I don't personally trust any revolution
where love is not allowed.

MAYA ANGELOU

It doesn't matter what industry you are in, someone, somewhere, right now is building a product, process, or business model designed to kick your butt. Someone is going to redefine what it takes to succeed in your business. Someone is going to start the revolution that will change your world.

Why can't it be you?

If it's you, then you have a significant opportunity to widen the gap of competitive advantage. If it's not you, then you better get comfortable playing by the rules created by one of your competitors. If you are an incumbent, the shelf life of your solutions keeps getting shorter and shorter. If you are a new entrant, the gap between what you can imagine and what you can do keeps getting smaller and smaller.

In recent years, who changed our world more profoundly: Google or IBM? With all due respect to IBM—a great company—the company's impact in the last decade has been minuscule compared to that of start-ups like Google, Facebook, and YouTube. They've created a revolution that's dramatically changing the world in which we live.

Now look at your industry. Who did the best job of leveraging change in your industry over the last ten years: the incumbents or the new kids? We are willing to bet that in most cases it was the new kids. Now consider the winners in your industry and ask, did they succeed because they were that much better operationally or because they changed the rules of the game? The answer is probably "Both," but we suspect that the majority of those in the winner's circle got there by radically shaking it up.

What does it mean to be revolutionary? Well, when people pull together and produce change on a massive scale—something that has a sudden and broad impact on society—the change is revolutionary. The catalytic agents behind these changes are often the hip, defiant nonconformists who can imagine the unimaginable.

This is what makes Ratan Tata such an anomaly and so intriguing. Distinguished yet edgy, defiant yet congenial, hip yet grounded, and uncompromising yet amenable, Ratan belongs to a rare breed of youthful thinkers who vibrate with new ideas. He's a seasoned entrepreneur, executive, and statesman in his early seventies who dreams as if he's in his twenties. He sits at the helm of a 140-year-old conglomerate that many believe represents the best of India's past, yet he has inspired one of the most revolutionary products in the world. In the twilight of his career, Ratan Tata isn't hamstrung by out-of-date beliefs; he isn't using old, worn-out charts to discover new frontiers; and he doesn't worship at the altar of "We've always done it that way."

To use management expert Gary Hamel's term, Ratan Tata is a "Gray-Haired Revolutionary."

SO WHAT MAKES THE NANO REVOLUTIONARY?

Let's start with its far-reaching impact. It is transforming the economics of the automobile industry with an entirely new product category, a potentially new distribution channel, an engineering process that has pushed the edge of the low-cost envelope farther than it has ever been pushed, and a cultlike following that would be the envy of any competitor. It represents a wave of low-cost innovation that is already beginning to change the value proposition in the global auto industry as well as most other industries. It is redefining customer expectations and supplier relationships by changing how people think—about work, relationships, mobility, and what is possible in India. And it is displacing current products and causing incumbent businesses to rethink the future. So let us unpack some of these ideas.

If being revolutionary is essential to Nanovation, here are some questions to help you determine whether your idea is revolutionary:

Is Your Idea Meaningfully New and Radically Different?

Nanovation is about creating something new that really grabs the attention of the user. If it isn't new, it probably isn't meaningfully different and thus not revolutionary. The Nano is revolutionary in two ways: (1) it is the first of its kind, a new category of car; and (2) it revolutionized the process of elegant, low-cost design.

We agree with the catchphrases "Differentiate or die" and "Be distinct or be extinct." In a world of mimicry and me-tooism, it's not enough to be different; you have to be *radically* different to stand out and get people's attention. You have to create something radically *new* to achieve fast and sustainable growth.

Whether it's in products, services, or business models, *radical* is hard to duplicate. It's also difficult to accept. Why? Because the minute you step into the realm of the radical, someone is going to label you a kook. Someone is going to say that you are being too speculative or too risky and irresponsible.

This is why most organizations are cautious, metered, and incremental with regard to implementing new ideas. There is nothing wrong with incremental innovation. In fact, incremental changes in products and services keep you in the game—at least for a while. Many of the great companies we've written about make continuous improvement a way of life. They make a habit of asking, How are we going to be two or three times better tomorrow than we are today?

Yet incremental improvements rarely create and sustain the kind of growth that is expected from investors, nor do they generate an evangelical response from customers.

How radical is *radical*? Well, it's radical when it produces an extreme change. When Southwest Airlines got into the business, its founders knew that they were not just competing with other airlines. They were competing with ground transportation as well. So their fares (sometimes as low as $10) weren't just lower; they were dramatically lower, often a third of what the competition was charging.

Amazon.com is another example of pushing the edge of the envelope. Jeff Bezos wasn't thinking about incrementally improving upon the 250,000 titles you could find at Barnes & Noble, Borders, or Books-a-Million. He wanted to change the game by orders of magnitude, giving Amazon customers access to more than 2.5 million titles. You know it's radical when people are stunned because they can't get their minds around such an extreme change; they can't grasp the fact that someone did the impossible.

Think back to Tata Motors' financial crisis of 2000 when Lord Bhattacharyya said a 1 percent cost reduction was a rounding error. Think about Ravi Kant calling for not one time, three times, or five times, but ten times what the Tata Motors team originally thought they were capable of when it came to reducing costs. And then there is the 1 lakh price of the Nano, almost a 50 percent price reduction from the Maruti 800, once the cheapest car on the road.

That's radical.

Nanovation gravitates to the seemingly lunatic fringe because this is where revolutionary products, processes, and services are often found. So if you're not out on the edge, you might be taking up too much space.

Consider these examples. Thanks to Skype, we can talk to people all over the world using the Internet phone service that allows us to hear and see them—at a fraction of the cost of mobile and land lines. In fact, the authors held regular video conferences on Skype, talking face-to-face with each other and to colleagues in India.

What can you do **faster, better,** or **cheaper** by orders of magnitude? How would that **improve** your **relationship** with your **customers?** How disruptive would it be for your competitors?

TiVo, the dominant brand in digital video recording, has sent shock waves throughout the advertising industry. TiVo owners not only use the DVR to record their favorite shows and then watch them at their own convenience, but 75 percent of them use it to skip through the advertisements. If you are a fifty-year-old consumer brand manager and your whole career has been steeped in perfecting the thirty-second television commercial, TiVo is probably keeping you up at night.

Nanovation recognizes that the shelf life of incremental improvements keeps getting shorter and shorter. How far will small improvements carry Sony, Samsung, Panasonic, LG, and the rest of the industry before the next major breakthrough in flat-screen televisions disrupts the whole market?

Question: What's the genius behind Apple's iPod?
Answer: iTunes.

No one questions that Apple revolutionized the home entertainment industry with products like the iPod and iPhone. They are sexy, cool, fashionable, and mind-blowing when it comes to functionality. But the real revolution was started with iTunes, a radically different business model that transformed the way we access music. iTunes represents a win-win model that gives consumers the ability to customize their music portfolios and protects the intellectual property of artists and music labels. Buy a song or a whole album. It's up to you. Get it when you want it, the way you want it, for a price that suits your budget.

Next Question: What's the genius behind Apple's iPhone?
Answer: iTunes + Multi-touch Screen + 3-Axis Accelerometer + GPS + Maps + 100,000 iPhone Apps.

The iPhone is a good phone and a great media player, but that's just the beginning. The extraordinary interface was a huge innovation when first introduced, as is the way the GPS, accelerometer, and maps can connect you with your environment. You can use it to find anything you need to find, anywhere in the world. And new, game-changing apps are taking full advantage of this power. Yelp .com is a great Web site that uses social networking to identify and rate businesses everywhere. But its iPhone app, Monocle, is spectacular. It uses the mapping to help you see what's right in front of you. Monocle lets you look through the camera lens at the street on which you are standing and visually projects ratings over the live picture of the shops in front of you. It helps you distinguish who's got the good hamburger from who's got the *legendary* hamburger.

If Ratan Tata has his way, there will be interesting similarities with the Tata Nano. Like the iPod and iPhone, the Nano is a revolutionary product. But the real stroke of genius may be yet to come. Imagine a small team of entrepreneurs who seek the investment capital to build a small assembly plant in a rural part of India. Now imagine Tata Motors shipping Nano kits (think Nano in a box) to this plant where the cars are assembled to unique customer specifications. Customers essentially get to express their individuality by designing and customizing their own Nanos while the entrepreneurs become part of a shade-tree industry that enables them to own a business and work for themselves.

"The idea would be to train people in the manufacturing process and get small entrepreneurs to buy our kits, assemble the car and sell it under their own badge," Ratan told *Autocar India*. "I would imagine that this . . . would give many people a livelihood and hence a low-cost assembly facility is important."

Does It Make Lives Dramatically Better?

Getting your family off a scooter and into a safe, comfortable automobile *definitely* makes life dramatically better. Doing it for the price of a scooter, with similar gas mileage and lower emissions, makes it even better. For a vast segment of the Indian population, the Nano opens the door to practical all-weather travel in ways that will make a huge difference in their lives.

Earlier, we showed how the Ace brought a dramatic change of lifestyle to more than a million rural Indian families. Not only did it help small farmers and tradesmen become more productive; it gave them the chance to take the whole family into the nearest town much more often than had ever been possible before.

The Nano is not only revolutionary in design and manufacturing; it is also creating a social revolution. Just as Southwest Airlines democratized the skies and Google democratized information and the way the world learns, the Nano will democratize the roads and make it affordable for as many as fourteen million more Indians to have safe, dignified mobility. And mobility creates opportunity.

With more than a billion people spread out over enormous distances, travel to and from the rural parts of India can be extremely difficult and often painful. Now for the first time people can leave the chaotic crowds of places like Mumbai, New Delhi, and Bangalore to visit and experience other parts of India.

In the United States, Southwest Airlines' message is clear as a bell: "You are now free to move about the country." The Nano does the same for the people of India.

(Southwest Airlines)

The Nano says the same thing to millions of Indians emerging from poverty. While they may not make many cross-country trips in their Nanos (at least not until road conditions improve), they could. And they *will* have the chance to get themselves and their families where they need to go in safety and all-weather comfort.

The Nano will have a significant impact on mobility in India in much the same way that the cell phone, computer, and Internet have done with communications. It democratizes the road in a way nothing before has done.

Imagine being unable to take your family to visit relatives in a village without jamming into a crowded bus or perching perilously on top of a train.

Imagine leaving your remote village and taking five hours to walk to a doctor, dentist, or pharmacy in the city.

You'd be extremely reluctant to make a journey like that. But what happens when you can do it in less than an hour in your Nano, protected from the heat, rain, dust, and mud?

NANOVATION produces change that MATTERS.

Imagine a young mother with a difficult pregnancy who will now get timely and proper medical attention because she can drive instead of walk ten miles to the nearest clinic.

Imagine a child who can go to a better school or a young woman who can get a better job because she can drive from the village to the city. What if the grandparents who could never make the walk several villages away could now drive to see their grandchildren?

Does that change their lives for the better? You bet.

Nanovation produces change that matters. Whether it is making something more affordable, more accessible, or more convenient, Nanovation is about creating breakthrough innovations that people care about and clamor for because it raises their quality of life and standard of living. By empowering lower- and middle-class buyers to go, see, and do things they couldn't do before, the People's Car is a major inflection point in a world that is becoming flatter right before our very eyes.

Does It Redefine and Raise Customer Expectations?

Before they had scooters, the emerging Indian middle class had bicycles, rickshaws, and water buffalo. When scooters became affordable in the 1960s, the expectations of most Indians took an enormous leap forward. With the Nano, the leap is just as big.

The People's Car is a monumental accomplishment that has created a whole new set of customer expectations—and not just in the auto industry. As we will describe in a later chapter, the Nano effect can be seen in everything from portable power generators to refrigerators and medical devices. But for now, how has the People's Car redefined people's expectations?

First, the Nano represents choice. Choices create options and options create freedom. Given the Nano's financial accessibility, more and more consumers will expect to have the freedom to own a car, and more will come to expect the freedom that personal transportation provides. Since car ownership is a symbol of climbing the socioeconomic ladder and the Nano is within reach, more people will aspire to do so.

Second, whether people buy the car or not, the Nano has shown us that it is possible to blow the door off pricing as usual and make a stylish car that works, that's real, and that's not an apology. The Nano illustrates that *inexpensive* doesn't have to mean "cheap." Consumers will come to expect greater accessibility and higher quality at lower price points across a variety of different industries. The argument will be, If an automobile manufacturer can do it, why can't it be done elsewhere?

"Fools ignore complexity. Pragmatists suffer it. Geniuses remove it."
Alan Perlis

Third, with the Nano's incredibly small footprint and turning radius, consumers will demand cars—particularly on crowded roads in emerging countries—that are more maneuverable.

Fourth, by getting more than fifty miles per gallon, the Nano will join a wave of products that are shaping our attitudes about environmental sustainability. Yes, much has been made about the additional pollution the Nano will create in India, but the critics who have taken this position haven't acknowledged that it emits no more pollutants than the motorcycles. Whether future Nanos are powered by electricity, compressed air, or something else, you can bet that Tata Motors will continue to develop greener versions of the car. This will solidify consumers' expectations that they can actually have an appropriate car that is easier on the environment.

Does It Dramatically Change the Rules of the Game?

The Nano is the most important car of our times because it has created a category of one. There is simply nothing else like it. Now, will this last for long? Probably not. Renault and its Indian partner, Bajaj, have announced a "Nano fighter" that they say will sell for less than the Nano. General Motors is reportedly considering a Nano competitor that would sell in Asia for under $4,000. China's Chery QQ is expected to sell in the Indian market for approximately $3,700. Good for them; we hope they succeed. But the Nano opened the door. It broke the mold by creating an ultra-low-cost segment that many manufacturers will have to consider if they want to build momentum in emerging markets.

By shattering the cost barrier and hurdling what many believed to be insurmountable engineering and design barriers, the Nano dismantled the prevailing paradigm and caused the automobile industry to rethink the merits of an ultra-low-cost car. It essentially introduced a very new value proposition to the market and launched an economic revolution. Now that this milestone has been achieved, surely there will be other manufacturers who attempt to break records in the areas of performance, emissions, fuel consumption, and alternative power sources.

Overdrive magazine's Sirish Chandran said it well: "Correct me if I'm wrong but the automotive landscape of our country, maybe even the world, will have a giant Nano-shaped footprint stamped all over it."

Game changer is a powerful term; unfortunately it has almost become a cliché in modern business. To change the game is to literally establish the new rules by which others must play, usually leaving them one of two choices: rush to catch up, or be eliminated.

Think about what it means to literally change the game. With the advent of superabsorbent polymers, resealable tape, Velcro, and elasticized waistbands, disposable diapers came into play in the 1970s. For parents and caretakers it traded a major household chore for an incredible convenience, all but eliminated the traditional diaper service, and created a new multibillion-dollar industry.

Changing the game is not only about creating new markets; it redefines existing ones as well. In the U.S. Netflix redefined the rules of the game by eliminating late fees for video rentals and making it extremely convenient to rent movies online. The hit show *Survivor* introduced reality television and spurred a whole new realm of entertainment across the globe. And Apple is rocking the world again by launching what will soon be a $4 billion industry that didn't exist two years ago—the apps (applications) economy. More than one hundred thousand apps for iPhones and iPads exist at the time of this writing. As Research in Motion (BlackBerry), Nokia, Motorola Google, and Microsoft struggle to build or regain momentum, there isn't a competitor who comes close to Apple—no one has even fifteen thousand apps. By creating something that is addictive to the consumer and easy for the developer, Apple has become the catalytic agent behind a renaissance in developing sexy software that enhances people's productivity while on the fly.

In India, Mumbai-based Novatium is making a $100 laptop with the intention of doubling the potential number of users with access to the Internet. Think about the game-changing implications of another couple of billion new people with access to your Web site, your products, and your ideas.

The People's Car will change the game on several other fronts. To what extent is yet to be seen, but the Nano has the potential to displace a number of existing products. First, because the cost is so low, many people will upgrade from two- and three-wheelers to the Nano.

A symbol of innovation and ingenuity, the People's Car disrupted an entire industry.

Second, until the unveiling of the Nano, the Maruti 800 was the benchmark for the most inexpensive car on the market. Now with the prestige and functionality of a stylish passenger car that meets safety and emissions requirements at almost half the price of the Maruti, the Nano will surely cause potential Maruti buyers to defect. It has already depressed Maruti prices by 20 percent and used car prices by 30 percent. Who wants a used Maruti—with its 1980s styling—when you can have a new Nano for the same price or less?

So Maruti, realizing the rules have changed, announced that it will focus more on mid-range cars and buyers higher up the socio-economic pyramid.

Third, what happens when Bosch goes back to Germany with new ways to take hundreds of dollars out of the cost of an engine control unit (ECU)? What happens when Delphi, TRW, and Visteon can make Nanovation cost cuts in their products in India? What will they be able to offer the American auto industry? As we'll show you in a later chapter, with the introduction of the Nano, cost performance and weight reduction are going to be the new touchstones of automotive innovation in the years ahead as carmakers realize that the tapped-out middle classes in Europe, North America, and Japan are not going to pay more for cars.

And that's *another* game changer.

> "We cannot dismiss India's competence in elegant design and frugal, 'Gandhian' engineering. In fact, we should learn from it."

When something changes the rules of the game, it challenges us to rethink the unthinkable. For example, with the successful launch of the Nano, the world has essentially said, "We cannot dismiss India's competence in elegant design and frugal, 'Gandhian' engineering. In fact, we should learn from it." This means that the Nano has laid the foundation for India to become a global hub for innovating low-cost products, manufacturing low-cost cars, and supplying low-cost, high-quality parts to automobile manufacturers the world over.

Prior to the Nano's arrival, this was unthinkable: most "experts" would have laughed at this idea. Why? Because many people have seen India as a country with incredibly bright people, tremendous engineering talent, and world-class doctors and scientists suffocating under a highly regulated, controlled, and corrupt economy. With no creative outlet, these very capable people had to leave India to leverage their gifts and talents. Now, with innovations such as the Nano paving the way, many believe that India, along with other developing nations, will be a leader in product development for the next twenty years.

Does It Ignite a Cultlike Following?

How do we define a cultlike following?

Think Starbucks. It has one of the most committed customer followings of any consumer brand in the world today. The answer is eighteen. What's the question? How many times does the average loyalist visit Starbucks in a month?

Think Nintendo. Anybody within shouting distance of a six- or sixty-six-year-old knows that Wii has creamed the competition and Nintendo is the comeback kid of the gaming world. It's a pop-culture smash hit of such proportions that Nintendo couldn't make enough product to keep up with demand.

Think Apple. People camp outside Apple stores for new product releases, like groupies waiting to see their favorite rock stars. Apple enthusiasts create fan sites on the Web.

Think Tata Nano. When thousands of people say, "It's extraordinary . . . I gotta have it . . . I want to tell you about it!" you probably have a cultlike product on your hands.

With more than two hundred thousand initial bookings, the Nano was one of the most successful product launches in the world—and this during a global recession! Yet Tata Motors did very little to hype the People's Car; it didn't need to. Just as Team Nano minimized the number of parts in the car, it also minimized its cost in marketing activities. There were only three major events: the unveiling of the car at the auto shows in New Delhi and Geneva, and the launch in Mumbai. That's it. There were no prelaunch campaign, no multimillion-dollar television commercials, and no multicity tour with Ratan Tata or Ravi Kant.

We've talked about how five hundred engineers came together, not just to create a product, but also to fight for the aspirations of Indians, to be part of a movement. In return, Indians have rallied around the little car with their own levels of passion and enthusiasm.

On our way back to Delhi from Pantnagar where we toured Tata Motors' Nano plant, we stopped at the famous roadside restaurant Namaka Gyani and struck up a conversation with the owner, Mr. Gyani. He told us about four Nanos that were being test-driven from Pantnagar to Delhi. The drivers stopped at his restaurant, approximately halfway between the two cities. He said, "The moment the four Nanos pulled up, everybody around this whole place flooded into the street to get a look."

After his test drive in Pune a week before the launch, Sirish Chandran, the editor of *Overdrive* magazine, said that the Nano was "staggeringly good . . . adorable" and showed "no signs of cost-cutting.

"Without a thread of exaggeration, this is the best car Tata Motors has ever made," he added. "Everywhere we went the car was mobbed, a million questions were fired at us, and were this our car we could have sold it at ten times the cost!"

The Nano is a symbol of rising India, a statement about the ingenuity of which Indians are capable as well as the freedom they desire. Is it any wonder, then, that people from all over India and around the world have literally logged on to be part of the buzz? The official Nano Web site received more than thirty million hits up until the launch in March 2009. All in all, there are approximately six thousand groups and forums on the Web regularly expressing views about the Nano. The highest Nano video view count on YouTube is nearly five hundred thousand, and bloggers from all over the globe wrote more than six thousand posts related to the car.

The attention garnered by the Nano is universal. Few products have generated the prelaunch hysteria that the Nano has created. Over two million search entries and two million images have been logged on Google. Scan the newspapers worldwide for Nano stories and you will find more than fifty thousand articles. The Nano ranked number one in the 2008 Brand Derby, a study conducted by the *Business Standard* in India, and *Time* magazine listed the Nano as one of the twelve most important cars in the world since 1908.

So you've got a new idea. Will it turn heads, stop people in their tracks, and create buzz? Will it make customers admire you and competitors envy you? Will it put you on the cover of major industry or business publications?

The Nano even had rivals such as Venu Srinivasan, chairman of motorcycle maker TVS Motors, gushing: "It's a red letter day for Indian industry, a day India should be proud of. Ratan Tata has the vision to create a new business model and all the naysayers are looking at it with concern. The Nano is a path breaker."

Nano has also made its way into the everyday lingo (think FedEx, Google, Xerox, Kleenex, Band-Aid, Skype, and Twitter) of Indians. The Indian radio stations created a Nano Day, television stations leave their scheduled programming for a Nano Break," and newspapers print news snippets called "Nano News." All of these activities came about through the media's own initiatives and added value to Tata Motors—at no cost.

That's revolutionary.

NANOBITE

How do you know if a product, service, or business model is *revolutionary*?

It produces change on a massive scale, and it has a sudden and broad impact on society.

It creates a cultlike following that is the envy of competitors.

It redefines and elevates customer expectations—it's addictive.

It is initially hard to accept (people can't get their minds around it) and ultimately hard to duplicate.

It produces change that matters, and it makes people's lives dramatically better.

QUESTIONS

- Who is most responsible for shaking up your industry: the incumbents or the new kids?
- Does your company think more like an incumbent or a new player?
- If someone accused your business of being radically different, would there be enough evidence to convict you?
- Someone, somewhere, is going to start a revolution that will disrupt your industry. What if it was you?

THIRTEEN
Nothing Short of Elegance

Making the simple complicated is commonplace; making the complicated simple, awesomely simple, that's creativity.

CHARLES MINGUS

O ne way you can identify a Nanovation is that it's not just revolutionary; it's *revolutionarily elegant.*

In 1957, four young physicists developed a theory of elementary particles that contradicted seven existing and well-known experiments. They had no data whatsoever to prove their theory, but they published it anyway because as one of them later said, "It was so beautiful, we believed it had to be right. And it was."

"If you can't explain something simply, you don't understand it well enough."

Albert Einstein

One of those young physicists, Murray Gell-Mann, went on to win the Nobel Prize for his work. "What is especially striking and remarkable," he told the TED Conference fifty years later, "is that in fundamental physics, a beautiful or elegant theory is more likely to be right than a theory that is inelegant."

According to Gell-Mann, who has spent a lifetime studying the most fundamental laws of the universe, elegance is an essential quality of both energy and matter. In fact, it underlies the equation of life. A theory appears to be beautiful or elegant when the mathematics is very simple and can be expressed concisely. That's what a physicist means by *elegance*.

Engineers use the word too. So do programmers, architects, designers, business book writers, and poets. Elegant work is always the best and most lasting work.

But if the universe is so elegant, why are we surrounded by so much junk? The short answer is this: junk is made by people, and people tend to make things complicated.

People also tend to look for easy answers and temporary solutions. If you can make something cheap that does its job well enough, somebody will buy it. So why bother with elegance? Why go to the trouble of adding elegance if you can sell it the way it is? If you're making a profit, why not milk it? It if lasts the length of the warranty period plus one day, what's the problem? If it emulates the performance of its peer group and commands a sizable market share, who needs to bother with elegance?

All good questions, but the second one is the money question because it goes to the heart of the most pertinent misunderstanding about elegant design. Design elegance can't be added after the fact, like icing on a cake or tail fins on a car. Either elegance is in the design from the beginning, or it will never be. Elegance is the *essence* of good design, not a by-product.

Elegance is ingenious simplicity and effectiveness in the solution of a problem.

Nanovation insists on elegant solutions. Someone has to wave the flag for the team (and for the customers) and say that what we deliver will be nothing short of elegance.

But what does *elegance* mean? It is one of those qualities we all think we can recognize but may have trouble defining. If you look through a few dictionaries, you come across a list of useful definitions:

- "Refined grace of form and movement. Ingenious simplicity, convenience and effectiveness" (the *Oxford English Dictionary*).
- "Elegance is the attribute of being unusually effective and simple" (Wikipedia).
- "A quality of neatness and ingenious simplicity in the solution of a problem" (Princeton University WordNet).

Ingenious simplicity and effectiveness in the solution of a problem: we can't think of a better description of the Nano than that. When we asked people at the Nano launch in Mumbai what they first thought when they saw it in person, that's pretty much what they said. *Unusually effective and simple*. And the deeper you dive into the ways in which the Nano team solved the problem of how to make a car for the price of a scooter, the more this description holds true.

So how did they do it? How did the Nano get to this state of elegance?

"Bad design is smoke. Good design is a mirror."
Juan-Carlos Fernández

Good design is a mirror of the thoughts and practices of the designers. It reflects both the intellectual and the artistic quality of their thinking. It provides a compass to their moral direction, their honesty. It reflects the head and heart of their connection to the end user. It shows you the clarity of their understanding of a problem. As the British author Bryan Lawson says, "Design is as much a matter of finding problems as it is of solving them."

We see five qualities in the process of elegant design. Five touchstones that are part of any really great design solution. Five elements that are certainly exemplified in the process of Team Nano and in the results of their work.

ELEGANT DESIGN IS . . .

1. Simple

H. M. Bangur is the managing director of Shree Cement, an innovative Indian company focused on being a great employer and a great member of the community. He's also known as the guy who ordered one thousand Nanos to give as rewards to his employees. When we sat with him, he said something that stuck with us: "The papers have all talked about the fact that Tata *did* it [produced the 1 lakh car], but no one has told us *how* they did it."

So we'll tell you: they did it by simplifying *everything*. Every single piece of material used on the car, every part, and every process. Every item had to justify its cost, even its existence. Every design was slavishly examined to see if there was a simpler, more focused, more disciplined way to do the same thing with less. Simple does more with less as a matter of course, but less is more only when less is better. And the genius of the Nano is that it does simple in the most brilliant and efficient ways.

David Pogue, the *New York Time*'s technology columnist, is adamant that simplicity is the key to great design. "Steve Jobs had always believed in simplicity and elegance and beauty," Pogue told an audience recently. "The truth is, for years, I was a little depressed because Americans obviously did not value it because the Mac had 3% market share. Windows had 95% market share. People did not think it was worth putting a price on it.

They made the NANO by simplifying EVERYTHING.

"But it turns out I was wrong, because the iPod came out and it violated every element of common wisdom. Other products had more features: they had voice recorders and FM transmitters. The other products were backed by Microsoft with an open standard, not Apple's proprietary standard. But the iPod won. This is the one they wanted.

"The lesson was: simplicity sells and there are signs the industry is getting the message. It's catching on.

"Be aware of good design and bad design. If you're among the people who create products, easy is hard. Pre-sweat the details. . . . Remember, the hard part is not deciding what features to add, it's deciding what to leave out."

"An idea should be as simple as possible, but no simpler."
Albert Einstein

And think about this: there is nothing at all simple about a modern automobile, even the world's least expensive little car. It's a complex system of interlocking and interacting parts and processes, an interactive system that resembles in many ways a living organism. (It's no accident that the original Volkswagen was also called a

"Bug.") So if you simplify a single part, you have to account for how that affects other parts and systems in the vehicle.

Take the fuel injection system. Bosch, the German engineering firm, has partnered with Tata Motors since it began manufacturing Mercedes trucks in 1954. Bosch signed on to Team Nano early in the project and had a big challenge: to take the costs out of the engine control unit and other high-tech elements of the car. The ECU controls engine times, fuel flow, pump pressure, and idle speed. On a typical German car, the ECU costs several hundred dollars. The fuel injection system alone can cost as much as $700. If your target for the whole car is just $2,000, that cost is going to have to come way, way down. So Bosch began simplifying.

"We wanted to be part of this from the start," Dr. Bernd Bohr, chairman of Bosch's Automotive Group, told us. "Normally we would adapt the products we use on premium European cars for use in the Indian market. And if our goal is to take 10 percent out of the costs, we can do that with 'value engineering.' But if your goal is to take 60 or 70 percent of the cost out, you have to start from scratch."

Bosch technicians looked at ways to reduce the complexity of engine management. They looked at all the parameters and began to sort them into those that were essential and those that were nice to have.

Where normal engine management systems have an injector for each cylinder, Team Nano found a way to make a single injector work for both of the engine's two cylinders. They found a way to integrate all the temperature and pressure sensors and management chips into the throttle body. They adapted a pump usually used for small engines that drive irrigation pumps and doubled its performance.

Simple, focused, and disciplined. And it works spectacularly well at a fraction of the cost. In the end, they didn't just take out 20 to 30 percent of the complexity; they reduced it by 80 percent. They simplified. And now the Nano has an ECU that costs less to manufacture, and it costs less to replace down the road. Because it is simpler, it lasts longer. And as an added return on innovation, both Bosch and Tata

Motors have a supersimple, low-cost product they can put to use in other applications around the world.

Here's another lesson. You don't have to have deep pockets and big budgets to design elegant solutions, but you do have to be willing to use constrained resources as springboards to creativity.

As the British mathematician Christopher Zeeman so elegantly puts it: "Technical skill is mastery of complexity, while creativity is mastery of simplicity." And simplicity doesn't necessarily mean plain. It just means thinking about the most ingeniously effective way to get the job done.

Elegance is simplicity, but that's not the end of the story. A unicycle is simple, but it's not elegant.

2. Focused

Simple demands focus: What is the problem you are trying to solve? Who are you trying to solve it for? What really matters in the end? Focus on function and on the end user means the clearer the focus, the clearer the design. Elegant design is a conversation between the designer and the user, a specific user. It doesn't try to be a Swiss Army knife. It tries to be a radically affordable scalpel by creating a new price-to-performance paradigm.

The essence of great design is being there. Being where the customers will be when they use the product. Letting the customer feel your presence there and think, *Someone was here before me; someone thought about this before me.*

Why are Apple customers so loyal? Precisely because they feel the designer's presence in their experience of the product; they sense the designer there with them.

Here's what Steve Jobs says about it: "When you buy our products, and three months later you get stuck on something, you quickly figure out [how to get past it]. And you think, 'Wow, someone over there at Apple actually thought of this!' And then three months later you try to do something you hadn't tried before, and it works, and

(Tata Motors)

A styling conference at the Engineering Research Center (ERC) in Pune.

you think 'Hey, they thought of that, too.' And then six months later it happens again. There's almost no product in the world that you have that experience with, but you have it with a Mac. And you have it with an iPod." And an iPhone too.

And you have it with a Nano.

"People ignore design that ignores people."

Frank Chimero

As they did on the Ace, Team Nano had a passionate focus on what the target audience needed and how they would use their Nanos when they got them. They knew, for instance, that Indians tend to travel in family groups, and that includes senior family members, who would be likely to ride in the rear. They also knew that, even with a Nano, because of the low cost of having a driver, some owners would choose to be driven. Again, they would be likely to ride in the rear. So making the rear seat roomy and easily accessible wasn't just a designer's whim. It came from a deep and passionate focus on the culture of their customers and how the end users would experience the product.

As we said, great design is a conversation—a deep, probing conversation, with the designers doing all the listening.

"You have to be interested in culture to design for it."
Lorraine Wild

We passionately agree with Lorraine Wild's comment (even if she was really referring to opera). To design effectively, you have to have a fanatically passionate interest in the people for whom you're designing. For all the attention that the idea of the 1 lakh car got, the Nano was never about a price point. It was about bringing mobility, safety, and dignity to the lives of India's emerging middle class (and soon, emerging middle classes around the world). Anyone in the world could start designing a superinexpensive car. But unless that person had a committed interest in the actual end user, he or she would never know the importance of those back doors and that roomy interior.

Take the steering angle, for instance. Indian streets and roads

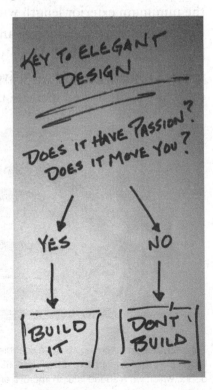

are often narrow, so it's important to have as small a turning circle as possible. The Maruti 800 has a turning circle of about twenty-eight feet, so Team Nano set their goal at twenty-six.

On average, small cars have a steering angle of about thirty-eight to forty degrees. That means, from center, the wheels can turn up to forty degrees in either direction until they reach the lock angle. The greater that lock angle, the smaller the turning circle. So chassis engineers Jay Bolar and Umesh Abhyankar went to work designing a steering system with a forty-three-degree lock angle.

This had never been done before, but because it was critical to the usability of the Nano, the team pressed forward. It was a risky decision, and they didn't know whether it was actually feasible or what problems this decision might cause in other parts of the system.

They soon found out.

An early design mandate had been that the Nano should have the minimum exterior length with the maximum interior space. But when you increase the steering angle, you suddenly discover you need larger wheel wells. And larger wheel wells encroach on front seat space. Early designs had the driver sitting very far forward, between the wheel wells. If you increase the size of the wheel wells but don't

(Tata Motors)

This early design rendering shows a snubbier nose on the Nano before the wheelbase was lengthened to allow for more driver legroom. Note the absence of air ducts behind the rear doors, which were added later to improve engine cooling.

want to take up passenger space, you have to move them forward, or you have to widen the car.

The decision was made to move the wheel wells forward by almost two inches. And while that solved the problem of interior space, it also solved another problem. The team felt the initial designs looked too flat in front. Lengthening the nose allowed not just more interior room and the targeted turning circle but also allowed for a more curvaceous and pleasing nose that gives the Nano an extra dose of likable personality.

But that happy occurrence never would have happened without a team focused on users and the functions that meant most to them. It never would have happened without a team deep in conversation with users, a team that had been there before them.

"A common mistake that people make when trying to design something completely foolproof is to underestimate the ingenuity of complete fools."
Douglas Adams

3. Disciplined

Focused design requires discipline. It's easy to start out thinking you know all the answers. It's easy to fall in love with a particular idea that tickles you. It's hard to put those ideas aside and keep digging for the right answer. Elegance barks to the would-be Nanovator, "Your first answer is not your best answer. Keep going!" Your first answer is tempting because it's your easiest and most obvious answer. But it is usually less than optimal.

Kim Goodwin is the vice president of design at Cooper, a leading design firm in San Francisco. She says this about discipline: "I think if you're starting out early in the process by talking about your ideas for solutions, you're already not listening. I think you need to enter into any design project with that Zen learner's mind of 'I don't know what I don't know.'"

If Team Nano had taken their first ideas and stuck with them, the Nano would have been a 2 lakh plastic-bodied golf cart. And we would not be writing this book. As much as anything, the Nano is the result of incredible discipline in looking for solutions, finding them, and then looking for ways to make them better. Improve; evaluate; repeat. And don't stop until you've got it right.

Of course, you'll never really get it right. As Salvador Dali once said, "Have no fear of perfection. You'll never reach it." So part of the discipline is to know when you've reached the point of diminishing returns, where there's no more return on innovation in cutting costs further.

Discipline is about editing, trimming, pushing beyond the first, easiest, and most obvious answer, and again, simplifying. Discipline knows when to keep pursuing a better solution and when to stop.

B. B. Parekh led the team that managed procurement of parts and materials on the Nano. He said, "We had very clear focus on what the ultimate product was going to be, and I think we could have done a much better job in terms of controlling cost and reducing the entire cycle. We kept pushing for improvements, doing things over and over. I think we could have done it faster and reduced the time to market."

Think about that: the executive in charge of procurement on the world's least expensive car thinks he could have made it even cheaper if they had been more disciplined.

That's discipline. That's what champions do. They don't pat themselves on the back for a great win. They're too busy thinking about how they can do it better next time. And that leads us to the next fundamental of elegant design.

4. Improved

If it doesn't work better, it isn't improved.

Recently the Discovery Channel ran a series of programs on design. In one of them, the producers asked a famous product design firm to redesign the backyard barbecue grill and then followed the best minds in the U.S. product design business as they put their heads together. What they finally unveiled was beautiful: a modernist design that was truly an object of architectural beauty.

But we were disappointed to see that they had missed what we think was the most important part of the exercise: they hadn't made it *better*. They came up with something prettier than the average backyard barbecue, but it didn't cook any better. In fact, we suspect it wouldn't cook as well.

What were we expecting? A new way of managing air flow perhaps, one that would cause the charcoal to light faster, burn hotter, and last longer. Perhaps they would show us a way to cook more with half as much charcoal.

If it doesn't work BETTER, it isn't IMPROVED.

Maybe something that would do all that and then fold up smaller. Something inventive. Something surprising. Something delightful.

We think it's great to make products pretty, but we assert that Nanovation has to offer *functional* improvement as well. If the function isn't improved over existing products—or delivered for a dramatically lower cost—it's not elegant design. Less is more only if less is better.

Nanovators don't innovate in a vacuum. A lot of engineers and designers, from a lot of companies, worked on Team Nano, usually focusing on a single part or system. And while each had to make his or her part of the puzzle as elegant as possible, they also had to consider its place in the whole. In other words, each part had to be *systemically* viable.

While the innovations they came up with might represent only an isolated part of something bigger, they considered the systemic impact of their solutions on other parts of the system. It's about asking, how will this solution impact other parts of the product, other parts of the organization, and the customer's experience?

If it does create new problems, the solution is less than optimal. The challenge then is to keep pushing beyond an easy or obvious answer to the one that *is* elegant.

> If a solution solves a critical problem in one area and doesn't create three new problems in other areas—it's elegant.

You can put the engine in the rear of the Nano, but in doing so you don't want to create a new problem. For example, you don't want to make servicing that engine a problem because it is very difficult to access. You want to create the tightest turning circle in the industry, but in doing so you don't want to crowd the driver's leg space by locating the wheels too close to the brake and clutch pedals. To reduce costs, you can use only one wiper blade, but you don't want to create a visibility problem in the rain.

Solutions that aren't elegant will limit your product. Why? Because over the long haul, another problem surfaces, creating an ugly symptom for either the company or the customer—usually both. This symptom shows up as increased cycle time, diminished customer experience, or increased manufacturing costs—all of which decrease the return on innovation.

Is the Nano an improved car? It can't outrun a Porsche. It's not as luxurious as a Rolls-Royce. It can't carry as many people as a Chevy Suburban. But what it does it does better than any car in history: it puts a family on a great set of wheels for less than ever before.

Half the price of the Maruti 800, formerly the least expensive car in India. One-fifth the price, in today's dollars, of the original Volkswagen. One-tenth the price of the first Model T, the first car that revolutionized and democratized driving.

Everyone said it couldn't be done, but the Nano did it. And when you drive it, you see that it drives just like any other small car and feels better built than many others costing three or four times more. The Nano does something more with less.

And it does it better.

5. Delightful

Here's the proof: the finished product is elegant if it delights the senses and stimulates the mind. You know it when you see it, even if you don't know why. It has a quality of likability. It makes you smile. It has wow factor. You want to pick it up. You want to know what it is.

When the world first saw the Nano, people grinned from ear to ear. And the closer they looked, the wider the smiles got. We attended the launch in Mumbai in the spring of 2009, when the Nano finally went on sale, and we talked with the people present. We talked to people on the streets. And when the car was delivered to the first owners later that year, we talked to them, too.

Everyone said the same thing: it was a real car, and they loved it. It was an ingenious car, and they wanted one. It was an elegant and delightful solution to a problem no one thought could be solved. And because it delights you, you want to see it do well.

Elegant design has integrity and communicates through your senses. Pick up a super high-quality pair of Japanese garden shears and you can feel it. They are balanced and sturdy, clicking together with intricate precision. There is no looseness in the locking bolt. They fall perfectly to hand. They delight you.

Many cheap products out there in the marketplaces of the world begin life as shoddy excuses and go downhill from there. The Nano, like other cars developed to sell for as little as possible, could have gone that route.

But it didn't. Team Nano, from the very beginning, made the Nano an exercise in elegant design.

FOURTEEN

Start with Less;
End Up with More

Less is more only when less is better.

ROY SPENCE, PRESIDENT, GSD&M

Part of elegant design is that it's simpler and it does more with less. But in an overcrowded world where sustainability is becoming a critical element of design—if not human survival—we think the less-is-more story is worth unpacking just a little bit more.

Suggest to many ambitious people focused on material gain that "less is more" and you can see them begin to panic. Their identity is caught up with things and possessions and having more, more, more. That's why the fastest-growing industry in the United States is storage lockers, which people rent so they can visit the stuff they can no longer fit in their already too-big houses.

So relax. We're not going to take your toys away. Instead, Nanovation shows you how you can have it all—including increased power, self-esteem, and peace of mind—by changing your relationship to the stuff around you.

Less is more only if less is better.

Doing more with less doesn't mean going without or depriving yourself. It doesn't mean making the best of a bad thing or settling for a disappointing level of performance or quality. It means being smart about how we solve problems and where we find solutions.

One of the tyrannies of our modern world is the idea that the bigger the budget, the more you can solve. And that's not necessarily true. In fact, far from it. As we've seen, limitations force innovation.

V. S. Ramachandran is the neuroscientist who runs the Center for Brain and Cognition at the University of California, San Diego. He is passionate about the benefits of low-tech experimentation because he believes it forces us to be ingenious. And if that's not saying something about Nanovation, we don't know what is.

For instance, consider the problem of phantom limb pain; amputees feel such excruciating pain in amputated limbs that they sometimes commit suicide. Doctors have worked on this and theorized about it for centuries; "treatments" included

San Diego's (and India's) V. S. Ramachandran says that low-tech solutions force us to be ingenious.

repeated amputations, cutting the limb higher and higher, on the theory that the nerve endings were inflamed; cutting the nerve at the spinal cord; massive doses of painkillers; or years of psychoanalysis—all with zero results. No wonder people killed themselves!

Ramachandran studied the problem and wondered if it was neurological, if the area of the brain that maps the body had been fooled somehow into incorrectly mapping the missing limb. He noted that lots of those who suffered this pain had had the limb immobilized for a long period before the amputation, in a position that would naturally cause muscles to cramp, so he tried an experiment. He took a mirror and had a young patient sit so that the reflection of his right arm in the mirror gave him the visual illusion that he had two whole arms. Then he had him wave his "arms" like he was conducting an orchestra. In seconds, the patient started screaming, "Oh, my God, the pain is gone!" Two weeks of this, for ten minutes a day, and he completely remapped the brain and cured the condition.

With a $5 mirror. That's the definition of an elegant solution.

What if the pursuit of high-tech solutions keeps us from seeing low-tech innovations? What if you spent your career trying to find a way to use electrodes in brain surgery to remap and rewire the brain cell by cell? What if you spent billions chasing that high-tech answer, imagining massive computer-aided, laser-guided ways to get all that done in the time you could have a patient under anesthetic? And what if your goal was a 20 percent improvement, with millions invested? And then Ramachandran comes along with a $5 mirror and ten minutes of arm waving. Boom, it's done.

What other innovations are we missing because we're so invested in the high-tech, high-dollar approach that we miss the low-tech answer? Why don't we always start

What if the pursuit of high-tech solutions keeps us from seeing low-tech innovations?

with an investigation of low-tech solutions before we start spending big bucks on R & D? Is there a gravitational field around the product development game that people can't break out of? Does investment in the game blind us to opportunity? Just because you've always done it that way doesn't mean it isn't incredibly stupid.

"Less is more" is also about efficiency, getting maximum output from minimum input. You don't need a military-inspired Hummer to get groceries unless you live in a mountainous war zone. If you need to carry a generator up a mountain to an isolated research station, a hefty four-wheel-drive pickup may be just the ticket. But if all you need to do is get the family to work and school, it's a pretty inelegant choice.

The creative and efficient use of motion to create a desired outcome is elegant. In his wonderful book *In Pursuit of Elegance*, Matthew May points out that elegance is about achieving an aha solution with the least amount of effort or resources. Team Nano took this as its mandate.

Consider these simple but elegant solutions that helped the Nano keep weight and cost down:

(The authors)

This is a BIW—body-in-white, in industry parlance—the single biggest component of a car. If you can save cost and weight here, without compromising safety, you're on the way.

THE BODY AND FRAME. The unibody construction, which combines the body and frame into a single, high-strength unit, was designed to use the maximum thickness of steel where it was needed for strength and the minimum where it was not.

THE ENGINE. Tata developed a unique all-aluminum two-cylinder engine and then tucked it under the rear seat to save room. At only 624 cc and 35 horsepower, you can describe power the way Rolls-Royce does: it's adequate, at least for Indian road conditions. And it fits the character of the car with its come-from-behind, beep-beep charm.

THE INSTRUMENT CLUSTER. Adapted from a motorcycle design by Delphi, the instrument panel is ultralight, simple, and perfect for this application. And placing it in the center of the dashboard means no more work has to be done to create a left-hand drive model.

(Tata Motors)

An early design approach for the instrument panel shows the first instrument binnacle far forward in the center of the asymmetrical dash. Later, it was moved forward for better visibility, and the dashboard was made symmetrical to reduce the costs of a left-hand drive model.

THE WHEELS. They're only twelve inches in diameter, which saves money, both on the wheels and on the tires. They're made with a new process that makes pressed steel look like an alloy wheel. And then some genius realized that having just three lug nuts could save more.

FUEL ECONOMY AND EMISSIONS. At over fifty miles per gallon, the Nano is getting into scooter fuel-use levels. It's the most fuel-efficient petrol-powered car in India. And it's clean-burning little engine has the lowest overall CO_2 emissions—101 gm./km—of any car in India. In fact, it's cleaner than most two-wheelers on the road in India.

The list of ways in which the Nano does more with less is long and impressive. And Team Nano got there because they kept pushing for more innovative solutions.

Limitations force you to do **more** with **less** in more **ingenious** ways.

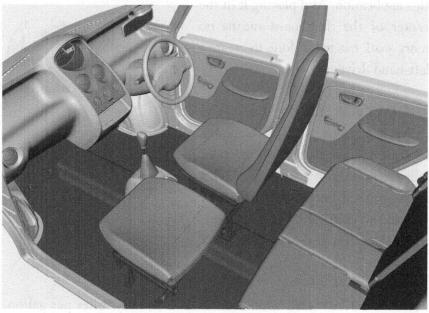

(Tata Motors)

The finished interior of the base version Nano shows the integration of the Delphi instrument cluster into a center ventilation and storage module. Seats are simple but adequate for comfort. Notice how the places people would touch are finished with plastic trim while other areas are exposed painted metal. Rubber flooring is easy to clean and helps dampen sound. And ventilation, on the 1 lakh version, relies on the ingenuity of the occupants to open the windows.

We've consulted with enough organizations to know that when an irreconcilable problem emerges, one of the first places people go to seek answers is more resources: "If we only had more people to carry the load, more time to develop it, more start-up capital to get it off the ground, more training to learn how to do it, or fewer regulations that impede it, we could produce something that's *really* creative."

There is no question that limited resources can stifle innovation, but all too often this becomes an easy and convenient excuse for not doing the critical and creative thinking required to push to the next level—the place where elegance is found.

For all of its life, resource and regulatory limitations have been a source of innovation for Southwest Airlines. The flight attendants know that the Federal Aviation Administration (FAA) gives no leeway on what must be said in the preflight safety announcements. Most companies would leave it at that, lamenting that they must live within the boundaries of those limitations or the FAA will revoke their right to fly.

Not Southwest. Its people see these FAA regulations as an opportunity to be creative. On many Southwest flights you will hear the flight attendant sing the safety announcement or incorporate it into a comedic routine. Here's the power that comes from exploiting these constraints. First, people actually listen and learn from the announcement, which creates the potential for a higher level of safety. Second, it takes the monotony out of waiting for the flight to take off and in some cases eases the stress of a nervous flyer. Finally, customers get off the airplane with a memorable experience—one that causes Southwest to stand out—and tell their friends and colleagues what happened.

Choosing to see a limitation as an opportunity instead of a liability unleashes the ingenuity and resourcefulness that establish a radical point of differentiation for the company. Figuring out how to break through limitations has become a badge of honor at Southwest and exemplifies the warrior spirit that pervades the company's corporate culture.

The Southwest example shows that limitations can either enable or disable innovation depending on how you look at them. It's a choice.

Team Nano took up the challenge of creating a 1 lakh car—even when materials costs soared by 40 percent! Were they afraid that they couldn't do it? Sure. But rather than cower from the incredible challenge posed by this constraint, they stepped through their fears and leveraged the limitation. They let it become a source of energy and creativity that fueled their imaginations. They went back to start-up mode—that place of a bootstrapping entrepreneur with a big dream and few resources—and chose to see their limitations as opportunities. It is as if they said, "If we can break through our limitations and take advantage of them, we will have done what no one else has been able to do, and we will have established a major point of distinction while doing something good for society."

AIMING LOW AND SCORING HIGH

E. Balasubramoniam initially—and then Prashant Saxena—headed the sourcing team on the Nano and, right from the beginning, set target cost figures for every single part they expected to get on the car, whether they were from internal sources or from suppliers. That doesn't mean that every part hit its original target price. Some came in higher, and that meant something else had to cost less. But some came in lower, and they did that because innovative team members kept pushing for better ideas.

Some companies just didn't get it. When Team Nano approached the tire manufacturers and showed them the tiny tires the Nano needed, they balked. They talked about their global planning requirements and the trends toward larger tires. They were getting out of the small tire business. There was no market for them! Why would they want to open that up again for an unknown little car in India? How could they make money on them?

Of course, after the Nano became a worldwide sensation and

they saw the value of having their name associated with the Nano brand, the big tire companies came back, full of ideas. By then it had occurred to them how big the tire replacement market might be for millions of Nanos and Nano imitators. But by then it was too late. MRF, India's largest tire maker, had stepped up and delivered.

The tire makers weren't the only ones who balked at first. One regular supplier absolutely refused to talk about the project, saying the cost targets for an engine component he was being asked to supply were so impossible that it wasn't worth the time to talk about them. So Balaubramoniam called Narendra Kumar Jain and explained the problem.

Jain said, "Look, I know their CEO. I'll call him and tell him I'm coming over." He didn't tell the supplier what the topic of the meeting was, but when he walked in with Subramaniam and his team, the man groaned. "Forget about it!" he said. "It can't be done."

"I told him to turn his cell phone off and make sure we're not disturbed," Jain remembered. "I said, 'You're well-known in this field, but we've got an idea we think will work.' And so we started sketching."

Once the vendor was involved in the conversation, he got engaged and then excited. Once he realized that Team Nano was serious about simplicity, he started putting his extensive knowledge and creativity to work.

By lunchtime, they came away with not just one way in which it could be done, but three.

It took a while for some vendors to understand what Tata was asking for. They kept pricing parts to EU specifications. But when they realized they could simplify, they became inventive. Team Nano got the prices down, but gave vendors exclusives to make it worth the investment. It was

Jain was diplomatically forceful because he believed in what the team was doing.

a risk for vendors, but when the car was revealed and the whole world cheered, their commitment to the Nano project was vindicated.

It took a while for some vendors to understand what Tata was asking for.

The limitations on cost were so extreme that they forced people to be innovative. Cutting the costs by 80 percent on most assemblies was beyond normal cost-cutting principles. It required people to change everything they thought about getting the job done.

And when that happened, they began to Nanovate.

NANOBITE

Less is more, but only when less is better. It's about . . . .

- achieving the most elegant solution with the least amount of effort and resources.
- choosing to see limitations as opportunities instead of liabilities.
- resisting the temptation to make excuses for lack of innovation.
- making the pursuit of low-cost, low-tech solutions a badge of honor.
- pushing boundaries because the prevailing paradigm will entice you to cry for *more*.
- avoiding the trap of "feature creep" and developing the discipline to keep it simple.

QUESTIONS

- Do the people on your team choose to see limitations as threats or opportunities?
- Assume, like Team Nano, that limitations can force creativity. How would this change your business?
- What are some limitations that are currently stifling innovation?
- How can you redefine those limitations as opportunities to radically differentiate you from your competitors?

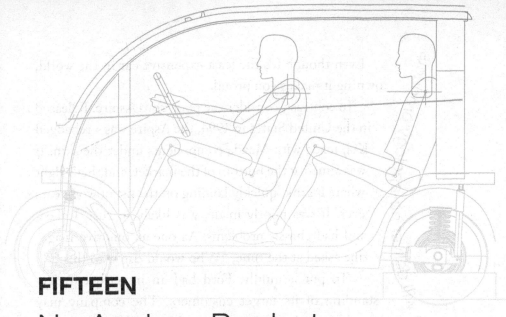

FIFTEEN

No-Apology Products

If I create from the heart, nearly everything works; if from the head, almost nothing.

MARC CHAGALL

Nanovation is about high-quality, high-utility products at a fraction of the normal cost. Nanovation seeks to balance the needs of the customer and the needs of the company. But more than that, Nanovation tries harder. Nanovation does well by doing good. In a sense, Nanovation partners with the customers to create something that meets their needs, that they would be proud to own, and that they can afford.

When the first few customers took delivery of their Nanos in 2009, they proudly basked in the media attention. No one thought they should be embarrassed for buying such an inexpensive car. Everyone thought they were celebrities.

Even though it's the least expensive car in the world, owning it makes you proud.

In contrast, consider the poor Ford Aspire. Released in the United States in 1994, the Aspire was a rebadged Kia, made with Mazda components under the skin. It was aimed at the bottom of the market, and that's right where it sank, quickly landing on the list of worst cars ever. It was poorly made, was likely to rust, leaked, and had chassis problems. As one automotive magazine asked at the time, "Who would *Aspire* to this?!!"

To put it mildly, Ford had an imperfect understanding of its target customers. The company may have had market research, may have had focus groups, and may have had reams of data. But Ford clearly didn't get in the shoes of customers. And worse, the company didn't commit to giving them something brilliant. Ford just gave them something cheap.

Why do companies filled with brilliant people fail to produce brilliant products? There's no question that Ford—like all car companies—attracts lots of bright people who love cars and want to do something great with their careers. So what happens?

First, when the focus is on price, not quality, you get shoddy goods by default. Second, when the focus is on profiting from a need instead of fulfilling it fully, you get no love from customers.

We suspect that if a team of bright, young designers had gone to Ford management and said, "Hey, what if we take the time to innovate a dramatically different kind of car that delivers true usability and customer delight and does so for half the price of the cheapest car in America?" they would have been laughed out of the conference room. And since no one wants to make a career-ending move, they would have gone back to their workstations and shut up.

Complacent, inflexible corporate bureaucracies

Nanovation takes, as a fundamental commitment, that it will deliver no-apology products.

quickly become cynical about customers. After all, they reason, what do customers know about cars? Managers (we won't use the word *leaders*) sit in conference rooms and convince one another that they make the best cars in the world, and their market share problems can be solved with better advertising and PR. And if that fails, try racing stripes.

> When the focus is on profiting from a need instead of fulfilling it fully, you get no love from customers.

John DeLorean, a former GM executive, laid it all out in his 1979 memoir, *On a Clear Day You Can See General Motors*:

> A cloistered executive, whose only social contacts are with similar executives who make $500,000 a year, and who has not really bought a car the way a customer has in years, has no basis to judge public taste.
>
> Our inability to compete with the foreign manufacturers is more due to management failure than anything else . . . the system and management are stifling initiative. Leadership and innovation are impossible.

DeLorean's words were prophetic, but automakers widely ignored his observations and recommendation. They dismissed him as a disgruntled employee. Maybe he was. Wouldn't *you* be?

You may have had the experience of working for a company and reading an interview by your CEO in which he talked about how great your company was, how much better your products were, and what a great place it was to work. Did you grit your teeth, realizing the man simply had no clue about the reality of your company's situation? As you realized your leader was living in a fantasy world of his own creation, you may have begun to wonder whether there was *any* sanity in the business world. Or worse, after the company had collapsed and the CEO walked away from the wreckage with the last few hundred million from the till, you read about him claiming the only problem was the media, the market, or government regulations.

So why didn't the same thing happen at Tata Motors? Certainly India has never lacked bureaucratic, shortsighted organizational cultures. You could hardly expect a company that dates from the British Raj to be innovative, fast moving, nimble, and visionary.

So why is Tata different? Pick a word: *leadership, values, focus, purpose*. Or try this word: *balance*. The Tata culture has always had a fundamentally different relationship with results, where success is measured in a balance of financial good and public good, where the benefits to customers and employees are considered to be as important as the benefits to shareholders.

Balance.

That means a very clear understanding that an apology product would be bad for customers, employees, and shareholders. Customers, trusting the Tata brand, might be fooled once, maybe even twice, but would be unlikely to return for that punishment again. Employees, ashamed of having their names on pathetically embarrassing products, would stop telling neighbors where they work. Shareholders, watching their returns diminish, would either take their investment elsewhere or send management packing.

"Designers have a dual duty; contractually to their clients and morally to the later users and recipients of their work."
Hans Höger

Pretty much all employees at Tata, from the chairman to factory floor workers, believe fervently that they have a responsibility to customers, to their community, to their country, and to the world to deliver quality and value. They take that responsibility very seriously.

"A promise is a promise," Ratan Tata said every time someone suggested not making the pricing goal or delivering something less than a great product. Look at all the moments of truth when the Nano team could have said, "This is good enough for a 1 lakh car! They're lucky to get this much."

- When they saw how much they could save if they made the Nano a two-door car, but insisted the Indian family needed the easier access of the two rear doors.
- When they saw how much they could save by not trying to tighten the turning circle, but pressed on because they knew it would have a dramatic effect on the Nano's practicality and character.
- When they made the decision to involve Italy's I.DE.A Institute to design the Nano because they knew these cars would be more than affordable transportation; they would become an expression of the fortunes of the world's emerging middle class.

Every decision had to be balanced. Yes, it had to be within the cost parameters, but it also had to be something the customers would be proud to own, something that would be as great to drive as it was practical to maintain.

One day in Pune, the team was reviewing the brakes and was quite proud of the braking performance, which was demonstrated to Ratan Tata. Performance was clearly better than that of the Maruti 800, even on the base model, on which the brakes were unboosted.

One young engineer, named Badal, was explaining this achievement when Ratan interrupted him: "Okay, young man, you can keep explaining that the brake performance is better without the booster, but I want the booster because I want the feel of the booster."

It was one more moment of truth. Young Badal stood his ground, saying, "Sir, you have to meet the cost plan."

Ratan stood his ground, too. He replied, "Okay, you can leave the booster off, but you have to give me the *feel* of the booster." And they did. Time and again, they made balanced decisions that delivered both price and quality targets. Reasonable compromises, all focused on giving the customers something worth owning. Something that would add to their dignity instead of challenging it.

It wasn't easy, and it kept everyone on the team awake at night. Remember how impossible the Nano seemed initially. "The biggest fear we all had," one of the engineers at Pune told us, "was that we might be able to deliver a 1 lakh car, but it would not actually be felt, seen, or appreciated as a car."

And yet, as automotive reviewers from around the world stepped out of the Nano after their first drive, almost all said the same thing: it's a real car. It drives like a real car, it feels like a real car, and it looks like a real car. So real, it has actually become a style icon.

And that's important if your goal is to make family transportation affordable for an amazingly large population of the world. Just because people are poor doesn't mean they are stupid. By making the Nano a car that people could aspire to, the team made it something worth owning.

Dave Hudson came to Tata Motors from Jaguar to focus on what auto engineers call NVH: *noise, vibration, and harshness*. Sure, as Ratan Tata said in that first Geneva interview, maybe the Nano did not have to be the quietest car in the world, but it had to be quiet enough. Developing the world's least expensive rattletrap would hardly be something to be proud of. NVH is one of the most important elements in our *perception* of quality. And this is one area where perception is reality.

But the Nano presented unique problems. With a

Time and again, they made balanced decisions that delivered both price and quality targets.

two-cylinder engine, there's more vibration than, say, a four- or six-cylinder engine. Even with the sophisticated design of the unibody frame, when you bolt on an engine and suspension and get it running, it acts like a large tuning fork, magnifying every rattle and hum.

(Tata Motors)

Dave Hudson tests noise, vibration, and harshness in an anechoic chamber at the ERC in Pune.

"You can't solve this by adding insulation," Dave explained. "You have to design your solution into every component. That means a balancing shaft in the engine to cancel the primary motion of the pistons; it means designing a mounting system that allows the engine more flexibility to move. When you do that, you need more clearance around the engine and more flexible connections."

It gets more and more complicated. Think about this: every object vibrates at a certain frequency. So Team Nano had to be very clever about exactly what frequency they allowed the engine to move; otherwise they would run into trouble with excitation from the frame, the road wheels, or even the ventilation system.

Balancing the investment of taking NVH out of the system while keeping costs down was a huge challenge. And because no one had ever done it at this level, team members had little previous experience to draw on. Levels of harshness that were acceptable on a truck like the Ace were not acceptable on a car like the Nano.

So they kept pressing. They kept balancing and refining to make the Nano better than anyone expected. And one of the biggest achievements was the body structure.

"Getting the body light meant you could save on cost and weight everywhere else," Dave continued. "You can use smaller brakes and suspension components. You can use lighter steering gear. That all takes costs out. But at the same time, this car has to survive on Indian roads, and it has to survive for many years. So, instead of saying that at one part of the body structure you had to have 0.8mm steel thickness, so let's use that everywhere, we looked for points that needed heavier gauge and points that could use lighter gauge. We went heavy where we needed the strength and lighter where we didn't. The body's the single biggest component on the car, so if you keep weight and cost under control, you're 90 percent of the way there."

And even though the Nano is extraordinarily light, it has conventional stiffness, enough to pass European and U.S. crash test standards with minimal modifications.

Remember, they could have made a golf cart with a motorboat engine and have met their cost target. And they thought about that early on. But because they had a commitment to no-apology products, they knew the Nano had to be a real car. A real car with no apologies at all. And although it's not the quietest car on the road, it is, as Dave puts it, "the quietest 1 lakh car ever built!"

When your focus is on the needs and dignity of the end users, and when you make their needs your cause, you start to get very focused on things that really matter. The Nano, from the inception of the idea on that rainy afternoon in Bangalore, was never about what was good for Tata Motors. It was always about what was good for millions of Indian families trying to crowd onto scooters.

ROOM TO MOVE

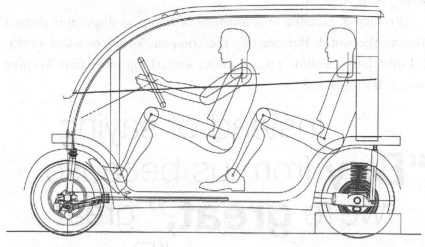

(Tata Motors)

Dignity starts inside, and that's where Team Nano started, too. This early design study focused on interior space with a priority to legroom and headroom. The team knew that if people put five or even six family members on a scooter, they'd try to put that many in the Nano. They also knew some of those rear seat passengers might be grandparents or ladies in saris, so four doors were needed for comfortable, dignified access. This early rendering helped the team develop the interior dimensions, around which everything else was designed. Members of the team smile ruefully when they tell us how much less expensive they could have made the Nano with just two doors, but the dignity of passengers drove the decision. In a very real sense, the Nano was designed *around* the passengers.

Once upon a time, General Motors said that what was good for General Motors was good for the country, meaning the United States. But it turned out that General Motors wasn't good for the country, and so the country turned against GM in favor of more innovative car companies that cared more about its needs.

Today, great companies are the ones that put the customers first and care more about their needs. Instead of saying, "Buy from us because we're great," they're now saying, "Buy from us because we want *you* to be great."

Procter & Gamble sells millions of Pampers disposable diapers around the world. But one day the company's leaders asked a critical question: "Shouldn't we be about something more than keeping babies' bottoms dry?"

Instead of saying, "**Buy** from us because we're **great**," great companies say, "Buy from us **because** we want *YOU* to be great."

What if P & G chose to expand its vision from selling diapers to being in the baby development business? What if its mission became to help mothers be more successful in those critical first few years of life? How could the company be a better partner? And if it put the mothers and babies first, would mothers, in turn, put Pampers first?

The answer is yes. After P & G's leaders asked those questions and committed to the answers, its business doubled. And Roy Spence, who helped the company navigate the process of rethinking what its business was all about, says there's a benefit to the company that's even larger: "As they made the conscious decision to get out of the dryness business and into the baby development business, new and innovative thinking spread like wildfire throughout the Pampers organization."

And that innovative thinking continues to pay dividends through-out the business.

In 1866, the Sherwin-Williams Company invented ready-mixed paint in a can because it believed passionately that home owners would benefit from being able to do their own house painting and decorat-ing. The result was an explosion of do-it-yourself home improvement across America in the 1880s and 1890s. In time, professional painters saw the value of not having to mix their own paint, too, and became a big part of Sherwin-Williams' business.

In 1999, when John Morikis was promoted to president of the Stores Group, the largest part of the Sherwin-Williams Company, he asked store managers to look at painting contractors in a new way. "We stopped looking at the pot and brush contractor as some-one we were just supposed to sell paint to," he said. "Instead, we asked how we could make them more successful. We turned the focus of our whole Stores organization toward finding ways to make millions of small contractors more profitable, more efficient and more competitive."

As a result of that focus on customers, the company's revenues doubled in the years that followed, and its stock value grew more than 200 percent.

Now the company's COO, Morikis says, "If you want to be suc-cessful, focus on making other people successful."

When companies are passionate about what really matters to their customers, even the *idea* of an apology product becomes unacceptable. When you're focused on making other people successful—getting them safe and dignified transportation so they can join the march to the middle class—you don't want to hear anyone on the team suggest you cut a corner either on price or on quality. For Team Nano, failure was not an option. The team would produce not just an inexpensive car but a *great* inexpensive car, with nothing to apologize for.

In business as in the movies, love means never having to say you're sorry.

NANOBITE

No-apology products . . .

- come from a designer's desire to make the customer proud. Cheap doesn't mean inferior.
  People are proud, not ashamed, to fly Southwest Airlines, shop Costco or Home Depot or Target, and yes, drive a Nano.
- focus on price *and* quality, not just price.
- passionately fulfill a need, knowing that profits will follow.
- come from designers who experience the customers' pain and pressure points by walking in their shoes.
- are balanced. Their success is measured in a balance of public good and financial good.

QUESTIONS

- Have your decision makers "lived" where your target customers live? Do they truly know what it's like to experience the problems you are trying to solve?
- Have your designers made the needs and dignity of the end users their cause?
- Do your customers aspire to own your products or engage your services—the way Apple customers do?
- Are you in the dryness (diaper) business or the baby development business, as is Procter & Gamble? Are you in the paint-and-brush business or the business of helping contractors be successful, as is Sherwin-Williams?

SIXTEEN
Return on Innovation

Everyone wants to be successful, but I want to be looked
back on as being very innovative, very trusted and ethical
and ultimately making a big difference in the world.

SERGEY BRIN, COFOUNDER, GOOGLE

Nanovation is not just about experimentation and inventing
things. It's about sustainability—building the capability for
ongoing innovations that offer a return. The return might be tangible,
intangible, or in the case of the Nano, both. It took six years, five hundred talented people, and an investment of approximately $400 million
to create the Nano. What did Tata Motors and the people of India get
for this effort? Was it worth the long, arduous ride? You be the judge.

NANOECONOMICS OF THE PEOPLE'S CAR

As we go to press in mid 2011, the commercial success of the Nano—revenue growth, market share, customer satisfaction, and percentage of sales from first-time car buyers—is yet to be proven. It's simply too early to calculate the ultimate return on investment, because we don't have the data.

What we can say is that with 206,703 fully paid bookings in just two weeks, the Nano is one of the most successful product launches in history. No car we could find has ever taken cash deposits from 203,000 buyers before the first car rolled off the production line. It's clear that if the Singur plant had opened as scheduled, every one of those 200,000 cars would now be on the road, and then next year's production would likely be fully sold.

In a country that sells 1.5 million passenger cars per year, there is much room for optimism. The initial bookings represent approximately $512 million to the company. That number of bookings is more than double what Tata will initially build due to the massive controversy in Singur that led to changing the location of its plant. However, when the new plant in Sanand is fully operational, it will have a production capacity of 250,000 to 300,000 cars per year. This, combined with its Pantnagar plant's yearly production of 50,000 Nanos, means Tata is prepared to meet future demand.

If the demand is there, Tata has proven its remarkable capacity to erect manufacturing plants in world-record fashion.

The potential market for the Nano in India alone is about fourteen to fifteen million buyers, which would represent the top third of scooter drivers moving up to new car ownership. Now add the potential sales of the Nano in other emerging markets, such as Thailand, Indonesia, Africa, Brazil, and Mexico. How about the Nano's distribution in Europe, the U.S., and Canada? The market opportunity and therefore the potential return on innovation become very big very fast.

Then there is the return on innovation that comes from new

categories of the base product. Tata Motors is currently exploring other energy sources, including diesel, electric, and hybrid energy, for new versions of the Nano. It will also continue to experiment with other types of construction material, including plastic.

Line extensions—such as wagon and delivery van options—could further extend the utility of the little car. And then there are improvements—already being made—as Tata Motors follows customers to learn how they are using the Nano.

Suman Layak of *Business Today* reported that the commercial success of the Nano will take a while. Speculating that it will take two million cars and six to eight years for the car to break even at an average operating profit of Rs. 10,000 (US$210) per car, he believes the Nano needs some big numbers.

Ravi Kant has a different opinion. The Nano was one man's dream, but as he emphatically told us, "It is a dream—despite all of the setbacks and travails we've had—that will make money from day one." According to Kant, a product like the Nano would normally break even in four to five years. But there is nothing *normal* about the Nano. He expects the People's Car to break even in two and a half years.

While the return on innovation appears to be quite significant, the Nano hit some speed bumps as we were getting ready to go to press. These issues are identified and unpacked in chapter 30, where we discuss the company's resilience and ability to bounce back from things that go wrong.

NEW CAR, NEW PLANTS, NEW JOBS

Innovation is everyone's business. It is the lifeblood of any economy. The return on innovation—for better or worse—affects everyone. The creation of a new innovation like the Nano means new factories in new places. And that means jobs. Jobs mean increased buying power, a stronger local economy, and a higher standard of living for the community. The new Nano plant in Sanand, along with its surrounding vendor facilities, will employ approximately ten thousand people. Consider the ripple effect on the nearby villages.

And let's not stop at job creation in new plants. How about the employment opportunities that will come to millions in the sales, service, finance, and insurance sectors? According to CRISIL, India's leading research and credit ratings agency, the Nano is expected to boost the Indian economy, expanding the car market by as much as 65 percent. Again, it doesn't take long for the impact of a small car to get big.

In the case of Tata Motors, the return on innovation goes way beyond job creation. The success of its Nanovation in the Nano will lead to new breakthroughs down the road. Just as the Ace gave the company the tools and disciplines needed to create the Nano, the Nano will give Tata Motors the tools to deliver even more radical innovations in the years to come.

And for the community at large, the return on innovation can be huge. As you will see, when Tata enters a community, it seeks to become a catalyst, a facilitator that will help make that community sustainable and self-sufficient. Getting your nation on the cutting edge of innovation means not only growth and jobs but also the potential for finding cures for deadly diseases, providing sources of clean water and sanitation, developing new ways of educating children, offering training programs to make adults skilled and employable, and building clinics to care for the health and well-being of the community.

"An investment in knowledge pays the best interest."
Benjamin Franklin

When each generation of Indians becomes more highly educated, more global in outlook, and more innovative, Tata Group then finds itself surrounded with its greatest asset: human intelligence and spirit. And that's the greatest return of all.

BRAND RECOGNITION SHOOTS THROUGH THE ROOF

This is not only how the people of Tata Motors see themselves; it's how the world sees them as well. Here, the return on innovation is brand reputation. For many years the Tata brand has been associated with integrity and ethical business practices. In fact, it is consistently listed as one of the most ethical companies in the world. With the unveiling of the Nano, the Tata Group leaped to number six on *BusinessWeek*'s World's 50 Most Innovative Companies list. With Apple, Google, Toyota, and General Electric, it was in good company.

"Goodness is the only investment that never fails."
Henry David Thoreau

The Tata Group has been on the world stage for many years, but the Nano is beginning to make Tata a household name. Within hours of unveiling the Nano at the New Delhi Auto Show in 2008, the Tata Group's global brand recognition shot up by orders of magnitude. What would it cost to launch a campaign designed to achieve this kind of recognition? The ultimate answer might be difficult to calculate, but Arun Nanda, Group CEO of Tata's advertising firm, Rediffusion Y&R, estimated that the unpaid media coverage for the launch day alone would be worth approximately US$21 million.

NANOMANIA

Perhaps one of the most powerful measures of return on innovation is a product that takes the world by storm. After his first test drive of the Nano, Hormazd Sorabjee, the editor of India's largest auto magazine, *Autocar India*, said, "Doubts about the Nano's celebrity status were immediately dispelled on a drive through Pune streets days before the launch. The car was mobbed wherever we parked. People wanted to touch it, jump into it, press their faces on the glass, and even pose for pictures next to it. In Chakan, we halted near a bus stop and commuters almost forgot their ride home." What company doesn't long for such a product?

What company doesn't long for such a product?

While the hysteria surrounding the Nano is undisputed, where does it come from? What causes it? When you kick the tires and see how it handles, and then consider the price, you are blown away. Its appealing design transcends gender, generational, and class boundaries. Yet quality, price, and design are only a manufacturer's admission ticket to the game.

Nanomania goes beyond these tangible elements and the product itself. The hysteria stems from how people emotionally connect to this car. Customers are buying more than an affordable form of transportation; they are buying status. In purchasing the Nano they are making a statement that says, "I'm successful. I have choices. I'm moving up the ladder." Give people choices and you give them dignity because choices say, "You're on our radar screen. You've got our attention. You matter."

The emotional connection with the Nano is also about trust. Customers told us that they are excited about the Nano and committed to buying the product because it is a Tata car. To most Indians, Tata stands for integrity, trust, loyalty, giving back, and a rising India—and they want to be identified with all of these values. It's personal, it's emotional, and it's real.

Reinforces a Culture of Imagination and Ingenuity

Corporate culture is an expression of the company's personality and genetic makeup—its DNA. Culture reflects the rites, rituals, traditions, and values that both describe and instruct how you handle big ideas, treat big thinkers, take extraordinary risks, and respond to dramatic change. Culture isn't something that is peripheral or collateral to the business; it's your very way of doing business. Thus, culture touches everything, influences everything, and affects everything.

Every time you step through fear, ridicule, and resistance and demonstrate the dogged determination to pursue your dream, you free the organization to attempt the seemingly impossible. Every time you examine the intersection between trends, face the brutal

The emotional **connection** with the Nano is **trust.**

facts of reality, and engage in opportunity-led innovation instead of crisis-led reaction, you declare war on complacency. Every time you push, prod, and cajole people into going beyond a good solution to find a better solution, you send a message to the entire organization about the power of elegance. Every time you ask a question about how a potential solution will bridge the gap between the user's experience and the cost targets you've established, you challenge the organization to climb higher up the ladder of creativity. And every time you refuse to compromise the user's dignity in order to cut a corner, you communicate what you value.

If you forget to do all these things, you still build a culture. It's just that you build a culture of disengagement, a culture of mediocrity, a culture that serves as a boat anchor to any forward progress you try to make.

Every time you do these things you unleash the imagination and ingenuity of your people and reinforce a culture of innovation. Nanovation blows mediocrity out of the water.

Nanovation blows mediocrity out of the water.

Like Ravi Kant's cost-cutting measures in 2000, like the launch of Indica, and like the creation of the Ace, this is what the Nano has done for Tata Motors. The creation of the Nano is yet another strand of cultural DNA that defines Tata Motors not as a stodgy, old industrialized giant from another era, but as a global powerhouse in touch with the people and on the move. Like the achievements that preceded it, the Nano has expanded the company's ability to think big and act bold, to move with speed and agility, and to create exciting products people want and need. Essentially the Nano has reinforced Tata Motors' self-image as a magnet for courageous people who believe in themselves, who welcome change, who dream about doing the impossible, and who have created a deep capacity for innovation.

Engagement: Return on Emotional Equity

How many people do you know who are truly emotionally charged at work—in your organization or in any other? *Imagining the future, creating, exploring, blazing new trails, fighting for a cause, working with a sense of adventure, making a difference*, and *changing the world*: these words describe what makes us come alive at work. They also describe the creative attributes in any recognized culture of innovation. But do they describe what goes on in *your* culture? Do they describe what *you* do?

What gets you up in the morning jazzed about coming to work? Is it conveying a spirit of hospitality for your guests, being on the verge of a technological breakthrough, creating peace of mind for a client, or experiencing the thrill of a scientific discovery? Unfortunately in most organizations the return on this kind of emotional equity is lacking. Why? Because too many people feel estranged from work that has meaning. This is a big problem because work that has meaning inspires and engages us. We are willing to risk rejection in order to doing something insanely great because there is meaning in it. We will stay late and go the extra mile for the opportunity to accomplish something amazing.

Most members of Team Nano will tell you that working on the Nano was an adventure. When you are going where no one has ever gone before,

What's your inspiration for innovation?

the road is full of surprises. You never know what obstacle, opportunity, or breakthrough lurks around the next corner. You never know who will come up with the next wacky idea and how you will react to it. You have to stay alert, you have to keep your mind open, yet focused, and you have to be nimble. Is it dangerous? Sure. There are multiple opportunities for costly mistakes to be made. There are rigorous debates over which way to go, and when your way is rejected, you need to have thick skin. But the journey is also exhilarating. You may labor for months and months to solve a critical problem, but when the breakthrough comes, it's invigorating.

When the crazy solution you came up with weeks ago—the one that was rejected—is finally proven worthy—eureka! The sacrifices you made and patience you exerted make the taste of victory all the sweeter.

Now, compare this with doing the same old, mundane, routine job every day. Where would you rather be? Where would your people rather be?

The Nano has been an adventure where the waters of innovation are constantly being stirred. As people did in response to Kennedy's moon shot challenge, people worked insanely long hours, making personal and professional sacrifices to make the dream a reality. Why did they do it? Certainly it was because they believed in the dream, but also because they wanted to be part of the adventure. When work becomes an adventure, people check in. They become more engaged, and they bring more of their imagination and discretionary effort to the game. Inspiration and engagement, in turn, drive innovation.

> As people did in response to Kennedy's moon shot challenge, people worked insanely long hours, making personal and professional sacrifices to make the dream a reality.

In addition to the adventure, consider this: when the company for which you work produces a game-changing product that creates a cultlike following and increases your brand recognition, it becomes a badge of honor for you personally. No amount of money can buy the sense of pride and enthusiasm that is generated (often for a lifetime) from this kind of innovation. Imagine how a member of Apple's original Macintosh team must feel when today, more than twenty-five years later, someone asks, "Wow! You were part of the original Mac team? What was that like?" Think about the pride one must feel to be at a party and say, "Early in my career I was a member of the team that built the first lunar landing module." We are absolutely convinced that many years from now this is how the members of Team Nano will feel. This is the return on innovation.

All of this pride translates into productivity. When we discuss what drives Nanovation, we are willing to bet that you will be blown away by the productivity of Team Nano and other Tata Motors' employees when one project (building the Nano) unexpectedly turned into four projects (building the Nano, disassembling one plant and building another in record time, reconfiguring an interim plant, and sourcing parts from all over the world simultaneously).

The fact is, companies with higher levels of employee engagement are more productive and more profitable. And building a culture of innovation can't happen without a highly engaged workforce.

Better Thinking: Spreading the Innovation Virus

Elegant solutions demand a higher level of thinking than the solutions that first come to mind. Team Nano was forced to deal with two competing targets. First, build a 1 lakh car. Second, do it while honoring the dignity of the individual and enhancing, not denigrating, the user's experience. That's a tough assignment, which requires a higher level of thinking. Perhaps the greatest gift of Ratan Tata's audacious dream, in addition to the People's Car, is that it forced the members of Team Nano to improve their thinking, to think in new ways. By improving their thinking, they expanded their capacity to solve problems.

Hormazd Sorabjee referred to the kind of thinking we are talking about. He said, "The whole car is what I call the triumph of Indian ingenuity because we have learned to innovate with very little at our disposal. Indians are phenomenally frugal so it is in the DNA of Indian culture to really push the envelope of innovation in a very finite cost structure."

"It is in the DNA of Indian culture to push the envelope of innovation in a very finite cost structure."

The Nano exemplifies the idea that when you raise the bar so high with an impossible dream, you elevate people's thinking. To the degree that this *improved thinking* can inspire and be exported to other companies in the Tata Group, there is a significant return on innovation.

Ideas are the lifeblood of any organization. Innovation comes in many forms: process innovation, product innovation, business model innovation, and others. With 350,000 people spread out across nearly one hundred operating companies the Tata Group stands to gain a lot from the lessons learned while creating the Nano. Whether it's finding the courage to think big and do the impossible (do their own Nano), reducing costs beyond what anyone thinks is doable, building trust with a new market at the bottom of the pyramid, or designing systems, processes, and products that are more elegant, Nanovation has something to teach all of us about how we create value.

A National Badge of Honor

Ask a random sample of people from around the globe what first comes to mind when they think of India. Until recently, you would hear them describe images of extreme poverty, malnutrition, and starvation. With few exceptions you would hear about the *Slumdog Millionaire* side of India or the *National Geographic* images of an ancient country symbolized by snake charmers, exotic palaces, sitar music, cross-legged Yogis, and the weathered faces of women who were wearing colorful saris and adorned with gold, carrying baskets on their heads. Missing would be a picture of the entrepreneurial fervor taking over the country, the incredibly bright and sophisticated leaders of tomorrow pouring out of the technical schools and pointing to a country that is truly finding its mojo when it comes to innovation.

India has suffered from the stigma of cheap, as in cheap labor and therefore cheap products and services. Prior to the

Nanovation has something to teach all of us about how we create value.

early 1990s, quality in India could be defined as good enough—most of the time. In other words, if the product worked and the service delivered more often than not, it was good enough. The brand reputation of India, Inc., has been—and in many respects is still—in need of a significant overhaul due to the stigma of "Made in India."

When Tata Motors made its initial bid for Jaguar and Land Rover, the head of a group that represents Jaguar dealers in the U.S. said that American consumers would question the "viability of the [Jaguar] brand [because they weren't] ready for ownership out of India of a luxury-car brand such as Jaguar."

There is no question that the IT and business process outsourcing firms have rapidly and dramatically changed the reputation of India, Inc., and solidified its place on the global stage. Yet to the frustration of many Indians, well-traveled people outside the country still regard India as the call center and back-office capital of the world, not a major breeding ground for innovation and ingenuity in consumer products.

Outsiders might think of India as the global center for holistic medicine, exotic spices, and beautiful fabrics, but if you had asked even the most sophisticated businesspeople from around the globe where the next revolution in automotive design would come from, few would have guessed India.

The challenge, then, is for India to convince the world

The **return** on **innovation** for India is that the Nano is a **badge** of **honor** for the nation.

that it is capable of building game-changing products the world is nuts about. Enter the Nano. The return on innovation here is that the Nano is a badge of honor for the nation. It has literally caught the attention of the world and become a symbol of India's ingenuity.

It essentially says, "We are not just imitators. We're not just leasing brains to create intellectual property or deploy business processes for the rest of the world. We are confounding the stigma of 'Made in India' by creating elegant, high-quality solutions to huge problems that will change the world." Arun Maira, a member of the Planning Commission of the government of India, said, "Nano has really put India on the map because we have been criticized for not being innovative. Now you have a modern car that has really made us proud and people are saying it was done by an Indian." Maira told us the Nano is a wonderful example of the Indian expression "Kar ke dikhayenge!" which means, "We will do it and then you will know."

"Kar ke dikhayenge!" means, "We'll show you!"

The chairman of Hero Honda, Brijmohan Lall Munjal, told us that the Nano is not only a badge of honor for the nation but also an inspiration for other entrepreneurs. He said, "Nano is a morale booster. It will give a lot of impetus to people who will think, *If Ratan can do it, I could also do it.*" Anup Banerji of the State Bank of India's National Banking Group agreed: "Nano will trigger more mass based innovation, mass based conveniences, and more affordability." According to Banerji, this is exactly what India needs. He said products like Nano "should be affordable, should be sustainable, and should be indigenous to a nation where the mass draws $500 a year. And if we can do all that ourselves, I am happy and proud."

Return on Saving Lives

Remember that rainy afternoon in Bangalore when Ratan Tata saw the family crash their scooter? Is there a greater return on innovation than saving lives?

Every time you move a family off a scooter and into a Nano—or any reasonably well-made auto—you reduce the chance that family will have a road-related injury by a factor of five. And when you move millions of people off scooters and into Nano-class transportation, you start to save hundreds of thousands of lives.

Road deaths and injuries place a huge burden on the Indian people and they also place a burden on its future. India is turning out very bright young people with some of the best educations in the world, and we'll need their fine minds to help us solve the problems of the future.

And that's the best return of all.

NANOBITE

Return on innovation—what's the payoff?

It increases revenue growth, market share, customer satisfaction, and percentage of sales from the new product or service.

It creates new jobs and improves people's standard of living and their quality of life.

It raises brand recognition and makes the brand stronger.

It reinforces a culture of imagination and ingenuity.

It inspires a critical mass of talented people to be more engaged in their work and more devoted to the business.

It's a source of pride for the company, the community, and even the nation.

It makes people's lives better.

SEVENTEEN
The Nano Revealed

A person with a new idea is a crank until he succeeds.

MARK TWAIN

For five years, from the time the first members of the Nano team met with Ratan Tata in 2003, the Nano was kept behind a curtain of such impenetrable security that team members couldn't even tell their wives or families about it.

"There were competitors who said it could not be done," Ratan remembered. "There were those who ridiculed us, who said it would be a toy, a cardboard car, so we kept media and spy shots and everything away as much as we could. We kept the Nano under very heavy wraps till the unveiling in Delhi."

In January 2008, the little car was still a big secret. But it was the moment of truth, time to bring the Nano to light. What would the world think? What would the press and their peers in the industry say? And most important, how would the people of India's emerging middle class respond?

The reveal of the Nano was planned for the Delhi Auto Expo on Thursday, January 10, 2008. In the months leading up to the Expo, the press was surprisingly quiet about the Nano. After the initial flurry of interest in 2003 and some follow-up articles in 2005, very little appeared in the press about the car or the promise. Word on the street, such that it was, was mixed. Some suggested that the launch would prove to be Ratan Tata's swansong; others suggested that international manufacturers were losing sleep. On the auto enthusiast boards, as car nuts in India got ready for the show, they posted lists of possible cars to be shown or revealed, including the Tata 1 lakh car. Not even the name appeared: that's how tight the curtain of secrecy had been drawn.

But that was about to change.

In December 2007, work was nearing completion on the first few Nanos, virtually hand constructed at the Pune plant. Ratan Tata came from Mumbai and, for fifteen days, virtually camped out in the ERC as the pre-production cars were being completed. With other engineers, he drove the cars on the test track and then joined them to fine-tune the details based on what they were learning.

One day, instead of driving, Ratan hopped in the backseat of one of the cars and went for a ride. "He just wanted to get a feel for the space in motion," lead designer Nikhil Jadhav remembered, "but what he found felt claustrophobic. The huge volume of the front seatbacks blocked the view forward. So, while there was plenty of actual physical space, the feeling was that you were confined."

After the drive, they stood around the car and discussed options. With just a week to go, they decided to reshape the seatbacks at the sides and shoulders to make them less visually obtrusive to passengers. While they were at it, they decided to move some of the foam from the sides to the lumbar area, to give the people in the front seats a little more support. A few days later, the cars had the new seats, and the team took turns riding in the back to test them out.

It's a small detail, but it shows the team's focus on getting the Nano right. Nothing could be "good enough" if the team could make it better and still meet the production budget. Even for the chairman, no detail was too small to warrant attention. The plan was for the public to be able to take a close look at the Nano, inside and out, and they wanted people to know that what they saw was what they were going to get. Above all, they wanted it to be a cool car, something worthy of their dream for the young Indian family and anyone else who wanted something more than mobility.

On the afternoon of January 9, the Nano team was hard at work inside Delhi's Pragati Maidan Exhibition Centre, rehearsing the next day's reveal. Although Tata Motors' ad agency, Rediffusion Y&R, was producing the event, Ratan was deeply involved in every aspect of the launch. Dressed in slacks and a pullover sweater, he began pushing one of the cars into place backstage. Jaydeep Desai and Abhay Deshpande were standing beside him and protested.

"What are you doing? We'll do that for you."

The chairman laughed and said, "I'm a human being. I know how to push a car!"

It was what Ratan himself described as a critical event. After all, it wasn't just Tata Motors' name that was at stake; his personal reputation was on the line. "I said really I want this to be different." He wasn't comfortable speaking before crowds, but both he and his friend Arun Nanda of Rediffusion agreed strongly that this had to be different from the normal car unveilings, which typically involve a show biz approach.

Together, Ratan and Arun scripted a show that basically revolved around a new video effect that appeared to project a hologram of Ratan onstage talking to the audience. As the hologram ended, the plan was that Ratan would drive the new Nano onstage, get out, and talk about it. Short, sweet, and simple.

"You won't have any politicians," Arun told him. "No guests of honor. This is your show. You do it yourself."

"As often happens," Ratan remembered, "everything went wrong in rehearsals. I was there until 2:00 a.m. and then back at 6:00 in the morning."

One of the challenges was driving the car onstage. They did a dry run, with Ratan at the wheel. He said, "It had to end up on one of those turntables, but you could not see the turntables because everything was dark onstage. I was afraid I'd drive right off the stage. And so, at two in the morning, you have somebody deciding, 'Okay, suppose you have two torches and you line them up with a marker in the car?' How do I stop at the turnaround? 'We'll have somebody in the audience clap their hands when you are on it.' It was nerve-wracking."

The morning of January 10 dawned rainy and cold, and all over Delhi, something unusual was happening. In one house, a couple leaving for the reveal were approached by their housemaid. "Sir, lady," she said, "if they are taking bookings for the car, please book one for me." Sight unseen, she already knew she wanted a Nano. Others were stopped by their gardener, the milkman, the man doing the ironing. One man reported that as his car pulled up in front of the Exhibition Centre, his driver turned to him. He, too, wanted to buy a Nano.

The executive was startled, but he understood. He said, "My driver spends an hour each day on a scooter coming to me and going home. Rain or shine, he is exposed. If he had a Nano, he would avoid the elements—the rain and heat—and arrive fresh."

But it was more than that. If you and your father before you had driven the cars of wealthier men, with no expectation of owning one of your own, then the idea that you could pull up to work in your own car . . . well, it changes everything.

Even before it was revealed, the Nano was beginning to disturb the balance of class and social power. People who had never dreamed of buying a car would suddenly have a real car within their reach. And the wealthy would suddenly find their maid or their driver arriving in a real car and parking beside their car. When both are car owners, the shift is profound. It expands the horizons not just of the poor, but of the society as a whole.

Inside Pragati Maidan, the atmosphere was festive, with the feel of a family gathering. Ironically perhaps, the unveiling of the People's Car was attended primarily by the elite of Delhi society. CEOs of various Tata companies and Tata suppliers came with their families. Politicians and other dignitaries did the same.

As Girish Wagh found his way to the front row, where he and other leaders of Team Nano were supposed to meet, he was awed by the emotionally charged atmosphere. There was a sense that something momentous was about to happen, involving something bigger than just a single car or a single company. As he got to the front, he found a number of the chairman's close family members already seated or milling around, talking to friends. But Ratan himself was nowhere around.

Girish had left the hall with Ratan in the wee hours. Now it was getting close to the 10:00 a.m. start time. Surely the chairman hadn't overslept!

"The function was about to start. I got a message that the chairman was backstage and wanted to see me. It was so crowded that it was hard to move, but I made my way backstage and found him in the green room." That's when Girish learned that Ratan had been there since six in the morning, rewriting and changing the program.

"Girish, I just wanted to tell you I've made a change in the program. I was supposed to come out in the red Nano, but now I am going to drive out in the pearl white one."

"Yes, sir. Thank you for letting me know, but there is no need for you to tell me that." But in Ratan's mind there was. Girish had led the project to this level of success, and this was his moment, too. In fact, the moment belonged to many, many people: to a team of five hundred within Tata and to partner teams at supplier locations in India and Europe. Symbolically Ratan had to represent the team, but he wasn't doing it out of ego. He would gladly have traded places with anyone else on the team. But this was his dream—the Chairman's Folly—and he had to take responsibility for it. If it failed, it should be on his shoulders and not on anyone else. But if it succeeded, if they had truly created a breakthrough new car, then the success had to belong to the whole team.

"I'm going to call you to the stage," he told Girish, who protested. Girish was uncomfortable with the idea of attention, but he also knew he had little choice in the matter. Fighting his way back to the front row, he felt floored by the excitement and press of expectations.

Years of work—innovation in the service of a great cause—and it all came down to this moment.

A hologram was a creative way for Ratan Tata to get the audience's attention and deliver his message.

As the lights went down, the audience fell silent. In front of them, a swirling cone of light appeared to float over the stage, almost like a DNA chain. It roared like a windstorm and tinkled like bells. Audience members described it as a hologram, but it was a video effect that made objects appear to float in space over the stage.

And then suddenly Ratan Tata appeared inside the cone of light as if he'd just been beamed down from a *Star Trek* episode. He was pre-recorded on video, but the effect was convincing: it looked as though he were standing onstage. He welcomed the audience and invited them to come with him on a journey, "a journey that symbolizes the human spirit of change, the will to question the unquestionable, the drive to stretch the envelope."

He spoke of the quest that led to the first manned flight by the Wright brothers: "Today, thousands of aircraft travel the skies, carrying millions of passengers in safety and comfort. The same quest for leadership and conquering new frontiers led to landing a man on the moon, an unheard-of and unbelievable achievement at that time."

He spoke of other evolutionary journeys, from the first bicycle to today's modern motorbikes, from the ENIAC computer, which filled an entire room, to the modern laptop computer with thousands of times more power.

"There are solutions for most problems. The barriers and road-blocks that we face are usually of our own making, and these can only be demolished by having the determination to find a solution, even contrary to the conventional wisdom.

"Today's story began some years ago when I observed families riding on two-wheelers. . . . I asked myself whether one could conceive of a safe, affordable, all-weather form of transport for such a family. A vehicle that could be affordable and low cost enough to be within everyone's reach. A people's car, built to meet all safety standards, designed to meet or exceed emission norms and be low in pollution and high in fuel efficiency."

He addressed the critics who said that this dream could never be achieved, that all they would see from Tata was a poor excuse for a car. "Let me assure you that the car we have designed and that we will present today will indeed meet all the current safety requirements of a modern-day car."

He spoke to those who had questioned the new car's effect on the environment. "The car we present you today will meet all current legislated requirements and will have a lower pollution level than even a two-wheeler."

And he spoke to those who feared a wave of people in Nanos would clog India's roads. He pointed out that if Tata sold half a million of the new cars a year for the next five years, they would constitute only 2.5 percent of the cars on the road in India, hardly the congestion that critics were claiming.

"Despite what the critics said, we pursued our vision to give India an affordable people's car that had not been produced anywhere in the world, a car that most people said could not be manufactured for that kind of price.

(Tata Motors)

The Nano's blueprint was the first image that the public saw, just seconds before the chairman drove the real thing onstage.

"Today, we will present what a young group of engineers and designers gave their all for years to achieve. I've said enough, ladies and gentlemen. *Now* I give you the new car from Tata Motors, the People's Car that everyone has been waiting for."

A deep chord of music filled the room as the chairman disappeared—the opening notes of Strauss's *Also Sprach Zarathustra*, more commonly known as the theme from *2001: A Space Odyssey*. Starbursts filled the area above the stage and began to sketch the outline of the car in midair. Backstage, waiting in the car, the real Ratan could hear the applause. His great fear was that he would miss the timing, arriving on the turntable in the moments of silence after the music ended. He recalled, "Having the music reach the dramatic crescendo and then stop and you have this little 'tak tak tak' car would have been a hell of a letdown!"

He needn't have worried.

As the pearl white Nano appeared onstage, turned, and drove onto the turntable, the audience leaped to their feet, their applause competing with the sound of Wagner's thundering kettle drums. If they had been playing the Indian national anthem, the men and women in the audience could not have been more proud to be Indians.

Other Nanos followed and parked on either side, a red one and a yellow one. They were filled with Nano Team members, dressed in their best suits. On the screen upstage, the world was introduced to the name, Nano, in large letters revolving overhead. "We decided to call it Nano because it connotes high technology and small size." He might have also pointed out the interesting fact that in his native Gujarati, *nanoo* also mean "small." Ratan explained the three models and their basic features and then introduced Team Nano. He began with Girish.

"When he called me to the stage," Girish remembered, "I think the audience was stunned. But all along he had been saying that whatever the Nano is today, it is a tribute to the young engineers who worked on it. It is a showcase of what is best about India."

"There are close to five hundred people in the team," Ratan explained, "and obviously not all of them can be here. So, on behalf of all of us, we'd like to acknowledge what the team has been able to do."

Next, he invited the top executives of Tata Motors—Ravi Kant, Prakash Telang, and Rajiv Dube—to the stage. They shook hands and stood with the chairman, and then Rajiv, realizing they were standing in front of the Nano and aware that the audience was more interested in seeing the car than them, moved to the other side.

Standing on the stage that day, Ravi Kant couldn't help thinking of the irony that one hundred years earlier, Henry Ford rolled the first people's car, the Model T, off the production line at the Piquette Avenue plant in Detroit. In 1908, the Model T revolutionized the roads, making affordable transportation available to the wide majority of the middle class in North America and, soon, the rest of the world. And now here he and his team were, revealing a new People's Car that would sell, in real terms, for one-tenth the cost of the original Model T. For a man who rarely shows emotion—and rarer still while standing on a stage—it was a moving moment, and he struggled to control his emotions.

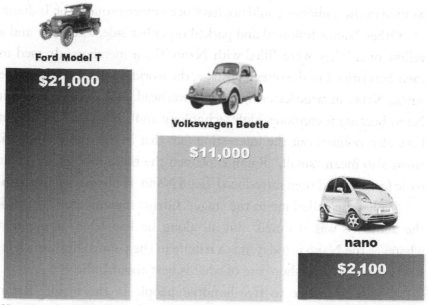

When new, the Model T cost $21,000 (in 2009 dollars), the Volkswagen cost $11,000, and the Nano cost $2,100.

"Let me say something about the car," Ratan continued. "As you can see, the cars have four doors. They'll seat four to five persons. In size, the car is approximately 8 percent smaller, bumper to bumper, than a Maruti 800. But internally, it's 21 percent larger in passenger space." That got big applause. So did what he had to say about safety, economy, and emissions. Designed to meet international crash test standards, delivering fifty miles per gallon on the road, and matching the most stringent European emissions standards, it was far beyond what anyone was expecting.

"Finally," he said, "all of you have been conjecturing about the price. Since we commenced this exercise four years ago, we're all aware that there has been a very steep increase in input prices of steel, tires, and other materials. Bearing all this in mind, I would like to announce today that the standard car will, in fact, have a dealer price of one lakh only."

And that got the biggest applause of all.

"To raise new questions, new possibilities, to regard old problems from a new angle, requires creative imagination and marks real advance in science."
Albert Einstein

"That is because a promise is a promise." It only took fifteen minutes to let the world know that the promise of the 1 lakh car had been delivered, and the world's response was overwhelming.

The moment the car was revealed onstage, people outside were breaking down the gates and rushing the hall just to get a glimpse. For the next two days, the Nano dominated the attention at the car show. There at the show, Anasuya Basu of the *Telegraph* described the excitement around the Nano as the crowds pressed in to get a better look. While other cars' stands were attended by lovely models, "the people's car, however, stood alone. It did not need eye-candy." To relieve the pressure of record crowds created by the Nano, the auto show's organizers asked Tata Motors to establish an additional exhibit at another venue.

Overnight, the Tata Nano Web site was swamped with hits (but never crashed!). In the following months, more than millions of visitors registered on the site. Across the Web, brand fans created more than six thousand Web sites and fan pages dedicated to the Nano. Yahoo! gave Tata Motors an award for the most searched words of 2008, *Tata Nano*.

Gavin Rabinowitz of the Associated Press said, "For millions of people in the developing world, Tata Motors' new $2,500 four-door subcompact—the world's cheapest car—may yield a transportation revolution as big as Henry Ford's Model T." *Newsweek* called the Nano a "new breed of 21st-century cars" that exemplify "a contrarian philosophy of smaller, lighter, cheaper that portend a new era in inexpensive personal transportation." The *Financial Times* touted the Nano as a symbol of rising India: "If ever there were a symbol of India's ambitions to become a modern nation, it would surely be the Nano, the tiny car with the even tinier price tag. The Nano encapsulates the dream of millions of Indians groping for a shot at urban prosperity."

The *Christian Science Monitor* reported that the car was greeted like a rock star with boys elbowing aside mothers and old men to get a look: "To all, it was proof in gleaming steel that India's engineers could do what was thought impossible: design a $2,500 car that does not require home assembly or a giant windup key."

"The launch of the world's cheapest car in India is changing the face of the country's automobile industry," claimed ChannelNewsAsia .com.

And "Tata Reinvents the Wheel," trumpeted the *Times of India*.

At a reception that evening, A. M. Mankad, the plant head in Pune, spoke to many of the assembled guests and dignitaries. He said, "They expected the Nano to be a patchwork car, but it wasn't. It was beautiful. Person after person came to me and said, 'I have two cars at home, but I will still buy a Nano, just to have one.' They fell in love."

Two months later, the Nano got the same response when it was shown at the Geneva Auto Show. "I'd been going to Geneva for ten to twelve years," Prakash Telang told us, "but I can't remember any time when a small car created so much excitement. We had the heads of all the car companies in Europe, Japan, and the U.S. coming to the Tata stand to see what we had done."

Carlos Ghosn of Renault/Nissan was just as impressed. "I should thank you. This is really fantastic," he said to Ratan Tata, grabbing his hand. "This is what we should try and achieve."

Luca Cordero di Montezemolo, chairman of Fiat, got behind the wheel and was impressed: "A modern and contemporary car design, sufficient internal volume, designed and developed entirely on your own."

And so, an operation shrouded in secrecy was exposed to the world. From ordinary people, car aficiona-

(Tata Motors)

The Nano goes to Geneva and makes new friends: Carlos Ghosn, CEO of Renault/Nissan, left; Luca di Montezemolo, chairman of Fiat, right.

dos, and the world press to foreign dignitaries, government ministers, and business leaders, the People's Car got an incredible reaction.

Ratan Tata, Ravi Kant, Girish Wagh, and Team Nano had come with the kind of hope and trepidation one has when unveiling a pioneering solution to the world—a solution to which you have given six years of your life. They came with no way of knowing the avalanche of accolades that would sweep them off their feet. It was a Tata product, but it was India's car. For the next year, India would bask in the limelight as news about its remarkable feat of ingenuity spread across the globe.

Meanwhile, the overwhelming response came with an overwhelming sense of responsibility for Team Nano. When the chairman said, "A promise is a promise," Girish knew that his team was accountable for delivering on that promise, and there was still so much to be done before the Nano would be launched.

NANOBITE

Simplicity, elegance, and impact are lessons learned from unveiling a proof of concept.

Keep it simple:

- The Nano was the star of the show; there were no beautiful models or dancing girls to distract or draw people's attention away from the car.
- Ratan quickly, but directly preempted each of the major concerns critics levied about the car.
- The whole presentation took no more than fifteen minutes.

Make it elegant:

- Instead of crowded text and PowerPoint bullets, the screen was filled with compelling images—including a blueprint-like rendering of the Nano—as Ratan took the audience on a journey.

Go for impact:

- Special effects and dramatic music were used to get the audience's attention. Ratan Tata appeared in a hologram-like cone of light—the audience was rapt.
- As Ratan closed his virtual presentation, the room went dark, and dramatic music signaled Mr. Tata driving a real-life Nano onto the stage.
- For dramatic effect Ratan waited until the very end to address the question everyone was waiting to have answered: What is the price?

The next time you present an idea or prototype to a room of VIPs, consider these questions:

- How will we get their attention?
- How can we make the idea the star of the show?
- Is there a compelling story through which we can unveil this idea?
- Can we convey our idea in just one slide?
- Can we use images instead of words to explain our concept?
- Have we addressed and/or developed counterpoints to the critics' concerns?

EIGHTEEN
A Legacy of Inclusive Growth

We can't solve problems by using the same kind
of thinking we used when we created them.

ALBERT EINSTEIN

If the tale of the Nano ended there on the stage in Delhi, it would be a great story. A visionary leader inspires a movement for innovation in the service of a cause and starts a revolution that brings mobility to millions and inspires the world. Great story, but it wasn't that easy. And because the greatest tests and some of the greatest disappointments were still to come, this is the time to take a deeper dive into Tata's commitment to making a difference while making a profit.

For Tata Motors, as with every Tata Group company, corporate social responsibility (CSR) is a way of life. It is paramount in everything they do, not because it's good public relations in a world of socially conscious customers, but because it is part and parcel of their very reason for being.

In chapter 19 we will tell you why Tata Motors decided to establish the Nano plant in a location that seemed as crazy as the development of the car itself. The company wasn't just interested in the ideal location for the Nano plant. As it had done with each of its facilities, Tata envisioned raising the prosperity of the entire region where the plant would be located. To understand the full weight of this decision, you must first understand Tata's commitment to nation building and giving back.

We also want you to grasp the extent to which Tata invests itself in a region, because as you will soon see, when the company is forced to pull out of a community, the missed opportunity can be devastating.

Tata Motors has a triple bottom line: People. Planet. Profit. The Tata mantra, "what comes from the people must go back to the people many times over," is deeply embedded in every project. Giving back. This is what Tata has been doing from the very beginning.

Tata Motors has a triple bottom line: People. Planet. Profit.

More than one hundred years ago the Tatas benchmarked against some of the best manufacturing facilities in the U.S. and the U.K., but came back determined to build Indian plants that were more people-friendly. Had *Fortune* magazine been conducting its 100 Best Companies to Work For research back then, Tata Steel would have been a very strong candidate to top the list.

When Tata Steel carved the city of Jamshedpur out of the jungle to create India's first steel plant, workers began by planting trees, digging lakes, and building schools.

Tata Motors did the same in 1964 when it built the Pune plant. Everywhere the Tata Group goes, it is not just going to build a plant. It is on a mission to build people's lives.

The cause of lifting India's people out of poverty has occupied the minds of Tata people over the years. Tata's legendary founder, Jamsetji Tata, said, "In a free enterprise, the community is not just another stakeholder in business, but the purpose of its very existence."

"I suggest that the most significant contribution organized industry can make," said J. R. D. Tata in 1969, "is by identifying itself with the life and problems of the community to which it belongs and by applying its resources, skills and talents—to the extent that it can reasonably spare them—to serve and help them."

And more recently here's what Ratan Tata had to say when the editors of *Global Giving Matters*, a Synergos publication, challenged him about the conflict between social responsibility and shareholder value creation: "My personal view is that they're not incompatible. What we've done in our discharge of social responsibility should be of value to our shareholders. Our efforts result in a more prosperous country, and lead to a greater quality of life that benefits all. Our failure to do so contributes to a poor India with continued shortages and inequities."

The primary reason to make money, the Tata Group believes, is to invest it in the welfare and future of the community. As we mentioned before, nearly two-thirds of Tata's stock is controlled by two charities that the Tata leaders established. In addition to their charitable work, when you look at the wages they've paid to their employees and to the employees of companies that grew up to supply them, they were the source of a great deal of wealth flowing into the communities where their plants were located. They regarded building a company as a way to build a community and a nation.

Take Pune, for instance.

In 1961, the Panshet Dam failed, flooding the city and destroying much of it, particularly the old central district built on the lowlands near the confluence of the Mula and Mutha rivers. The devastation might have disabled other cities, but with the help of companies like Tata, Pune chose to rebuild.

> **"The most significant contribution organized industry can make is by identifying itself with the life and problems of the community."**

Around the new plant, Tata built schools and hospitals, roads and bridges, parks and community centers, technical colleges and training centers. Even housing developments where their workers could live in dignity.

That word again. *Dignity.*

Tata began by planting trees, creating a forest where there had once been stony wastelands. The company dug a lake that would provide water for the plant. And it made trees available for free to any neighbors who would plant them around their homes.

The first buildings erected in the Pune plant were for the training and housing of apprentices. Families that had known only poverty soon had sons and daughters training for well-paying jobs. And their children became the educated class that is now making India a world power.

Those training facilities eventually grew into the Engineering Research Center and the Tata Management Training Center, where— under those same trees planted when the plant was built—engineers, managers, and leaders from around the world come to improve their critical thinking, leadership, and creative skills.

Ravi Kant stated it very clearly: "Corporate social responsibility is the real DNA of Tata. As much as cost control and profit, service to the community is integral to the culture. And it's not about public relations, although it has that important benefit. It's about being of service to a higher cause. When you invest in training and research, you're not just investing in the person or project at hand; you're investing in the long-term future of your company and your community."

LEADING LIKE "INDUSTRIAL GANDHIS"

Gandhi rallied the people of India around the idea that it was their birthright to be an independent nation. The Tatas supported that movement not just financially—they were present at the creation of the Congress Party of India—but also by taking the lead in building the industries an independent India would need.

They were "industrial Gandhis," dedicated to the vision of an India that could compete globally. As industrialists. And as innovators. Although a steel mill might look like the opposite of a spinning wheel—Gandhi's symbol for Indian independence—it was just as important. An independent India would never survive on subsistence farming and homespun cloth. It would need the means to compete in the global marketplace, and the Tata companies helped provide the means—the investment and the technology—to make independence work.

Mahatma Gandhi helped the Indian people think of themselves as people worthy of a great nation. Jamsetji and J. R. D. Tata helped the Indian people think of themselves as a great *industrial* nation with the ability to create wealth; an educated nation with the ability to lead. Ratan Tata is helping the Indian people think of themselves as an innovative nation with the ability to compete globally and inspire the rest of the world.

Trees. Lakes. People. Tata builds the community as it builds the plant.

What comes from the people must go back to the people.

We had a fascinating conversation with M. B. Paralkar, head of corporate social responsibility at Tata Motors. He said, "When you establish a factory or a business, the society in which you operate suddenly becomes your partner. You will draw many things from society and nature, and you try to give back by using your resources to make society better.

"I cannot say to the people, I will do well and you cannot do well. I cannot say, I will eat well and you cannot eat well. I cannot say, I will be prosperous and you cannot be prosperous. You need to bring people along with you."

For the Tatas, CSR is not an afterthought to be pursued once a venture is up and running profitably. It is part of every project from the very start. Prior to breaking ground on a new manufacturing plant, CSR teams are already on location, seeking to understand how to improve the quality of life in the surrounding communities. In fact, Tata embraces the development needs of more than one hundred thousand villagers from more than one hundred adopted villages around each plant.

If you have ever traveled to an Indian village, you can immediately see that the needs are overwhelming. So, knowing where to start can be daunting. Tata Motors focuses its social responsibility activities in four major "thrust" areas:

Health

With its partners such as UNICEF, the government of India, Care India, and others, the company offers preventive and curative health services. These include regular health campaigns and awareness talks on hygiene, family planning, sanitation, and diseases common to the region. The United Nations estimates that 638 million people in India still lack access to basic sanitary facilities. These health campaigns are usually followed by construction of sanitation facilities and the provision of equipment and training to produce safe drinking water.

Most villagers can't afford or don't have access to proper medical care. This often means ailments go unchecked, and critical conditions develop as they are left untreated. Tata Motors brings health care to rural communities via mobile clinics. Each week a team of nurses and doctors visits each village surrounding the company's facilities. These teams provide medical consultation, administer medications, and conduct laboratory tests.

Four major thrust areas: Health. Environment. Education. Employability.

To increase sustainability, the company also puts village health workers (VHWs) through intensive training. These activists are equipped to address minor health issues, give basic medical treatment, and offer prenatal and postnatal care.

For example, one very special Tata Motors' project focuses on restoring a sense of dignity and giving people a second life. In 1981 the Jamshedpur plant established a front-end society, Nav Jagrat Manav Samaj (NJMS), to treat leprosy. Although the disease can be cured through modern medications, it continues to spread due to ignorance about leprosy and a resulting lack of treatment. As you can imagine, the stigma for the patients and their families is terrible. Many people with leprosy are deserted by their families and forced to beg just to survive.

Through NJMS, Tata Motors established a hospital for infected patients, a home for the elderly who have no family, and a rehabilitation program. Recovering patients and their families are also supported with residential quarters, water treatment facilities, and the social and vocational training to earn a living and proudly stand on their own. Tata Motors also sponsors education for the children of these families, and many are now studying in their fields of interest. Today, NJMS has seven different settlements of lepers with approximately thirty-five hundred residents who are making their way back into mainstream society.

Tata Motors is changing people's lives by addressing what must have seemed like an overwhelming problem a decade ago. Since its inception, NJMS has decreased the rate of leprosy from twenty-two out of one thousand people to less than one in one thousand. The ultimate goal is to totally eradicate the disease.

Environment

Tata Motors employs green practices that maximize resources while protecting and preserving the environment. Through its "reduce, reuse, and recycle" program, the company uses robust effluent water treatment and waste management systems at plant sites to prevent potential harm to the environment.

Recycled water is then used in a variety of other ways, including horticultural purposes within the plant, eco-lakes that are a haven to many species of rare migratory birds and plant species, and reservoirs used for fishery. Sludge, a by-product of the effluent treatment plants, is used to make recycled bricks and paint.

In many regions where Tata sets up plants, the land is dry and infertile. Solely dependent on the rainy season, most farmers are limited to a single crop each year. And village youth are forced to migrate to other regions for work. Now, through Tata's lift irrigation program, farmers have access to water throughout the year from irrigation outlets. Now they can grow multiple crops each year, substantially increasing their income, and young villagers can stay close to home.

Tata Motors is also working to create a greener environment through large-scale tree plantation drives. In 2009 alone, the company worked with villagers to plant more than two hundred thousand saplings during the monsoons. Groups of villagers are responsible for the survival and growth of trees in their areas and then get to keep the revenues from the fruit-bearing trees. Together the partnership is restoring greenery to their regions, reducing soil erosion, and making the land more fertile.

To reduce CO_2 emissions, Tata Motors' Pantnagar plant has replaced vehicles transporting people and parts between buildings every day with conveyor belts and a shuttle bus system. All of these activities are symbolic of Tata's passion for preserving the environment.

Education

The Bhamchandra High School of Vhanboli Village in Pune is a good example of how Tata involves the community to give students an opportunity to get a quality education. The school, developed by Tata Motors and privately run by members of the village, has received government recognition for its exceptional academic performance.

Tata Motors partnered with farmers from Vhanboli who donated their land to build a school so that children in the community could continue their secondary education. Tata provided the teaching facilities, infrastructure, and capital to get the project off and running. Today, the school is mostly self-sustained. Villagers assume management responsibility, and Tata managers from the Pune plant play an advisory role. But this success story doesn't end here. Bhamchandra High School is now providing secondary education to students from seven neighboring villages.

Tata Motors also promotes education by giving numerous scholarships to students from various backgrounds and by recruiting Tata employees to volunteer their time. Employees are involved in helping underprivileged students with their education and helping schools improve their teaching, curriculum, and learning environments. These employees are instrumental in reducing the dropout rates, particularly among girls, in higher education.

Employability

In this thrust area, Tata Motors is equipping youth and women to generate income on their own through training, technical skill development, and entrepreneurial activities. The company has bestowed financial independence on many women and produced many entrepreneurs who are now successfully running their own businesses. Here's how they are doing it.

WOMEN, INC.: UNLEASHING THE POWER OF HOUSEWIVES

In the early 1970s Tata Motors encouraged its employees to unite as shareholders and establish industrial cooperatives. The idea was for employees and their families to earn extra income by supplying the company, and eventually other customers, with a variety of products from cables for its vehicles and scrap wood turned into packing crates to chapatis (Indian flatbread) for its onsite cafeteria.

Imagine you are in the tree-shaded residential section of Tata Motors' Pune plant. You come upon a facility where women are busy laughing, cleaning, and operating huge mixing cauldrons, grinders, and ovens. This is one of many women's cooperatives initiated by the company called Grihini Udyog. This particular cooperative makes a variety of office products, including files, diaries, and registers, and a variety of food products, such as pickles, chutneys, and dry masalas (curry powders).

There are other cooperatives as well. One makes cables, switches, and instrument panel connectors; a tailoring cooperative makes gloves, canvas tool bags, and uniforms; and an electronic cooperative assembles flashers, horns, and timers. There is also a chapati cooperative that produces fifty thousand chapatis a day for Tata Motors' huge canteen.

(Tata Motors)

The brainpower available in the minds of Indian village women is an unbelievable natural resource, and Tata is determined to help the women develop it.

While most of the products are sold to Tata Motors, some—pickles, chutneys, and bags—are accessible in the open market. The cooperatives are independently owned and operated by women dependents of Tata Motors. Leaders of each cooperative are elected, the women set their own hours, and production facilities are spread out around Pune, making it easier for them to commute to work. The women can also get financial aid to buy equipment, such as sewing machines, so they can work from home.

Each cooperative is mentored by a senior manager at Tata Motors. They offer advice when needed, but the businesses are run by the women themselves. They usually ask for no financial assistance after the start-up years. It's all part of the company's larger

Women from one of the cooperatives in Sanand have established a food preparation business.

initiative to raise the dignity of a region by equipping people to help themselves. An otherwise dormant talent pool now becomes a wonderful example of how the entrepreneurial spirit can change society by changing people's lives.

If you are interested in making your business a better citizen—to build products that have great social value, to make things in a way that preserves the environment, and to raise local communities to a higher standard of living and better quality of life—we think Tata Motors offers a blueprint for success. The company is not perfect, but with its CSR activities touching the lives of more than a million people, it provides a model for positive change.

So, what can we learn from Tata Motors about being socially responsible? How do you go from just being generous to genuinely changing society? What contributes to a successful, sustainable intervention?

Let the Community Teach You

Cultivate a sense of ownership and belongingness among the people you are helping. Tata never goes in as the big corporate conglomerate assuming that it knows what the villagers want and need. Instead, each Tata Group company deploys a rigorous process for sustainability that includes:

1. A community-needs assessment via survey.

2. Prioritizing needs in consultation with the community via town hall and small group meetings.

3. Designing appropriate projects.

4. Partnering with the community, government, and other stakeholders to secure resources needed.

5. Monitoring and evaluating projects with active participation from the community.

This process ensures that community members have a voice and actively participate in the design and implementation of a solution from

(Tata Motors)

Here women engage in a town hall meeting with Tata's CSR team to identify community needs.

the very initial planning stages. More important, there is dignity in the process because the villagers are an integral part of solving their own problems.

The Tata Group has been involved with CSR for 140 years and has accumulated a wealth of knowledge and experience. It sees many of the same needs in different geographies, yet the Group resists a one-size-fits-all approach to social responsibility. Instead, the company goes in with humility, expecting to learn something new each time.

Make It Sustainable

Paralkar and his team also understand that building confidence and trust among villagers takes time. The Tatas have learned to be very patient.

Listen to Paralkar: "We do not believe we know everything. We do not believe that we can do everything or that we *should* be doing everything. We do believe that the people know their own problems, they have the capabilities to improve, and they can stand on their own. What we need to give them is the encouragement, seed capital, seed thoughts, and some hand-holding. They can do it better, and if *they* do it, then it becomes sustainable."

Tata Motors seems to subscribe to the philosophy that if you give a person a fish, you feed him for a day, but if you teach that person to fish, you feed him for a lifetime.

Paralker pointed out that Tata Motors isn't interested in making anyone codependent on the company. He said the company is a facilitator in making the villages strong: "We cannot put our hands in our pockets and just give money. That can happen only once, but then you cripple a person. We are here to help, but we are not going to create a model that makes people dependent upon us. We are going to create a model that makes people interdependent first and then, hopefully, independent."

Stay Lean and Agile

When you consider the number of people and resources dedicated to CSR across the more than one hundred Tata Group companies, the investment is huge and the impact is very broad. Yet in any one location the company will not have more than two or three people spearheading CSR activities. When we asked Paralkar why, he said, "We do not want to create a kingdom or another institution that must fight to survive. We want a very small and agile team that creates activists who, in turn, take over."

Paralkar believes that like a pebble hitting the water, Tata can help create the first ripple or two, but then the villagers are in the best position to extend that ripple effect.

INTEGRATE YOUR BUSINESS—BUILD AN ARMY OF VOLUNTEERS

Tata Motors creates a strong link between its business and society by providing employees with the means to better the communities in which they work. It recognizes that workers want to be actively involved in making the world a better place. Factory integration is about rallying Tata employees and associates around social causes and getting them involved in deploying CSR activities. For example, when the company engages in education programs such as building a computer lab or a library, establishing an adult literacy program, or educating farmers, factory workers and their families become volunteers. When villagers start businesses, Tata managers become advisors and advocates to those entrepreneurs.

Seek Credible Partners

Tata Motors also creates a public-private partnership with the government to address community needs. "Once we do the needs analysis, we take the government people with us. They are our partners," Paralkar told us. "We might find a way to do it better and raise standards. We might help create a benchmark way of doing it, but we are not replacing them; we are supplementing their efforts."

Build Synergy

Perhaps because it has been at the CSR game for so long, Tata Motors is particularly adept at bringing together businesses, governments, employees, villagers, and investors to solve problems. Using the power of a common cause, compelling vision, and clearly defined values, the company has created synergy among a wide variety of stakeholders. Doing this enables it to move faster, cast a wider net, and achieve sustainability in the communities it serves.

Few people would disagree that corporations have a tremendous opportunity to positively change the world by becoming model citizens. Yet some cynics are suspicious about the motives behind CSR. Hard-line business analysts suggest that CSR runs in diametric opposition to making a profit and providing a return to shareholders. Obviously Tata doesn't agree.

The examples that we have shared here are but a raindrop in the sea of CSR projects being deployed at Tata Motors. But they demonstrate Tata's genuine compassion for the planet and especially those who inhabit it. They also show that Tata Motors has a clear vision of what it means to be a good corporate citizen. This commitment is not a public relations ploy. And it is not driven by some trendy,

Social responsibility is integral to Tata's core competence and strategy.

new approach to maximize profits, be more competitive, or attract world-class talent. It's driven by a commitment to social responsibility that goes back generations!

At Tata Motors, CSR is a values-based response to the social and environmental challenges confronting our world. It is not collateral duty; it is tightly woven into Tata's

The way you spend your money says a lot about what you value.

cultural DNA. Consequently CSR has become an integral part of the company's core competence and strategy. Perhaps this is why Ratan Tata is noted as one of the most trustworthy executives in the world and the Tata Group enjoys a global reputation for being transparent, accountable, compassionate, and generative. In a 2009 survey of six hundred global companies, the Reputation Institute ranked the Tata Group as the eleventh most reputable company in the world.

Now with a deeper understanding of Tata's commitment to social responsibility, you have the background and context for the next revolutionary decision that Team Nano was about to make—a multimillion-dollar decision that would impact Tata Motors and two particular regions of India for years.

As we will see, it's not enough to build a car. You have to build a car company. And even that's not enough, because unless you can build the community to support that car company, you'll never really get it in gear.

QUESTIONS

- In a world of socially minded customers, employees, investors, and media, do you see CSR as a threat or an opportunity?
- Does your company have a clear vision of what it means to be a good corporate citizen?
- Do you understand the criteria your customers use to determine whether you are a good corporate citizen?

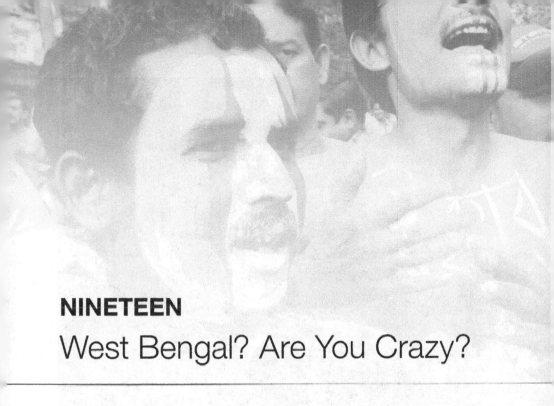

NINETEEN

West Bengal? Are You Crazy?

Opportunities to find deeper powers within ourselves
come when life seems most challenging.

JOSEPH CAMPBELL

O ne of the first things Ravi Kant and Girish Wagh began working on when Girish took over leadership of Team Nano was
where to build the new car. Ideally car companies have as little excess
manufacturing capacity as possible. A company that makes soup can
change its production line over to a new recipe in a matter of hours.
A car company doesn't have that kind of flexibility. The production
line is designed around the needs of the specific car that is to be built.
It's usually located as close as possible to vendors and transportation
hubs. And of course it should be close to lots of good, experienced
line workers.

In the Indian auto industry, three hubs have emerged in the

A Nano body assembly at the Tata plant in Pantnagar.

last few decades that would meet those needs. One is in Gurgaon, near Delhi, where Maruti built its plant. In Chennai, in southeast India, another hub has emerged around Hyundai's plant. And in Pune there is one around the Tata plant. In addition, Tata had two other plants at that time: the original Jamshedpur plant and a plant in Lucknow, both of which produced commercial vehicles. They were starting construction on a new plant at Pantnagar, in the state of Uttarakhand, which was built to produce the little Ace truck. As head of the Ace project, Girish had been instrumental in the early development of the Pantnagar plant. When he took over leadership of Team Nano in 2005, he was confident in his ability to oversee the plant development.

LEADING UP THE ROAD LESS TRAVELED

Building a plant in any of these established areas would have offered Team Nano an easy path to production, and it was with this in mind that Girish and other executives headed to Mumbai to make a presentation to the chairman. There, they were in for a surprise.

"Why don't you look at Punjab or West Bengal?" Ratan Tata asked them. "Government leaders from both states have approached me informally. They would like to have us. Why not go look?"

Later on, Ratan Tata explained, "To go to West Bengal was breaking tradition. It was a part of the country that had been ignored, a part of the country that all industries stayed away from." The East lagged so far behind the rest of the country that it presented a danger of destabilizing the rest of India if it couldn't be brought into the new century.

The Punjab was a different story. The second richest state in India, it's an immensely fertile agricultural area whose people are known for their industriousness. With an educated workforce ready to join the Tata ranks, it was an inviting proposition.

Girish found both state governments extremely cooperative, and the West Bengal government the more competitive of the two, with good reason. While Punjab wanted new industry, the state was not desperate for it. West Bengal was.

By 2005, under the leadership of reformist Chief Minister Buddhadeb Bhattacharya, the Communist West Bengal government was actively looking for industrial development. And the chief minister himself—"Buddha" as he's popularly known—had spoken to Ratan Tata privately, urging him to throw Tata's support behind his efforts at building an industrial base. As the most trusted and respected group of companies in India, what better than Tata to open up the state to manufacturing?

Girish was surprised at how forthcoming the West Bengal government was: "They gave us very good incentives, and those incentives were actually comparable to the incentives that we got in Uttarakhand. So then we came back and we started comparing on a lot of other factors."

Going to West Bengal was breaking tradition. But then nation building runs through Ratan's blood. And what better than Tata to open up West Bengal to manufacturing?

On those other factors, West Bengal looked less attractive. Transportation was poor, few automotive suppliers had operations there, and there was already significant opposition to the government's redevelopment plans, not just in West Bengal but in neighboring states.

The South Korean steel company Posco had spent years trying to invest $12 billion in the neighboring state of Orissa and had been rewarded with demonstrations and the kidnapping of two executives. The London-based mining company Vedanta Resources had pledged $20 billion in investment to develop the impoverished state's mineral wealth, only to be challenged all the way to the Indian Supreme Court by locals who opposed the mining.

(Ilya Mauter, Creative Commons per Wikimedia.org: http://commons.wikimedia.org/wiki/File:Village_girls_West_Bengal.JPG)

Girls in a West Bengal village get ready for school.

But Orissa is not West Bengal. Other Tata Group companies already had operations there. Maybe things would be better there.

They weren't. In May 2006, when Tata Motors executives went to West Bengal to inspect several possible sites being offered by the West Bengal Industrial Development Corporation, they were met by organized protests, led by the political opposition, the Trinamool Congress.

Still committed to reindustrialization, Ratan Tata overruled the team and encouraged them to look at a broader goal. "Let's go to West Bengal," he insisted. "We have an imbalance in India. The North, West, and South are thriving. We have to take it upon ourselves to help the East. They are asking our help and we must go."

As they had done for the rest of India with hydroelectric power, steel, and air transport, they would set out to provide West Bengal with the means to build a viable automotive industry that could compete globally someday. An industry that would be known not just for low-cost manufacturing, but for quality, value, and innovation.

Jaydeep Desai, assistant general manager, Small Car Group, was surprised by the decision. "We certainly had greener pastures elsewhere," he remembered, "but after the chairman explained his views, we started looking at it with a new perspective. He told us it would be tough going in the initial stages but that we would get the benefits at the end of the day. After all, the whole reason we are making the Nano is to help the poorest people come up. So why not help them also by where we locate the plant? Why not let them be part of building it?"

And so in June 2006, the decision was finalized. If the Nano could do more than just provide safe, dignified mobility for India's emerging middle class, if the Nano could be the beginning of bringing some of the poorest regions of India into the rising tide of Indian prosperity, that just made the whole project all the more audacious and meaningful to the team and to the nation.

Remember that we define Nanovation as an impossible dream in the service of a cause. And taking on the problems of West

What if the Nano could be the beginning of a rising tide of prosperity?

Activists from the Trinamool Congress shouted antigovernment slogans, December 2006. Tragically the agitation was about internal state politics and not what was right for the local people.

Bengal—when so many easier paths were available—was certainly revolutionary. And it was also consistent with Tata's commitment to doing what was right for the people and the country. It was a significant leadership moment, and like many leadership moments, it involved significant risks. But as Team Nano viewed the situation, they were risks worth taking.

No one thought it would be easy. In July 2006, even before Tata Motors took possession of the land, the Press Trust of India reported that Mamata Banerjee, the former Trinamool Congress party chief and currently India's minister for railways, was threatening bloodshed if any arable land was converted to industrial use. Since most of West Bengal is in the fertile plain of the Ganges Delta, that position would present an almost insurmountable obstacle to development.

Planting a symbolic rice seedling beside the Durgapur Expressway, Mamata mocked Tata Motors, suggesting it was greedy for free land and asking if the government planned to give the company anything it asked for. If the government did, she warned, if land was forcibly acquired, "blood will flow."

Then on January 13, 2008, three days after the world first saw the Nano, Mamata Banerjee called a press conference to protest against the way the government had acquired the land it had made available to Tata for the plant. She demanded that Tata should give away a million Nanos for free.

"Tatas were given land valued at $200 million free, as also $30 million in incentives such as power and water. Everything is free. After getting so many things free, the Tatas should give one million cars free," a reporter from the *Daily Hindu* quoted her as saying. In the face of the wave of positive comment coming from around the world, few people took notice of Banerjee's somewhat comical demands. After all, she was just one contrarian person.

And how much trouble could one person cause?

Despite the disgruntlement, stirring of malcontent, and ill will being spread by the agitators, Tata Motors had already been in full motion with its CSR activities. M. B. Paralkar's Corporate Social Responsibility team preceded the development team into Singur. They had conducted a needs assessment of the area and were well on their way to building rapport and establishing trust with the villages in and around Singur.

"Even before the operation started, we had our CSR team members at Singur doing a survey of the communities that were directly impacted," Paralkar told us. Even though Singur is only about an hour away from Kolkata (formerly called Calcutta), the capital of West Bengal, it was extremely impoverished. "First and foremost the women were quite vocal. They wanted jobs."

Few people were under the impression that all of the women and youth would get jobs in industry, but they were excited about acquiring the skills that would make them employable anywhere—skills that would be useful for a lifetime.

According to Paralkar, "Health was also a problem. There were no facilities. Even though there is a good supply of water everywhere, the quality of drinking water was very poor." Then there was education. M. B. said, "The schools were there, but there were no facilities and no books. Many children would sit on the floor or in the middle of the street."

So, the CSR team went to work in the four thrust areas—education, health, employability, and environment—described in chapter 18.

They partnered with local primary and secondary schools, developing infrastructure with things like better buildings and computer labs. They also trained teachers, created extracurricular activities, offered career guidance for students, and partnered with technical institutes in West Bengal to give promising students a path to both higher education and, when they were ready, meaningful careers at the Nano plant.

They brought the mobile health vans, staffed with doctors and nurses, into the villages and organized health awareness meetings on critical health issues. They started women's self-help groups, helping them earn money and improve their social and financial standing. Borrowing from the idea they had pioneered in Pune, they organized a women's cooperative group to provide training, job opportunities, and eventually a share of the profits. The Pune group had begun with seven women; it then had more than twelve hundred and generated more than a million dollars each year. They took a group of Singur women to Pune and introduced them to the concept, then brought them back to open a canteen at the construction site to feed workers.

The Pune group began with seven women. They now have twelve hundred and generate more than a million dollars each year.

Anarupa Pal was one of the twenty-five women who started the cooperative. "She told us how she never, ever thought she would leave the four walls of her home," Garima Dutt, a member of the CSR team, remembered, looking at a picture of her that appeared in a Tata calendar. "She never thought that without any formal education, she could earn an income."

"It's not just for my own self," Anarupa told Garima, "but even in the village, people look up to me now because I am independent. I earn an income and can contribute to the education of my children. This is fantastic for me."

Unfortunately, as all of this was going on, Tata's CSR people had to put up with protesters who were opposed to the location of the plant. Imagine working to eradicate extreme poverty and to address the absence of sanitation, health, and education with the constant threat of violence looming over your head. Imagine not being able to engage in this noble work without police protection. What if the very people you were trying to help were afraid to be associated with you?

Mrs. Anarupa Pal of Beraberi village in Singur in Hooghly district of West Bengal. Tata Motors which is setting up its Small Car plant at Singur has helped her and 25 other women residents of Singur to enhance their families' income by forming a self help group and set up a canteen that supplies food to people working at the project site. One of the myriad ways, Tata Motors sparks sustainable change by supporting livelihood generation.

October			Octubre			Octobre					
Sun	Mon	Tue	Wed	Thu	Fri	Sat	Sun	Mon	Tue	Wed	Thu	Fri	Sat
			1	2	3	4	5	6	7	8	9	10	11
12	13	14	15	16	17	18	19	20	21	22	23	24	25
26	27	28	29	30	31

TATA MOTORS

(Tata Motors)

Tata Motors set out to help women such as Anarupa Pal of Beraberi village in Singur in West Bengal and twenty-five other women residents of Singur to enhance their families' income by establishing a canteen that supplied food to people working at the Nano plant.

If you are part of the Tatas, you gut it out and press on because the mission of community building isn't adjunct; it is central to everything else you are doing.

And so Tata Motors went to West Bengal seeking to do what it has done in India for more than a century. It went to help a nation rise by bringing industry to a region that had been left behind. It chose an unconventional place to build a revolutionary car with the idea of reigniting an industrial revolution.

The decision to build the Nano plant in West Bengal is another example of Ratan Tata's extraordinary vision and risk-taking ability. A leap of faith? Yes. But it was a well-thought-out leap. His intent and expectation were to give the people of West Bengal the tools and the opportunities to leave behind subsistence living and become a vital part of the global economy, along with the rest of India.

The challenges had just begun.

A LAKE OF WORRIES

In late 2006, Girish Wagh stood on a highway in the Hooghly District of West Bengal, outside the village of Singur. Before him was the one-thousand-acre plot of land the team had chosen as the site of the new Nano plant.

"It was a significant choice," he told us. "The site had good frontage on a major highway. That's important for a big plant because we wanted the substantial logistical benefits." Tata also wanted the plant to make a statement. A view from the highway would tell people driving by that India could build one of the most advanced, state-of-the-art facilities in the world. "Part of our vision was that this would be a futuristic plant, a world leader, and we believed we would have a lot of visitors coming to see it, from India and from around the world.

"Unfortunately we missed a few important details," he added. "Like the fact that this land was one of the lowest pieces of land in that part of the country." The head of construction for the Nano plant, M. B. Kulkarni, and his team had studied the site and calculated how much fill would be needed to keep the plant above flood level. But even the best-laid plans can go awry.

"Unfortunately we missed a few important details."

In September 2007, the Julkia River that goes right through a portion of the property burst its banks after a downpour. The drainage system for the one-thousand-acre parcel hadn't been completed yet, and to add insult to misery, two more things happened for which Mother Nature could not be blamed. First, someone opened a river gate that was supposed to remain closed, and second, a group of troublemakers had dug small canals on the outskirts of the property, allowing water to gush in and flood the site.

Standing in the same spot where he had stood a year earlier, Girish fought back the tears. He was devastated. The one thousand acres had become a lake with a half-built plant rising out of it. Policemen in a small powerboat patrolled the waters to chase off looters.

"It was quite depressing," Girish said as he looked at pictures of the moment, the same pictures he showed the chairman a few days later at Bombay House. "I was extremely tense. How do I take this news to the chairman because, at that point, no news could be as bad as this? I mean, he could have pointed out that flooding was one of the most basic things we should have checked at the site. And he would have been right. We had made a mistake."

(PTI 20090909)

When the monsoons come, they turn much of low-lying West Bengal into a lake. Here, the 2009 floods displaced villagers in the Howrah District.

But after only a couple of photos, Ratan Tata immediately grasped the situation and, instead of pointing a finger, chose to become part of the solution.

"I was floored. He looked at the photos and said, 'Okay, what's the solution?'" Girish later told Tata's Group Publications, "After our meeting got over I told Mr. Tata, 'Sir, I was extremely strained coming into this meeting. I was worried about how you were going to take it.' He patted me on the back and said, 'Don't worry. Whatever has happened has happened. You have an action plan; now go ahead and implement it.' This, after we had lost time and money by ignoring a basic requirement. It was a tremendous gesture."

And so they went to work. They redesigned the ground plan, raising roads and buildings to above foreseeable flood levels. They replaced fifty-four thousand square feet of flooring. Then they went to work on preventive measures. In the following months, they worked on a flood control plan with the West Bengal government.

Team Nano plunged ahead to get the planned production deadline of October, then just months away, back on track. Despite continuing political agitation around the plant, construction was largely complete, and the assembly lines were being installed. Vendors were beginning their own construction projects at or near the site, and the Nano could see light at the end of the tunnel.

Hiring began as early as the spring of 2006, and one of the first employees to arrive in Singur was young Surya Banerjee—in fact, he was the twentieth employee on the project. He was a third-generation Tata family member. His father and grandfather had worked for the company, so joining the company's most visible project in a generation was a thrill for the young engineer. And as an assistant plant manager, he was part of the team responsible for building the plant.

"In building a car factory," he told us, "there are five processes you have to build—in effect, five separate factories that must be constructed and equipped.

"First, the press shop, where sheet metal is formed into body parts. This is where the highly technical hydroforming and roll-forming processes take place.

"Next, the weld shop, where the body-in-white is fabricated. This is the basic unibody frame of the car, including the roof, front and rear structure, and the underbody. This is also where the doors and other body parts are assembled.

"From there, the body parts go to the paint shop. At the same time, engine and drive-train components are being assembled in the engine shop.

"And finally all these parts arrive in the final building, where the assembly line is. This is where the cars are assembled to specifications from marketing plans. Different colors, different trim levels, different accessories. All the parts come in at one end of the line, and the plan is that every fifty-eight seconds a new Nano will roll off the other end of the line."

Now imagine building all this. Five factories in one, each with specialized equipment—machines as big as houses—that is complicated to install and set up. Designing a factory is not much different from designing a car. A factory is a machine that needs to run flawlessly for sixteen to twenty-four hours a day. And if it's a lemon, you can't trade it in. You're stuck with what you build for generations.

At the same time, *building* a car factory is nothing like building a car. It's a one-off project that can't be mechanized. There is no "assembly line" for factory construction, and when you get on site, things don't always fit the way they did on the design screen or in the blueprints.

Other than the architects and some contractors, few on the project had ever built a car factory—or any other kind of factory—before. So, while you're building the plant, you also have to build the company. You have to hire, train, lead, and supervise on the fly, all while under extreme deadlines.

The construction planning had to be like clockwork, and the design had to be extraordinarily well thought out. If the huge machinery arrives before you have the building ready, where are you going to put it?

For young engineers like Surya Banerjee, it was a thrill ride of an assignment, and by the time the Nano was revealed in Delhi, everything was on time and on budget. The first cars would roll off the line in October 2008, and in spite of political demonstrations outside the gate, everything was looking good.

But distant thunder was beginning to cloud the Nano's future again, beginning with problems from an unexpected direction. If the flooding didn't derail the project, then perhaps the rising costs of materials would.

COMMODITIES AND RAW MATERIALS PRICES SHOOT THROUGH THE ROOF

In the spring of 2008, prices of oil, metal, and other commodities began to skyrocket unexpectedly. For Team Nano, in the summer of 2008, the commodity price crisis couldn't have come at a worse time. After all, the entire premise of the Nano was predicated on reaching a specific price for the base model. If they backpedaled on that promise, they risked alienating the public and possibly risked turning them off to the entire idea of the Nano. And they surely didn't want to face the ridicule of the press and competitors or give the demonstrators outside the gates another reason to mock them. But they also didn't want to create a losing proposition that couldn't sustain the company financially.

When oil prices rise, they drive up the prices of everything else. Plastics derive from petroleum. Manufacturing and processing of all sorts of raw materials depend on petroleum, and transportation does, too. So when copper wire doubles or triples in price, as does the petroleum to make the plastic casing for the wiring, it affects the manufacture of the finished product. It costs more to transport the wire to the plant that makes the wiring harness for the car. It costs more to make the wiring harness and to transport it to the assembly plant. The incremental costs multiply, and you have to throw your projections out the window and start again.

Team Nano had to go back to **work** on ways to cut costs even **further** than **expected.**

In many cases, Tata Motors had contracts with suppliers to deliver goods at prices set months before. And while that would help somewhat, if the commodity prices continued to rise, they couldn't expect suppliers to deliver at prices that no longer were viable in the new market conditions.

With less than six months to go before Tata's 1 lakh car was set to go on sale, Team Nano had to go back to work on ways to cut costs even further than expected. It was like preparing a dinner for four and then opening the door to discover your friends had brought an additional ten friends. How do you deal with something like that?

It was a leadership moment, and Team Nano was up to the challenge. As they had done in the crisis in 2000, Girish and Ravi Kant and their teams went back to the drawing board on every single cost item, looking for new levels of innovation in process and materials, anything that could help them combat the rising cost not just of commodities, but of doing business. While it was too late to reconsider design, it wasn't too late to work on cost-cutting ideas that anyone had.

But as oil prices headed toward $200 a barrel, there was an upside for the Nano. "The Model T created a revolution," Ravi Kant told us. "And if there was ever a time for a new revolution, this is it. When people see oil prices going up past $200 a barrel, they start thinking about fuel efficiency. And here comes the Nano, getting fifty miles a gallon. You can't ignore it."

If they could get it to production, there was no doubt the Nano was a car for its time.

Most auto manufacturers develop a car and then establish its price. Not Tata. The price was established the day Ratan Tata chose not to amend John Griffith's headline "Tatas Plan Rs. 1 Lakh Car" in London's *Financial Times*. The question was, in the face of materials costs going through the roof, would Ratan amend the price of the car now?

As we mentioned, Ratan spent the better part of two weeks at the Pune plant just prior to the Delhi Auto Expo in January 2008. He worked with Girish going over every detail necessary to make the unveiling a success. Curious about whether the chairman would confirm the price at the auto show, Girish asked, but he got no response. Hinting for an option to delay the pricing decision until the Nano was actually launched, Girish discussed the escalating commodity prices. Still, Ratan didn't say anything.

Then five years and a thousand seemingly insurmountable hurdles later, Ratan Tata showcased his dream to the world and confirmed that the launch price of the base model would be 1 lakh. Why did he do it?

Because as he told the audience, "A promise is a promise."

The challenges caused by the flooding in Singur and the skyrocketing materials costs tested Team Nano severely; they would pale in comparison to the crisis lurking over the horizon. With the world looking on, Ratan Tata and Team Nano were about to be confronted with an extremely painful decision.

NANOBITE

When things go wrong, you bounce back and build momentum by . . .

- owning your mistakes instead of pointing fingers.
- focusing on the solution instead of ruminating on the problem.
- making things happen instead of making excuses.
- spending energy on things you can control (innovative cost cutting) instead of whining about things you can't control (rising prices).
- unifying the team by instilling hope instead of discouraging the team by spreading doom and gloom.

TWENTY
Leading Through Crisis

I know God will not give me anything I can't handle.
I just wish he didn't trust me so much!

MOTHER TERESA

As Mother Teresa would have been the first to tell you, going out of your way to help other people is not going to make your own life or work any easier. In the months following the reveal in Delhi, with construction nearing completion, with equipment installed and workers in training, with the ramp-up to production progressing at record pace, Team Nano was about to learn just how much trouble it could handle.

A STORM BREWS IN WEST BENGAL

Tata Motors was not involved in the land acquisition process. The Singur site had previously been assembled by the West Bengal

Industrial Development Corporation for industrial development. When the land was offered to Tata, there was no hint of any problems with the title. Had there been, the Tatas would have gone elsewhere. Other sites in West Bengal were considered, but Singur was chosen primarily for two reasons: (1) the location on a major highway would allow the plant to be a showcase and give easy access to transport, and (2) there was the need for investment in a part of the state that had been so ignored.

> In Singur, twelve thousand people asked for compensation on less than one thousand acres.

In Singur, on the edge of the factory grounds, was an office dedicated to dealing with payments to local landowners for their property. And because of the protests and legal challenges, there were delays in closing on the land transfers. For the 997 acres allocated for the Nano plant, twelve thousand people were lining up for compensation. Some were landowners and some were sharecroppers. Some farmed the land themselves, and some were absentee owners who had rented their land while they sought more lucrative employment in the city. That meant more than ten stakeholders per acre of land.

While most of them were very supportive of the plant and excited about the prospects for the future, some were fearful. Many worked land that their families had worked for generations. They didn't know any other way of life. It didn't take many of them for Mamata Banerjee and her party to create a movement. In the end, 243.66 widely scattered acres belonged to farmers unwilling to part with their property, but those were enough to build a campaign around, and Mamata brought demonstrators from all over West Bengal to demonstrate against the plant.

It was clear that although there can always be legitimate issues regarding the transfer of landownership, the primary impetus was political. Mamata's Trinamool Congress wanted to cause the maximum amount of embarrassment to the Left Front government of Bhattacharya, with an eye on taking over the state assembly in the next round of elections. Since the Nano is one of the most visible business stories in Indian history, huge public attention was guaranteed, and the opposition exploited the press around the Nano to the fullest. There were even allegations—not fully articulated and never proven—that one or more auto industry competitors, desperate to slow the Nano project, were fueling the fires with donations to Mamata.

So Mamata Banerjee's demand that Tata give away a million Nanos for free, while nothing more than comedy for the evening news, was part of a powerful political wave that was about to swamp the rising Nano plant in Singur, worse than any natural flood. The oncoming deluge would be a tragedy for everyone except the politicians.

THE CRISIS ESCALATES

In June 2008, less than five months after he stood on the stage in Delhi to unveil the Nano, Ravi Kant was the target of violent demonstrations when he tried to visit the Singur plant. Protesters stormed the guard wall and stoned policemen at the gates. Many protesters were landowners who had come to believe that the compensation they were offered was not adequate, some were curious locals, and a large number were brought in by Mamata Banerjee's organizers from around West Bengal. As the rocks rained down on the police, they retaliated with batons and tear gas. It wasn't the first time this had happened, and it wouldn't be the last.

For weeks, Mamata Banerjee had been ratcheting up the rhetoric, personalizing it against Ratan himself. "Tata Babu, you may be rich," she shouted over a public address system as she addressed a swelling crowd of activists outside the plant, "but no matter how many times you say Nano, we say no-no."

(The Times of India Group © BCCL Times Content)

Firebrand politician Mamata Banerjee made a national name for herself by stopping the construction of the Singur plant.

She was mocked and laughed at throughout much of India, particularly among educated people, but her message had a strong ring with many in West Bengal, which was what she cared about. It was a battle for political advantage in which the Nano and the local farmers were being used as pawns, and there was little either could do.

Approaches were made to Mamata Banerjee to sit with Tata and government leaders and work out a solution, but she declined to negotiate. She was making national headlines, and perhaps she didn't want to jeopardize her new visibility with a settlement, even one the farmers were happy with.

In polls of local residents, people were overwhelmingly in support of the plant. Of the farmers who had been paid, more than 90 percent opposed the agitation, and 89 percent thought their standard of living was already on the rise, even before the plant opened. At the

(The Times of India Group © BCCL Times Content)

You can't feed the poor with slogans. Here, the highway to Singur reopened after angry contractors brought political pressure.

same time, 55 percent of locals had come to believe the compensation for landowners wasn't enough. And nearly 80 percent thought the West Bengal government hadn't handled the situation well. As often happens, it was easy to shift the argument around in ways that tended to confuse more than they illuminated.

Reports of suicides by distraught landowners helped fuel the fire. The more heated the opposition rhetoric became, the more desperate both sides began to feel. Mamata played to the emotions of the poor, painting them as victims of greedy industrialists, gaining herself a national platform. The tension rose higher when in an unrelated protest against land acquisition in the nearby town of Nandigram, police opened fire on rioters, killing fourteen people.

Inside the plant, work **progressed** in the belief that the **politics** would be **settled.**

Inside the plant, work progressed in the belief that the politics would be settled and Nanos would roll out on their expected release date in October. But the stress was taking its toll. Most engineers had moved their families from places like Pune or Chennai. There were Japanese, Korean, British, and German engineers and consultants, as well. Most of them commuted from Kolkata, and as the agitation intensified, they were forced to take ever more circuitous routes to avoid being attacked by increasingly violent protesters. They traveled in caravans of cars and buses, sometimes with police protection, and the trip was beginning to take anywhere from three to five hours each way. Often, team members didn't get home until past midnight, only to turn around and start traveling back at dawn.

(The Times of India Group © BCCL Times Content)

On August 22, police tried to hold back the crowd, while Girish Wagh and Team Nano were trapped inside.

Logistics became a nightmare. With crowds of protesters blockading the plant, it became difficult to supply the teams inside.

"We had a responsibility to feed people," Surya Banerjee remembered. "We had employees and vendors and we had to get food inside the plant, and the protesters were stopping all deliveries of food. They were trying to starve us out." It was a situation that required innovative action, and Team Nano came up with the solution. "We got ambulances and loaded them with food and cooking supplies. Every day, the ambulances came, and they didn't stop them outside the plant. Nobody checked."

Although police guarded the plant entrances and tried to keep the protesters at bay, the plant security manager, Colonel Bhatra, and his team of young guards had their hands full.

Surya remembered their bravery: "They manned the gates with the police, and they took some beatings. They patrolled the fences, stopping intrusions of protesters who found holes in the fence and came inside to sabotage the construction equipment. They assaulted our people, even invading the guard's mess and beating young off-duty guards and threatening them with death if they didn't leave immediately. But they stood their ground." Surya went to the front gate frequently and saw that as the protesters charged with fists and clubs, as rocks came soaring over the gates and fences, Colonel Bhatra and his men never backed down.

Throughout those days, the community services teams tried their best to continue their work in the villages. In the villages surrounding the plant, people had different political influences. When the teams went to one area that was on the side of the government, no problem. But when they went to an area that was on the side of Mamata, there might be some risk. Even though they had police protection most of the time, there were beatings and kidnappings. Community workers trying to get medical care to villagers were held hostage. The situation was becoming untenable.

"Even until the last moment," Surya Banerjee recalled, "everyone was optimistic. No one believed we would have to leave what we had built. We were trying to negotiate with the various parties. Even we realized leaving was a possibility, but we thought we would work it out."

They were wrong.

On the evening of August 28, 2008, Girish Wagh had to make the very difficult decision to stop work at the plant. "I took the decision," he told us, "not that we were going to pull out, but that we couldn't work in these circumstances. Workers were coming with torn shirts, with bloodstains, beaten up on the way to work. The danger was on all our minds."

But the decision to stop work left him with the problem of what to do with the four hundred white-collar workers and more than eight hundred apprentices. He and the team agreed to send them home, still on payroll, until the situation improved. But as the first buses left the plant, demonstrators stormed them, banging on the sides and windows with rocks. One bus got through, and the rest returned to the relative safety of the plant.

They were being held hostage.

"I was in one of the shops," Girish remembered, "when I got the call that there was a problem and went to the gate. There were very senior-level police there and they were very helpful, but the demonstrators were unrelenting. And probably quite rightly the police decided not to use violence because the situation was so explosive. Police violence would only have served to build up sympathy from the public at large."

Inside the plant, engineers from all over the world were being held hostage.

Inside the plant, the tension was palpable. After weeks of increasing fear, they were now under siege, and some workers began to have emotional breakdowns. Things were going worse than anyone could have imagined.

"It was pretty tense," Surya Banerjee told us. "We had about one thousand employees with one thousand police guarding us. But outside it was a war zone. What might happen?"

For the men and women trapped inside the plant, it was a grim moment. Indian mobs, for all the peacefulness of the Indian disposition, are notorious for turning suddenly murderous, and as the employees sat together inside the plant, everyone knew how bad the situation might possibly be. Outside the plant, on the other hand, the mood was more like a carnival. Feeling as though they had the Tatas—and by extension, the Bhattacharya government—on the ropes, they began to celebrate what they saw as a victory for their cause. As the night wore on, the demonstrators first sat and then lay down in the road, blocking the only exit from the plant. Soon, they were asleep, a mass of contented activists sleeping it off.

And then in the middle of the night, it started to rain heavily. Suddenly awakening to find themselves soaking wet, the demonstrators moved off in search of shelter.

A terrified Japanese consultant ran into the night. He didn't want anything more to do with the plant.

"I got a call from the police, who said the road was clear," Girish explained, "so we started loading the cars and buses. And I remember a Japanese consultant had become so upset—I think I can use the word *unstable*—that he refused to get in a car. He said he would walk. He would go on his own. He didn't want anything more to do with Tata Motors."

While in the days that followed, Girish and small groups of executives and engineers continued to go to the plant to take care of business, he didn't allow any more foreign nationals on the property, out of a moral responsibility to keep them—and all employees of Tata and its vendors—safe.

It was a huge decision to put on the shoulders of a young executive. Ravi Kant stayed in touch with him via phone and text messages and communicated his full support. And Ratan Tata went on national TV to add his support, saying the safety of employees could not be compromised.

One of Girish's huge concerns was that after having built up Team Nano with some of the best people in the business, he would lose them as everything seemed to be unraveling. He needn't have worried. From their hotel rooms and homes in Kolkata, the team kept in touch and kept working toward the launch of the Nano.

Girish canvassed the team daily from their various locations away from the plant site. If the decision to leave had to be taken, he wanted to make sure everyone on the team had his say and was on board with the decision. But it was terribly hard to do.

"Cell phone communication was good," Girish said, "but I think in such circumstances if you go to where people are and personally meet them, it makes a lot of difference."

Within a few days, Surya Banerjee returned to the plant and joined Colonel Bhatra and his security team in keeping the plant safe. He said, "There was machinery that had to be maintained, or it would be lost. And the infrastructure was incomplete. Buildings were unfinished. The water supply had not been completed."

Over the next few weeks, they continued training apprentices in remote locations away from the action. And Girish and the rest of Team Nano began to ask the question they could no longer avoid.

What happens next?

THE BEGINNING OF THE END

On the morning of September 25, Team Nano should have been less than a month away from starting full production of the Nano. At the Singur plant, five cars had been built already, testing and trouble-shooting the production line and giving new workers their first taste of hands-on training.

"Anyone who isn't confused here doesn't really understand what's going on."
Attributed to a participant in the Northern Ireland peace talks

But in Singur, everything was on hold as Girish and the Nano team waited to see what would happen next. On September 25, they found out.

At the plant, the office of the Singur block development officer (BDO), Prasenjit Roy, was ready for a special day. Compensation checks were to be handed over to more than 354 farmers, a significant move toward the eventual compensation of all. At 11:30 a.m., the first checks were handed out to the waiting farmers. Outside the office, an increased police detail was on hand to keep order.

An hour later, after 256 checks had been distributed, a leader of the anti-acquisition forces, Becharam Manna, entered the office with a dozen supporters. Presenting documents he said proved the wrong people were being paid, he demanded the process be stopped. The local magistrate, Vinod Kumar, was called and rushed to the scene. But while he was explaining to the people inside that the process was, in fact, paying the right people, protesters outside suddenly attacked the building and began ransacking cars. Police moved to stop the violence, and soon things were getting out of control again.

(The Times of India Group © BCCL Times Content)

How bad does it have to get before you make the decision to abandon the investment in the plant and in the people of Singur?

While those inside the BDO office continued to try to hand out checks, demonstrators blocked landowners, eager to be paid, from entering. A farmer named Achinta Polen, who had come to collect his check, made it nearly to the door before he was badly beaten. Magistrate Kumar tried to leave, but protesters blocked his way, and police had to rescue him. By then, the crowd had swelled to more than ten thousand protesters, and a stalemate had ensued.

At 5:30 in the evening, Mamata Banerjee arrived and effectively laid siege to the payment office, entering to talk to the magistrate and refusing to let him or anyone else leave.

"By then," Girish told us, "we couldn't put off the decision anymore. We knew we were probably going to have to leave Singur." The entire project was at risk, and the Nano was more important than a single plant. But it hurt him to think of the local people who had supported them and the local employees who, just months before, had been so excited about the possibilities that lay ahead of them and their families.

Did Mamata and the protesters realize they had gone too far? They claimed that they weren't against industrial opportunity; that they were just fighting for the rights of the little people. But when, near midnight, she emerged from the building to address the jubilant crowd, she was belligerent: "We are not against industrialization, but the state government is seizing land in the shadow of the night like a thief and with police help. We are campaigning against this, and it will continue till the state government gives up its plan to acquire land here."

And it was clear that she would not stop.

On October 3, 2008, Ratan Tata had had enough. He saw no end to the violence and threats to workers' safety. After a ninety-minute meeting with the chief minister in which Buddhadeb Bhattacharya was very persuasive in trying to convince him not to relocate the Nano plant, Ratan made it final: Tata Motors would pull out of Singur.

He explained to the chief minister that "the well-being of my employees is my responsibility. We cannot run a plant with police protection when the walls are being broken, bombs being thrown, people being threatened and intimidated." It was a lonely decision after a long day that came with a lot of pain.

The *Indian Express* reported Ratan Tata as saying, "I think two years ago I once mentioned that if somebody puts a gun to my head, you pull the trigger or you take the gun away because I will not move my head. I think Ms. Mamata Banerjee has pulled the trigger."

Her accusations were far from true, but her threats were real. Perhaps she and her supporters really thought they were winners. But there were no winners in Singur. And the biggest losers of all would be the local people who had been caught in the middle.

There would be no plant. No jobs. And no future filled with education for their children. No health care. And far fewer business opportunities. If the state's Communist rulers, once notoriously hostile to big business, hoped the Nano project would rebrand West Bengal as a region open to new investments, it was not to be. One can't help questioning whether the legacy of antibusiness politics had really changed. If anything, the agitators reinforced the stigma that West Bengal is not investor friendly. As the world watched this event unfold, you can be sure that companies considering a move to West Bengal would think twice.

(Tata Motors)
October 3, 2008: at a press conference in Kolkata, Ratan Tata announced that Tata Motors was pulling out of Singur.

For the families of Singur, there would be only empty buildings in a flooded plain.

Moving out of Singur was one of the hardest things many on Team Nano had ever had to do. Prior to the announcement to pull out of Singur, Atul K. Vaidya, a senior engineer with the planning team, arrived at the plant for one last visit. He was one of the few people to know in advance that the pullout was for real. Standing in an empty industrial shop surrounded by tons and tons of idle equipment, he was reduced to tears.

He told Philip Chacko of Tata's Group Publications, "We had started from scratch with the plant, we had put in so many months of hard work. The investment, the manpower, the enthusiasm, the effort—all wasted. It was too much to take."

Atul was with a security official and his colleague Jaydeep Desai on this last "good-bye" tour of the plant. Neither of them was aware of Ratan Tata's impending announcement. "Jaydeep was baffled," Atul continued. "He kept asking me what was wrong, why I was getting emotional. I couldn't tell him what I knew. This week you are rearing and ready to manufacture a path-breaking product, the next week you begin to pack up and leave. It was so painful."

Everyone felt the pain. For Ratan Tata personally, it was a terrible disappointment because the only reason they went to West Bengal was to help the people and the state.

"We thought we had conceived a product that made an impact on the low-end consumer, with an opportunity to have an all-weather affordable vehicle, so we were doing it for that segment of the economy," he told us. "And it seemed supportive to think that, well, you did this project in an area of the country that was ignored, where there are a vast number of intelligent and reasonably educated people without jobs, and so you are bringing something in to help them. We had this feeling that, in addition to the product, we were helping regenerate a part of the country. It made you feel that you were doing something that was doubly good."

And it was doubly disappointing to have to abandon Singur.

The move to West Bengal was to help build a nation; it was also done to keep a promise, as Ratan made clear in an interview with the *Economic Times* of India (*ET*).

"Earlier this decade we had some problems with the Haldia petro-chemicals complex and we decided to withdraw," he explained to *ET*. "I told [Chief Minister Buddhadeb Bhattacharya] at that time that, 'I am going, but trust me I will come back.' Later he invited me to set up an automotive industry there."

In the end, Ratan reflected upon the Singur travesty with humility. He told *ET*, "What happened there was sad. But I must take responsibility. They offered the land in Kharagpur. We would have gone there. But, I rang up Buddhadeb and asked him, 'don't you want to showcase this project as a world class enterprise. We can bring in our best people, best schools.' It was in deference to my wishes that Singur was offered and the location was most suitable. We really hoped that investment would flow into that part of the country that has been ignored so far."

Losing the Nano plant took a huge human toll on the residents of Singur, most of whom hoped the plant would help their children make the move out of poverty.

"We were emotionally attached to Singur," Surya Banerjee explained. "People set it up with their own hands. People in the paint shop installed all the equipment. It was *their* plant. But they realized that we had to move on."

An elderly village woman in West Bengal reacted to the political violence.

Jaydeep Desai also remembered how hard it was emotionally: "We knew there would be challenges, but we also knew that we could bring Singur up from poverty. There was a clear understanding in everyone's minds that we were changing a part of India because of our work, and so there was a lot of emotional involvement with the people working at the plant and the people of the community."

After all the work they had done with education and health care around the area, it was hard to think they would have to say good-bye.

"I remember one old woman," Ramesh Vishwakarma told us. "She was literally crying when we were moving out because we were giving her a particular injection free of cost, which she would not get once we left. She was eighty years old, I think. She started crying 'Who will give me medicine? Tata do not go, do not go away.'"

But the commitment wasn't just to the people of Singur. There were professional considerations as well. "We were 95 percent there when we had to stop work. We only had another 5 percent left to do, and the Nano would be rolling out on Indian roads. It was devastating to let that go."

Ravi Kant called Girish to discuss the situation, and Girish spoke frankly of his anger and frustration: "I told him, I'm an engineer. But I'm not doing any engineering work, even for a minute. I'm just dealing with business problems." It had been his only chance to vent his real feelings, something he couldn't do, busy as he was keeping the rest of the team intact, focused, and calm.

Ravi understood the pressure that

(Subhabrata Das)

Girish Wagh led the team through incredible difficulties, but learned that resilience is essential to leadership.

Girish was under, something few leaders in the history of the Tata companies had ever had to endure. "I know," his boss told him. "But you have to learn to do this kind of work also. When there is engineering to do, you will do it. But now, you have to deal with this." Both Ravi Kant and Ratan Tata backed Girish's decision to stop work. Both let him know that they would support him if he felt they had to pull the plug. But they also wouldn't put the decision all on his shoulders.

While politicians from all over India tried to intervene and find a solution, the opponents of the plant were adamant that their demands had to be met, without compromise. There was a strong feeling of disgust throughout much of India.

Biswadip Gupta, joint CEO and managing director of JSW Bengal Steel, told the *Times of India*, "Here, we had a project on the verge of completion—that could have changed the industrial landscape of Bengal—before it was suddenly forced to relocate. The move crushed the hopes of the entire state. I wonder whether anyone, including those who had their eyes on votes alone, is celebrating … in Bengal because the sense of loss is so great."

> **Nanovators are fighters with a "never say die" spirit because they deeply believe in what they are doing.**

Poet Subodh Sarkar was more sarcastic: "Tata's shifting their Nano factory to Gujarat is a puja gift to [Gujarati chief minister Narendra] Modi by our opposition leaders. The opposition, while trying to oppose the government's decision, has ridiculed its own credibility."

In the end, the Tatas made the choice to look elsewhere.

Ratan took responsibility for making the call and remembered the moment he told Girish the decision he'd made: "If you look at what Girish went through, you've taken on an impossible task and astonished the world with what you created, you've gone through a total commitment of a plant in West Bengal and given it everything, you've worked at dealing with adversity as they built it, violence, even flooding. He dealt with all those things. Then, one fine day, the chairman says, 'We're moving.'

"I remember the day when Girish said, 'We've gone so far. Can't we find a solution?'

"I said, 'Girish, it won't work. We've got to move.' I could see the disappointment.

"He said, 'You know, we're 95 percent done. We'll be out in production in weeks.'

"But once he realized he couldn't change the decision, he was committed. I've worked with many people who say, 'Well, okay. If that's what you want.' And undercurrents keep on happening that sabotage what you're trying to do.

"Not so with Girish."

Surya Banerjee, during those few weeks, became an expert in crisis management. From October to April, he stayed in the plant, unable even to see his family.

After two years of building—both plants and people— and just steps from the goal line, the game in Singur was over, but the Nano story wasn't.

As the country song says, "You have to know when to hold 'em and know when to fold 'em." The cause in West Bengal, though worthy, was subservient to the greater cause of the Nano. Ratan Tata and Team Nano had the sense and the guts to do an about-face and make the difficult choice of walking away from a fight that wasn't worth winning.

Nanovators are also willing to let go for the sake of the larger cause.

NANOBITE

Innovation is fraught with roadblocks and missteps. When things appear to be going south . . .

- stay focused on the bigger picture, the larger cause.
- pick your battles wisely. Nothing is worth compromising the well-being of your people.
- focus forward on the solution; casting blame and ruminating on the problem are wasted energy.
- fight smart. Remember the unchecked ambulances hauling food and supplies past protesters into the plant?
- dig deep. You are usually more capable of coping than you think you are—and coping can be contagious.
- if, after honest debate and good feedback, the coach calls a play you don't agree with, it's your job to make that play work.

QUESTIONS

A culture of innovation is built on trust, and trust is often created or destroyed depending on how one leads through crisis.

- When faced with a crisis, where do you find your leaders? On the front line? In the trenches? At the point of action? Or somewhere else?
- The courage of conviction exemplified in a leader's unbending resolve to do what's right gives followers hope and the willpower to persevere. How do you measure up in a crisis?

TWENTY-ONE
Moving at the Speed of Yes!

> Compromise: An agreement between two
> men to do what both agree is wrong.
>
> **LORD EDWARD CECIL**

While the decision to withdraw from Singur was painful, there was little time for grieving and second-guessing. The catch-22 in which Tata Motors found itself might have generated great fodder for the media, but the marketplace was more interested in how the company was going to move forward and meet the incredible demand for the People's Car. The meltdown in West Bengal would test the speed and agility of Team Nano as well as a host of state governments. Team Nano and one particular state rose to the occasion.

Even as early as December 2007, they had begun contingency planning, in the event that Singur was unworkable. Girish Wagh had the courage and foresight to face the brutal facts of reality by asking tough questions. What if the political agitation can't be resolved? What if we lose part of our workforce due to intolerable working conditions? What if we have to move? And how will we meet immediate demand for the car in the midst of a potential shuffle? Everyone hoped they would not have to address these questions, but *hope* is not a strategy.

They decided that if worse came to worst, the Nano's engine would be made in Pune and the rest of the car would be manufactured and assembled at the Pantnagar plant in Uttarakhand. It was a backup plan that would at least enable Tata Motors to establish limited production of the Nano while they sorted out the major issue of where to find a home for the mother plant.

When fracture lines started to show in Singur, the calls from various state governments in India—Maharashtra, Gujarat, Andhra Pradesh, and Karnataka—came in, inviting Tata Motors to build the plant in their respective regions.

Here is where Tata Motors shifted into high gear and demonstrated its remarkable abilities to say yes fast. In the four days following Ratan Tata's announcement that the company was withdrawing from Singur, Ravi Kant rallied a team of senior leaders including Girish and Amarjit Singh Puri, Tata Motors' point person for government liaisons, and did what normally would've taken months to do. They flew from one state to another, conducting half-day meetings with government officials to evaluate the merits of each potential location for the plant.

As Ratan Tata aptly observed, it was important for the same team to go to each state so they could compare the pros and cons. At the end of this whirlwind tour, Sanand in Gujarat got the nod.

YES TO OPPORTUNITY

The speed with which Chief Minister Narendra Modi's government moved to seal the deal was nothing short of heroic. By October 7, just ninety-six hours after Ratan's dreadful announcement in Kolkata, a

Memorandum of Understanding was signed by Ravi Kant and Gauri Kumar, Gujarat's principal secretary (Industries). It took the Gujarat government just ten days to get all the clearances and tie up all the details to make the land ready for possession.

Ironically the land the Gujarat government had in mind was part of a plot that, long ago, Jamsetji Tata had given to Gujarat during a famine to save cattle.

What made Gujarat so attractive? Well, Narendra Modi has a reputation for running the state like the chief executive of a business, and he was very clear that the Nano was not just a Tata project, but a project endorsed and supported by the people of Gujarat as well. Modi also pledged to provide full support to the project in terms of infrastructure facilities such as roads, power, water, drainage, and effluent discharge systems.

(Tata Motors)

From left, Ravi Kant, Ratan Tata, and Narendra Modi prepared to announce Gujarat as the Nano plant's new home.

Two organizations demonstrated the power of a "yes-fast" culture and achieved a remarkable outcome.

Ravi Kant pointed out that the difference between Gujarat and West Bengal is that in Gujarat there is bipartisan collaboration that supports big projects. This political consensus favors what's best for the state versus what's best for any particular political group.

In addition to the friendly political temperament, Sanand had eleven hundred acres of flat land, under one land survey number, already under the possession of the state government, that wasn't in a low-lying flood plain, with soil that was harder and more conducive to building an automotive plant. On top of this, Sanand is approximately sixty miles from a new port being developed at Dholera, to the south of Ahmedabad. With eight jetties, Tata Motors could cut costs by using the all-weather port to ship cars along the coast to South India.

In the final analysis, Gujarat's sense of urgency got Tata's attention. Modi and his team have built a "yes-fast" state. Governments that are looking for industrialists to come and invest in their areas would do well to take a lesson from Gujarat. The efficiency with which they pursued this project showed their vision, attitude, and total commitment to building Brand Gujarat.

Ratan has rarely missed an opportunity to express his gratitude to Modi and his government for moving unbelievably fast. According to Ratan, things moved so rapidly that had it been possible to transport the plant from Singur to Sanand in a day, the Nano would've been back in production overnight. When asked about moving from Mamata to Modi, Ratan quipped, "There is a bad *M* and a good *M* and we have made the transition."

Pulling off a miracle: Singur to Sanand in a Nanosecond.

The mood in Gujarat was exuberant. In Ahmedabad (Gujarat's business capital), a two-hour drive from Sanand, the streets erupted with whooping, dancing, and bursts of firecrackers. The *Times of India* reported one jubilant reaction after another. "We are on the world map, thanks to the Nano. We are very happy as it is a win-win situation for all. Farmers will gain not just with good land deals but also through better employment opportunities," said Habibkhan Pathan, a resident of Chharodi village. And Murazkhan Pathan, a farmer from Kalana village, said, "We have been charged up since the Nano project was declared as it will transform the entire landscape of Sanand just as the Tatas changed the scenario in Jamshedpur and Mithapur."

The *Times of India* also caught up with business leaders who weighed in. Dr. Bakul Dholakia, former director of the Indian Institute of Management, Ahmedabad, and advisor for the Adani Group, said, "[The Nano plant] will reposition the state in the eyes of foreign investors as an ideal investment destination." Pankaj Patel, chairman and managing director of Zydus Cadila Healthcare, one of the largest pharmaceutical companies in India, said, "It's a unique, world class project that will put Ahmedabad once again on the global map. It will give a major impetus to the city's economy, will bring more ancillary industries here and will increase employment opportunities."

Team Nano was no longer an **orphan** in search of a **home.**

When the decision to move to Gujarat was made public, Ratan Tata told the press, "This is a momentous day for us. We have been through a sad experience, but so quickly we have a new home. We now have a chance [to function] in a conducive and friendly environment." The *Economic Times* asked Ratan if he was relieved. "Well, it's a sense of settlement," he said. "We are not exactly orphans looking for a home."

On November 5, 2008, Tata Motors officially took possession of the land at Sanand. The very next day they were on their way again to building a new facility. It was like climbing Mount Everest all over again. The bad news is that you are physically and emotionally spent. The good news is that you have done it before and have the benefit of leveraging the lessons learned on the first trip.

YES TO A MIND SHIFT

Imagine the mind shift that had to take place when the decision was made to pull out of Singur. Employees had moved their families from all over India to West Bengal to build the Nano plant, vendors had followed Tata Motors to Singur, the people in charge of corporate social responsibility were well into serving the community and establishing relationships with the locals, and with five test cars already off the production line, everything you've been working for, everything you've invested in and sacrificed for, was about to come to fruition.

Then the chairman said, "We are leaving."

The financial loss was staggering, but the emotional loss might have been even more significant. Ramesh Vishwakarma, head of manufacturing in Gujarat, told us, "In that moment in time, the amount of effort we had put into training, construction, erecting equipment, CSR activities, and overcoming the flooding problem made us feel proud that, yes, we had achieved something." Even with the construction of the new Sanand plant going on in the background of our interview, the painfulness of this decision was evident.

Jaydeep Desai, assistant general manager of manufacturing, said, "We were emotionally very attached to West Bengal. We had hope against hope that leaving would not happen."

Even Ratan Tata showed his regret when referring to the political protests in Singur. In true servant-leader fashion Tata explained to the *Times of India* that political opposition and political aspiration should always be subordinated to the better welfare of the country or the state.

"I wonder what we have left behind," he mused. "I am sure West Bengal can attract other investments . . . and we will be as supportive as we can in attracting new investments. But what about the people who had aspirations for jobs . . . will they prosper? Many of them are below subsistence levels—they say so themselves. I mean, who is doing anything to improve their lot?"

The move to Sanand was also going to require a "yes-fast" mind-set from vendors. And that wasn't easy. Component suppliers who were promised huge volumes that hadn't yet materialized were now facing a global economic slowdown. It would be a year or more before the Nano was in full production. Yet Team Nano was relying on these partners to help with additional cost reductions and design modifications. Girish Wagh told Tata's Group Publications, "We wanted to help our vendors come out of this stronger. We wanted to repay their faith in us." So Tata put a compensation package in place for vendors to help absorb the sunk costs.

It's difficult to fathom the disappointment. It's like running a marathon, being only a mile and a half from the finish line with friends and family cheering you on, and then being told, "You can't finish. And to make matters worse, we are going to start running a new one—tomorrow. Except this one is going to require a new set of skills."

Who could blame Team Nano for being physically and emotionally wasted? Who could criticize them for being cynical? For resisting the change and dragging their feet?

But that's not the culture of Tata Motors. Nor does it represent the cultures of Tata's partners. Sixty-some vendors, critical to the success of Nano, committed to moving to Sanand.

YES TO A SACRIFICE

Perhaps the most significant mind shift and the ultimate sacrifice were paid by the families of everyone associated with the plant. Imagine uprooting your family, moving to a new, unfamiliar place, and having your children change schools to start something new. You do it because you believe in the project and the opportunity to be part of one of the most exciting innovations in the world. Now, imagine having to do that all over again.

Yes, there is a sense of relief, having just come through an

The greatest sacrifice came from the families. experience where, every day, you didn't know if you would get to work or come home from work safely. Yes, anxieties are high, everyone's on edge, and it would be nice to put this behind you. But to move all over again? It's almost too much to fathom.

Workers came from all over India—Chennai, Pune, Mumbai, and other places—to help build the plant in Singur. Leaving meant they had to find new homes again, register their children in new schools (many right in the middle of the academic year) again, and establish new routines again. Many working spouses, having just gotten settled, had to leave their jobs and hope they could find employment in their new locations. And it's not like all of the workers got to move as one big family. Some were needed in Pantnagar, where the Nano would be assembled; some were needed in the power train shop in Pune; and many of them went to the new plant in Sanand.

Girish and other members of Team Nano worked long and hard to establish a plan that would disrupt people's lives as little as possible. Unfortunately, in the middle of the crisis it was impossible to meet everyone's needs. Too much had to happen all at once for the project to get back on track.

Of all the major struggles Girish had to face, this one affected him most deeply. He told Tata's Group Publications, "For us workers, the shifting was easier than it was for the families. We were going to a similar kind of work environment, meeting the same people, but *their* lives changed completely."

Girish is a consummate professional, but he's also human. In one of our final interviews with him, it was obvious that the emotional stress of this experience had left an indelible mark—the mark of a caring leader.

As is always the case, the most powerful form of leadership and influence is by example. Although he would never mention it, we suspect that Girish's family sacrificed as much as any of the families.

How could you seemingly be everywhere at once for two years or more and not pay a significant price?

Somehow in the midst of this incredible transition, Team Nano, families and all, held together. They, too, were willing to say yes. Girish estimates that they lost only 1 to 2 percent of their people during the move.

YES TO A SENSE OF URGENCY

Team Nano had one critical piece of data when it started construction on the plant in Sanand that it did not have when building the Singur plant: demand.

The unveiling in Delhi gave the company a sense that the demand for the Nano would be strong, but it wasn't until after the car was launched in Mumbai that they really knew they had a tiger by the tail. We will unpack this further for you in the next chapter. For now, suffice it to say that demand created a heightened sense of urgency. People had to be action oriented, but their actions had to be focused on critical issues central to getting the new plant up and operational as fast as possible. The sense of loss coming out of Singur was quickly overshadowed by a pressing need to meet the expectations of frenzied customers. It was also being driven by a renewed vision for building the best automobile manufacturing plant in India.

As Jaydeep Desai pointed out, "Now we know the demand, we know the future, and we know we have to make things happen very fast because the customer is not going to wait. So for everyone in the system the orientation to delivering things on time was very high."

Surya Banerjee, an assistant plant manager in Singur and one of the last to leave, quickly got engaged with the mission to rebuild in Sanand. "The whole world was watching us," he remembered, "and that was a big motivation. The world was excited about the Nano. People were anxious to get their hands on it. It was good pressure. We had something to work for."

> It takes twenty-one to
> twenty-three months
> to erect an auto
> manufacturing plant
> in India. It took Team
> Nano fourteen months.

The activities to bring the new plant online happened simultaneously. While building construction was going on in one area, people were unloading equipment, dismantling huge crates, and fabricating machines and structures in other areas. As soon as one part of the building was complete, people were poised, ready to move in and install the necessary equipment. It takes approximately twenty-one to twenty-three months to erect an auto manufacturing plant in India. It took Team Nano fourteen months. This was the result of radical collaboration between construction companies, suppliers, the government of Gujarat, and Tata Motors—all of whom had a "yes-fast" orientation.

Keep in mind that one major project—building the world's cheapest car—immediately turned into five projects: disassembling the Singur plant, building the Sanand plant, manufacturing the Nano at the Pune and Pantnagar plants to meet initial demand, sourcing parts from all over the world, and working with vendors (who had also established a home at the Singur plant) to make the move to Sanand. Then consider the fact that while all of this was happening, Team Nano was making engineering changes on the car and working diligently to perfect its design.

Desai was impressed with Girish Wagh, who seemingly was everywhere at once. "He was in Pune, Singur, Pantnagar, Sanand, and Mumbai," Desai told us. "He was here and there and he always looked fresh; he never looked tired. He always kept smiling even though he must have felt a huge amount of pressure."

What Team Nano accomplished is even more astounding when

you consider the infrastructure failures in India. Nirmalya Kumar reports in *India's Global Powerhouses* that on average, in India, it takes 225 days to obtain a building permit, 16 days to clear exports through customs (compared with 6 days in China), and 4 years to enforce a contract. India is also known for acute power shortages, which force many companies into the power generation business.

According to Kumar, "Captive power costs 50 to 100 percent more than that from the grid. Unreliable power supply and power outages are estimated to cost Indian businesses 7 percent of sales, six times that in China."

One has to admire Team Nano's ingenuity and passion to succeed when faced with these bureaucratic obstacles.

YES TO NEW SKILLS

Tata Motors had the skills and experience to erect a manufacturing plant, but taking one down and moving it was a whole new adventure. Do you move it by sea, rail, or on the roads? After getting numerous bids from transporters, the team found that the most cost-effective way to do it was using trucks.

(The authors)

Transporting expensive equipment by truck took on a whole new meaning when it was done on Indian roads.

Meticulous planning went into the move. When you are dismantling a giant robot or stamping machine, how do you do it? What number do you give its parts for traceability? How do you clean and pack it so that it won't be damaged with vibration or while bouncing over potholes? What packing materials do you use? What equipment needs antirust protection, and how do you apply it so it doesn't damage the machine's functionality? Where do you store it while the new plant is under construction?

The answers to these questions came from talking with equipment manufacturers and vendors. It also required many of the engineers to go back to school—in this case the Internet—to get reacquainted with the basics of physics and chemistry.

Ramesh Vishwakarma, head of manufacturing, was the person responsible for moving the plant with lightning speed. He told us that Team Nano literally wrote the book on dismantling equipment and establishing antirust procedures for transit. Every part was meticulously tagged, photographed, and then loaded onto trucks. At any given time Vishwakarma said he could track the trucks carrying equipment and find the part he was looking for. As you can imagine, it required tremendous planning and discipline to ensure that when a crate was opened, it had the right machinery and the right materials in the right condition.

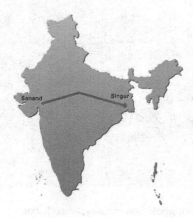

"We were used to installation, but we were not used to dismantling and transportation," Jaydeep Desai told us. "So we had to learn fast. Literally, for the first six months we were converted into a logistics company. Nobody had a background in logistics, but the way people took up this challenge and contributed, thanks to Mr. Vishwakarma, was amazing."

Imagine the logistical nightmare

of dismantling a plant in Singur, moving it twenty-one hundred kilometers (thirteen hundred miles), and recommissioning it in Sanand. This is roughly the equivalent of moving it from Milan to Stockholm, Melbourne to Brisbane, Los Angeles to Chicago, or Sapporo to Hiroshima—except you are doing it on dilapidated Indian roads. Just to put this in perspective, a trucker in the U.S. can haul a load approximately a thousand miles in a day. In India that same load would take four to five days.

(The authors)

Imagine loading and unloading thirty-two hundred trucks like this and then keeping track of every piece of equipment. It was a gargantuan task.

Vishwakarma recounted a meeting in which Ravi Kant and Prakash Telang asked him how many trucks it would take to transport all of the equipment. In many organizations that would have

Every piece of equipment was tagged, tracked, and staged according to when it was going to be installed. Here robots are being assembled in the new Sanand plant.

required a day or two to assemble a committee, a few days to study it and develop a plan, a week to put it in a report to management, and two weeks later you have an answer. Vishwakarma did quick calculations on the spot, conferred with a colleague, who immediately did his own calculations, and then declared that it would take three thousand trucks. All in all, it took the team thirty-two hundred trailer-trucks less than four months to move the equipment from Singur to Sanand.

YES TO EMPOWERMENT

When one project turns into five, how do you accomplish the objectives with the same team and the same number of people? You put people on multiple fronts, have them work simultaneously, and trust them to execute the plan. But that means you have to say yes to empowerment. The move from Singur to Sanand created an opportunity for many team members to step into the breach and do things they didn't even know they were capable of doing. In the face of a seemingly insurmountable task, champions rise out of a deeply rooted belief that their leaders have in them.

"We had unflinching support from the top," Desai told us. "Mr. Ravi Kant, Mr. Telang, and Mr. Tata said, 'Whatever you need, you come to us, and we will see that it is done.' So all of the decisions were made with electrifying speed because they had faith in Mr. Vishwakarma. And they kept that faith irrespective of all of the challenges we faced."

We've all seen scenarios where a huge assignment is delegated to a team without the commensurate authority. Someone questioning you every time you make a decision drags you down and wears you out. It turns up the volume on fear, and fear paralyzes people. That's not empowerment, that's not "yes-fast," and that's not the way to stimulate the resolve and creativity needed to pull off a heroic task.

For example, it normally takes approximately thirty months to set up a paint shop in a traditional manufacturing facility, at a cost of more than $60 million. Team Nano set up the one in Singur in just eight months for less than $11 million. It was a phenomenal accomplishment.

Now, Jaydeep Desai and his colleagues from the manufacturing and planning group had the complicated task of shutting down the paint shop in Singur. Paint and chemicals, if not neutralized and treated properly, create a hazard for the environment. The challenge was keeping the paint alive by circulating it for three to four hours a day. They figured out how to do this for four months until the entire shop could be transported.

Sometimes people who have the authority to do something heroic fail to run with it. They don't want to be accountable for the consequences of their decisions. They pass the buck, throw things over the firewall, or put other people through unnecessary revisions while they try to get the perfect plan. Decisions dragging on endlessly kill the creative spirit of the organization and make it sluggish.

In the move to Sanand there was simply no time or margin for such indecisiveness and procrastination. Tata Motors executives said yes to a team that had no experience in dismantling a plant. But it was a team that had already proven it could say yes to getting the job done while navigating uncharted waters.

YES TO OWNING IT

Imagine being given the responsibility to commission a brand-new, state-of-the-art manufacturing plant. You do it in a record eleven months—from recruiting three thousand people to constructing the buildings to installing equipment—for a product that is wildly successful. You are two years into production, you've worked out the kinks, and things are going very smoothly. Then you get a call asking if a part of your plant could be transformed to build a new, radically different product.

The person who received that call was Prasann Chobe, the head of Tata Motors' Ace truck plant in Pantnagar. As we mentioned, with the decision to pull out of Singur final and Nanomania in full force, Team Nano had to come up with an interim plan for fulfilling the demand, and they had to do it fast.

Chobe was asked if it was possible to take one of three distinct welding shops on the Pantnagar campus and transform it into a production line for the Nano. Producing 750 Ace units a day, Prasann Chobe's young engineers had their minds around truck production, not a small passenger car, so the Nano was completely new to them. But the question itself was a stamp of endorsement to Prasann and his team. It validated what they had been able to do in getting the Ace plant up and running with unprecedented speed.

Nanos make their way through the assembly line that Prasann Chobe and his team helped build at the Pantnagar plant in Uttarakhand.

You can imagine the pride people felt in stepping into the breach, making a contribution, and moving the project forward.

"We had a young, charged team," Prasann explained. "We had put up a plant in eleven months, which was definitely a much tougher task than bringing in the Nano. This was an opportunity for us to prove that we could do it in such a short time. It required a lot of engineering input to make the necessary changes, but the entire team was sure that we would be able to do it."

Give people a series of challenges, give them an opportunity for adventure, say yes to their entrepreneurial spirit, and your business will become their business.

The Pantnagar engineers quickly locked arms with the ERC team in Pune, who helped them understand the Nano as well as what would be required to change out equipment and ramp up a production line. In less than four months, Team Nano had produced five cars in Pantnagar. At the time of our visit they were producing one hundred cars a day and working toward a maximum output of fifty thousand cars a year.

> # Give people an **opportunity** for adventure, and your business will **become** their **business.**

A parking lot of Nanos at the Pantnagar plant, waiting to be delivered to their eager owners.

Pantnagar was chosen to assemble the high-profile Nano for many reasons, not the least of which was Chobe's ability to build a team of players who were willing to do whatever it took. When they were called upon to bridge the gap, their answer was yes. Then it was full speed ahead.

YES TO CHANGING LIVES

In his interview with the *Economic Times*, Ratan Tata described his feelings about finding a home in Sanand: "We look forward to the new location with a great deal of enthusiasm. We are looking not just at manufacturing a car, but being a good corporate citizen as well." By now you understand that those were not just words; they were words backed with action.

As with Singur, Tata's CSR team hit the ground running even before the first bulldozers were excavating the site at Sanand. The company selected twenty villages within a six mile radius of the plant. The vision is to improve the quality of life and standard of living for a population of approximately forty thousand people. Specifically Tata aims to make the villages self-reliant by collaborating with the residents on various development programs.

(Tata Motors)

This map shows the twenty villages around the Sanand plant that are the focus of Tata Motors' CSR initiatives.

The community needs assessment revealed a lack of sanitation and health in the area as a big problem. The villagers also want to set up small businesses and improve their agricultural practices. The CSR team also learned that there is a strong penchant for entrepreneurial activities within the community.

Based on these needs, what has the company accomplished since taking possession of the land in Sanand on November 5, 2008? For starters, more than thirty-four hundred patients have been treated through mobile health clinics, and 134 health awareness camps have been conducted with a special emphasis on maternal and child health care.

Tata is also working with the villagers to raise the standards of

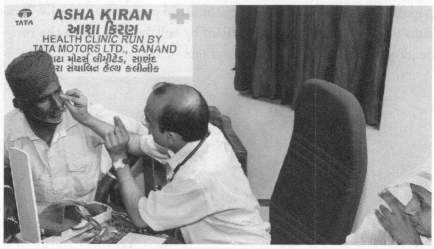

One of many mobile health clinics that bring prevention and curative health services to the villages.

sanitation by helping them understand the importance of cleanliness, personal hygiene, and new sanitary practices. Currently only 20 percent of the households in the project area have sanitary facilities. So far, the company has helped construct 250 low-cost toilets, and 1,300 more are slated to cover 100 percent of the homes in all twenty villages.

Here's what one woman had to say about improving the sanitary conditions in her village:

"As there were no toilets in our village, I had to wake up at early hours and stay up late at night and walk long distances to go to the fields. With Nano factory coming to the nearby area, several awareness camps were organized on health and sanitation. First, we resisted since we were used to our routine, but after several meetings with 'Nanowale' [CSR employees and the doctor who came from the Nano factory], we began to realize that sanitary habits are important for our own health. I even took my husband for some of these meetings and he, too, agreed for the need of a toilet in our house. Then, the question was expenses. We, being from a poor family, could not afford to build a toilet. The CSR team told us about how the company collaborated with the government to bring the Total Sanitation Campaign to our village. Now I have a toilet in my house at a cost that we can easily afford. I can sleep for extra hours and am glad that I do not have to go out in the open!"

In partnership with the government and the Sumant Moolgaokar Development Foundation, Tata is bringing safe and potable drinking water to every village. The partnership plans to provide reverse osmosis plants to all twenty villages.

In the area of education, the CSR team at Sanand is working to mitigate the dropout rate by conducting counseling sessions with teachers, students, and guardians. Conducted in partnership with the State Education Board, the meetings are designed to introduce innovative ways of teaching to make learning more interesting, organize extracurricular activities, and conduct career counseling for the students. So far, ninety primary school teachers have been trained to improve their teaching. The goal is to get teachers from all 112 primary schools of the Sanand Block involved in the training.

Additionally Tata Motors is upgrading the facilities—benches, desks, and teaching tools—in each of the 112 primary schools. Overall, more than ten thousand students will benefit from this program.

To help people throughout the community become more employable, Tata is partnering with Industrial Training Institutes (ITI) to bring technical skills to more than one thousand students who want to go into the automotive sector or want to start businesses in vehicle maintenance and repair. Tata has provided vocational skills

More than ten thousand students in primary schools like this one will benefit from Tata Motors' initiative to upgrade facilities. Students will no longer have to sit on the floor or meet in the street to learn.

training in various trades to more than sixty youth and plans to train five hundred more.

The company is partnering with the Gujarat Knowledge Society and Education Department to conduct computer training for women who want to become employable. And seven self-help groups of women have been trained in food processing, sewing, embroidery, and nursery. In the next five years Tata will train more than one thousand women through this initiative.

For Tata, employability is also about equipping people to become entrepreneurs. When Tata Motors was still in Singur, the CSR team wanted to set up young drivers in their own businesses. The idea was to offer them a loan on very easy terms to buy an Ace truck so they could transport people and goods commuting between Kolkata and Singur—a twenty-five-mile trip. The problem was that people in Singur were more interested in getting jobs than starting businesses.

When Tata came to Sanand, they discovered a strong entrepreneurial desire among the people. M. B. Paralkar told us that the first person to volunteer for the program was a young man. He bought an Ace truck and started driving his own shuttle service. Pretty soon, he was back, asking for a loan on another vehicle. He had hired a driver and was expanding his business. "I am quite sure that the opportunity in Gujarat will be taken by many more people," M. B. said. "Our job is to give them the right perspective, to show them that they can do it." The CSR team believes that one enthusiastic entrepreneur like this young man will have a contagious effect on others. That's how you move beyond employability to sustainability.

The CSR team has brought a number of environmental initiatives to Sanand. In an effort to enhance the green cover in the region, it is engaged in extensive tree plantation. Imagine a dust-barren schoolyard being transformed into a lush shaded area. They are not there yet, but this is what the students in one of the nearby schools are doing. Each child has planted a sapling and is responsible for nurturing and growing it—even on weekends, when the school is not open.

Through its massive tree plantation drive, Tata has planted more than five thousand saplings and has plans for one hundred thousand more trees over the next five years. Increasing agricultural productivity is another initiative in which Tata Motors is involved. The company partners with experts who help farmers acquire the best crops and the best farming methods for their land. In partnership with Rallis India, more than sixty farmers have been trained in multiple cropping, hybrid seed, and effective use of fertilizers, all with the intent to increase crop yields. The goal is to raise farm productivity by 20 percent in all twenty villages by 2012.

Children transform a barren playground by planting saplings. Each child is responsible for the health and well-being of a tree.

Finally the company is helping villagers understand that indoor air pollution can be as fatal as smoking. Approximately 75 percent of Indian homes use chullahs (indoor stoves that burn wood, charcoal, twigs, leaves, and agriculture residues) for heating and cooking. This makes families susceptible to chronic obstructive pulmonary disease. The CSR team encourages the use and construction of smokeless chullahs. Smokeless chullahs have been constructed in two villages, and the objective is to have a smokeless chullah in every household in every village in the near future.

Tata says yes to changing lives by saying yes to a lot of partnerships with organizations (government and private) that share the same vision. While we were in the village of Rupavati, southwest of Sanand, the village leader organized a town hall meeting in which we were able to talk with the villagers. When we asked, "What has it meant to have a company like Tata Motors help you achieve your dreams?" one of the village elders used the term *nirmal gaon*, which means "the ideal village." He said that Tata has helped them develop a picture of what they can become and been a catalyst in giving them access to government programs like the ones mentioned above.

We also talked with twenty-five women who were part of a food-processing cooperative. They were beautifully dressed in colorful saris and adorned in gold jewelry. It was quite obvious that they were very happy to be earning money. They might be very poor, but they have an elevated sense of dignity and pride because they now have the know-how to contribute to supporting their families.

So as you can see, in addition to creating ten thousand new jobs directly and indirectly, the new Nano plant is having a dramatic effect on people's lives in and around Sanand. And Tata Motors is just getting started.

YES TO A BRAND-NEW PLANT

On June 2, 2010, shortly before 1:00 p.m., Chief Minister Modi and Ratan Tata drove a sunshine yellow Nano off the assembly line and inaugurated the new plant at Sanand.

Built in a record time of just fourteen months, the $417 million facility integrates the Nano plant, spread over 725 acres, and an adjacent vendor park spread over 375 acres. When the plant phases up to full production, it will build 250,000 cars a year, and if the market demands, it has the capacity to produce 350,000 Nanos a year with some modifications.

Visit the lake at the Sanand plant (left) in five years, and it will look a lot more like the lake at the plant in Pune (right) while providing the same beauty and functionality. That's the power of a bold vision.

"Life must be understood backwards.
It must be lived forward."
Soren Kierkegaard

The intelligent automation plant or smart factory is equipped with energy-efficient motors, sophisticated robotics, and variable frequency drives and sensors to predict bottlenecks and breakdowns in the plant before they happen. The plant can automatically order parts from suppliers as needed and has a genealogy program that tracks every part in the car. So if there is a defective part, Tata Motors has the ability to track down the car that houses the component. The state-of-the-art facility can also measure and monitor carbon levels, uses solar energy for lighting, and will eventually have the capability to tap into smart electrical grids and align production with the most economical and robust sources of energy available.

(Tata Motors)

In a celebratory moment that symbolized the end of a long journey, Ratan Tata and the chief minister of Gujarat, Narendra Modi, inaugurated Tata Motors' brand-new Nano plant at Sanand.

In many ways the inaugural ceremony signified the end of a trip that was as heroic as the development of the car itself. Through floods, escalating materials costs, and protests that erupted into violence that threatened people's lives, Team Nano showed the grit and determination to make another part of the dream come true. The People's Car had made its way from the mind of a dreamer to its home in Sanand. In the midst of all this heroism, the Nano was also making its way to a launch in Mumbai.

How does your organization stack up on the twelve characteristics of a "yes-fast" culture? A "yes-fast" culture . . .

1. anticipates and plans for future scenarios instead of waiting and reacting.
2. is known for organizational flexibility instead of rigidity.
3. majors in opportunity-led change instead of crisis-led change (both exist in companies that Nanovate, but the former dominates).
4. asks, "What if?" and "Why not?" instead of "Yeah, but . . ."
5. redeploys talent where needed. It chooses being fast instead of fighting over the best players.
6. chooses cross-functional collaboration over tribalism, silo building, and turf protection.
7. is decisive; it does not procrastinate and pass the buck.
8. has people who think and act like owners instead of being complacent and indifferent.
9. has people who take initiative, not orders.
10. employs people who assume responsibility for developing new knowledge and new skills instead of waiting for the company to offer training.
11. has leaders who trust people to get it done instead of resorting to command and control.
12. establishes a record of constant, ongoing experimentation rather than perfect it, then try it.

QUESTIONS

- What is your organization's dominant default response to new ideas, new ways of doing things, and unusual customer requests? Yes or no?
- When crisis or disruption dictates the need to move with speed, how quick and agile is your company?
- When they are faced with adversity and major setbacks, how much encouragement and support do your leaders extend to the rest of the organization?
- When they are faced with doing something they've never done before (think dismantling an entire plant), are your people reticent or willing to do whatever it takes—to learn, adapt, and move?
- If Team Nano and Narendra Modi's government are the benchmarks, is your culture adaptive?

TWENTY-TWO
Now You Can

The story of the human race is the story of men
and women selling themselves short.

ABRAHAM MASLOW

On March 23, 2009, we flew to Mumbai for the much-awaited
official launch of the Nano. When we arrived at the pavilion
a short distance from the famous Gateway of India, the first things
we noticed were rows upon rows of trucks with satellite disks on top
representing media from all over the world.

Even though the Nano had been revealed a year earlier in Delhi
and in Geneva, camera crews stationed themselves on the tops of
buildings across the street in an attempt to get an advance look at what
was going to happen.

Tata Motors had taken what looked like a vacant block and
turned it into an elaborate stage with a giant ball, the size of a hot

air balloon, in the middle. As the three thousand people flooded into this outdoor arena, the place felt like a rock concert with fans joyfully anticipating the appearance of U2.

(The authors)

Press from all over the world showed up to capture one of the most awaited product launches in history.

As the lights went down, a huge wall covering the full length of the stage was transformed into a giant video screen. The Nano story was about to be told in yet another entertaining and awe-inspiring way.

The opening video captured the attention of the audience with a compelling narrative that put the Nano in a league with some of the boldest accomplishments in history.

Here are some still shots that capture the video along with the narrator's words:

It is said that behind every great answer lies a greater question. And more often than not, that question starts with "Can you?"

"Can you?" is a challenge not just to yourself, but to all that has been labeled "impossible."

"Can you?" incites you to rebel against logic, against the norm, against all odds.

"Can you?" is the journey of exploring possibilities, of discovering solutions.

Can you seize the extra in every ordinary? The reality in every dream?

It was to the question: "Can you see in the dark?" that Edison answered with the lightbulb.

"Can you be on top of the world?" was the question that conquered Everest.

And, "Can you go beyond?" put a man on the moon.

(Tata Motors)

"Can you be stubborn enough to win?" got us our freedom.

"Can you roam the world, but still be connected?" was the birth of a cell phone.

"Can you work at the speed of your thoughts?" gave us the computer.

"Can you make the world hum your song?" put India in the limelight.

(Tata Motors)

Even the Nano dream started with "Can you?"

(Tata Motors)

"Can you imagine a car just three meters long, seating a family in absolute comfort?"

"Can you have the smallest four-door car as safe as the big ones?"

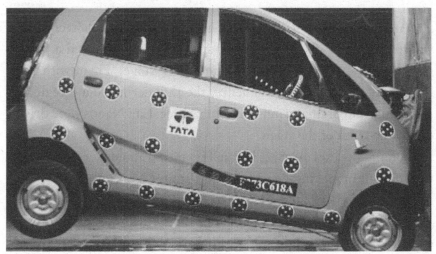

(Tata Motors)

"Can you have a car that delivers fuel efficiency bordering that of a two-wheeler? Can you imagine a car that impacts the environment the least? Can you imagine a car that breaks all class barriers?"

And, "Can you imagine a car that will change the world—again?"

And to all these "Can yous" we just have one thing to say, "Now you can!"

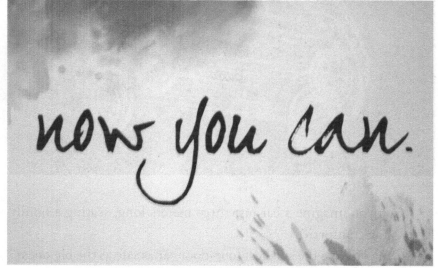

now you can.

(Tata Motors)

As the last line of this inspiring video clip was delivered, the wall on which it was shown slowly split apart and revealed a pair of distinctly Nano headlights on a pitch-black stage. Then, with laser lights swirling around the audience, the thundering sound of drums pounding, and dramatic music blaring, three Tata Nanos were driven out to the front of the stage.

Joining the cars onstage, Ratan Tata talked about working against tradition and breaking many barriers through a period of time when most people believed it could not be done.

"This is really a reflection of tremendous teamwork, not only to conceive the car, but now under the difficult circumstances of moving a plant, building another plant, and also, putting in an interim measure to provide the market with a car at an earlier date."

(Tata Motors)

He then invited Team Nano to the stage and continued, "Ladies and gentlemen, this team that is here with us are the people that defied conventional wisdom, broke those barriers, and wrote a new equation for the transport."

After resounding applause, Ravi Kant added, "It's been some time in coming. As you know, we have gone through very difficult periods. We've gone through many ups and downs. But I think it shows the determination, the grit, and the 'never say die' attitude of this entire Nano team."

A great story ends with something memorable. Ratan Tata wrapped up by saying, "In looking back those six years, you reminisce about how many people disbelieved in what you set out to do. And I'm sure many of the Nano team members felt the same way. And yet after five or six years, you end up with something that tells you that whatever you undertake, if you really pursue it, you probably will make it.

Nothing is really impossible if you set your minds to it. I think what we have done is given the country an affordable car. A major part of our country consists of young citizens. And I hope in some ways, directly or indirectly, we can dedicate this car that has been developed by a team of young people, to the youth of India, to inspire them to believe that we can do what most countries felt could not be done."

Then Ratan Tata invited everyone to the adjacent pavilion to experience firsthand the production cars. For the next couple of hours the place was abuzz with people taking pictures of friends and colleagues as they pushed their way into the Nanos on display.

Between dignitaries, invited guests, and the media, people had to wait in line to interact with the star of the show.

It was an event that made an indelible impression on the guests for several reasons. First, it retold the Nano story in a fresh, new way, and it invited the audience to a new way of life. It showed how the Nano opens up undreamed-of possibilities and says to the people of India, "Now you can."

Second, it wasn't just another product launch. The event touched people at an emotional level. You couldn't help feeling a sense of exhilaration for Girish Wagh and Team Nano. It was like watching an Olympic athlete step up to the podium to receive a gold medal, knowing the hard work and painstaking sacrifices that got him or her there.

Finally, you couldn't help feeling a sense of pride for the Indian people.

Perhaps the late C. K. Prahalad, champion of "the bottom of the pyramid," said it best: "The Nano lays to rest the skeptics who as recently as five years ago assumed that India cannot compete in manufacturing. Yes, Indian engineers given the right challenge and leadership can outinnovate and outengineer others. Seldom does a single product introduction challenge the received wisdom in the industry so radically."

THE LINE FOR A NANO STARTS HERE

"A design isn't finished until somebody is using it."
Brenda Laurel

On April 9, 2009, after a six-month delay caused by the events in Singur, the Tata Nano went on sale. In one thousand cities around India, at more than thirty thousand dealerships, banks, and stores, thousands of people lined up to buy the application form, for which they plunked down Rs. 300 (about $6 at the time). With only one thousand Nanos on display at Tata dealers around India, most of those people were paying to order a car they'd never seen before.

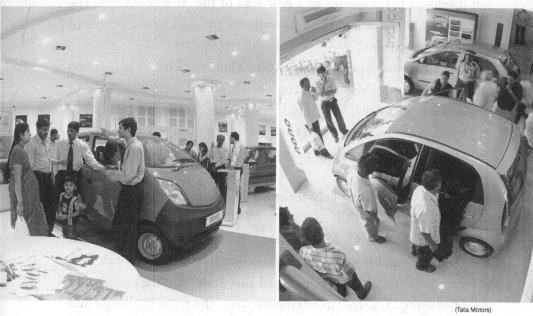

(Tata Motors)

Is it a car or a rock star? The crowds swarmed the Nano to touch it and see if it was real.

In the dealerships, it was chaos. In Srinagar, showroom manager Ghulam Nabi Baba told a reporter that the phone hadn't stopped ringing for months with people wanting to know when they could buy one. Now that the time had come, there were traffic jams in the street and people lined up outside. Dealers had to bring in security guards to keep order and hire temporary sales staff to handle the flow of orders. At K. B. Motors in Kolkata, director Shilpa Kedia told the press that they had recruited ten salespeople just to handle the rush. "We are expecting a huge turnout," he said.

In Mumbai, an eighty-two-year-old former police commissioner placed an order and told reporters he used to drive a scooter but now wanted to drive a car. And a ninety-six-year-old woman—India's first woman press photographer—sold her fifty-five-year-old Fiat to pay the deposit on a Nano.

(Tata Motors)

Potential buyers lined up outside Wasan Motors in Mumbai to book their Nanos. Dealers had to take on extra help to handle more than four hundred thousand applicants.

In the first three days, more than fifty-one thousand applications were sold. By the time they stopped taking bookings on April 25, more than four hundred thousand people had purchased forms.

Buying an application didn't get you a car. The next step was to submit the form along with the booking fee.

And here's where the story gets really interesting. Everybody knew that because the new Nano plant in Sanand wasn't complete yet, there wouldn't be nearly enough cars to go around. So Tata Motors was running a lottery: you signed up, paid your money, and took your chances on getting one of the first one hundred thousand cars being offered. It might take two years, but you paid your money.

A ninety-six-year-old photographer sold her fifty-five-year-old Fiat to pay the deposit on a Nano.

All of it, or just about.

That's right. To book your Nano, you had to put down an amount from Rs. 95,000 to 140,000, depending on the model. Some people paid cash, but most had to take a car loan from one of the thirty banks participating. And if your income was only a couple of hundred dollars a month, that was a big step to take.

How many people would do that?

The answer, once all the bookings were in, was 206,703. In just sixteen days, more than 200,000 people paid about $2,000 each to get on the waiting list for a Nano. And if they could have driven their car off the lot immediately, we suspect that number would have been two or three times higher. Quite reasonably many people decided to wait until production caught up with demand. For those who didn't get a lottery allocation, Tata offered 8.5 percent interest on their money. And if they waited more than a year, that went up to 8.75 percent.

Parthasarthy Guha went to see the car in Kolkata when it was displayed and loved it. "[For the] last 30 years," he posted on the Nano Web site, "we haven't [had] any car in my family. In 2005, I purchased a Honda Scooter. Tatas understood our problems and made this car for scooter owners like us." He paid his money for the lottery and then got an allocation more than a year away. No problem—he was thrilled. In fact, his eighty-six-year-old grandmother told him he would get a Nano because it was meant for people like him.

Of course, once the dust settled and people realized their place in line put their car as much as two years away, they had the right to cancel and get their money back, and as many as 10 to 15 percent did.

Still, it was the most pre-preproduction orders on any car in history. To put it in perspective, the Ford Mustang was one of the most successful car launches ever, selling more than half a million cars in the first year of production in 1964 and 1965. But how many of those people would have paid 90 percent of the full price in advance, knowing they might have to wait as much as two years to see their cars? We suspect the number would have been far less than two hundred thousand.

The State Bank of India (SBI) has had a long-standing relationship with the Tata Group and played a key role in the booking

It was the most pre-preproduction orders on any car in automotive history.

process. Anup Banerji, managing director and Group executive of SBI, said he was initially worried about volume: first, in terms of traffic congestion, and second, how the bank would handle the number of Nano bookings.

"I was in Kalma Chowk area [a landmark intersection in Mumbai known for horrendous traffic jams] and it struck me, if Nano comes, then how will we manage the congestion? That was my first impression." Banerji continued, "Nano also has helped us run a drill on ourselves internally, to see how robust our cash management systems are. We collected two hundred thousand applications. That means we got the people to come to three thousand SBI branches and put their money there. We pooled it all together and passed it on to the Tatas. So it tested our systems and we came out on top."

Banerji went on to tell us that the Nano experience has become a certificate of credibility for the bank. When a potential client questions whether the bank has the horsepower to handle extraordinarily large volumes of transactions, his response is, "I will do it."

On June 23, 2009, the list of lottery winners was released on tatanano.com. First on the list was Ashok Raghunath Vichare, a fifty-nine-year-old customs officer in Mumbai.

"I am very happy; I can't say how happy I am," his wife, Shaila, told reporters as she got in the car and drove away with her family, paparazzi on scooters following them and snapping pictures.

(Tata Motors)

Ratan Tata hands over the keys to the very first Nano family.

Vichare was asked to write his impressions of the car after he'd had it a month. Here's what he said:

My life has not been the same ever since. Even after a month, the interest from media and public has continued. People, especially children, rush to the car on traffic signals just to shake hands with me or take photographs of the vehicle. I can understand their curiosity. Before booking the car, I went to the showroom three times to see the car from inside. I realized that although the car looks compact from outside, it is quite roomy inside. I had a look at all the interiors, seats, engine location several times. My daughter chose the silver color for the car. Although, I could not take a test drive, the Tata name was enough to inspire confidence in me to book the car.

When we caught up with Vichare in Mumbai two months after he took delivery of his car, he and his family were still glowing with enthusiasm.

"I think Mr. Ratan Tata is a social person. He thinks for the social welfare of the common person. Hundreds of thousands of people can now afford a car," he told us. "There are so many friends of mine who want to purchase it from me. So I refuse and say this is an antique piece for me. This is the first in the world, so I cannot give it to anybody."

We also talked with nineteen-year-old Jigar Parikh in Mumbai, who won an early spot in the Nano lottery. Jigar told us that his whole family has always been big fans of the Tatas, so they have always owned at least one Tata car. When he was informed he would be one of the first to own the Nano, nobody believed it.

When we asked if he thought the Nano would appeal to a lot of people his age, he responded, "Parents are concerned. Students like us need to travel here and there, so parents who can afford it would rather go for a car than a bike because it is much safer. I think we all know that bikes are much more convenient, but when you buy a car

(Tata Motors)

When they drove the first Nano off the lot, Ashok Raghunath Vichare and his family became instant superstars. Or was it their Nano?

in India, you know, it is pretty much like, 'Oh, you got a car!' You get that dignity and that proud feeling."

In the months that followed, everyone who drove the Nano had a similar experience. *Autocar* magazine launched an ambitious journey, driving the car all the way across northern India, tracing the symbolic route of the Nano's journey from the abandoned plant in Singur to the new plant in Sanand.

Everywhere they went, they found the same excitement and curiosity. Everywhere they went, people surrounded the car. Policemen volunteered to guide them. Motorists gave them the right of way. Everywhere they went, "the cute-as-a-button Nano [drew] more attention than even a Porsche."

Their experience reflected that of every Nano reviewer and owner we talked to: "The car has proven to be trouble free as well as very efficient all through. Initial fuel economy figures in Mumbai's stop-start traffic also tell us that this car is easily the most fuel-efficient petrol car in India. . . . The Nano's compact dimensions are a boon in the narrow gullies. The dashboard snoops can hold an amazing amount of knick-knacks."

They were surprised at how comfortable and user-friendly the Nano was: "Before the trip began, we had visions of aching lumbar and monotonously puttering down the road as an autorickshaw blitz us. Things turned out a little bit different. No complaints from the spine. And the Nano, in a manner, is fun to drive."

(Tata Motors)

Girish Wagh explaining the wiper to Kevin Freiberg. Kevin is over six feet tall and found plenty of room in the backseat as well as behind the wheel.

That's just what we found when we drove the Nano on the test track at the ERC in Pune. Far from being the rattletrap some Americans and Europeans predicted it would be—made of bamboo and canvas, held together with twine and sticky notes—it was solid and well built. On the road, it has a surprisingly springy feeling, a sense that the car can handle potholed roads. It's fun to drive. It has a zippy, can't-stop-me feel that suggests you can go anywhere—the Nano has held its own on the highest mountain passes of the Himalayas.

The quick steering and amazingly narrow turning circle add to the active feeling. As cars have become heavier and tires wider, people have forgotten what it feels like to drive a light and maneuverable car. It's fun and toylike in the best sense of the word, meaning it feels playful and eager.

No, it's not fast, but it's fast enough. Anyone who ever drove an older VW Beetle will remember the routine of driving with your foot either all the way on or all the way off the throttle. And if a Nano ever gets out of city traffic, that's how you'll drive the Nano, too. It begs for it.

But in city traffic, with its narrow track and ability to slip through tight places, the Nano is really in its element. Vinoo Mammen, the chairman of MRF, the Indian tire company that makes the Nano's tires, bought one for the company, thinking his engineers would like to study it. But he found himself using it for his daily commute. Speaking to the *Hindu*, he said, "When you are in the Nano, you have a sense of being on the move. While the big cars are stuck, Nano always manages to find a way out."

One thing we found remarkable was how many Nano owners are packing the family in the car and hitting the road. Although the Nano was conceived as an alternative to putting the family on a scooter for trips close to home, Nano owners are taking road trips in surprising numbers. Sunil and Rinku Budwani of Pune took a driving tour all around the state of Maharastra, covering more than five hundred miles in their racing red Nano. "I drove it in the worst of road conditions without any problem. It drives perfectly with a great pickup. It is spacious, good-looking, and a value-for-money car."

Ravindra Joshi, a retired water works engineer and proud new Nano owner, told us, "It is a dream to have such a vehicle, and it is a gift by the Tatas to our country. I travel throughout India by so many means: by railways, by roads, and we often go to Shirdi [a very sacred and important place of pilgrimage in India, approximately 266 kilometers or 165 miles from Mumbai]. So this car will be an asset to us as we move from here to there."

Even Ashok Vichare, the very first owner, wasted no time getting his car on the road. He said, "Recently, I took my family from Mumbai to Pune in the car, via the express highway. I drove up to a top speed of sixty miles per hour. The vehicle was completely stable throughout the journey. Overall, the Nano meets all my requirements. The suspension ensures a smooth ride. The engine makes almost no noise. The headlights are powerful and effective for night driving. On the highway I got a fuel efficiency of twenty-four kilometers per liter."

That's 56.45 miles per gallon, if you were wondering, on a freeway with a family of four or five. It was a kind of pilgrimage, taking the Nano home to the place of its development and birth. Not a long drive for a family from Mumbai, but quite a journey for the idea for the little car with dignity that was born on a rainy afternoon in Bangalore, all those years before.

"While the big cars are stuck, Nano always manages to find a way out."

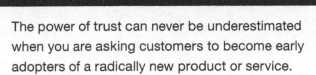

NANOBITE

The power of trust can never be underestimated when you are asking customers to become early adopters of a radically new product or service.

Many people put deposits down on the Nano, sight unseen, because of their trust in the Tatas and the Group's reputation for integrity.

Many people bought the Nano because of what it symbolizes—concern for the social welfare of others.

Many people bought the Nano because they were surprised at the engineering feat of creating so much room inside a snazzy car with such a little footprint.

QUESTIONS

- When you introduce a new innovation to the world, is your launch as innovative and entertaining as the creation itself?
- On a scale of one to ten (ten is high) where would your customers rate your organization on ethics and integrity? Do they trust you?
- People don't want to be sold; they want to be served. Do your customers believe that your products and services have been developed with the social well-being of others in mind? Are you making that link and telling that story?
- Have you made enough deposits in the public's trust account to cause potential customers to take a leap of faith on your new breakthrough product, service, or business model?

Part Three
Finding What's Next!
The Eight Rules of Nanovation

If you open up the mind, the opportunity to
address both profits and social conditions is
limitless. It's a process of innovation.

JERRY GREENFIELD

If I had played by the rules, I never would have got anywhere!

MARILYN MONROE

W e make the assumption that there is creativity in everyone. If
this is true, then creativity is waiting to be unleashed in every
organization. But what unleashes it? What makes it flow? Those who
figure out how to inspire, drive, and support Nanovation have a significant competitive advantage.

What follow are eight rules for driving Nanovation. These rules
are critical because they create the atmosphere for Nanovation to
flourish. Without these rules, Nanovation comes to a halt.

Part Three
Finding What's Next
The Eight Rules of Nanovation

JERRY GREENFIELD

MARILYN MONROE

TWENTY-THREE

Rule 1: Get Wired for Nanovation

When you innovate, you've got to be prepared for everyone telling you you're nuts.

LARRY ELLISON

WHAT NANOVATORS BRING TO THE GAME

While we firmly believe that everyone has the potential to be innovative, it does appear that Nanovators are wired a certain way. There is a difference between innovating and being an innovative person, between being a company that innovates and an innovative company. In each case the latter is known for having a deep-seated, ongoing capacity to Nanovate. It's a permanent part of the bloodstream flowing through the person and into the organization.

Who are the Nanovators? How do they think? What makes them tick? What do they bring to the game that makes Nanovation possible?

X-Like Integrity

If you are familiar with the X Games you know that they are for athletes engaged in hair-raising sports (think kite surfing, snowboarding and skiing, mountain biking, motocross, and skateboarding, just to name a few) that all involve big air and a lot of risk. *X* stands for "extreme," and that is an apt description for the brand of integrity for which the Tata Group is known. Although no company is without its faults, the Tata brand is synonymous with the words *honesty, integrity,* and *trust.* Anyone who knows Ratan Tata or has studied the Tata Group knows that he delivers on his promise and does what he says he is going to do. Yet in the midst of India's well-known corruption and malpractice, he has never been willing to buy political favors to get things done, nor can his influence and power be bought—for any reason.

The Tatas have walked away from any number of deals, such as Bollywood films, due to questionable ethics. Perhaps that is why government officials seeking bribes don't even attempt to solicit Tata executives.

In November 2005, Ratan Tata told the *McKinsey Quarterly,* "What I feel most proud of is that we have been able to grow without compromising any of the values or ethical standards that we consider important. And I am not harping on this hypocritically. It was a major decision to uphold these values and ethics in an environment that is deteriorating around you. If we had compromised them, we could have done much better, grown much faster, and perhaps been regarded as much more successful in the pure business sense. But we would have lost the one differentiation that this group has against others in the country. We would have been just another venal business house."

Nanovation is an adventure into the unknown. If you are leading a revolution, people want to know at least three things: (1) Is your idea or mission worth supporting? (2) Do you have the competence to build a critical mass of activists and pull it off? and (3) Do you have integrity, can I trust you, and will you look out for my best interests along the way? The most difficult is trust because you have to earn it every day. And here's the thing: radical innovation is a magnet for conflict. From major crises and formidable resistance to minor setbacks, each step in the journey tests the honor and integrity of a leader and gives followers an opportunity to evaluate whether he or she can be trusted.

As chairman of a $71 billion conglomerate in a society that is still very caste and class oriented, Ratan Tata had the respect of the young engineers on Team Nano, but it was his willingness to roll up his sleeves, encourage dissent, and become one of them that earned their trust. It didn't happen overnight. For several months he pushed, prodded, and invited people to speak up. As soon as people saw that they wouldn't get their heads lopped off for expressing their opinions, trust was solidified.

Ratan Tata delegated the Nano project to Girish Wagh, but he and Ravi Kant were passionately involved. When the team got bogged down, they offered ideas. When the team got discouraged, they offered hope. When the project hit roadblocks, they were there to support, using their considerable power and resources to break the logjams and move things forward. Whenever the team stopped on the easy answer, Ratan's restless and probing nature, combined with Ravi's penchant for getting it done, challenged them to reach for more.

When the first test mule disappointed, Ratan made sure everyone saw it as a forward step, not a setback. Sure, the team members were depressed that they had failed to impress the chairman, but the experience helped them define boundaries of power and size that, in the end, made the Nano so successful.

All of this created a bond among members and strengthened the team immensely. It also established a crucial first step: building a sense of unity that Team Nano would need to accomplish the impossible.

A revolutionary innovation like the Nano involves risk. This is a given. Yet risks are taken only when people trust their leaders. How much risk is really acceptable? How will they deal with our mistakes? What information can we share and with whom? Whom can I rely on, and who really "has my back"? These are questions of trust.

To do what Team Nano did, there had to be a steady flow of seemingly off-the-wall ideas among its members. But people are willing to be vulnerable and "put it out there" only if they trust each other.

The first engine the team used in a test bed was a two-cylinder marine engine from another division. Who puts a boat engine in a car? But the fact that it failed was not the point; the point was a new way of thinking that eventually led to the development of the innovative two-cylinder engine that powers the first-generation Nano.

To pull off the Nano project successfully required a huge amount of collaboration. But people are willing to extend a hand and reach across boundaries only if there is trust. Trust and innovation are inseparable, and trust is built upon integrity.

Authentic to the Bone

True Nanovators like Ratan Tata have a strong sense of who they are, what they stand for, and how they want to live their lives. They have an enviable freedom. They don't give much credence to what people think about them. There's an inner security that gives them the liberty to pursue big ideas. They aren't swayed by the current of public opinion. They say what they say and do what they do based on their higher calling—the heroic cause we discussed earlier.

They don't let the analysts, media, or management gurus run their businesses. They are independent and interdependent at the same time. They set their own course and blaze their own trails, yet they are keenly aware that they can't get there on their own.

But having a strong sense of who they are doesn't mean they're arrogant. In fact, it's just the opposite: they have a strong sense of their own "bull" and work hard to control the grandstanding part of their personality. They know the louder and more dogmatic they are, the less creativity and engagement they'll get from others.

Talk to Ratan Tata in private and you quickly discover that there is a refreshing realness in the way he communicates. He's not a poser. He doesn't get on a soapbox, and he doesn't pretend to be someone or something he's not. His authenticity lends credibility and authority to his words. We find these characteristics in a lot of great leaders. They don't try to fit into the world's notion of what a supersmart, extremely confident, in-control, savvy, and sophisticated executive should be. They are just themselves.

You can't be a leader playing follow the leader. Frankly, business authors like us have probably done readers a disservice. We extol the virtues of iconic leaders such as Ratan Tata and show the many things about his leadership worth emulating; then we tell you it is impossible to be yourself if you are trying to be like someone else.

Ratan didn't try to be like Jamsetji or J. R. D. Tata. There is no question that he learned from them, but we seriously doubt Ratan would've have been as successful with the Tata Group as he has by trying to emulate his predecessors. Even when authenticity is quirky, eccentric, or rough around the edges, people are inspired by and drawn to it.

Our advice: learn from the best and make it your own.

Confident Humility

A number of years ago, we were flying out of Washington Reagan National Airport on an MD-80 passenger jet. Upon takeoff, just as we were approaching full thrust, the pilot jumped on the brakes. In a whiplashlike effect, people's heads were catapulted into the seats in front of them. Knowing the Potomac River was at the end of the runway, we wondered if he could stop the plane before we skidded into the water. He did—barely.

As the smell of burnt rubber filled the cabin of the aircraft, the pilot got on the public address (PA) system and tried to quell our fears and lighten the moment. In a strong Texas accent he said, "We had a warning light go off in the cockpit just before takeoff, so we aborted. We're going to pull over to the side of the runway and clean out our shorts while we let the brakes cool down. Then we'll have maintenance come out and take a look at it." People laughed, but we could still sense a lot of tension in the cabin.

After approximately thirty minutes, we started to taxi onto the runway again. Maintenance had been onboard and fixed the warning light, so everyone assumed that it was okay to fly, but you can imagine the anxiety people were still feeling. That's when the pilot came back on the PA and said, "Ladies and gentlemen, I've been married to the same woman for thirty-five years and I love her. I have two daughters waiting for me at home, and I can't wait to see them. Let me reassure you, if this plane were not airworthy, we would not be taking off. Please give our flight attendants your full attention as they share our safety announcements with you."

In less than two minutes this pilot conveyed a tremendous level of confidence combined with the humility to be vulnerable. In the midst of a potential crisis, he was inspiring. He earned the confidence of the passengers and turned a scary experience into one that was positive and quite memorable.

"A coach is someone who asks you to do things you don't want to do so you can be the player you want to be."
Coach Tom Landry

That's what great leaders do. Their confidence creates a presence that captures our attention, and their humility makes them real. They have the confidence to take us places we wouldn't go on our own, but they do it in a way that makes them feel like one of us.

One thing that makes Ratan Tata such an exceptional leader is this yin- and yanglike integration of confidence and humility. His confidence makes him believable; his humility makes him approachable and teachable. Ratan is no pushover—he has very strong points of view—yet he is humble enough to know that he hasn't cornered the market on insight—there is always something missing. He openly shares his ideas and expects those ideas to be challenged and improved. He encourages others to take risks by candidly admitting his mistakes and vulnerabilities and talking about what he has learned from them.

When we think about game-changing innovation, we don't think about being cautious, metered, and incremental. We think about leaping over industry paradigms, letting go of personal preconceptions, ignoring self-doubt, and hurdling the criticism of those who say it can't be done.

That takes confidence. It takes guts to stand up among your industry peers and define the target, make it public, and stick to it, no matter what obstacles you face. The Nano was a defining project for Ratan

It takes **humility** to build a global **powerhouse** that says, "We have so much yet to **learn.**"

Tata. His reputation was on the line. He could've refuted the *Financial Times*' interpretation of "affordable." Instead, he chose to let that become the goal—gutsy!

But it also takes humility to build a global powerhouse that is taking on the world in IT, steel, power, tea, automobiles, and other industries and say, "We have so much yet to learn about internationalizing our business."

It takes humility to meticulously forge a web of distinctly modern twenty-first-century companies that think big and act assertively and say, "We need to make bigger plans and keep up with the countries around us. We have been a very conservative house, and we have been applauded for our conservatism, but today we need to take more risk."

And what is it, if not humility, that causes one of the most powerful business leaders in the world to sit down with engineers forty to fifty years younger than himself and say, "Treat me like any other member of the team"?

Positively Disruptive

From his first leadership position at Tata, Ratan Tata was disruptive. As we showed earlier, when he took over as chairman, he made dramatic changes to the Group's lineup of companies and management.

Nanovators are notoriously disruptive because Nanovation is about breaking rules, doing what seems ludicrous, displacing existing products and services, and disrupting the equilibrium of an entire industry. That's what the Nano did.

Nanovators might be afraid, but they are always up for a spine-tingling ride to the edge of disruption because they are constantly seeking to renew themselves, reenergize their organizations, and reestablish their edge on the competition. That's why they are always seeking the next big thing. And they know that the "edge" is where it will be found. This optimism is contagious. Have you ever interacted with someone who really thinks big? Did you leave the conversation inspired to think bigger? It's magnetic. People get next to it, experience its impact, and want to feed off it.

Nanovators know that the key to accelerated growth is to be distinctive, and to be distinctive, you have to take chances. You have to blow the doors off business as usual. You have to challenge people to think differently. Nanovators are notorious for pushing people out of their comfort zones and expanding their capabilities. Because that's where breakthroughs come from.

You know Pixar as one of the most successful studios in the history of movies and almost certainly the most critically acclaimed. By 2010, the company had produced eleven animated feature films, all of which have met with success. But you may not know that once upon a time, all the company wanted to do was sell computer systems.

Originally called the Graphics Group, the company was purchased by Steve Jobs as a high-end computer hardware firm focused on developing graphical imaging systems for government and scientific work. But the core product, called Pixar Image Computer, struggled to find a market. Desperate to generate sales, one young employee made short animated films to demonstrate the system's capacity, films with names like *Luxo Jr.* The little films were simple but clever, and they demonstrated the incredible power of the system. That young employee's name was John Lasseter.

Although it was able to sell a few systems—Disney bought several to take the manual work out of animation—the company struggled, and Jobs considered selling it. Then it did something utterly disruptive. Desperate to generate revenue while waiting for computer sales to pick up, Lasseter's little animation team created a service revenue stream, doing contract animation for television commercials. Disney started giving them work, and eventually Disney offered a $26 million deal to produce three animated films, the first of which was *Toy Story*.

Like a lemon farmer about to lose his farm, who discovers he can make more money selling lemonade, Pixar was disruptive out of desperation. But out of that disruption was born one of the greatest, most creative companies of all time.

(Pixar)

Little Luxo Jr. was only intended to sell computer systems, not become the guiding light of the most successful movie studio in history.

Having found their winning formula, most companies would stick to it, strenuously avoiding further disruption. Not Pixar.

After their initial wave of success producing three blockbuster hits, *Toy Story*, *A Bug's Life*, and *Toy Story 2*, Pixar leaders Steve Jobs, Ed Catmull, and John Lasseter worried about complacency. So they asked director Brad Bird, a veteran of Walt Disney, Warner Brothers, and Fox, to join the Pixar team. This invitation is particularly interesting given that Bird had just come off a financial failure called *The Iron Giant*.

Bird pushed people beyond their comfort zones, gave outcast animators a voice, and encouraged dissent. When someone in a large meeting asked if *The Incredibles* was too much of a stretch project, Bird said that if there was ever a studio that needed to be doing something too ambitious, it was Pixar. He argued that doing something scary, which pushes you to the outer limits of your capabilities where you might fail, maintains the creative edge.

(Pixar)

Brad Bird and the team at Pixar created *The Incredibles*. What can your team do that's incredible?

One day, when they were struggling to contain the huge budget and insane schedule, Bird suggested using a rudimentary "cheat"—filming a pie plate flying across the screen to simulate a flying saucer instead of using an expensive computer animation. The purists were horrified. The idea was heretical. But Bird understood that kids didn't care how technically cool the advanced animation was. They cared about the story and where the flying saucer was going. Even though Bird never actually threw the pie plate, his threat disrupted the animators' conventional thinking and forced them to become more imaginative.

The disruption worked. Under Bird's direction, Pixar won two Academy Awards for the innovative animation in the box-office hit movies *The Incredibles* and *Ratatouille*.

Ask Ravi Kant, Girish Wagh, and anyone on Team Nano if the Nano disrupted their company and their lives, and you will get an emphatic yes! But they will also tell you that the project ripped the lid off their self-imposed creative limitations. It unleashed a level of confidence that gave them the courage to think for themselves.

There are many examples in the story where it looked as though Team Nano were doing something ludicrous. But many of the people who worked on this project would now tell you that they are now more comfortable being uncomfortable. They now know that when you are doing things that have never been done before, it all looks ludicrous.

Compelling, groundbreaking, and game-changing, Team Nano got a taste of what a "wow project" is like. Doing something radical is extremely difficult; it is also intoxicating. They now know that their hunger for the kind of ongoing transformation that creates competitive advantage while changing the world supersedes their uneasiness and anxiety.

Undoubtedly Ratan Tata's disruptive spirit has rubbed off on a team of young people who dared to be different. They are now less afraid of the untried, the unpredictable, and the unexpected.

And they are the future of Tata Motors.

If they will take the baton of disruption and keep looking for the new, the unconventional, and the unfamiliar, the Nano will *not* be the last word coming from this band of mavericks.

Maniacal Focus

"Once the problem was stated, its
solution came to me in a flash."
Anton Fokker

The power of a well-defined problem is that it comes with well-defined constraints. And constraints provide focus. They help you determine what you can and cannot do as you go forward.

Ratan Tata was very clear about the problem he was trying to solve. He made a choice: design an all-weather form of transportation for Rs. 1 lakh (at the time, about $2,100). That choice set the direction and put the project in motion, but it also constrained all the other choices that Team Nano would have to make.

Although no one knew what the final product would look like, everyone was laser clear about what the Nano would and would not be. It would be a basic car, not one with a lot of bells and whistles. It would not be just incrementally better than a Maruti for slightly less money; it would radically shatter the current cost barrier and redefine the price-to-performance paradigm. It wouldn't be an apology. It wouldn't look like a thrown-together Erector Set. It wouldn't be uncomfortable. It would be roomy, yet maneuverable. It would have style. And it would meet regulatory standards. Jaydeep Desai remembered that the chairman was very clear from day one that it should meet all of the safety and emissions norms: "It should be seen as a car, not a compromised car."

"A problem clearly stated is
a problem half solved."
Dorothea Brande

Clarity created a relentless focus and a dogged, uncompromising determination in which Ratan Tata paid attention to the smallest design details. He wanted the team to get inside the customers' heads and build a car that would create not the ultimate driving experience, but an experience that told customers, "You were front of mind each step of the way. We thought about how you would experience the car, and we want you to feel like the value far outweighs the price."

Clarity also created a maniacal focus in which Ravi Kant kept pushing the team to engineer costs out of the car. Very few managing directors would go over a bill of materials line by line, but that's what Ravi did. When the team said, "We can't squeeze any more cost out of this part," Ravi's response was, "Then we will have to squeeze it out of another part."

When cost constraints threatened to diminish the user's experience, Ratan Tata wouldn't take no for an answer. When creating the right experience threatened to raise the cost of the car, Ravi Kant sent the team back to the drawing board. Together they brought a maniacal focus to the team that, in turn, enabled the team to manage thousands of trade-offs without giving up until they got it right.

"Desire is the key to motivation, but it's the determination and commitment to an unrelenting pursuit of your goal—a commitment to excellence that will enable you to attain the success you seek."
Mario Andretti

There were many other times when Team Nano could've lost focus: when credible experts said it couldn't be done, when the cost of materials went up by 40 percent, and when the political opposition threatened their lives and their ability to complete the Singur plant. Each episode could've easily taken the team off course. Instead they stayed committed because they knew what they wanted to accomplish and the solution was worth fighting for. When the roadblocks came (literally and figuratively), they drove around them, over them, and through them.

Hunger for Change

Have you ever been hungry—really hungry—for something? When you are hungry, your desire intensifies, and your craving runs wild. Hunger unleashes ambition. If you're hungry to win, you crave getting back into the game to find an opportunity to win again. If you're hungry to learn, you crave books, seminars, and experiences that will teach you. If you're hungry for food, you become frustrated and agitated until you satisfy your desire and get what you crave. If you're hungry to grow a business, you're constantly searching for the changes necessary to position your organization for growth. Put it in any context you like; the word *hungry* means you move from what C. K. Prahalad calls "wait and react" or "sense and respond" to "anticipate and create."

The one thing most people don't hunger for is change. We fear it and resist it. We live in denial of it, sometimes for an entire lifetime. And yet it's inevitable.

Nanovators, on the other hand, are *hungry* for change. While most people take change like medicine, Nanovators eat change for breakfast and make their competitors eat it, too.

Why? Because change is opportunity.

Nanovators see broad, sweeping, and uncertain change as the new norm, not as something that is here today and gone tomorrow. They aren't lulled into a false sense of pace—where everything slows down at some point long enough to catch their breath and retool. They accept that the rate and speed and variety of change will continue to increase—no more predictable patterns. They firmly believe that the winners of tomorrow will be those making the bold moves

While most people take change like medicine, Nanovators eat change for breakfast.

today. If they are certain about anything, it's that the world will continue to be uncertain. Doing nothing is not an option.

Right now, wherever your business is at this point in time, you can make one of two choices. You can expand your capacity to change quickly and successfully, or you can become impotent and obsolete.

You can inspire the ongoing flow of radically new ideas, or you can be destined to play follow the leader.

You can make strategic, ongoing change a core competence, or you can become equipped to live in a world that no longer exists.

You can play "catch up" by reacting to trends in the market, or you can lead the market by anticipating and shaping change.

Nanovators would rather drive change than be driven by it. They would rather run with shakers and movers who truly believe that change happens *through* them, not with victims who believe that change happens *to* them.

Nanovators refuse to be confined by geographical or cultural boundaries. They bring a global mind-set to the game. This means they will go anywhere to find the right talent, form the right relationships, acquire the right assets, and develop the right capabilities to create new business models and new products that can be deployed anywhere in the world an opportunity exists.

> **You can expand** your capacity to **change,** or you can become impotent and **obsolete.**

Even though he has an incredible legacy to uphold and a lot to lose, Ratan Tata is more interested in creating the future than protecting the past. If you review the major decisions he has made since becoming chairman of the Tata Group, it's pretty clear that he sees innovation and change as the way to protect the company's 140-year-old legacy. As a young executive in his early forties working with an iconic figure like J. R. D. Tata, Ratan Tata could've fallen into the trap of complacency. Instead, he declared war on it.

Whether it came from his education at Cornell, the time he spent working as an architect in Los Angeles, or the opportunity to travel the world, Ratan Tata acquired an international perspective. He could see that the world was moving fast, and many of the Tata companies had grown comfortable, if not complacent. In his mind they were not prepared for the explosive opportunities that globalization would present—they weren't hungry for change. Insulated by government policies prior to liberalization, few of them had ever faced stiff competition from abroad on Indian soil. If the Tata Group was going to continue its legacy of growing a nation, it would have to overcome its strategic inertia and figure out how to be a global player.

He restructured and reduced the number of companies within the Tata Group, kindly and fairly ushered the old guard out and brought the vanguard in, and then put the Tata companies through a rigorous process of growing people, reducing costs, improving quality, and fostering innovation. He did all of this because he wanted the Tata Group to be equipped for a new world order that was just cresting over the horizon. The result was a twenty-five-year journey that transformed the Tatas from an Indian powerhouse into a global powerhouse.

Inspired by the boldness and audacity of China's growth, he essentially laid the groundwork for a radical and unprecedented global expansion. Think we are overstating the case? Go to Tata .com under the section "Our Businesses" and check out "Mergers and Acquisitions." From Tetley Tea to Corus Steel and most recently Jaguar–Land Rover, the acquisitions have grown more bold and daring over time. In his compelling book *India's Global Powerhouses*, Nirmalya Kumar points out that over the last decade, Tata has conducted thirty-seven international acquisitions valued at $18 billion and, in 2008, generated revenues of $38 billion from outside India.

What have you done in the last twelve months to expand your capacity to change?

Between 2000 and 2008, Tata Group companies either acquired or invested heavily in scores of growing companies around the world.

With each acquisition the Tata Group learns something new—about integrating corporate cultures, tapping into the intellectual capital of the world, finding the best capabilities, expanding its capacity to change, and realizing the full potential of its partnerships. Yet even with all of the experience they've gained through multiple mergers, most of the managing directors of the Tata Group companies will tell you that they are still early in this process. Even with such humility, there can be no doubt that they are creating a conglomerate that is hungry for change.

CHANGE: OPPORTUNITY-LED OR CRISIS-DRIVEN?

Consider the last five major changes that your organization has been through. What drove them? Was it a really cool, unprecedented opportunity or an impending crisis? Nanovators are hounded by the question, why is substantive, dramatic change usually preceded by crisis, and more important, how do we get ahead of the curve and let opportunity, not crisis, excite transformation?

When the commercial vehicles market fell through the floor by 40 percent in 2000, the dramatic cost-cutting changes undertaken by Tata Motors were crisis-driven. Ravi Kant garnered important lessons from this uncomfortable experience.

Tata Motors would have to reinvent itself.

The company already had 55 percent of the maturing commercial vehicles market. How much more could it grow? Ravi and his team had to ask, "If the commercial vehicle market is cyclical, how do we capitalize on the fact that different markets go through different cycles at different times?"

The answer: diversify.

Diversify the product offering, diversify the customer base, and diversify geographically.

(Tata Motors)

Tata Motors' vice chairman, Ravi Kant, at the press conference of the Nano launch in Mumbai.

Kant commissioned a study that would scan the globe for new market opportunities. This led to the Tatas building trucks in Korea; to a joint venture with Marcopolo Motors of Brazil to set up the largest bus manufacturing facility in India; to a strategic alliance with Fiat; and to the now famous Jaguar–Land Rover acquisition. The study also showed that the ground was fertile for Tata-type products that have the potential for price disruption in emerging markets such as Africa, Southeast Asia, China, Brazil, and Korea.

If a business case was needed to support Ratan Tata's dream for the People's Car, this was it.

Are You Ready to Capitalize on Opportunities in Other Parts of the World?

Sophisticated market research notwithstanding, you have to wonder what crystal ball Ratan Tata and Ravi Kant are looking into. Building a relationship with Fiat gave Tata Motors drive-train technologies it needed for its Indica and Indigo cars, and it could be the key to what some have dubbed the Tata World Nano. Ratan Tata has said he would like to introduce the Nano in the North American market. Sergio Marchionne, Fiat's chief executive, has routinely stated his desire to have a price disrupter that could be offered at a lower cost than its already economical range of products.

The question is, how do you reengineer a car to meet safety and emissions standards and bring it to market where you have absolutely no sales presence? The Fiat-Chrysler union might be the answer. What about an American version of the Nano without the Tata branding? What if the Nano revived a dormant brand from Fiat's past—a brand that symbolized innovation? Fiat gets a low-cost car and, through Chrysler, a foothold in the American market. Chrysler gets a car that people might actually get excited about and positions itself to meet the rigorous new emissions standards that take effect in the U.S. in 2012. At more than fifty miles per gallon, the rebranded Nano could appeal to multiple generations of U.S. car buyers who are conscious about sustaining the environment.

And if that scenario doesn't pan out, many of the Jaguar–Land Rover dealers told Ratan Tata when he visited the U.S. that they would welcome the Nano to their showrooms. If Mercedes has the Smart Car, why couldn't Jaguar–Land Rover have the People's Car?

Are your people
equipped to think and
act like global citizens?
Are you "locally
relevant" in countries
where you want to
grow, or are you using
a domestic team to
drive your international
business?

Many firms have learned that strategic paralysis is a formidable enemy. The people of Tata Motors have discovered this enemy is best fought offensively. Yes, the economic crisis of 2000–2001 was a wake-up call for Ravi Kant. But Ravi answered that call by seizing opportunities that put Tata Motors in a position to learn, adapt, and grow with less crisis-induced trauma. It's a continuous process. With each attempt to renew its products and reinvent its business model, Tata Motors increases its appetite *for* and capacity *to* change. And by the way, it has also created a change-ready organization that has been pretty impressive in responding to crises—such as the closing of the Singur plant—when they do arise.

Are you hungry for change?

Remember Surya Banerjee, the assistant plant manager who stayed on to shut down Singur? He wasn't involved only in crisis management. He was also part of the team driving change. He recalled, "When we knew the situation in Singur was lost, we said, '*Chelo* [Let's go]. We should forget the past and move forward.'"

So they began planning how to move the entire factory from West Bengal, in the far eastern part of India, to Sanand, in the far northwest. Instead of using the plant closing as an excuse, instead of feeling sorry for what they'd lost, they threw themselves into one of the most ambitious logistical projects ever, like archaeologists planning to move an ancient monument, numbering each part and piece and readying it for shipment to a distant location.

They barely missed a beat. What had taken two and a half years to build in Singur, they dismantled and rebuilt in just fourteen months in Sanand.

"The whole world was watching us, Surya said, "and that was a big motivation. The world was excited about the Nano, and they were watching. People wanted their Nanos. It was good pressure. We had something to work for.

"Now, we have a tremendous sense of confidence. We can move and re-set up a plant in fourteen months. We can do anything."

Are You Wired to Be a Nanovator?

Doodling on napkins and tinkering with ideas is one thing, but turning ideas into commercially viable products, services, and business models is quite another. What Nanovators bring to the game is their willingness to go the distance needed to make a dream a reality. They have more than the vision; they have the drive to lead, the focus to stay on target, and the integrity to win the trust of their teams.

They are wired to win, wired in such a way that they turn creative genius into innovations that can change the world.

NANOBITE

Get wired for Nanovation by taking the following points into consideration:

THERE IS A NEW WORLD ORDER. A global economy fueled by the Internet shrinks the distance between people from different places. Today, four billion people around the world have cell phones and computers. They are connected to the Internet and to each other via social networks. You know what this means? Connectivity and real-time collaboration enable us to communicate more easily, connect dots faster, spread ideas quicker, find solutions sooner, and bring new innovations to market with unprecedented speed. You are going to be part of this new world order, or you're going to wake up one day and wonder, *What happened to me?*

CRAZY IDEAS WILL REVOLUTIONIZE INDUSTRIES. What seems bizarre today could be tomorrow's established way of doing it. You can lead that change, or you can be swept along by it. In the end, you'll have to live with a little of both.

YOU MUST LET GO. Right now, someone, somewhere, is creating a product or service to displace yours. It will be better, faster, or cheaper. It will be more accessible or easier to use. It will solve a problem or address a need your customers didn't know they had. Nanovators are hungry for change because they know that if they don't let go of old products and services and replace them, someone else will do it for them.

YOU MUST BEWARE OF PAST SUCCESS. Success is never final. You have to earn it again and again. Each success only keeps you in the game. The problem with success is that it makes you vulnerable to arrogance, inflexibility, and complacency because it dupes you into thinking that you have all the answers. If you think that you're smarter than you are, it's easy to become closed to learning and hard to be open to new possibilities. Now, not leaning on yesterday's headlines doesn't mean you throw out everything you've learned from past wins. It just means that you are not going to let those successes limit your thinking about the future.

CUSTOMERS ARE ON THE MOVE. Their wants and needs are in a constant state of flux. Stand still and they will blow right by you. Maybe you'll be able to catch up; maybe not. Wouldn't it be better to keep moving, too? Wouldn't it be better to play a critical role in shaping their expectations?

QUESTIONS

- Do you make change happen *through* you? Or do you just let it happen *to* you?
- Is your organization changing faster than the industry? Are you changing faster than your organization?
- Think about the majority of major changes in your organization. Have they been opportunity-led or crisis-driven?

TWENTY-FOUR
Rule 2: Lead the Revolution

Over time and cultures, the most robust and most effective form of communication is the creation of a powerful narrative.

HOWARD GARDNER

BE COMMITTED AND INVOLVED

Take a good, hard look at some of the most innovative companies in the world. They carve out time to do what Team Nano did. They move from buzzwords and lofty aspirations to rubber-meets-the-road commitment. Their executives are engaged, lending support in the form of ideas and resources, removing roadblocks, and making connections.

This is because innovation is a strategic priority.

LEADERSHIP FRAMES THE STORY

The ability to see what's possible and then mobilize people to make it happen is one of the scarcest resources in the world. Consider the companies like Apple, 3M, P & G, Pixar, Medtronic, and Nokia with a world-renowned reputation for turning out one game-changing innovation after another.

What makes them unique? Each of these icons has a leader who frames the story and creates an expectation for Nanovation.

"Stories are the single most powerful tool in a leader's toolkit."
Howard Gardner

If you have a powerful idea, house it in a powerful story. Don't kill it with spreadsheets and Pareto charts buried deep down in a cumbersome report. And don't stitch it together in a string of one hundred PowerPoint slides. Make it accessible; put it in a story. This distinctly human and time-tested way of conveying information has been around only a few millennia.

What made Jesus such a magnetic and iconoclastic teacher? It was his ability to convey critical information to his followers in parables. Go back to tribal behavior. One of the most important people in any tribe—primitive or corporate—is the shaman, who tells stories that reinforce the fundamental values and culture of the tribe. When you meet someone on a plane and strike up a conversation, what happens? You start telling each other stories, and through those stories, you get to know each other.

Stories are powerful because we remember them and the lessons housed in them. We hear on the television: "Indian Ocean earthquake causes tsunami. Terrorists attack the Taj Hotel in Mumbai. Michael Jackson dead at fifty." These sound bites capture our attention and intensify our need to get the story. And of course, we convey moral principles and character virtues to our children by telling them bedtime stories. Unfortunately somewhere between putting our children to bed and making our way into the office the next morning, the art of storytelling gives way to complicated analysis and sophisticated reports that cause people's eyes to glaze over.

The Nano gained worldwide attention and became one of the most anticipated product launches in history because the story is epic. It has all the drama of a great novel: Compassion. Adventure. Danger. Sacrifice. Betrayal. Risk and loss. Unsung heroes. Insurmountable odds. Setbacks. And triumph.

It also has a credible and competent storyteller.

In his book *Leading Minds: An Anatomy of Leadership*, Howard Gardner argues that the ability to share a compelling story and enroll different audiences (employees, customers, and the world at large) in it is one of the key characteristics of leadership. That's a bold statement, but we agree.

Every great leader we've met or written about over the last twenty years has the ability to markedly influence the behaviors, thoughts, and feelings of followers who, in turn, become activists and missionaries for the cause.

Ratan Tata is no exception. He is the Tata Group's storyteller in chief, Team Nano's shaman.

An Epic Story

As you remember, when the Nano was revealed at the auto show in Delhi in 2008, Ratan appeared before the audience in a hologram-like video and did an amazing job of telling the story. Let's revisit some of the things he did so we can identify the main ingredients of a compelling story. Our intent here is to help you create an agenda—a template, if you will—for building a business case that rallies champions and believers who are inspired to pursue your ideas.

A Compelling Story Almost Tells Itself

Earlier, we shared the story of the reveal of the Nano in Delhi in 2008. Rather than display the typical hoopla that surrounds the unveiling of a new car, Ratan chose a more authentic and understated presentation, which was in keeping with his persona. The Nano was born out of compassion and a sincere desire to serve, so he chose to let the Nano tell its own story.

Compelling Stories Challenge Us to Think Differently

Nanovation finds its legs when people are mobilized, and Ratan rarely talks about the Nano without some reference to the fact that there are solutions to most problems if we are only willing to break down self-imposed barriers—starting in our minds.

Compelling Stories Are Simple and Succinct

The Nano story is powerful because it requires little explanation—it's simple. People immediately identify with the problem (it's right there in front of them every day), and they understand the scope of the problem and, therefore, the scope of the opportunity.

Ask Ratan Tata to explain the genesis of the idea and the mission of the project. You will get a crisp, tight business case that conveys the Nano's value proposition—all in the time it takes to ride the elevator. Jack Welch once told us that if an engineer pitching a new idea couldn't explain it using one PowerPoint slide, the person didn't have a firm grasp on the idea. Welch would ask the person to come back and pitch it again when he or she could explain it more succinctly.

Compelling Stories Preempt the Critics

When you have only a brief time to share your idea, go on the offense. When the critics seek to throw a wet blanket on an astounding achievement, tell the truth and find the high road.

Compelling Stories Have Unsung
Heroes who Defy the Odds

When you listen to Ratan Tata talk about the initiative, ingenuity, hard work, collaboration, and sacrifice that Team Nano exemplified, it's hard not to be moved. An organization draws its strength from its heroes. They are the personification of its highest ideals. They exemplify its highest values. Team Nano was a group of ordinary people who made the extraordinary human and attainable. They have shown us the heights to which the human spirit can rise. When we look up at their accomplishments, we are drawn up to achieve our own. Heroes show us who we aspire to be and give us permission to act.

(Tata Motors)

Ratan Tata, the Tata Group's storyteller in chief, shared his vision for the Nano with Kevin Freiberg. His ability to think big is extraordinary, and his passion is contagious.

Compelling Stories Are Vivid

Stories bring the abstract into focus and make the intangible tangible. A vivid story paints a picture; it creates a mental image that puts you there. When Ratan Tata shares his story about the Indian family crashing on the motorcycle in the rain, instantaneously you are there, drawn into the experience. The problem you are trying to solve is no longer abstract; it's visceral.

A vivid story is also quantitative, but it doesn't drown you in numbers. By making it quantitative, you are making a commitment that you will deliver on a promise. Ratan made terms such as *low cost* and *affordable* measurable. He was very clear and specific about the Nano's value proposition. The audience doesn't need to know all the facts and figures, but when you've got only a few minutes to pitch an idea, the ones that exude value can be immediately persuasive. And in an era of advertising spin, real facts make you stand out from the crowd.

"The key to leadership was to have a simple message and repeat it as often as you can."
Harold Geneen

Compelling Stories Stick

Like every great leader, Ratan Tata frequently repeats himself. He never tires of speaking about the Nano's potential to raise the standard of living and the quality of life for Indian families. He also knows that in terms of "getting" the story's central message, the lightbulb goes on for different people at different times. If people hear the story enough, they can see it, grasp it, and internalize it. Then it becomes *their* story. In time, Ratan's story became Team Nano's story and eventually India's story.

A good story is difficult to stop. It travels and takes on a life of its own because it is repeatable. And with today's media, a simple, yet powerful story has a rapid trajectory—it can literally spread (virally) overnight. Ratan may be the storyteller in chief, but through repetition, he has created a critical mass of corporate shamans around the globe who are now the Nano's ambassadors.

On the Nano project people paid close attention to the way he allocated his time and the organization's resources, they listened to the questions he asked, they scrutinized what he rewarded and punished, and they watched how he reacted to critical incidents. Everything he did said something about who he is, what he values, and what's important to him.

He framed the story of the Nano as a quest to save lives.

Every member of Team Nano knew what Ratan cared about. He not only envisioned the project; he also rolled up his sleeves and got involved. So they knew how he defined the difference between a real car and an apology. They got in tune with his drive for elegant solutions. They understood his respect for the dignity of the end user. And they were well aware that he would not compromise on the price of the car. His demeanor, attitude, and actions gave Team Nano the freedom to challenge assumptions, cross boundaries, and break barriers.

By now, it is pretty obvious that Ratan Tata would not take no for an answer. A leader who won't back down on a heroic cause instills confidence in the rest of the team. Ratan's relentless pursuit of doing something magnificent for the people of India made the dream desirable, and it made Team Nano believe that it was possible. He set the tone for doing insanely great work. He created a story and invited people to step into their roles.

ARE YOU A LEADER PEOPLE LOVE TO FOLLOW?

Ravi Kant, Prakash Telang, and Rajiv Dube also played critical roles in setting the tone for the success of the Nano. Unlike the stories you hear that accompany most radical innovations, the story of Team Nano had no corporate bureaucracy to slow things down.

Imagine being on the design team. Coming up with the elegant solutions to do what's never been done before requires intense concentration and focus. The project you've undertaken is hard enough as it is. Every time you are distracted by having to fight for another resource, you have to restart the creative process. Distractions slow you down, and they create undue frustration. This, in turn, inhibits creativity.

Tata Motors' senior executives did what all great leaders do. They served. They operated in a way that made the organization fluid and dynamic. They made sure the team had the necessary resources, equipment, and facilities to move through each phase of development. No cumbersome reports to appease nervous managers, no getting wrapped around the axle of human resource policies, no unnecessary legal hoop jumping, and no political jockeying to make something happen. The executive team set a tone for removing roadblocks, paving the way, and doing things fast.

Tata Motors' executives demonstrated real courage. Take yourself back to the beginning. The experts in the industry are telling you it can't be done. The emotional costs are high, not to mention the actual investment costs. The outcomes are uncertain—there is no guarantee that the project will work. You've been charged with protecting the legacy business as well as finding new ways to grow. The small-car project could be seen as a threat, if only in the fact that it will take resources away from the existing business. Do you lean into it with all of the knowledge, skill, and experience you have, or do you ever so diplomatically disassociate yourself from it in case it fails?

Rajiv Dube, former president of the passenger car division for Tata Motors, told us, "I think it was fortuitous that the project became a company-wide project versus a passenger cars division project because it required resources to be pulled in from wherever they were available within the company. Resources were pulled from within commercial vehicles and from within the commercial vehicles' vendor community. So the project got fresh momentum. There was a renewed sense of fervor that took place."

With Ravi Kant leading the charge, the executive team became irrepressible. They charged the hill with Ratan Tata and provided the support that every radical project needs.

Prakash Telang told us that while the 1 lakh target seemed like a huge stretch, he had faith in the chairman's vision. Telang knew that Ratan Tata had done quite a bit of thinking about the design and the price of the car on his own. He also knew that the chairman would not have committed to the scope of the project if he didn't think it could be done.

Telang said, "It also helps that we have a 'never say die' approach to this type of project."

Ramesh Vishwakarma, head of manufacturing in Gujarat, and Jaydeep Desai enthusiastically remembered Telang's involvement. Desai said, "Whenever I would meet with Mr. Telang, even if it was 9:30 p.m., he always had time for this project."

You can't legislate creativity, and you can't order out for it. You can't give lofty speeches about thinking big and acting bold and expect that people will get it. Culture is not some quick-fix, instant-gratification program.

A culture of Nanovation is a way of life that develops over time, and it affects every part of your business. This way of life, for better or worse, is established by the tone you set. Everything you do tells a story, and your story shapes the culture.

Whether it's a culture that makes radical innovation a more natural, desired way of doing business or not, it will be a culture defined by your leadership.

CHAMPIONS CREATE BELIEVERS

Remember how after the dream was articulated and the vision cast, the Nano project stalled for a couple of years? Ratan Tata sat in review meetings and would get quite upset because the lack of creativity in these discussions indicated that people didn't really believe in the project.

That's when Ratan and Ravi Kant decided to shake things up by redeploying talent. Ratan asked for Girish Wagh to lead Team Nano. According to Ratan, what Girish brought to the game was not just imagination, creative genius, or the ability to conceive of a futuristic product.

What he brought was great leadership, along with expertise in doing this kind of project. His success in developing the Ace let everyone know that he was a leader who had been down this road before, at least partway.

He knew where he was going.

There is an interesting lesson about disruption in this decision. A Nanovation certainly has the potential to shake things up, but only if it takes hold. Truly disruptive innovation needs a champion, someone to rally a critical mass of believers in the trenches who can swim against the current and see a "wow project" through to its intended result.

"I think if the older segments of our company had run this project, it probably would never have happened," Ratan told us. "You have to challenge what people think is sacrosanct and try to break the barriers and the resistance that come from people who have been doing something the same way and do not believe that there is another way to do it."

Girish Wagh had already demonstrated that he was up to the challenge of breaking barriers. He led a team of 350 engineers on the highly successful Ace project. With unwavering support from the chairman, Ravi Kant, and the executive team, Girish was empowered to lead. But he also had to make a choice—to be accountable and assume the mantle of leadership. And that's exactly what he did. Girish rallied a team of young engineers, the average age of whom was twenty-five, and inspired them to see that if they could help make the chairman's dream come true, they could change the world.

Here's another lesson we learned. Youth has no age limits. Ratan Tata is in his early seventies. He had the wisdom and the guts to turn this project over to people who were many years younger than he. Think of the difference in their perspectives and their experiences. Ironically many of these young engineers remarked to us that the chairman very well might have been the most youthful thinker at the table.

CONNECTION, CHEMISTRY, AND COLLABORATION

Organizations don't produce game-changing innovations; people do. Think of the most innovative companies in the world. They are characterized by healthy, vibrant relationships where people feel connected—to each other and to the larger cause that draws them together. Yet connection alone doesn't describe them completely; there has to be chemistry as well. People have to like each other, feel valued, and work well together. Then when people get connected and feel a sense of chemistry, the stage is set for radical collaboration.

What should you look for when choosing someone to champion a radical innovation? What did Ratan Tata and Ravi Kant see in Girish Wagh that made him a good candidate to lead Team Nano? They saw the ability to connect people, create chemistry, and promote radical collaboration and accountability.

Connecting People

Ratan Tata had the idea for the Nano, but it took more than five hundred engineers working together to turn that idea into a life-changing product with huge potential for commercial success. Girish demonstrated the ability to bring a diverse group of technical

Do you **embrace** your suppliers as **innovation partners** or as an **afterthought** in the **process?**

champions together and help them believe in the chairman's dream—to the point where it became their dream, too.

Girish knew who to go to for what he needed. He established a network of talent within Tata Motors that enabled Team Nano to marshal the right resources at the right time. But he didn't stop there.

Girish also built a relationship with suppliers who were instrumental in making the dream possible. The connection with these suppliers was unique. Respected for their expertise, they were invited to be full-fledged members of the team, not order takers. Team Nano trusted that its suppliers would exceed expectation by coming up with creative solutions that they didn't even know were within the realm of possibility. By having a seat at the table, suppliers were able to see where and how they could make the greatest contribution.

After all, they knew their capabilities and potential better than anyone.

Creating Chemistry

If the innovation you are pursuing is far-reaching, chances are good that you will need an eclectic group of people with some eccentric personalities on your team: dreamers and doers, old-timers and Gen Yers, creatives and analytics. You get the point. It's not easy to lead odd ducks and people with diverse perspectives. Girish had to contend with it all, but people liked working for him.

"Girish never lost his belief in what we could do," Jaydeep Desai remembered. "He kept pushing us all together. It didn't matter if it was the planning team, research team, or anyone else, he kept the flock together. He kept us focused on the target."

By creating a relaxed and informal environment where people could express their ideas freely and openly, Girish made sure the chemistry among team members fired up creative action. He struck the right balance between agreement and dissent. Girish understood that too much agreement would lead to mediocre ideas, something less than the elegant solution the chairman had envisioned. He also knew that too much dissent would make it difficult for people to work together—no matter how great their ideas.

Girish encouraged dissent and debate as long as they were con-structive and focused on moving the project forward; not on conflicts between personalities. He encouraged unity by keeping people focused on the vision. If a vision is like the picture on a jigsaw puzzle box, Girish built a sense of community by keeping each group focused on how its "pieces" contributed to the ultimate picture.

"Creativity is allowing yourself to make mistakes. Design is knowing which ones to keep."
Scott Adams

As you might imagine, when you start with a clean slate where no idea is out of bounds, talented people with diverse perspectives will be passionate about advancing their ideas. Chemistry is established when a strong leader leverages the creative tension that emerges from such a group and then keeps people moving forward.

Girish was able to create an environment where people were able to leave their egos outside the door. When someone brought a new idea to the table, it was open for examination. Team members could question it, challenge it, modify it, and do whatever they thought was necessary to make it better. Girish had a knack for balancing the critical issues of cost, quality, and time. He knew how to listen to people's ideas, identify what was realistic, and then bring all of the inspiring possibilities together.

(Tata Motors)

Girish Wagh (left of the Nano) and part of the young Team Nano dedicating one of the first cars to leave the Pantnagar plant.

Girish did something else that established chemistry and inspired loyalty among the members of Team Nano. He buffered the team from outside resistance so members could concentrate on the task at hand. And when he could no longer do this because the situation became too dangerous in Singur, he stayed with them on the front line until all of the team were ushered to safety and the plant was secured.

Radical Collaboration

Girish understood technology, but he wasn't only a technologist—he became a critical link between the business units, departments, and functions that needed to work seamlessly if the "impossible" was going to become possible. He fostered relationships among engineers, suppliers, construction workers, and Tata Motors' senior executives that encouraged individuals to reach beyond themselves for creative solutions to the many challenges they faced.

Through this interface, he inspired a spirit of cross-functional collaboration. When the team was confronted with unforeseen obstacles, he would attack each one of them by getting people together and coming at the problem from a new perspective. Through collaboration, the team was able to cut cycle time, increase speed, eliminate waste and redundancy, and lower costs.

Collaboration also made Team Nano a magnet for world-class talent. Imagine looking from the outside in at a team that appears to operate seamlessly. Morale is high. And the frustration that so often comes with getting to elegant is tempered by forward-focused, solution-oriented colleagues who rally around each other. Wouldn't that be an awesome force to be reckoned with? Wouldn't that be a team you want to be on?

When he was offered a chance to join the Nano team in 2008, Dave Hudson was thrilled. Even though he was leaving a coveted job at Jaguar, he was thrilled with the challenge. But only a year before, it would have been unthinkable in the industry that one would leave a post at a top European carmaker like Jaguar or Mercedes to work for the unknown Tata Motors in India. Now it's hot!

Accountability

At the end of the day you can cultivate connection, chemistry, and collaboration within a team, but you still have to get results. Girish "owned" this project and assumed responsibility for driving it toward the market. He set the performance bar for the team extremely high and held himself to the same high standards—even when things became extremely difficult.

With escalating materials costs the expectations of the team were always being raised. Inspired by the weightiness of Ratan Tata's vision and Girish's collaborative style, team members cared deeply about what they were doing. They adopted a "never say die" approach to the project. There was no room for complacency. Team members demonstrated the self-discipline to take their assignments seriously and be accountable for producing results. The harder the challenge of rethinking a part or subsystem, the more intellectually and emotionally engaged the team got.

And that was as true of Tata Motors' team members as it was of vendor teams.

Was Team Nano a textbook example of a high-performing team? Yes, but it wasn't perfect. Did people get defensive? Sure. Was there conflict to be managed? Yes. But ultimately conflict gave way to connection, chemistry, and collaboration.

Call it whatever you want—chief facilitator, tour de force, catalytic agent, junction box for ideas, or the overall systems architect—if you want to transform a radical idea into a game-changing innovation, you need a champion who knows how to bring team members together and turn them into believers. So choose carefully.

DRAWING THE BEST OUT OF OTHERS

Nanovation requires a leap—a leap of faith in your ideas as well as in the ideas and capabilities of your colleagues. Leadership is about how you make people feel. In addition to his own big thinking and unbending resolve to accept nothing less than the elegant, perhaps the most powerful thing that Ratan Tata brought to Team Nano was a deep-seated belief in its ability to do what had never been done. By constantly communicating his faith in the team—particularly when elegant solutions seemed nowhere to be found—Ratan helped each member expand his views of his own capabilities.

Everyone wants to know that someone believes in him or her. In these uncertain times, it's easy to lose faith in one's sense of direction. It takes courage to drive innovation forward, and courage thrives on knowing other people believe in you.

How many truly creative ideas never found their way to the light of day because the innovators lost the courage of their convictions and the confidence to leap? Because no one was there to encourage their risk taking?

Time and time again Team Nano found the courage to overcome defeats and roadblocks (literally) because they knew that everyone, from the chairman to the project leader, had faith in them.

Many organizations overlook this important point. We expect innovation and creativity will occur spontaneously, but we're unaware that abstract authority and fear, bureaucratic paper chases, and organizational politics strangle grassroots creativity and problem solving. We give lip service to valuing the voices of those lower in the organizational hierarchy, but when it comes right down to it, the systems, processes, and structures of the organization—along with senior executive behavior—clearly communicate the truth: "We really don't trust you."

If you want to lead the revolution, you have to give power to the people.

NANOBITE

What's your story?

So you've got a great idea. Before pitching it to your board, investors, CEO, suppliers, or the media, ask your team, "Do we have a compelling story that will make this idea stand out?" Then consider these questions:

- Will our story get people's attention?
- Is it simple? Will they understand it?
- Is it succinct? Will they remember it?
- Does it paint a picture? Can they see themselves in it?
- Does it engage them emotionally? Will they care about it?
- Does it stick? Is it worth repeating?

One way you know that Nanovation has become a permanent part of your cultural DNA is that there is a constant buzz and excitement about the cool things that people are working on. A spirit of hopefulness about the future pervades the place.

- Whether it's on the shop floor, the cafeteria, or the executive suite, what stories do people tell?
- Are they talking about the next big thing, a new idea that a group is working on, or a new marketing/advertising campaign that people can't wait for you to see?
- Are people talking about the latest blockbuster product that is sending shock waves throughout the industry? Are they talking about the ways in which your latest innovation has changed a customer's life or transformed the way another one works?
- Or are the stories more about making quarterly numbers, coping with new regulations, raising productivity, and having better execution? Or are there any stories being told at all?

TWENTY-FIVE

Rule 3: Build a Culture of Innovation

Good design is obvious. Great design is transparent.

JOE SPARANO

CREATE A PLACE WHERE NANOVATORS CAN THRIVE

Those who don't know the company well might be tempted to say that with the Nano, Tata Motors got lucky—once. As we have shown, that just isn't true. One only has to look at products such as Indica, Ace (and now its smaller transportation variant, Magic Iris), and Tata Motors' commercial vehicles to see that the Nano is not a one-off innovation. Rather, it is the latest among a string of examples of incremental engineering steps that led to breakthrough products.

That's what makes Tata Motors an innovative company, not just a company that innovates.

The little Magic Iris is a public transport variant of the Ace to show how an inexpensive small van can replace autorickshaws as small taxis in India.

The Tata Group is loaded with examples that demonstrate its commitment to innovation.

- After the 2004 Indian Ocean tsunami, Tata Consultancy Services (TCS) and Tata Teleservices joined forces to develop a text message weather alert system for fishermen on the high seas.
- Titan developed the Titan Edge, the world's thinnest watch.
- The Group's Pune-based Computational Research Laboratories (CRL) built Eka, the fourth-fastest

supercomputer in the world, and they did it in just six weeks for less than $30 million.

- How about a beverage dispensing machine that doesn't use electricity? That's what Tetley, Tata Tea's U.K. subsidiary, did.
- Then there is Ginger Hotels, another business model innovation geared to the bottom of the pyramid. Ginger launched the Smart Basics concept and created a revolution in the world of Indian hospitality. Appealing to the GenNext market, Ginger symbolizes simplicity, convenience, informality, style, warmth, modernity, and affordability.

These are just a few examples that represent a conglomerate that is serious about expanding its capacity for Nanovation.

How do you know when innovation has become a way of life in your organization?

There are plenty of signs: if restlessness is tolerated, curiosity is encouraged, passion is inspired, creativity is expected, and people are always talking about what's next, then you're on your way.

Even now, Ratan Tata is asking people throughout the Tata Group, "What's the next Nano?"

Perhaps the most glaring sign that innovation has made it into the bedrock of your culture is no sign at all. The organizational mind-set changes so significantly that when you are innovating, you are not all that conscious of it.

If you have to talk about it, you're probably not being innovative yet.

The whole conversation about innovation and the process of engaging in it becomes very natural. It's a bit like a fish that doesn't know it's wet. For most organizations this is an unreal expectation, yet this is what the Tata Group is striving to accomplish. Tata Motors and the Tata Group are making perpetual innovation part of their culture.

LIVING INNOVATION OUT LOUD

Since the day in 1981 when Ratan Tata first took on the task of re-organizing the Tata Industries think tank, the Tata Group has made innovation a strategic priority. At Tata, Nanovation is not a flavor of the month; it's a way of life. In fact, Ratan has challenged all of the managing directors of the various Tata Group companies to make innovation a deeply embedded, systemic way of doing business, a groupwide movement.

Here is what Ratan Tata had to say in Voyagers, a Tata Group in-house publication:

> We have to be a Group that innovates, that starts creating intellectual property, that breaks new ground rather than be the one that always follows established processes and technologies. We have an immense task ahead of us, to move from where we are to a new level. The start has been made and that is very, very welcome. (*Voyagers*, 2007)
>
> In many cases, innovation happens at unexpected moments of time and is done in a different context. But you have to have the environment which enables you to do that. You have to think of how you can make a difference to the world we live in. As we move into the future, we should endeavor to be a group that makes a difference and that leaves a mark, not because of the profit it makes but because of what it has done to mankind around us. (*Voyagers*, 2008)

And note the emphasis on what is good for humankind over what is good for profits. Not that they don't focus on profits, but because they recognize the need for balance.

Now, these are just words, right? A lot of business leaders are good at platitudes. But as we've pointed out, the people in the Tata Group, starting with Ratan Tata, have a reputation for X-like integrity. If they say it, they mean it.

So, what is the Tata Group *doing* to give Nanovation validity and support? What is it *doing* to demonstrate that it *is* a strategic priority?

In 2006 Tata Quality Management Services started the Tata Group Innovation Forum (TGIF). The purpose of TGIF is to encourage innovation within the Tata Group companies, help them expand their innovation capabilities, and establish a groupwide community of champions and believers dedicated to creating a culture that nurtures new ideas.

It is about creating a place where people don't feel threatened and are encouraged to explore.

In an interview with *Quest*, R. Gopalakrishnan, executive director of Tata Sons and chairman of TGIF, said, "In the case of a 140-year-old organization like ours, we obviously have layers and layers of systems and cultural DNA embedded in the very way we work. Where we need to improve is in trying to peel those layers off and in democratizing innovation so that more and more people see that innovation is the core of their job; that's what they are paid for."

Freedom to Think, Dream, Create

How comfortable would you be putting your feet up on a desk for a few hours a week just thinking about the future of your business, connecting dots, or asking a series of "What if?" questions? If you walked by someone's office who had his feet up on the desk, how would you react? If you were in a board meeting and saw one of your directors, or even the chairman, doodling, how would you feel?

Innovation can't be chartered; it doesn't just show up when ordered. It takes time—to be alone, uninterrupted, and think. Consider any single event or activity that you are frequently engaged in; how long is it before you are interrupted or distracted or switch to something else? Ten, fifteen, twenty minutes? If you're average, it's approximately three minutes. And if your friends and colleagues can IM, text, or tweet you, it's zero.

This doesn't necessarily bode well for innovation and creativity.

The beauty of living in a digital world is that we can get back to someone or get a response from someone on an urgent matter almost immediately. But we pay a hefty price. The volume has been turned way up on what people expect in terms of a timely response. Consequently we live in a hurry-up world of fragmentation.

Like a thief in the night, our preoccupation with the urgent and the immediate robs us of the time needed for creativity and blue-sky thinking. When we do have time, we feel guilty. When we don't have time, we feel frustrated. In our execution-driven, results-oriented culture, there is often no immediate result to our pondering, no direct cause and effect. And so we develop a commonly accepted, but equally skewed view of what it means to be productive. We agree with the concept of taking time away from supporting the legacy business to work on new ideas, but when it comes right down to doing so, we're not all that comfortable with it.

The bottom line: if you don't have time to think, creativity suffers, and innovation goes out the door.

In companies where innovation truly is a way of life, people have the freedom to engage in dabble time. For example, 3M expects people to spend 15 percent of their time on their own projects and ideas. At Google it's 20 percent, and at Genentech it is also 20 percent. The point is that time creates the oxygen for new ideas to ferment, the mental space for creativity to grow, and the opportunity for dreams to take shape.

Of course, all of this balances on a fulcrum of trust. Innovative companies don't have a need to control people's time. Instead they

If you don't have time to think, creativity suffers, and innovation goes out the door.

treat people like adults, trust that they will leverage their time wisely, and manage the exceptions. Mandating people's schedules leaves little room for spontaneity. When opportunity knocks and everyone is going ninety miles per hour with their hair on fire, there's no time to explore and reflect. This is why so many companies fall behind the change curve and end up playing by someone else's rules.

It also helps to have a place where people can get away to think. Tata Motors has the Lake House specifically for this reason. As we mentioned earlier, the Lake House sits in the parkland that Tata built across the street from the company's main factory in Pune. It's where Ravi Kant convened a group of leaders that included Prakash Telang and Girish Wagh in 2000 to figure out how to do the impossible: cut 10 percent from the company's operating costs.

(The authors)

A view of the lake from Tata Motors' Lake House on the campus of its factory in Pune. Sometimes, when you step outside and stop thinking, the great ideas come.

This retreat sits in a beautiful, serene tropical setting overlooking a man-made lake. Tata employees are encouraged to hold meetings and entertain guests there as well as use it for reflection time. Ratan Tata, who could go anywhere in the world to get away, frequently chooses to go to the Lake House for think time.

CAN YOU EXPAND YOUR TEAM'S CREATIVE CAPACITY?

It's an important question because most people feel that creativity is a natural gift: you have it or you don't. If you have it, great: you are responsible for coming up with ideas to move the business forward. If you don't have it, you're off the hook. We've got news for you. *Everyone* in your organization is creative, people's capacity for creativity can be expanded, and people are more capable of changing than you think. The challenge is getting people to believe it. Take a closer look at these three assumptions.

Everyone Is Creative

Creativity is distinctly a part of what it means to be human. It's in our nature. It's how we were made. Ignore this at your own risk. Your organization is made up of people who, with the new tools of technology, are creating Web sites, streaming YouTube videos, recording music, and podcasting to the world. They have a need for creative expression. That need will either find an outlet in growing your business or not—it's up to you.

Everyone's Capacity for Creativity Can Be Expanded

You're not sure about this? Then ask yourself, How do art conservatories, film schools, dance academies, creative writing labs, and culinary institutes survive? Certainly some people are more naturally gifted than others, but how much of the intellectual and creative capacity of your organization is really being tapped right now?

"I think there are two types of people in this world—people who can start things and people who can finish things. And while I place great value on the finishers, it's the starters who are rare because they can envision what isn't there."

Ed Frank

Everyone Is More Capable of Change Than You Think

Humans are incredibly adaptive. We change diets, careers/jobs, spending habits, and the way we treat our environment. Whether it's learning to live with a lifetime partner, rising to the challenges of raising kids, or moving on in the wake of losing a loved one, we frequently adapt. We change hairstyles, costumes, cars, homes, and neighborhoods every day. The problem isn't that we aren't creative and we don't know how to change; the problem is that we often don't know how transformative we really are.

There is a deep chasm of incongruity between who we are and what our companies encourage. Most organizations aren't very good at developing people's creative potential. Most organizations are routine and robotic, sluggish and uninspiring, inflexible and dead.

Most organizations do not encourage creative virtues such as artistry, curiosity, nonconformity, originality, and playfulness. Yet significant progress in any business depends on these character strengths. This is why we have so many dead people working—people who show up DOA (dead on arrival), go through the motions, give the bare minimum, and dream about working somewhere else (somewhere they can still contribute nothing but hope to be better paid for it).

Conversely, in places known to be hotbeds of creativity—Google, Zappos, Southwest Airlines, Genentech, Medtronic, and Tata Motors—there is a sense of aliveness. People are vibrant and excited about their work.

No wonder creativity flourishes.

HANG WITH OTHER NANOVATORS

Nanovators are adept at establishing a network of other Nanovators. Ratan Tata is a connoisseur of innovation, and guess what? Connoisseurs like to run with other connoisseurs—in this case, other people who also live, eat, and breathe innovation. It's where they find stimulation and get their creative juices flowing.

As we were discussing innovation over breakfast in Los Angeles one morning, Ratan told us about his involvement with the X PRIZE Foundation. The X PRIZE is a $10 million award created to facilitate radical breakthroughs for the benefit of humanity. The mission of the organization is to invite and inspire innovators to find solutions for some of the greatest global challenges through incentivized competition.

White knight/estars.com

X PRIZE winner Scaled Composites won with *SpaceShipOne*, soon to be offering space tourism through Virgin Galactic.

For example, how about developing a car that gets more than one hundred miles per gallon? With the likes of world-class entrepreneurs such as Google founders Sergey Brin and Larry Page, revolutionary inventor Ray Kurzweil, *Huffington Post* founder Arianna Huffington, and many others, Ratan Tata has put himself in an incubator with visionaries like himself. But not any old incubator; this one operates at the intersection of ethics and capitalism, rewards curiosity, and fosters cross-disciplinary innovation. Imagine the ideas that flow within this group!

The same thing is happening within the Tata Group of companies. Inspired by 3M's Technology Fest and IBM's Innovation Jams, TGIF has created a process that brings technologists from across all the Tata Group companies together. People unite in one of five clusters (Plastics and Composites, Nanotechnology, IT, Engineering, and Water) to identify projects that are of common interest to everyone in the cluster. Participants pool their knowledge and resources to create new products and services.

TGIF is also taking collaboration outside the Group by identifying projects of common interest with companies such as Corning, DuPont, Honeywell, Intel, and Philips, to name a few.

For example, seven Tata Group companies are connected to eight hundred scientists at DuPont. Together they have created a forum to pursue potential innovations in biotechnology, biofuels, specialty proteins, and carbon dioxide absorption. In this sense the Group has embraced open innovation, knowing that breakthroughs will often come from outside the Group. These collaborative efforts are yet another way the Tata Group is making perpetual innovation a way of life.

NANOVATION IS EVERYONE'S BUSINESS

Answer: Anyone, anywhere, anytime.

Question: Where does innovation come from?

Who do you hang out with? How do they inflame your innovative thinking?

If this is true, then everyone is responsible for innovation, not just R & D, the lab, or the design studio. Nanovation knows no titles. It is not bound by hierarchy, geography, gender, or generations. Yes, Ratan Tata has a big title, but without grassroots innovation, without the ingenuity of five hundred engineers operating with entrepreneurial freedom, there would be no Nano.

What if you changed not only the rules of the game but also the rule makers in your organization? What if you literally changed who decides what projects have merit, who works on what, and who collaborates with whom?

Perhaps you think there would be utter chaos and a whole lot of time and energy spent on aligning people and projects. Maybe. But how much time is wasted in a command-and-control system where you have to ride herd on people through scads of review meetings, multiple levels of approval, and thick, convoluted reports? What's the cost of great ideas that get lost in the closets of slow decision making, budget negotiations, and management indifference? How much energy lies dormant because people who are working on their boss's pet project—not the one they really care about—trade full-blown commitment for compliance?

We've been talking about the *voice of the customer* (VOC) for a long time in management circles. If your goal is to be one of the most innovative companies in the world, it's time to think seriously about how you empower the *voice of the employee* (VOE).

Nanovators believe that ordinary people are capable of doing extraordinary things. They operate on the assumption that problem solvers, creative idea generators, and change agents can and should be found anywhere in an organization. This is why they are comfortable encouraging people at all levels to step up and let their voices be heard. The more people who step up, the more ideas will be generated.

Consider this passage from Ratan Tata, writing in the journal *Quest* in 2009:

As a Group, apart from setting high standards for ourselves, apart from looking at the issues of how we run our enterprises, we need to encourage and foster an environment of innovation. We need to empower our young people to have the freedom to dream, to have the freedom to innovate and to provide them the encouragement to convert that into reality.

The challenge therefore, for all of us in managerial positions is, in fact, to create that environment, that environment of encouragement, that environment of motivation. I believe that it is that new level and that new plateau that you could reach which would be the most fitting tribute to JRD Tata in the years to come.

If you went on a treasure hunt for the creative genius that fuels Nanovation in your organization, where would you look? Would you find it in the ranks of your frontline people? Would it exist solely in your R & D areas? Or would you find it all over the place? Where will the next blockbuster idea come from in your organization? Our bet is that it will come from someone, somewhere, you wouldn't expect.

What we *do* know is this. It is easy to say, "Everyone is responsible for innovation." In companies where this is more than mere lip service, people have the freedom to choose projects they care about, projects they can own. Then they have the freedom to run with those projects and see what they can do with them.

Encourage Entrepreneurial Freedom

Mostly we've talked about breakthrough innovation as it applies to the design and engineering of the Nano. But there is another powerful example of Nanovation that lies outside the realm of engineering.

We're talking about the marketing story that ran parallel with the launch and first sales of the Nano.

Imagine leading the team responsible for marketing the Nano. That was the job of Nitin Seth, head of the Car Product Group. You know that a "promise is a promise," which means that in order to honor the 1 lakh price, there is very little margin on the car, which also means little or no marketing budget. Now, add to this that it will be one year from the time you unveil the car to the time it will actually be available. How do you keep people interested during this period?

Seth was given a huge challenge, not unlike the development of the car itself. And not unlike the designers and engineers, Seth's marketing team rose to the occasion.

Seth and his team created a Web site where you, the consumer, can design and save your own Nano with your own accessories. Microsoft built a chat engine that enables consumers to get immediate answers from a bank of eight hundred frequently asked questions about the Nano. You can also play games with the car. For example, the site has a two-dimensional game that allows you to drive the Nano. More than three million people have virtually driven the People's Car. Seth also ran a contest inviting people to guess the exact price of the Nano on the launch date. The winner got an all-expenses-paid trip to Mumbai to attend the launch.

Then, for the first time in the Indian automobile industry, consumers could book a Nano online and make the payment using net banking through thirty-four banks.

Seth had another challenge. With the closing of the Singur plant, production of the car was delayed. With only four hundred cars to distribute throughout India, he was not able to have a car in every dealership showroom. What to do?

The marketing team bought LCD televisions (at a 50 percent discount) from Tata Group sister company Croma, the electronics superstore, and installed them in every dealership. Potential buyers could see the car—interior and exterior—from every angle.

To extend the marketing reach even further, Seth worked with other Tata Group sister companies—like Croma and Westside, one of India's largest and fastest-growing retail clothing stores—to display the cars in their retail locations.

Other Tata Group retailers—Titan Watches Limited and Tata Indicom, one of India's leading mobile phone, Internet, and broadband service providers—were too small to house the Nano. Instead both companies displayed Nano material in their stores, and Tata Indicom sent text messages to thirty-two million subscribers, inviting them to book a Nano.

It created a win-win scenario.

Tata Motors was able to display or promote the Nano for free in more than fifteen hundred retail outlets, and the Nano drove retail traffic into the stores. This combined with four hundred dealership outlets created a total of approximately two thousand brick-and-mortar touch points to complement the virtual campaign. In each of these retail outlets, people had to be trained to answer questions about the Nano because they had never shown a car in their lives.

Here's the amazing thing: Nitin Seth didn't solicit a message from Ratan Tata or Ravi Kant asking these sister companies to cooperate. Nor did he go to the managing directors of Croma, Westside, Titan, or Tata Indicom to get their buy-in. He simply went to his marketing colleagues in the other companies and asked them to participate.

"I said, 'This is what I am trying to do. Will you cooperate with me?'" Nitin told us. "They said, 'No problem. We also see the benefit for us.' So it was win-win for all of us."

"Win-win" is right. The crowds did come to the retail stores. In the twenty days preceding the Nano's launch, an additional 1.4 million potential customers flowed into the stores because the cars were displayed there. And while the people were there, they could buy a Nano Phone (Tata Indicom), a Nano Watch (Titan), Nano Apparel (Westside), and a Nano Mouse (Croma) for their computers.

Seth also struck a deal with Amul Butter to put a Nano on its packaging—at no cost. Amul, a cooperative of 2.8 million milk producers, is perhaps the most recognized brand in India. With five hundred thousand retail outlets across India and a market share of 85 percent, Amul Butter is loved by Indians. And so is the Nano. So having India's favorite car on a pack of India's favorite butter was a no-brainer for all concerned, including the shoppers who picked it up to show the family.

Nitin Seth didn't ask for permission from on high. He didn't plan or process it to death. He moved. He didn't drag his feet because he was confronted with huge limitations. He let the budgetary constraints and the limited number of display cars inspire his team's creativity.

"I had never heard of this," he told us. "We wanted to sell, but we had no budget, no cars, yet we still had to reach the masses. It forced us to think differently."

Nitin pointed out that after the team accepted the limitations it faced, it went into "try it" mode. Since it was too costly to use an outside design firm for Web site development, they downloaded free Web pages from Google and started there. This move became the impetus for developing their own site, which changed three times between the unveiling of the Nano at the auto show in Delhi and the launch in Mumbai. Not bad for the most visited Web site in the country.

And as we mentioned earlier, the most-searched term on Yahoo in 2008.

Measure Innovation

In chapter 16, "Return on Innovation," we talked about some ways to measure innovation. Here we see how the Tata Group takes the temperature of innovation into the Tata culture with a tool called the Innometer.

The Innometer is an assessment tool originally developed by Professor Julian Birkinshaw at the London Business School. Consider it a thermometer that one can quickly stick into a company, department, or team and test the group's temperature for innovativeness.

The Innometer tells you whether your environment is conducive to innovation and compares your company to a baseline of other companies. It's like an annual physical exam for organizations. It provides a diagnosis that ultimately helps leaders develop a plan for treatments. The assessment tool essentially measures innovativeness on two dimensions.

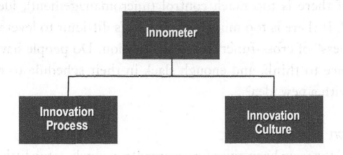

First, how robust is your process for innovation? How well do you ideate? If you cannot ideate, you cannot innovate. This part of the assessment evaluates the degree to which ideas are generated

- from within the business being assessed;
- in collaboration with other business units across the Tata Group; and
- in collaboration with partners outside the Group.

The Innometer also evaluates the process by which new ideas are converted into new products with commercial success. In other words, are there criteria for screening new ideas and a process for getting the initial funds to explore them?

The process part of the assessment examines how well an idea that has been converted is diffused. That is, does the team have a strong process for disseminating the innovation across the organization or into the market?

Second, how robust is your culture of innovation, based on the perceptions of employees? The Innometer measures whether the culture is too constrained, too loose (undisciplined and chaotic), or in the target zone for innovation.

Here, four dimensions come into play:

Space

Do people have the right amount of autonomy to pursue an idea? If there is too much control (micromanagement), ideas get choked. If there is too much autonomy, it's difficult to leverage the "goodness" of cross-functional collaboration. Do people have time and space to think, and enough slack in their schedule to experiment with a new idea?

Direction

Has the team been given (or assumed) too much or too little direction? If there's too much direction, the team's thinking can become constrained, causing them to miss an elegant solution. If there's not enough direction, the team can lose focus and momentum.

Boundaries

Are the boundaries defined enough to provide guidance and direction, but not so well defined as to inhibit creativity? Do the boundaries encourage or constrain risk taking? Open communication? Experimentation?

Support:

Do the systems, structure, and policies of the organization accelerate innovation or slow it down? Do managers' behaviors pave the way or get in the way of innovation?

On each of these dimensions, then, business leaders get a quick snapshot of their culture. They can determine where they are out-performing their peers and where they need to improve. Most important, they develop a deeper understanding about how culture affects innovativeness and a deeper commitment to creating a culture that inspires innovation.

Sunil Sinha is CEO of Tata Quality Management Systems. He stated, "Since much of the Tata culture was driven by numbers, so people are driven by the numbers, and we thought that it may be a good idea to create a framework for evaluating innovation. The Innometer creates a healthy and functional kind of competition among businesses as they compare results."

Sinha explained how business leaders look at the outcomes: "Oh, my neighbor got a 4.5 in process. How come I have got only 4.2? Let me learn from the neighbor what have they done. And why is my culture piece low while somebody else's is so high?" Sunil believes the Innometer is a good tool for top management to get their thumbs on the pulse of what is happening in their organizations.

In addition to the Innometer, the Tata Group conducts a study on the state of innovativeness in the Tata companies. TGIF commissions a group of officers who meet with a large number of people across the Tata Group to figure out what is going right and what is going wrong. From these interviews, business leaders can zero in on what needs to be reinforced and what must be eliminated.

Celebrate Innovation and Innovators

Sunil Sinha is also excited about Innovista, a competition within the Tata Group companies designed to stimulate, support, and institutionalize innovation.

"It was very important for us to bring the innovators to the forefront as heroes and make them role models," Sinha said. "We wanted to showcase innovation and send a message to people that common people can innovate."

Awards for the competition focus on three categories of innovation:

1. Promising Innovations: those that have been successfully implemented
2. The Leading Edge: those that are in the idea stage
3. Dare to Try: those that teach what doesn't work

The whole idea behind Dare to Try is to encourage a culture of risk taking.

The Dare to Try award is given to projects that have failed—ambitious projects that could not be completed because of certain impediments in the process. They might not have worked due to certain cultural issues, deficiencies in technology, or possibly an inability to commercialize the idea.

"I haven't failed. I've found 10,000 ways that don't work."

Thomas Edison, on delays in the development of the lightbulb

"We encouraged people," Sinha explained. "We said, 'Come on and share. We want to learn from you.' But to our great horror, we found that in the first year, after so much cajoling and encouraging people, after telling them, 'You will not lose your pay and bonus,' only three projects were registered from all over our India operations."

Teaching people to stick their necks out runs counter to following deeply entrenched conventions in almost every country and culture. You really have to train people to understand you're serious.

Dare to Try wasn't the only award that had a modest beginning; the whole Innovista program got off to a slow start. In a company with 350,000 employees and a global footprint, only one hundred projects were submitted for the other two award categories.

Sinha remembered the disappointment: "Only one hundred projects! That told us where we were in terms of innovation."

So TGIF took it as a challenge and started to strengthen its communication with all of the Group companies. Gopalakrishnan, Sinha, and their colleagues hit the road and talked to people. They engaged CEOs in discussions about the future of the Tata Group. They echoed Ratan Tata's call for a culture of innovation. And they asked various Group companies how they could make the Innovista process better.

Eventually a lot of recommendations started to bubble up, and gradually the project grew. In 2008, Innovista registered seventeen hundred entries. The number of participating companies increased from thirty-three to sixty-two, and the number of Dare to Try submissions went from three to one hundred fifty.

Sinha appeared to be most proud of the Dare to Try awards.

"We were not comfortable talking about failures," he said. "Too much of our culture was about good news. Our meetings were designed to talk about the good news. Now, the whole paradigm is changing. People are passionately telling us what has failed and more importantly what they have learned about why it failed."

Sinha told us that Dare to Try has another important benefit: when senior managers see a high-potential project that didn't make it, they get behind it, revive it, and help make it successful.

Create a "Yes-Fast" Culture: Yes Is a Distinctive Attitude

In 1966, John Lennon walked into an art gallery in London to preview an avant-garde showing of work by a Japanese artist from New York. At the center of the gallery was a white ladder, above which were hung a magnifying glass and a white canvas. Lennon climbed the ladder and peered through the glass at the tiny, single word printed on the canvas.

The word was *yes*.

"It if had been any other word, I would have walked out of there," he told an interviewer years later. "All the so-called avant-garde art at the time, and everything that was supposedly interesting, was all negative." The artist was Yoko Ono, and while few people could comprehend her work, Lennon got it right away. To climb the ladder was to search for an answer. And the answer was yes.

Isn't that the answer we're all looking for?

Remember our discussion about moving the Nano factory from Singur to Sanand? Time and time again Team Nano found a way to say yes when it would've been so easy to say no. How many organizations would have given up when faced with the same obstacles?

Whether it is the emergence of a new technology, a demanding customer who wants it a particular way, a major crisis, or a market shift that necessitates a new way of doing business, what is your culture's default reaction to these scenarios—yes or no?

Yes is about what's working well, what you want to achieve, what resources you *do* have, what's happening that can give you momentum, how you are going to be part of the solution, and how you *can* get it done.

No is about what isn't working, what is in your way, and who is to blame.

Yes is energizing, vibrant, optimistic, and hopeful.

No is indifferent, apathetic, skeptical bordering on cynical, and demotivating.

If you want to energize your organization and make Nanovation part of your cultural DNA, you need to help people get to yes. And get there faster than ever before.

If you can create a culture that says yes to people speaking up, yes to people pursuing their passions, yes to people on the front line (the true experts) not being quarantined from senior executives, yes to obliterating the barriers that keep people from serving their customers, and yes to blowing the doors off bureaucratic bloat and making decisions fast, the best and brightest will beat a path to your door.

CAN YOU SUCCEED AT WARP SPEED?

Consider some of the market realities driving the need for warp-speed change. Thanks to Web companies like Facebook, Twitter, eBay, and Google, you can now reach a global market lightning fast. You don't have to spend months or years building the infrastructure to get into the game. And in industries that do require infrastructure, global outsourcing allows you to build a team of experts and scale up with incredible speed.

In a sea of sameness, where most businesses are operating in over-supplied markets, customers have more choices. They have instant access to competitive price information. The result is rapidly eroding margins, driving the need for new products, services, and business models. On top of this, the lead time for bringing products to market has been dramatically reduced. This means that your innovations have a much shorter freshness window.

CAN YOU FEEL THE NEED FOR SPEED?

In a world where products and services rapidly become commoditized, speed is your friend. Competitive advantage goes to those who can move with speed, agility, and alacrity. This means fast approvals, open, direct, and forthright communication (no meeting after the meeting), and a seamless spirit of cooperation instead of tribalism across departments and business units,

Speed is exhilarating.

When things move fast, people stay interested and give more discretionary effort. When things move fast, people get more done—people who are more productive stay inspired. When things move fast, the competition has a more difficult time keeping up. All of this is well and good, but it won't happen unless you have a culture that declares war on complacency and thinks "yes-fast."

"Yes-fast" is an attitude, a way of doing business. In a "yes-fast" culture people work smarter, better, and faster on high-leverage things that matter, things that give the organization traction and propel it forward.

YES TO NEW IDEAS

If the Nano story has shown us anything, it is that "yes-fast" cultures are idea hungry. Everyone says, "People are our most important asset." Although we don't like the terminology—the word *asset* objectifies people—we agree with the statement. People *are* your most important asset, but only if they are firing on all cylinders, only if they bring a constant flow of fresh ideas into your business. The fuel for Nanovation is ideas.

In a "yes-fast" culture people don't just *tolerate* new ideas; they are hungry for them. They aren't casual or indifferent toward new ideas ("Oh, that's interesting"); they welcome them—like a child opening a birthday present, they are quick to unpack and explore them to see what's there.

> When **someone** comes up with a **creative, unusual,** or **unheard-** of idea in your **organization,** what **happens** to it?

Does it go into a political or bureaucratic black hole and emerge six months later after the window of opportunity has closed? Is there a process for collecting, testing, and developing new ideas? Who decides what ideas are valuable: those closest to the point of impact or those twice removed from the trenches? With regard to new ideas, do the people in your culture feel that they have a voice, that they get support from others who value their ideas and want to build on them? Or do they more often than not feel that they are rejected, that they are wasting their time? When an idea is rejected, do people know why? Is there an invitation to resubmit a new and improved idea?

Your future will be determined by how you answer these questions because new ideas are the very lifeblood of your business. If people don't see something happen with their ideas quickly, they lose interest. If you don't have a system, a repository where new ideas can be shared, they will get lost. Tapping into the collective brain trust of your organization, being able to see what has and hasn't worked, and having a place where people are willing to build on an idea because they see it from a different perspective are powerful ways to expand your capacity for Nanovation.

When innovation becomes a way of life, capturing the collective wisdom of the organization is a high priority. Systematically retrieving ideas and transforming them into business models, products, and services that have commercial viability become a practice.

As you can see, making innovation a way of life is a lot of work, and it doesn't come easily. Anyone within the Tata Group will tell you that the Group is far from having arrived. After all, building a culture of innovation means that you're always reinventing, redesigning, and redirecting your entire organization.

NANOBITE

What would it look like if your organization had an all-encompassing, corporate-wide culture of innovation?

Maybe it would look like this:

Innovation would be a strategic priority among senior leaders. They would invest a significant amount of time and energy in supporting, encouraging, and enabling innovation.

Every employee would be considered a problem solver, innovator, and change agent. Employees would know how to build a compelling argument and a solid business case for chasing a new idea.

People at all levels across the organization would be challenged and equipped to live up to their creative potential. Innovation would be part of everyone's job description, performance evaluation, and bonus check.

Innovation forums would frequently give people an opportunity to come together, share their ideas, build mentor relationships, and pursue projects of mutual interest.

People would be expected to carve out a chunk of time to think and dream about the next big thing. No one would be embarrassed or ridiculed for having his feet up on the desk for thinking time. People would be encouraged to pursue off-the-wall ideas.

The rule makers would change. Clusters of peers, not just C-suite executives, would decide which projects are worth pursuing.

People with great ideas would know how to get pilot projects funded without an act of Congress. They would also know how to tap the organization for the technical resources needed.

Diversity fuels the fires of innovation. Do you have the courage to surround yourself with eccentric people who don't think, act, or look like you do?

QUESTIONS

- How often do you hear the question "What if?" in your organization?
- How much "thinking time" do your people get each week?
- Do the people surrounding you fuel your creativity or dampen it?
- Does your organization measure and celebrate innovation? Does it recognize and reward those who dare to try?
- What is your culture's default reaction to new ideas, demanding customers, new business models, and major crises—yes or no?

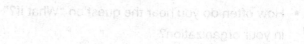

TWENTY-SIX
Rule 4: Question the Unquestionable

An outsider's point of view is always handy.

PAT OLIPHANT

Outsiders ask a lot of questions because they don't presume to know how things work or why something is done a certain way. They don't know what is unquestionable. They aren't held hostage by history because they have no history. They aren't shackled by "we can't" because they don't know "we can't."

Is it a stretch for insiders to think like outsiders? Sure. The good news is that you can borrow a page from the Ratan Tata playbook. You can develop an outsider's mind-set through the discipline of questioning the unquestionable.

What is the
unquestionable?

UNQUESTIONABLE=DEEPLY
EMBEDDED WORLDVIEW

New ideas are dangerous—especially to those who helped create and perfect the status quo and who benefit when nothing changes. Culture is designed to protect itself. People who have a financial, historical, or emotional stake in the old culture and old regime rarely want to change. Question the deeply embedded assumptions underlying the existing culture and you awaken a sleeping giant. As human beings, we naturally feel the urge to protect and defend instead of question what we believe about the way the world works. So, we spend our energy defending the status quo instead of using it to focus on creating the next big thing. Without even knowing it we become prisoners of our thoughts, held hostage by history and incarcerated behind the iron bars of dogma.

When you are wrapped around the axle of protecting the status quo—which usually happens because you helped establish and perfect it—the temptation is to spend your energy defending it instead of using your resources to create the next big thing.

What if Herb Kelleher and Rollin King hadn't questioned the "hub and spoke," "assigned seating," and the "diverse aircraft" paradigms in the airline industry? There would be no Southwest Airlines.

What if Muhammad Yunus hadn't questioned the banks' "the poor are not creditworthy" paradigm? We wouldn't have the Grameen Bank or the tens of thousands of businesses it inspired that are turning poor people into self-sustaining entrepreneurs.

What if Dr. G. Venkataswamy hadn't questioned the "massive blindness can't be cured" paradigm? We wouldn't have the Aravind

Eye Care Hospitals, the largest and most productive eye care system in the world. And three hundred thousand people a year—70 percent for no cost—wouldn't receive twenty-minute cataract surgeries.

(Aravind Eye Care System)

It just takes one picture to see the vast numbers of people who are being helped by the Aravind Eye Care System.

It's difficult to achieve ongoing strategic innovation unless you are willing to periodically think like an outsider and reexamine your closely held assumptions. Here are a few questions that will help you step outside your comfort zone and see with new eyes:

- What are our dominant beliefs about our products and services? Customers? Market? Competitors?
- What do we believe about where great ideas come from and who can innovate?

- Where did these beliefs come from? How do they limit our view of what's possible?
- How has the world changed since we developed or inherited these beliefs? Are they still relevant? Useful?
- What if our beliefs are no longer relevant? What new alternatives are possible?

UNQUESTIONABLE=WHAT PEOPLE BELIEVE IS ABSOLUTELY IMPOSSIBLE

Everybody knew that it was impossible to build a real car for Rs. 1 lakh. And yet the Nanovators did it.

Nanovators know that if you live long enough, time has a way of poking a finger in the eye of conventional wisdom. We now know that the world isn't flat; that Everest can be climbed; that a person who experiences more than eighteen g-forces in a space vehicle won't die; and that a surgeon in a leading medical center can operate on a patient three thousand miles away.

We now know that a person with the most technical expertise doesn't always make the best leader; that an individual can work from home and be just as productive as a person logging face time in a cubicle; and that it is possible to build an incredibly successful business with no bosses, no hierarchy, and no rules.

We know these things because *someone* questioned the unquestionable.

We also know that a little-known Indian car company can turn the global auto industry upside down with a product no one thought was possible. It happened because Ratan Tata has a habit of asking provocative questions like these:

"What's next?" gets everyone focused on the future. It keeps the organization from being comfortable with where it is. Want to get Ratan Tata's attention? Get him to talk about *what can be*, not *what has been*. What's the next big thing for Tata Motors? Or India?

"What if?" brings an idea out into the light where it can be exposed to the thoughts of others who can shape it, mold it, and build on it. What if we expanded the market by making it more affordable for more people to own a car? What if we changed the traditional dealership distribution model and shipped kits to certified assemblers in various regions of the country?

"Why not?" forces the skeptics and unbelievers to step out of the critics' corner and at least consider the idea from the Nanovator's perspective. It challenges the organization to examine whether it has the capability to do it.

"Why not us?" We've tried to generate interest among other manufacturers, but no one is biting. Why shouldn't we be the ones to do it? If not us, who will?

"So what?" challenges everyone to think about the relevance of the idea. Does it matter? Will it solve a significant problem? Is it marketable? Is it worth doing?

Vaclav Havel said, "We must not be afraid of dreaming the seemingly impossible if we want the seemingly impossible to become a reality."

Vaclav Havel asked why Czechs shouldn't rule their own country, even when Soviet rule seemed unquestionable.

Havel should know. He was the dissident who led Czechoslovakia's Velvet Revolution and played a pivotal role in freeing his country from Communist rule in 1989. Questioning the unquestionable opens you up to new ways of seeing the world, to pushing the edge of the envelope and stretching the boundaries of what you think is possible.

UNQUESTIONABLE=WHAT'S POLITICALLY CORRECT?

One thing you quickly discover about Nanovators is that they are notoriously irreverent. They are not afraid to challenge the sacrosanct, speak up, or air their disagreement with people in positions of authority, even when they are the minority voices in the room. Depending on where you stand, irreverence can become a bureaucrat's threat or an innovator's imperative. If you believe that great ideas trump title, status, seniority, and power, irreverence is an imperative.

We've pointed out that Ratan Tata, Ravi Kant, and other members of the executive team were intimately involved in the Nano's development. Yet the younger members of Team Nano weren't afraid to engage in an open, spirited debate with the chairman and his team. Were they interested in pleasing Ratan Tata? Of course. Developing the Nano was his dream, and they knew how much it meant to him. But they also knew that he didn't want to put something "out there" that would embarrass the company, something for which he would later have to apologize. He'd rather scrap a bad idea or even a brilliant idea ahead of its time before that happened, even if it was his idea. *Particularly* if it was his idea!

Remember Ratan's penchant for building a plastic car? When we talked with Anil Kumar and V. Katkar, two members of Team Nano, they remembered the eight to ten months the debate raged over whether to build the car with plastic or sheet metal. Four to five times the engineers seriously studied the issue, and each time they had to tell the chairman what he didn't want to hear: *plastic will work from an engineering point of view, but we have yet to make it work from a manufacturing point of view.*

"Even with as passionate as he was about plastic," Kumar told us, "he never put us down or implied that we weren't good enough to realize his vision."

If realizing the dream was the goal, telling the chairman what he wanted to hear wasn't the way to get there. The way to get there was to take chances and bring the very best ideas to the table, regardless of who opposed or promoted them.

Here's another example of questioning the unquestionable. When the decision was made to move the engine to the rear of the car, the suspension and handling of the car changed—and not for the better. The steering became sluggish and less responsive. Rohit Vaidya proposed having the rear tires larger than the front tires to handle the weight of the rear engine, improve suspension and balance, and correct the problem.

Talk about being politically incorrect. There was complete disbelief.

"Irreverence is the champion of liberty and its one sure defense."
Mark Twain

Abhay Deshpande said, "Nobody accepted this weird idea. It did not fit the model." Even Mr. Arora, the head of marketing for MRF, the tire supplier, thought these guys were crazy. So the only option was to build a prototype and see if the larger tires improved the dynamics of the vehicle. They did. According to Vaidya and Deshpande, they could tell the difference immediately.

Rohit Vaidya stuck with his idea, even when it opened him up to ridicule. When we asked him what kept him believing when his colleagues thought he was nuts, he said, "I just chose to remain patient and eventually let the mule [prototype] speak for itself." And it did.

This is the bright side of irreverence. It opens the door to independent thinking and compels people to step out on their own to pursue a radical idea without waiting for someone to give them the go-ahead. Without irreverence, Nanovation is nearly impossible.

Just to be clear, we're not promoting insensitivity, obnoxiousness, or hyperdriven personalities who must always have it their way. We are not talking about the kind of irreverence that is disrespectful and dehumanizes people or deprives someone or something of its sacred character.

We are talking about a healthy disregard for the uncontested, taken-for-granted assumptions that usually define what it means to be politically correct.

UNQUESTIONABLE=HISTORY AND HAND-ME-DOWNS

The Grandma's Roast Theory is a classic story told in the U.S. that illustrates this idea. It turns out that the young bride cut off both ends of the pot roast before cooking it and cooked them in a separate pot from the main portion of the roast. When her husband asked why, she said, "I don't know. That's just the way my mother always did it." Several weeks went by, and the couple was invited to the parents of the bride for dinner. What was on the menu? You got it: pot roast.

So the husband asked his mother-in-law, "What's the reason for cutting off each end of the roast and cooking them in a separate pot?" The bride's mom said, "I've never really thought about it. I guess I just did it the way my mom always did it. Let's call her and find out." Fortunately the grandmother was still as sharp as a tack, so they called and asked, "Granny, how come you cut the ends off the roast and cooked them in a separate pot?"

The grandmother said, "We were very poor. Ovens hadn't come out yet, and the only thing we could afford were small pots, so I had to cut off the ends of the roast and cook them separately."

It's laughable, except that the same thing happens in both small and large companies. Things—ways of doing things—get handed down from one generation to the next without ever being challenged. Doing it the way it's always been done without questioning its relevance or utility to a new world is dangerous.

If you're selling insurance, real estate, cars, or anything else the same way your grandparents did, you're probably in big trouble.

If you're running a company the way your predecessor did—even if he was Jack Welch—you're probably headed for a wake-up call.

If you're trying to motivate a multigenerational workforce based on what motivates you, you could have a mass exodus on your hands.

If you're marketing to customers through the same communication channels you were using yesterday, tomorrow could be very disruptive for you.

Here's a question: What's *your* pot roast?

The future can be very unforgiving to those who stubbornly cling to what was fashionable yesterday, or those who are unwilling to explore the rationale behind the hand-me-downs. What are you doing today that people will be laughing about tomorrow?

Nanovators declare war on complacency and ask, How can we be three times better tomorrow than we are today? Every rule, policy, and process is on probation constantly. Consider the way your organization does things from the perspective of an outsider. Here are a few questions a skeptic might ask:

- Why do we do it this way?
- Whose idea was it? What do they believe, and why?
- What's in it for them? Why are they invested in it?
- What limitations did they have at the time? Are those constraints there now?
- What other options did they explore? Is there a better alternative now?

A word of caution. When we say question the unquestionable, we're not talking about the kind of skepticism or cynicism that can kill enthusiasm or suck the life out of a new idea. We're taking about a level of curiosity, a passion to know, and a desire to make things better that propels you toward expanded understanding. It literally forces you to think outside the box of usual experience.

If you are taped up inside the box, it is very difficult to read the shipping label on the outside unless you have the mental agility of a contortionist—or the discipline to challenge your theories and let yourself out of the box.

How do you get
OUTSIDE THE BOX?

"I have no special talents. I am only passionately curious."
Albert Einstein

It starts with acknowledging that great ideas are everywhere. Then it's followed by the curiosity to explore and the humility to learn. If you don't want to do what everyone else in the industry is doing and you don't want to play by the same set of rules, then put yourself and your company in a position where you are challenged to look at it differently. What does it take to think like an outsider? Here are some suggestions:

Find a Burning Question and Pour Gasoline on It

Do you have to be a creative genius to engage in Nanovation? No. But you do have to be curious enough to ask questions that others aren't asking. You do have to be inclined to explore the unusual and investigate things that, at first glance, might appear to be off-the-wall, like building a plastic car for 1 lakh or distributing that car in kits to be assembled at satellite facilities.

You have to be fired by a burning question.

Nanovation is as much about identifying the right problem and asking the right question as it is about finding the right answer and solution. With all due respect, Ratan Tata and Team Nano weren't successful because they are smarter or more creative than everyone else. They weren't successful because Tata has more money than everybody. Trust us: there are plenty of very smart people in India, and there are a lot of companies with the capital to invest in a project like the Nano. No, what made them different is that they were obsessed with a burning question: Can we build a really basic, affordable, all-weather form of transportation that will elevate the dignity of the people who drive it?

We remember being young graduate students just starting a master's program at San Diego State University when Steve King, the chairman of the Speech Communication Department, confronted us. "What's your burning question?" he asked. "You should come here to study because you have a critical question that, when answered, will advance the field of communication."

In time, *our* burning question became this: What's the difference between a really great company and everybody else? Answer that, and we can teach people to build great organizations.

Ratan Tata's burning question, in the case of the Nano, was this: What if we could give these people safe transportation they could afford?

Were it not for Ratan Tata's inquisitive nature and passion to explore, were it not for his burning question, the Nano would not be. Had Girish Wagh and Team Nano not dedicated themselves to doggedly pursuing this question, the Nano would not be.

"Never doubt that a small group of thoughtful, committed citizens can change the world; indeed, it's the only thing that ever has."

Margaret Mead

Great ideas don't come out of nowhere; they come from people who have been asking questions to satisfy their curiosity for a long time, even if only behind the scenes. Ratan Tata had been thinking about a safe, affordable form of transportation for at least four years prior to witnessing the family crash on the motorcycle. Maybe he had been thinking about it most of his life, whenever he returned to India from a trip to Europe or the U.S. and saw how different life was for so many Indians.

Have you ever had the spark of an idea and known that you were onto something significant? It haunts you, doesn't it? It burns inside you and you become agitated. It calls you to explore. And until you eventually do something with it, it makes you restless. The motorcycle accident was the spark that brought many of Ratan's questions to the flash point and caused him to act. But make no mistake; he had been tinkering with the idea of a new and better way for quite some time.

Where is *your* burning curiosity?

Curious people see a world that others don't see. Not because they are smarter or more imaginative, but because they look harder, deeper, and more often. They spend a lot of time noodling on ideas and doodling on napkins. Their passion to explore triggers the trial-and-error experimentation that quenches their thirst to know.

Let your curiosity run for a while and it will take you down many roads, some of which will place you in unfamiliar territory. When you look up, you might just find yourself on the outside of your industry, looking in. From this new vantage point you might be inspired to ask a fresh set of questions. If this happens, resist the temptation to fall back into "industry speak," and go for it. Ignore the voice in your head that says, *This would never work*, and keep thinking like an outsider.

Expose Yourself to Radically Different Perspectives

Where do new ideas come from? They don't come from sitting in the same office, talking to the same people, looking at the same computer screens day after day. Spending the majority of your time with people who share your beliefs and assumptions doesn't unleash your creativity. It sharpens your prejudices. It doesn't promote discovery. It leads to close-mindedness.

Nanovators know that great ideas often come from people in unexpected places. That's why it pays to think like an outsider.

The late management guru Peter Drucker made it a habit to study a new subject intensely for three years. Whether it was economics, Japanese art, Greek sculptors, or the opera, every three or four years over a sixty-year period, he picked a new topic. Doing this gave him a substantial reservoir of knowledge, and it forced him to become open to new disciplines, each with its own assumptions and each employing a different methodology.

Ratan Tata has the benefit of overseeing one hundred operating companies in a wide array of industries in different parts of the world as well as several charitable trusts. Every day he is exposed to people who see the world from vastly different perspectives. Every day he is challenged to learn something new and consider the world from a different point of view. With this much diversity, there is a gravitational pull to look at one company from the perspective of another company.

Where you stand determines what you see. Like Drucker, Tata often stands in the place of an outsider. It forces him to garner the learning from one discipline and use it to challenge the taken-for-granted assumptions in another field. His radar screen constantly scans other industries for breakthrough innovations that could be applied to something he is currently working on.

The creativity needed to spawn Nanovation often comes from taking yourself out of a familiar environment and going into one that is new.

Is this uncomfortable, even difficult? Yes. Is it time-consuming? Yes. Does it take more energy? Yes.

But if you want to stimulate the creative juices of what-if and shake things up, you've got to force yourself to do it.

Very few of us have globe-trotting jobs like Ratan Tata has. So much of our daily work is routine. It can have a numbing effect on us. Our brains get lazy, we go on autopilot, and we tend to become comfortable with the status quo. Breaking away, putting yourself in a place that's new, whether it's a new location, a new field of study, or a new group of people, enables you to stimulate the creative side of your brain.

Cast a Wide Net

Toronto-based Goldcorp ran a contest on the Web inviting people to help it find gold in an ailing gold mine in the Red Lake area of Canada. More than fourteen hundred people downloaded the not-so-supersecret data on the fifty-five-thousand-acre property. People from fifty-one countries around the world submitted seventy-seven proposals using methods and technology that in many cases, Goldcorp had never heard about. For $500,000 in awards, the company and its global brain trust found more than $3 billion in gold, making Red Lake the richest gold mine in the world.

Or consider Nintendo. By the end of 2005, Nintendo's storied gaming business seemed to be over. Nintendo, if you remember, ushered in the modern age of video games. But it was bleeding market share to Sony and Microsoft. Sony's PlayStation 3 and Microsoft's Xbox 360 had faster processing, better graphics, more memory, and more functions.

So Nintendo took a big leap, and game developers started spending large amounts of time with gamers. They learned about what excited them and what seemed old-school. They listened to the questions the gamers asked and then forced themselves to ask even tougher questions. What if, they asked, we quit playing follow the leader and took the gaming world in a new direction?

The result? The Wii, a pop-culture smash of such proportions that Nintendo couldn't make the product fast enough to keep up with demand. Anybody within shouting distance of a six- or sixty-six-year-old knows that Wii smashed the competition and made Nintendo the comeback kid of the gaming world.

Each year IBM hosts a worldwide event called Innovation Jam. Everyone from the company's employees and their families to outside experts is invited to join a virtual brainstorming event.

For example, topics might include using clean coal to produce jet fuel, building an electronic marketplace for retirees, and creating an employee exchange between a company and its customers. People log on and post ideas, others react to and build on those ideas, and then everyone votes for favorites.

The Jams started in 2001 with the belief that an open dialogue of fresh ideas could find solutions to huge challenges faster than IBM's researchers trying to solve problems secretly on their own. The largest Jam ever was in 2006. More than 150,000 people from 104 countries and 67 companies came together. The result? IBM invested more than $100 million and launched ten new divisions with the ideas that were shared at the event.

What do these companies have in common? They are tapping into the intellectual capital of the world outside their walls. They are bringing the world to their doorsteps and inviting some of the brightest, most creative thinkers into their businesses.

In a flat world where the Internet offers unprecedented access to human imagination and ingenuity, innovation is global. Never before have we had the bandwidth to engage a global community in a conversation designed to address our biggest challenges. The potential for far-reaching exploration and problem solving is magnificent.

Jettison the Incumbent Mentality

Incumbents are vulnerable to the often-fatal trap of thinking like insiders. Riding the wave of a great innovation, they can be tempted to see the future as more of the same only better—more choices, better features, and better design—all incremental improvements on yesterday's headline.

Nanovators see the future as a whole new game and leapfrog "better" with entirely new rules. Incumbents seek to grow market share by being better than the competition. But even if they are better, competitors catch up, innovations become commoditized, and incumbents eventually get forced into a price war.

Nanovators sidestep the price-value discussion by creating new markets and making the competition irrelevant.

When the first iPhone was released, very few people complained about the $600 price tag. But all of the incumbents scrambled to catch up, and they are still catching up. Very few incumbents (think IBM, Coca-Cola, Kodak, even Apple) make it without a crisis. And many don't make it at all.

Nanovators are ambidextrous. To jettison the incumbent mentality, you have to learn how to manage the creative tension that comes with pouring yourself into something the world is ecstatic about and then letting go of it or changing it up to pursue the next big thing. It is balancing the passion, dedication, and discipline necessary to create a blockbuster product like the Nano or a new business model like iTunes without getting stuck in the assumptions and beliefs that created it in the first place.

How did Steve Jobs and the team at Apple come up with one game-changing innovation after another for more than twenty-five years? One could hardly accuse the people at Apple of not being fanatical about what they believe or devoted to what they have created. Yet they have demonstrated the incredible discipline to challenge those beliefs and let devotion to one product give way to another. They had enough outsider vision not to think narrowly of themselves as a computer company and realized there was a world beyond even the most innovative and well-designed laptops.

They envisioned a world of personal mobile devices that have changed our world.

Apple has been known for being fiercely proprietary. The first iPod was slated to be a Mac-only device. The assumption was that once consumers experienced how cool and friendly the iPod was, they would switch from Windows to the Mac. Apple challenged this either-or assumption and eventually built a Windows-compatible iPod with USB2 connectivity. Drawn by the seductiveness of the iPod, Windows users still flooded Apple's retail stores and experienced the elegance of the Mac. But here's what happened next. Prior to making the iPod Windows-compatible, Apple had sold a million iPods. Within a year of making the switch, the company sold another three million units. Yes, Apple gave up a few Mac sales by ditching its previous business model, but in the next eighteen months the company sold another nine million iPods!

The Nano has received accolades from all over the world. Without a doubt, the man who conceived it and the team that produced it are very proud of what they've accomplished. As you could imagine, they are emotionally connected to the Nano and tangibly invested in it, but you can bet that they are thinking beyond the assumptions and approaches that created the first 1 lakh car.

Ratan Tata said as much when he told us about one of his disappointments with the Nano. He had conceived of a car that would be truly unconventional in terms of materials and manufacturing. Talk about blowing up the old rules and starting over from scratch. Can you imagine exploring the idea of building a car with bamboo or even soya materials? That's what Team Nano did. Mr. Tata told us about another approach he thought would represent a real breakthrough, the idea of a lightweight, easy-to-assemble plastic car. It was an idea both he and Jeff Immelt were sure was the right thing to do. But it turned out to be more expensive than steel.

Speaking like someone from outside the auto industry, Ratan continued, "Had I had a plastic Nano, I would have had to overcome another stigma—that this was not a real car. Our critics would have said that a plastic Nano would not stand up to the rigors of a car. So having a steel car has overcome that somewhat, to my dismay initially, but in hindsight it has made the credibility of the product much better."

Perhaps a plastic car might have been too early, too far out in front of the curve to be accepted by the industry or the consumer, but when we suggested that it leaves room for the next Nanovation, Ratan responded with a mischievous grin, "Yes, it does."

While the Nano is his dream, his "baby," we get the distinct sense that Ratan Tata is far more attached to the next big thing than he is to the car itself. In the end, it's not about the product; it's about the people who find it useful.

NANOBITE

When are you most creative?

Think back to some of your best ideas or the most creative ideas that have come to someone you know. When you got the idea, where were you? What were you doing? Who were you with? The answer to these questions will help you identify how and when creative ideas come to you. They also might lead you to finding or creating an environment that is conducive to Nanovation.

Create a Nanovation board of advisors. Invite five energizing, disparate, disruptive, and unpredictable people to join your board of advisors. Find five diverse people (the weirder, the better) from outside your company, outside your industry, and outside the dominant gender and generational makeup of your employees. Ask them to participate in a forum (virtual or face-to-face, it doesn't matter) designed to look at your business model, products, and services from their unique perspectives. The mission is for them to ask questions and challenge you to think like an outsider. For example:

- What would we be doing differently if we operated our business in your industry?
- What assumptions drive our business that don't make sense to you?
- What are we doing right now that you would kill immediately?

QUESTIONS

- What taken-for-granted assumptions drive your organization?
- What do people in your industry believe is absolutely impossible?
- What is politically incorrect to question in your organization?
- How would you define the *incumbent mentality* in your company?

WHAT IF . . . ?

Challenge

Set aside a day three times a year to get away from the office and have a "What if . . . ?" session with your team. Get as many ideas out on the table as possible, and then choose two or three to explore further.

- What if we had no hierarchy? No bosses?
- What if employees decided for themselves what they would work on?
- What if all meetings were voluntary? What if we conducted all meetings standing up?
- What if we went from voice over IP to everything over IP?

TWENTY-SEVEN
Rule 5: Look Beyond Customer Imagination

Innovation comes from the producer—not from the customer.

W. EDWARDS DEMING

As we've seen, Nanovators start a lot of conversations with "What if?" and respond to a lot of push back with "Why not?" Their imaginations are always on the go to places that others have never been. It's as though they can see over the horizon, beyond the buzz of the market, and beyond the articulated needs and desires of customers. This is how they end up with products and services that were never asked for, but are devoured by customers when they finally get them.

Think of products like TiVo (digital video recorder), iPod and iTunes, and Nintendo's Wii. Does the word *addictive* come to mind?

These first-of-a-kind products empower customers to do things they didn't even know they wanted to do. Customers never asked for these products, but now can't live without them because they've opened up a whole new world.

> When you design a car around customer wishes, you get cup holders. When you design a car around innovative thinking, you get a Porsche.

Inside companies all over the globe, the term *customer-driven* means that the customer is the focal point of the business. Customers should articulate their expectations, and suppliers should rise to meet or exceed them. Right? But that's not the way it played out with some of the greatest product and business model innovations in the world.

Who asked Douglas Engelbart to create the computer mouse or Roy Plunkett to discover Teflon or Freon? Who asked Starbucks founder Howard Schultz to create a comfortable and inviting third place between home and work to have coffee—for $4? And what about people selling used goods or doing research? They weren't shouting out for the invention of eBay or Google, were they?

How could they? They could hardly have imagined them.

When Ferdinand Porsche, the inventor and designer of the earlier people's car, the Volkswagen, decided to build a sports car that would be incredibly fun to drive, he didn't ask wealthy Germans what they wanted. If he had, they'd have helped him design a prewar 1932 Mercedes-Benz SSK, which in 1947 would have been their idea of the ultimate sports car. Instead, he innovated a superlight, rear-engine sports car called the 356, which later evolved into the legendary Porsche 911, the single most successful and long-lived sports car in automotive history.

When you design a car around customer wishes, you get cup holders. When you design a car around innovative thinking, you get a Porsche.

CUSTOMERS ARE #1—BEWARE OF THE CUSTOMER!

Customers are smart and never to be underestimated. But customers don't always know what they want, and if they *do* know what they want, they can't always tell you. Listening to customers might even derail you from pursuing breakthrough innovation and changes that will radically differentiate your business.

Does this sound like heresy? Maybe, but how many customers are on the cutting edge enough to know what's possible in your industry? How many customers are aware of your future capabilities? How many customers are in the right frame of mind to share their ideas for an innovative new product when it will displace the one they just bought?

You might be thinking, *How does this square with all the talk about co-creation [collaborating with customers to create new value] and open innovation [like Linux and open source software]?* No doubt, these approaches have led to incredibly meaningful innovations. The cardiologist who contributes to the development of the artificial heart and the radiologist who advances ultrasonography are pushing medical equipment manufacturers because the status quo doesn't meet their specific needs.

We get it. Customers can contribute to the fantastic fusion of ideas that create blockbuster innovations. Customers—particularly in specialized fields—are a cauldron of creativity that should be tapped when you are looking for fresh insights. We're simply suggesting that you shouldn't take their word as sacrosanct. Even Nintendo's hard-core gamers scoffed at Wii's rudimentary graphics and minimal functionality. Fortunately Wii was aimed at a dormant market—nongamers.

Ask most customers what they want and you are likely to get suggestions for incremental improvement based on the current state of things—a faster laptop, a thinner widescreen, a mobile phone with GPS, better service, or a more realistic game. This feedback is helpful and might be better than not having it at all, except that it tempts you to pursue good when good is the enemy of wow! It tempts you to be iterative and incremental when transformational gets people's attention.

Transformational gets people's attention.

Had Steve Jobs asked consumers what they wanted before developing the iPod, what would they have said? "Give us something smaller, with more features for the same price as what's already on the market." What was on the market sold for $60 or less. How many focus group members would've said, "We're okay with your $400 price"? How many of them understood the future of technology enough to know that a solid-state device would trump a CD scanned by laser? And how many of these people could've conceived of software such as iTunes replacing CDs—one song at a time?

"If I had asked people what they wanted, they would've said faster horses."
Henry Ford

If Tata Motors had relied solely on the market to inform product design, where would it be today? The Nano might be an enclosed motorcycle or a pepped-up autorickshaw. The Ace might be a better three-wheeler or a better standard-sized truck.

Suppose, back in 2003, the designers in Pune asked a focus group to paint a picture of the car they wanted to drive in six years. Isn't it likely that customers would've described something similar to what was currently in dealership showrooms—only slightly better?

No one, not even Team Nano, understood what was possible in terms of technology, design, and engineering acumen. No one was asking for a 1 lakh car because everyone thought it was out of the realm of possibilities.

So, what do you do? Like Girish Wagh did, you keep asking questions until you get the answers no one expected.

Keep customers in the front of your mind and at the heart of everything you do. Talk to them, listen to them, but don't rely on everything they tell you. Use your intuition. And read between the lines of what they *aren't* telling you. How do you do that? Stop distancing yourself from your customers through the mediation of focus groups and sales force anecdotes. Don't just analyze the spreadsheets; engage all of your senses. Borrow from the best methods in social science, and get to know them firsthand:

Anthropology: understanding how a particular group of people developed their assumptions, beliefs, and customs.

Phenomenology: understanding what it's like to be a particular person or group by understanding how *they* subjectively experience and make sense of their world.

Ethnography: understanding a particular group by immersing yourself in their context as much as you can: living where they live, eating what they eat, doing what they do, and using your product or service the way they do.

Be the customer. Get into her head. Experience his world firsthand. How do they do things? What are their aspirations? What do they *really* care about? Do they use existing products and services "as is," or do they modify them? What makes them happy? What causes them frustration? Where do they find fulfillment? Where do they spend their energy? What stories do they tell again and again?

The answers to these questions come primarily from observing, not from doing interviews. Often, you don't know what to ask until you've witnessed the excitement. And you don't know the importance of a question until you've experienced the frustration or picked up on an offhand comment.

In his book *Authentic Leadership*, Bill George, former chairman and CEO at Medtronic, recounted an experience that illustrates this point.

Ratan Tata's natural inclination toward *design thinking* inspired the team to go beyond customer input.

Medtronic is the world's largest manufacturer of implantable biomedical devices, such as neuro-stimulators, heart valves, pacemakers, and defibrillators. George was observing an angioplasty case where the surgeon was using a Medtronic balloon catheter to open up blocked arteries.

"The product literally fell apart in the doctor's hands as he was threading it through the patient's arteries," George recalled. "He was so angry that he took the catheter, covered with blood, and threw it at me. I ducked as it went sailing across the room!" You can imagine how motivated he was to find a solution to that problem. The result was a much-improved product. But if he hadn't been there with the end users, would he ever have known why the product stopped selling?

During his tenure at Medtronic, George observed more than twelve hundred surgeries. These firsthand observations keep your thumb on the pulse of the customer and simultaneously enable you to break new ground where even the customer has yet to stand.

By the way, Medtronic annually targets more than 70 percent of its $14 billion in annual revenues to come from products introduced in just the last two years.

If you talk to the Nano designers, they will tell you that the customer was front of mind every step of the way. Every move that was made, every design feature, and every compromise was evaluated from the customer's point of view. Ratan Tata's deep-seated empathy for customers and how they would experience this car set the tone. But his natural inclination toward *design thinking* also inspired the team to go beyond customer input and follow their creative instincts.

Unarticulated needs are recognizable, but you have to look beyond the obvious. After all, if they were obvious, someone else would've come up with a solution.

So how do you develop the discipline of looking beyond customer imagination? Here are some ideas.

See More Than What's There

What if the seed-bearing burrs that stuck to George de Mestral's pants in an open field could be emulated to create a unique, two-sided fastener that is extremely convenient and user-friendly? Voilà: Velcro!

It's not enough just to look; you have to expand your capacity to see. This means seeing the obvious and asking, What else is going on here? Is there a story behind the story? For example, if you walk into almost any children's hospital in the world, what do you see? You see kids with routine cuts and bone fractures as well as very sick children who are fighting for their lives. That's the heartbreaking obvious. The *siblings* of those who are sick are not so obvious.

Mark Schmitz founded environmental design firm ZD Studios in Madison, Wisconsin. ZD specializes in visual branding—designing physical environments for clients that help tell the brand story. As we were discussing his work with American Family Children's Hospital in the U.S., Mark said, "We designed the hospital for the siblings of sick kids [not the sick kids] so they would want to come and hang out."

In most children's hospitals the children who are sick get world-class attention and care, but their siblings—who often take a backseat to everything that is happening—quickly grow tired of visiting.

That's because there's nothing to do in hospitals that are sterile, quiet, and boring.

(ZD Studios)

ZD Studios designed the hospital's entrance to be active, vibrant, and inviting—like a theater marquee.

If knowing that you are loved gives you a reason to get better, and continually being surrounded by loved ones is critical to this outcome, you have a problem. So Mark and his team designed the hospital to be attractive and compelling with lots of activities for kids. "It's truly a transformational environment," Schmitz told us. "Everywhere you look, there is something to learn, watch, and admire." Schmitz saw the same thing everyone else sees, and then he saw something different. Now the hospital is a cool place to hang out.

The ability to "see more" than what's there makes Nanovators unique. Thousands of people who travel in emerging countries look at families riding motorcycles and see nothing. Ratan Tata saw an opportunity to change the world.

When the family on the scooter crashed in front of him, Ratan saw the bigger story. He saw a family with aspirations that represented the best of India. He saw the indignity of what it must be like to show up—anywhere—disheveled from traveling exposed to extreme weather conditions. He saw a company with entrepreneurial blood running through its veins and "doing the impossible" in its cultural DNA. And he saw—out there somewhere—a team of designers and engineers with the extraordinary capacity to solve an exceptional problem.

Ratan Tata saw a story—born of compassion—taking shape at the intersection of some very interesting trends.

Trade the OR for the AND

In their book *Built to Last*, Jim Collins and Jerry Porras talk about how companies get caught in the "Tyranny of the OR" instead of embracing the "Genius of the AND." The tyranny of the OR—the belief that you cannot live with two contradictions at the same time—comes in many shapes and sizes. You can give employees a voice or you can have order and control, but you can't have both. You can have fun at work or you can have increased productivity, but you can't have both. You can focus on radical innovation or you can keep the legacy business running, but you can't do both. You can take care of your shareholders or you can be a responsible corporate citizen, but you can't do both.

Nanovators refuse to get caught in this either-or thinking. They've seen what can happen. During the dot-com boom, everyone went crazy thinking that e-commerce would drive a stake through the heart of bricks-and-mortar companies. When the smoke cleared, it wasn't an either-or proposition; the genius of the AND (clicks and mortar) won out. Either-or is so obvious and so limiting. It's usually the first answer, not the fourth or fifth one. And as we've said, pressing beyond the obvious and allowing limits to inspire creative solutions is a trademark of the Nanovator.

When a Nanovator hears either-or, it signals a potential opportunity—a chance to find the AND. The either-or mentality of incumbents gave Ted Turner the idea for CNN. Turner simply wanted to stay on top of what was going on in the world, but with his time-constrained schedule he never saw the news when it was offered. The major networks essentially said, "You can watch the news at either 6:30 or 11:00 p.m." Turner bet on the AND—the fact that there were people like him who wanted the convenience of checking the news anytime twenty-four hours a day.

What if you look for the opportunity in the tyranny of the OR while everyone else is lamenting it?

Linux taught us that you can have an operating system that is tailored to your needs AND you don't have to pay a fortune.

Disney and Pixar taught us that you can make a movie that's entertaining for kids AND adults.

Southwest Airlines taught us that you can have low fares AND the best customer service in the business.

Apple showed us that you can have incredible functionality AND intuitive operation AND world-class design.

(The Hershey Company)

Perhaps the most obvious and famous symbol of the "Genius of the AND" is Reese's Peanut Butter Cups.

You get the point. In each case the opportunity for innovation came from the AND, from someone who reconciled what others thought was irreconcilable.

In a 1936 essay first published in *Esquire* magazine, F. Scott Fitzgerald wrote, "The test of a first-rate intelligence is the ability to hold two opposed ideas in the mind at the same time, and still retain the ability to function."

The genius of the AND gives you an opportunity to stand out and distance your business from the competition. Why? Because most people are surprised by anything that defies what they intuitively know to be true.

With the exception of Brijmohan Lall Munjal of Hero Honda and Carlos Ghosn of Renault/Nissan, why did the automotive world believe the Nano was an impossible dream? Perhaps it was because most people were caught in the tyranny of the OR. They didn't believe the AND was possible. It went like this: "Yes, Ratan Tata might build something for 1 lakh, but it won't be a real car." In other words, you can have the mind-blowing affordability or you can have a real car, but you can't have both.

> They kept pushing
> the team to transcend
> the trade-offs and
> find the AND: a
> proper car that one
> could afford AND be
> proud to own.

The majority of people couldn't reconcile the contradictions. The trade-offs between price and quality were too big and too many. After all, cheap means cheap. Right? Not for Ratan Tata. Not for Ravi Kant and Girish Wagh. They kept pushing the team to transcend the trade-offs and find the AND: a proper car that one could afford AND be proud to own.

When the Nano was unveiled at the auto show in Delhi, we think the utter shock in the room came down to this: for at least three years prior to the unveiling, a lot of cynics and naysayers questioned every aspect of the car from its emissions and safety to the quality of manufacturing. But there, right before the critics' very eyes, was the real deal—a substantive, stylish car that was beyond what anyone imagined it to be.

Girish Wagh told us, "Generally people stand up when the national anthem is being played, and sometimes they won't even stand for that. When Mr. Tata drove out onto the stage in the Nano, everybody stood up and clapped. There was thunderous applause."

Why were people so blown away? Because their either-or paradigms had just been shattered. The Nano was simply beyond their imagination.

NANOBITE

Are you waiting for customers to tell you what they want?

If you are, you might already be behind and be forced to play catch-up in a game where someone else is making the rules. Here's why you should listen to customers, but not take their feedback as sacrosanct:

- Customers don't always know what's possible in your industry.
- Customers aren't always aware of your future capabilities.
- When a new product will displace the one they just bought, customers aren't always in the right frame of mind to help you think futuristically.
- Ask most customers what they want and they will tell you they want the same, only a little better, which tempts you to be iterative and incremental instead of transformational.

QUESTIONS

- When was the last time you really lived with your customers, like Girish Wagh trying to understand what villagers wanted in a small truck or like Bill George of Medtronic watching over twelve hundred cardiac surgeries?
- How does the "Tyranny of the OR" hinder your organization from being more innovative?
- What would it look like if you sidestepped either-or thinking and embraced the AND—a real, affordable car AND one you can be proud to own?

TWENTY-EIGHT
Rule 6: Go to the Intersection of Trends

> Red lights are meant to slow or stop movement. Taking
> a left on a red is dangerous, a little crazy, and certainly
> a lonely sport not for the weak-willed. If you have the
> guts and smarts to try it, the rewards are well worth it.
>
> **BILLY GLYNN**

Let us say it again: you can't be a leader playing follow the leader. Nanovation is about getting ahead of the leaders, about getting to the intersection of trends first.

Nanovators aren't necessarily futurists, but they do pay close attention to the early warning signs that precede major cultural, societal, and market shifts. They tune in to the ways that seemingly unrelated patterns are shaping our world.

In their outstanding book *Innovation to the Core*, Peter Skarzynski and Rowan Gibson call it "harnessing discontinuities." Discontinuities hold the potential for tremendous opportunity. Where most people see an isolated trend, Nanovators see combinations. They connect the dots by relating one trend to several others. The intersection or convergence of these trends represents an opportunity for innovation.

It's amazing what you will see when you make a concerted effort to study changes in social and economic patterns, fashion, technology, and consumer behavior.

- How are people living their lives differently?
- How is the geopolitical landscape changing?
- Where is technology going?
- How are demographics shifting?
- How are energy availability and policy changing?
- How will climate change affect your industry?
- How will the businesses of the future be organized and managed?
- How will the regulatory environment shape the development of new products and services?

Do these trends cross paths in any relevant or meaningful way? Where they intersect, are there any hidden fault lines? Do these fault lines have the potential to create seismic shifts and disrupt the world—at least your corner of the world?

At the **intersection** of trends lies **"the next big thing."**

NANOVATION AT THE INTERSECTION

Right now, Nanovation is all about the convergence of three specific trends.

Miniaturization

Everyone speaks of the miniaturization of computing power, from tube-based computational machines, which took up the space of a suburban house to calculate basic mathematical problems, to today's mobile devices, which most of us carry. Today, scientists are developing wearable computers, such as MIT's Media Lab and their Things That Think project that inserts biomedical devices inside marathoners to track their vital signs during a race and transmit the data to doctors. And for the last decade, scientists around the world have been working on molecular computing, data stored on individual atoms, software made of DNA. That means you could store thirty thousand feature films on a device the size of an iPod. Technology is making things smaller and smaller while doubling their capacity every eighteen months, according to Moore's Law.

But it's not just in computing that we're seeing the power of miniaturization. One of the authors owns a watch made by the Citizen Watch Company that runs on power from light and will likely do so until a point slightly before the end of time. Put it in a drawer, and it will continue to run in total darkness for eighteen months. Take it out and, in seven hours, it's fully recharged. The cost of this incredible, earthshaking invention? About $100, anywhere on the Web. The pace of change of innovation in small things is proceeding at an ever-accelerating pace. And it's changing the way we think about what's possible.

The Bottom of the Pyramid

There are nearly seven billion people living on earth today, as many as half of them so far beneath anything a person reading this book would think of as the poverty line that their problems would seem incomprehensible to us. Thirty eight percent of the world's population lives on less than $2 a day, without access to education, health care, transportation, information, sanitation, nutrition, clean water, or anything we would think necessary for life. Add to those numbers another few billion who live just above the poverty line, the lucky ones whose economy helps them eke out $2 to $3 a day, and the picture of the world in which most human beings live seems bleak. Their needs—and our need to enfranchise them into the global culture and economy—will be a driving force in innovative thinking throughout this century, at least.

(Tata Motors)

Visionaries see the bottom of the pyramid not just as a market but as the source of future brainpower. Here are future leaders at a school the CSR team is investing in, near the new Sanand plant.

On the one hand, most of these people cannot afford to buy a single thing your company produces. On the other hand, we can't afford to ignore them anymore. From the point of view of global economic and political stability, we can't afford to have this many people disenfranchised. And from a human point of view, it's not right. They're poor not because they're stupid or lazy; they're poor because they don't have access. As C. K. Prahalad said, "While cases certainly can be found of large firms and multinational corporations that may have undermined the efforts of the poor to build their livelihoods, the greatest harm they might have done to the poor is to ignore them altogether." Understanding and responding to the needs of the bottom of the pyramid are critical today.

Doing More with Less

These days, it doesn't take a genius to see that we need to rethink our use of resources. As we said earlier, doing more with less is one of the key drivers of Nanovation. As the global economy has stalled, all but the most fabulously wealthy have had to reexamine their relationship with materialism, with efficiency, and with energy use. As the world watched BP's disastrous well in the Gulf of Mexico belch millions of barrels of oil into the ocean, it was hard not to think that it was past time to examine our out-of-balance dependence on harder-to-find fossil fuels. And as we watch our climate change, the idea of being more thoughtful in our consumption—the idea that it's always smarter to maximize one's resources than it is to squander them—becomes increasingly compelling.

But it's not enough to just do less with less. The key is to use our ingenuity to find ways to do more with what we have: that necessity is the mother, as they say, of invention.

The intersection of these three trends is driving Nanovation to the forefront of global business, technology, and design thinking. The irony that the most important market of the future may be the market with the least to spend is hard for some people to wrap their heads around, but it's true, as is the irony that we really can do more with less. And it's true because our technology is making it possible.

If your goal is to be a creative, innovative person who can make a difference in this world, there's never been a better time to be alive.

We live in the age of mass innovation. Competitive advantage goes not to the strongest, smartest, or richest companies, but to those that develop the capacity to see what others can't see and turn those insights into innovations faster than their competitors do. At the intersection of these trends, Tata Motors discovered a niche that complacent competitors and unsuspecting customers could not see.

Where did they find it? At the intersection of trends.

First, they saw the bottom of the pyramid, something that's more visible in India than it is in Europe or North America. And on the top edge of that segment of the population, they saw an emerging need. From this new market segment, an explosive number of Indians are becoming more prosperous and moving into the middle class. Their purchasing power is on the rise, and so is their desire for more freedom and autonomy. And this is not only true in India; it's happening in emerging markets all over the globe.

Second, thanks to technology, the miniaturization of information and communication technology and their resulting child, the Internet, the new, emerging global middle class is more educated and sophisticated than ever in history. They talk to each other. They do their homework. And these hyperinformed customers demand products and services with higher value and lower cost.

Third, again thanks to technology, the ability to take costs out of the supply chain, out of design, and out of manufacturing has loomed as a vast frontier of opportunity for the past couple of decades. The ability to do more with less isn't just a nice green catchphrase; it's been one of the defining and driving forces behind the business success of the world's best companies.

Finally, socially conscious customers, employees, suppliers, and shareholders are more dedicated than ever to corporate social responsibility (CSR). Talent, money, and resources will flow to purpose-driven companies committed to safety, energy efficiency, sustainability and community service. This was a key motivation for the Nano team. Like Ravi Kant, they really cared about what happens when a whole family rides on a scooter on a rainy afternoon.

> At the intersection of these trends Ravi Kant saw a vast white space that could be filled by a simple, inexpensive product.

Kant had done his homework. He is a keen observer of what's going on in the world markets. He knew that these trends foreshadowed the future, yet unarticulated needs of a global citizenry concerned about value, committed to independence, and passionate about protecting natural resources and developing alternative forms of energy.

At the intersection of these trends Ravi saw a vast white space that could be filled by a simple, inexpensive product. There weren't any competitors in this space because only a few would even admit that it existed.

The trends were evident. The signals were there for anyone to see. Yet many chose to discount what they were seeing as irrelevant to the context in which they were doing business. They fell into the "you just don't understand that our market is very different" trap. Perhaps others saw these trends as real, but couldn't see how they were related. Meanwhile, Toyota connected the dots and got way out in front of the industry with its hybrid Prius and its youth-oriented Scion.

Even when the Nano was unveiled, many in the Western world became cavalier. They rationalized that a basic, bare-bones car like the Nano could've been designed in the West, but customers would never buy it. Even if they were right, what about the emerging markets around the world? We're in a global economy. Didn't that represent a huge opportunity for diversification? What about reverse innovation—creating a product for the developing world and then distributing it globally? Even when carmakers considered this market, they couldn't conceive of anything like the Nano.

It's easy to be a sideline critic and ask these difficult questions in retrospect. But the lesson should not be lost on any of us. Like that of any great strategist, Ratan Tata's and Ravi Kant's radar was tuned in to the trends of our time. But they didn't just take what they found at face value; they put it through the decision-making grid. Were these trends consistent with their experience—as Indians, as industrialists, and as globe-trotting executives? Where did they converge? What is the probability of these trends being permanent and pervasive? If they are here to stay, what impact will they have on the short- and long-term future of Tata Motors? Is anyone else—in our industry or another—addressing these trends? Do we have the inherent capabilities to address them?

Fueled by Ratan Tata's deep sense of empathy for the common person and his passion to solve a huge global problem, and by Ravi Kant's belief that the trends supported the dream, Team Nano went "left on red" at the intersection of trends and created one of the greatest breakaway products in the world.

FOCUS ON NEXT PRACTICES VERSUS BEST PRACTICES

Nanovators put little stock in what everyone else is doing. There is always a temptation to imitate the strategies that make the most successful companies successful. If it's good for Southwest Airlines or Google or Amazon or Tata or Infosys or . . . , it must be good for everybody. Well, maybe and maybe not. It depends on what you're trying to accomplish.

Best practices might be appropriate because they keep you in the game. As long as you understand that, the best you will ever be by following someone else's best practice is *second best*. That is, unless you flip that *best* practice into the *next* practice.

"They can steal our ideas but they can never steal our culture."
Bruce Nelson, Office Depot

Almost every airline in the world has taken a shot at emulating Southwest Airlines. A few, including Jet Blue and Virgin America, have been successful. Most have failed because they didn't understand that the secret sauce to Southwest's success lies more in an entrepreneurial culture committed to creativity and innovation than in operating strategy. The business model and the operating strategy are much easier to copy than Southwest's one-of-a-kind, fun-spirited, and irreverent culture. If all you have are best practices, that is better than nothing, but it won't lead to game-changing innovation.

If you are okay with incremental change and iterative innovation, best practices are fine. But if you want to make a quantum leap in terms of impact, you've got to look for what C. K. Prahalad calls "next practices."

Prahalad says you can't play a game of "wait and react"— or even "sense and respond"—if you are going to find the next big thing; the future belongs to those who "anticipate and create." It takes guts to be a leader in developing next practices; you're always in uncharted waters. How many captains of industry, particularly the auto industry, thought Ratan Tata had gone off the deep end when he announced *his* next practice?

Following best practices is essentially the equivalent of looking in the rearview mirror. You are looking at what has already been done. Best practices can be deceptive. They can put your company on its heels, forcing it to play a constant game of catch-up. Many people intellectually admit that their organizations' best practices will someday become obsolete. But most of them are unwilling to admit that it will happen sooner rather than later.

Where do next practices come from?

If you want to go beyond "best in class" and establish a class of your own, you have to take a different approach. You have to be a student of where things are moving and what's going to happen next. And then get out in front of it—fast. By the way, this can't be relegated to your own industry. You have to know the trends in any number of disciplines unrelated to your own and then be able to synthesize divergent insights and competing ideas.

Where do the new ideas that create next practices come from? Out in the world. Myopically focus on your own industry at your peril. It limits your sources of creative stimulation and causes you to miss critical market shifts.

What is the next big thing in your industry? Chances are good that the genesis of it will come from somewhere outside your current thinking.

Outside, at the intersection of trends.

QUESTIONS

- What trends are reshaping the world in which you live?
- Where do these trends intersect?
- Do any of these trends or combination of trends have the potential to disrupt your business? Do they signal room for a new product, service, or business model?
- Given these trends, where isn't your competition?
- How do you become or stay relevant to customers who are already living these trends out loud? What are the implications for the way you market to and connect with these customers?
- Are you in touch? Are you connected to the sources of information (reports, Web sites, magazines, journals, blogs, etc.) that will help you identify future trends and the next big thing?
- What if the best practice in a completely unrelated field became the new next practice in your industry?
- What if your company had a portfolio of next practices?

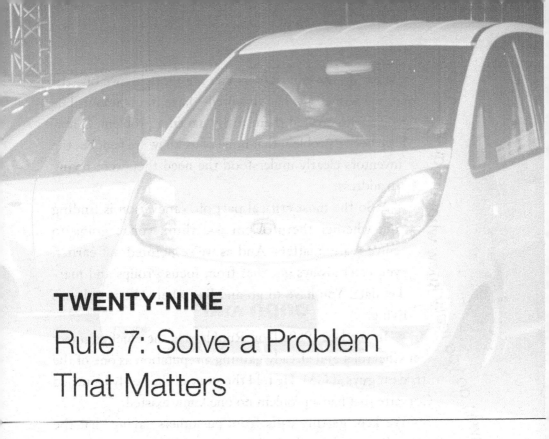

TWENTY-NINE

Rule 7: Solve a Problem That Matters

Design is directed toward human beings. To
design is to solve human problems by identifying
them and executing the best solution.

IVAN CHERMAYEFF

IF YOU BUILD IT, WILL THEY REALLY COME?

A difficulty with solving a problem that matters is this: How do you
know the problem you want to solve really matters?

When we study a radically new business model like iTunes or an
"impossibility" like the Nano, the temptation is to pay more attention to the solution than the problem. After all, there's a lot more
glory and sex appeal in the solution.

What do the innovations you are most in awe of—the ones *you* wished *you* had invented—have in common? The people who created them really nailed a problem. It may have been a problem that none of us knew we had, but the inventors clearly understood the need they were trying to address.

So the most critical part of Nanovation is finding out whether the problem you think you're going to solve really matters. And as we've pointed out earlier, you can't always get that from focus groups and market data. You have to go and live where the people are living.

In the late 1980s Don Runkle was the chief engineer at Chevrolet and already gaining a reputation as one of the true car guys at GM. He told the story of the newly launched Corvette that had a problem no one knew existed.

"We kept getting calls from customers saying that the roof of the new coupe leaked in the rain. We tested the cars, hosed them down, drove them in the rain; we couldn't get them to leak." Finally frustrated and suspecting that the owners were just a bunch of nuts, he sent a team of engineers to the home of one of the complainers and asked him to show them the problem.

The Corvette owner took a hose, hosed down the roof of the car, then turned the hose off and opened the driver's door. Water streamed off the roof and down onto the driver's seat.

"Once we understood what the problem was," Runkle remembered. "It was easy to fix."

And they couldn't understand the problem until the engineers went and lived with it.

But it's one thing to have customers calling and telling you there's a problem. What do you do with a problem that no one has identified?

HOW DO YOU KNOW WHEN A PROBLEM REALLY *DOESN'T* MATTER?

There's no easy answer to that. Late-night television is filled with pitches for products that may be inventive but don't really matter. Do you really need one more appliance to chop and dice your vegetables? Maybe you do. But does the rest of the world? Do you really need a blanket with sleeves when you watch TV? Somebody must, because they sell them, but why?

Finding world-changing problems to solve is massively difficult to do. But here's a hint: if you're more interested in the technology than in the solution, you're probably heading for a fall.

(Chris Mayne)

For Ratan Tata and his colleagues, getting these kids the education and health care they need to live up to their potential is a problem worth solving.

WHAT CAN WE LEARN FROM SERIOUSLY COOL INNOVATIONS THAT DIDN'T MAKE IT?

Let's look at three examples of what we believe are seriously cool innovations that didn't make it or haven't performed to expectations yet. In sharing these three stories, we are painfully aware that hindsight gives us an advantage that people never have on the front side of an innovation. The men and women behind these three innovations are way smarter than we are. So why didn't their ideas take root?

The tragic flaw in all three of these stories is that they are love affairs with technology rather than love affairs with people and their problems.

The Segway: The Answer to Ultracool Urban Mobility?

(Segway, Inc.)

In 2001, word started to spread about a new invention that would revolutionize transportation and change the world. The hype was huge. Insiders assured us that the invention, code-named Ginger, would reshape the way cities were laid out and would be a catalyst for urban renewal. It had the endorsements of big-time innovation mavericks Steve Jobs and Jeff Bezos. And the venture capital people predicted it would rack up its first $1 billion faster than any company in history had reached that goal. Lots of people thought that, even before they knew what it was.

The Segway, a computer-controlled, self-balancing human trans-porter, is a seriously cool invention. We marvel at the technology and absolutely love it. You've probably seen shopping mall security guards, postal carriers, or police officers in airports riding them. Highly maneuverable, easy and safe to use, and radically different from anything on the market, the Segway is definitely a category of one.

But the Segway hasn't even come close to performing to the over-inflated expectations of the media and its brilliant inventor, Dean Kamen. Why?

To call the $5,000 Segway a failure would be unfair. According to the *Wall Street Journal*, Segway sold 23,500 units in 2006. The company's Web site says it has 47 global distributorships with 350 authorized retail points in 80 countries. It also boasts an annual growth rate of more than 50 percent. Still, Segway's commercial

How do you **avoid** going too far **beyond** the customer's **imagination?**

success has fallen far short of expectations. In its second year, Kamen predicted that Segway, Inc., would be producing 10,000 transporters a week. Confident that he had a blockbuster on his hands, Kamen leased a 77,000-square-foot warehouse and hired people to work around-the-clock shifts. He even enlisted scores of lobbyists to persuade state legislatures to loosen their laws allowing Segways to be used on sidewalks.

What tanked the widespread success for which this technological wonder was destined? First, it is an advanced technical solution that solves a loosely defined problem—or perhaps one that doesn't exist at all. To say that it's unbelievably cool and radically different doesn't make a very strong value proposition. What will the Segway do for people that other products can't? Yes, it offers law enforcement officials the flexibility to cover more ground with less effort in places such as malls and airports, but are these niches large enough to sustain it?

Second, the elitist price, too expensive for most consumers, is a barrier to creating critical mass. It fails to compete effectively against less expensive alternatives. For $5,000 you can buy a used car or a new motorcycle. On top of the high acquisition cost, the proprietary batteries are expensive, making the maintenance cost high as well.

Finally, Kamen essentially took a page from the Steve Jobs playbook and said nothing during the year leading up to the launch. His secrecy stirred a media and online frenzy of speculation about what Ginger would be. Then after the launch, Kamen boldly proclaimed that the Segway would be to the car what the car was to the horse and buggy. The product had been overhyped. How many cities have been redesigned around the Segway? How many Segways have you seen scooting down the sidewalk?

How can you tell if the market is ready for what it hasn't yet asked for? You have to be willing to get out into unfamiliar territory, but if you are too far out in front, customers won't follow.

Webvan: The Amazon of Grocery Shopping?

In 1999 Webvan launched one of the boldest, most ambitious, and well-financed efforts to rewrite the rules of retailing and revolutionize the grocery industry. Founded by Borders bookstore cofounder Louis Borders, Webvan set out to provide time-starved shoppers with the convenience of ordering groceries online twenty-four hours a day. A fleet of customized delivery vans would then deliver the goods within a thirty-minute window the next day.

The idea was that every time customers ordered online, Webvan would get smarter about who they were and what their preferences were. The second time they ordered groceries, what would happen? Customers would simply revise their original lists. What originally took most people an hour or more in the store became a seven-minute process.

Webvan started delivering groceries to just 10,000 homes in the San Francisco Bay area before a rapid expansion plan took hold. In the end, the company was making deliveries to about 750,000 customers in Chicago, Los Angeles, Portland, San Diego, San Francisco, and Seattle.

So why did Webvan go bust? There are many reasons, but one stands out. The success of the business model required customers to radically change their buying behaviors. If it's true that people don't always know how to ask for what they haven't experienced, it's also true that sometimes the experience isn't compelling enough to cause them to change. Customers had to order their groceries the day before they needed them, and life doesn't always work that way. People just didn't get into the swing of creating new habits and playing by new rules.

The company was built on a fundamental premise: people would prefer to buy groceries online and have them delivered at home rather than go into a supermarket. Unfortunately the assumption was flawed. The customer base never reached a critical mass fast enough to support the enormous investment made in building Webvan's massive distribution centers.

Webvan made another fatal assumption. It would have to grow explosively to ward off competitors. Had the company slowed down and let demand drive capacity, then conceivably some customers would have learned to be more proactive in organizing their shopping needs. Who knows? With a little time on its side Webvan, like Amazon and Apple, might have attracted a younger generation of online shoppers who loved the convenience and made this disruptive business model work.

You have to ask, Are the trends that launched this project still relevant, or are they changing? If they're changing, do these market shifts lend more or less support for what you are doing? In either case, do you have the agility to adapt?

Iridium: The Edsel of the Sky

Imagine being in a remote Indian village, on a secluded island in the Bahamas, or on a boat in a rarely traveled Alaskan waterway and having to connect with your offices in Singapore, Europe, and the U.S. Sounds rather exotic, doesn't it? This is what Iridium, the sixty-six-satellite global phone communications service, was designed to do.

The brainchild of Barry Bertiger, one of Motorola's brightest engineers, Iridium was a response to his wife Karen's complaint that she couldn't reach clients using her cell phone from the Bahamas. In 1985, working with two other engineers at Motorola's Satellite Communications Group, Bertiger envisioned a low-earth-orbiting satellite system that would allow subscribers to make calls from any place on earth. After being rejected by his superiors, Bertiger got the green light from Motorola's chairman at the time, Robert Galvin.

On November 1, 1998, having just launched a $180 million advertising campaign, Iridium was in business. Sadly by August 1999, the company had only twenty thousand subscribers. Confident that it had its thumb on the pulse of the market, Motorola invested $6.5 billion in the project. This meant that Iridium needed fifty-two thousand subscribers to meet loan covenants and more than six hundred thousand to eventually break even. It wasn't even close. Two days later, after becoming what one writer dubbed the "Ford Edsel of the sky," Iridium made history by filing one of the largest bankruptcies in U.S. history.

The satellites were launched successfully, but why didn't the business ever really get off the ground? Iridium failed to anticipate the rate and speed with which cell phones would become ubiquitous. As the spread of cellular increasingly met business travelers' needs for connectivity, Iridium found itself pursuing a market that was shrinking fast—military contractors, oil drillers, and geologists wouldn't carry the day.

The phone itself was a sight for sore eyes. The $3,000 brick-sized handset was bulky, heavy, and unattractive. To make matters worse, the handset depended on strict line of sight between the phone's cigar-sized antenna and the orbiting satellite. Calling required the user to step outside a building or a car; even if you were out in the open, you had to be positioned just right so as not to drop a call. To say that Iridium was design challenged is probably an understatement.

How many CEOs are willing to leave a meeting and step out of a building onto a street corner in the middle of Mumbai just to make a call that will cost them $3 to $8 per minute? It's easy to see how the market for potential buyers narrowed very quickly.

On top of all this, Iridium was a partnership of eighteen companies with Motorola holding the majority stake. Unfortunately less than six months before product launch, the partners, who controlled marketing, pricing, and distribution, apparently hadn't taken the project seriously. Marketing plans were behind schedule. Sales teams hadn't been created. There were no distribution channels. Many of the partners were huge telecoms that regarded Iridium as a tiny thing and failed to give it the zealous support it needed.

NANOVATION REALLY MATTERS

In the end, all three of these companies created brilliant solutions to nonexistent problems. And even when their solutions were elegant, as in the case of the Segway, their pricing was such that they made themselves irrelevant in the marketplace.

Nanovators have to be very clear on the problems they seek to solve. Albert Einstein's famous remark, "If I had twenty days to solve a problem, I would take nineteen days to define it," suggests that defining the problem is as critical as designing the solution.

In the real world, walking is not a problem, at least not a $5,000 one. But entire families perched on scooters in the rain? That was a problem everyone knew needed a solution. That was a problem that *really* mattered. The "Now You Can" campaign, as depicted in the following print ad, captures the significance of the problem the Nano solves.

NANOBITE

Consider these lessons learned from the experiences of Segway, Webvan, and Iridium founders:

KNOW THE REAL PROBLEM YOU ARE TRYING TO SOLVE. Think about the underlying interests of the people who would buy your product. What are they really trying to accomplish? Are they buying a hammer, or are they buying a wood deck overlooking a gorgeous canyon? Do they want to know the weather conditions or what they should wear today? Are they buying a car or a symbol of freedom, safety, and status?

DOUBLE-CHECK THE ASSUMPTIONS UPON WHICH YOUR BUSINESS CASE RESTS. Before you launch a marvelous technological achievement, ask, How do we make money on it? Is the value proposition clear and irrefutable? Don't let the glamour of sexy technology blind you from a weak business model. The Nano certainly doesn't have the stigma of sexy technology, but it isn't design challenged like the Iridium, and it is being launched in one of the fastest-growing car markets in the world.

Do the trends still hold true—particularly if you have a long product development cycle? In Iridium's case the trends shifted dramatically, but the company failed to adapt.

Is your product or service compelling enough for consumers to change their behaviors? Webvan thought people would gladly change their grocery-buying behaviors—they didn't. There is no question that a global economic crisis has intensified frugal consumer buying behaviors. This will serve the Nano well. What percentage of the approaching eighteen million two-wheeler market can the Nano convert? This remains to be seen.

CAN YOU BUILD IT FOR A PRICE THAT CREATES CRITICAL MASS? Segway and Iridium established price points only the elite could afford in markets where there are cheaper alternatives. The Nano, on the other hand, has the potential to expand the number of households that can afford to own a car by 65 percent.

CAN IT BE GRADUALLY SCALED? Do you have to bet a significant portion of the farm (as Webvan did) before you learn whether the thing you are creating has traction, or can it be "road tested" first and then ramped up gradually?

QUESTIONS

- Does your next big product or process or business model innovation solve a significant problem and serve the world in an important way, or is it a result of your fascination with cool technology?
- Have you really nailed it in terms of defining the problem you are trying to solve?

THIRTY

Rule 8: Risk More, Fail Faster, Bounce Back Stronger

In order to succeed, people need a sense of self-efficacy, to struggle together with resilience to meet the inevitable obstacles and inequities of life.

ALBERT BANDURA

O ne could argue that Nanovation has less to do with having superintelligence, great genes, or creative illumination than it does with being fearless. We don't want to mislead you here. Everyone is afraid of something. We're afraid of people who look, think, and act different from us. We're afraid to *suck*—at anything. We're afraid of ideas that are foreign, strange, and weird. We're afraid to tell it like it is because we're afraid to be challenged. Mostly we're afraid of making a mistake or being wrong, being rejected or being alone, losing control or looking foolish, and we're afraid of the embarrassment that usually comes with these things.

Consider two young children in art class playing with clay for the first time. One won't pick up the clay for fear of being laughed at and ridiculed. The other is joyfully shaping and molding away, careless about what the world thinks of his lopsided candy dish. Both kids are creative, but fear inhibits the first child's imagination and stunts his creativity.

FACE THE FEAR AND KEEP GOING

This is an important character virtue since fear is an integral part of Nanovation. Radical innovation almost always involves doing something untried, unproven, and unknown. When you pursue a creative idea that takes you way beyond what anyone thinks you are capable of, fear tempts you to make agreements with the doubt that antagonizes you. But if you push through fear and doubt, you often arrive at something that has truly never been done before.

If it isn't scary, is it really creative?

People such as Ratan Tata aren't fearless. They simply have more control over their fears than many people do. They have less fear of embarrassment, of what will happen when they risk big.

Fear is one of the great enemies of Nanovation. Fear steals our dreams, weakens our resolve, lowers our esteem, paralyzes us, and hinders us from pursuing big ideas. Fear—if we succumb to it—suffocates the creativity that fuels economic growth and vitality.

"The only thing we have to fear is fear itself."
Franklin D. Roosevelt

When fear gets a chokehold on a leader, the result is a toxic, fear-based culture where people are afraid to do anything that resembles radical. Businesses die every day because of this. Fear stops the flow of new ideas. Then the river of creativity dries up, leaving a crusty, old riverbed of rocks and missed intentions, remnant of something that was once vibrant.

The problem is that most fears are irrational, but they get a grip on us before we know it. Run from your fears, and they will grow stronger. Ignore them, and they will own you. The key to stepping through fear is to recognize it for what it is, face it, and bear down on it. When you do, fear loosens its grip and makes room for the creativity and risk taking that drive Nanovation.

(Chris Mayne)

These women and their families live on less than $2 a day. What do *you* have to fear?

The best way to destroy fear is to do the very thing that frightens you. Just for the record, we are not talking about BASE jumping off the Petronas Towers in Kuala Lumpur or going on *America's Got Talent* when you really don't have any.

We're talking about real-world risks and the courage to stick your neck out for something you believe in. Courage takes practice, and practice comes from putting yourself in situations that activate fear.

Ratan Tata has risked often, and oftentimes he has risked big. Undoubtedly doing this has forced him to deal with fear. But each big risk was always about serving people, advancing the company, or building the nation. In other words, his passion for the bigger yes clearly stood on the other side of the chasm (leap of faith), calling him to step through his fears. But it didn't happen all at once. One bold move led to another and then another. And with each new risk the pipeline of self-confidence expanded.

Exploration is about adventure, and adventures are often dangerous. The Nano project was an adventure wrought with danger: public ridicule, escalating materials costs, flooded land, and political unrest. Nanovators aren't more courageous than everyone else; they've simply found more reasons to step through their fears and into the adventure. Their ambition to make a dent in the universe intensifies their desires to control the fears that stand in the way.

What If You Had Less Fear and More Exploration?

Would your imagination grow? Is it possible that people in your organization would see diverse others as a source of creativity and embrace them? Could this increase the flow rate of fresh ideas? Would it help you connect dots that were previously unconnected? Would there be more openness and transparency? Would people speak up and tell the truth so the organization could move faster?

Building a greater bandwidth for innovation, finding out what your organization is really capable of, starts with a bigger yes and ends with a gutsy, visceral decision of the will to step through fear. This, then, is the prerequisite to risking more, failing faster, and bouncing back stronger.

RISK MORE

Risk is about avoiding negative consequences while pursuing something positive, yet dangerous. Between the fear that something bad might happen and the excitement that something good might happen lies risk.

Nanovation and risk go hand in hand. It's almost impossible to

Nanovation is about discovery. You can't discover if you're not willing to risk.

have one without the other. This doesn't mean you have to bet the farm, but it does mean you have to create an environment where risk taking is not only acceptable; it is expected.

In the late 1990s two corporations, Whirlpool and Maytag, were operating in a sea of sameness. Each had the same products, the same declining margins, and the same flat growth rates. And to make matters worse, global competition was coming on strong. Whirlpool embarked on one of the most massive transformations in corporate history while Maytag hunkered down, embracing a strategy of cost containment.

In their book *Unleashing Innovation*, Nancy Tennant Snyder and Deborah Duarte document Whirlpool's full-blown, company-wide journey to make innovation a way of life. As they report, the charge from then CEO Dave Whitwam was bold and clear.

"Innovation will come from everywhere and everyone, and when we are successful, every job at Whirlpool will change," Whitwam declared. The initiative that Whitwam launched made risk taking a deeply embedded part of Whirlpool's DNA.

What happened? Whirlpool became an idea machine with more than seventy thousand employees who see risk taking and innovation as an integral part of their jobs. Maytag, the once iconic American brand, leaned on yesterday's headline—reliability—when the market was crying for something new. Whirlpool has become a $20 billion global powerhouse with more than 20 percent of its revenues coming from innovative products—up from zero ten years ago. Maytag self-destructed by cost cutting its way into the ground. Whirlpool has been lauded as one of the most innovative companies in the world. In 2006, Whirlpool bought Maytag.

We have yet to find an organization where innovation is a way of life that doesn't also have a culture that encourages people to try new things and test new ideas. The problem with Maytag was that it thought playing it safe (hunkering down) would be *safe* when, in fact, safe was risky. Choose your approach: big leap of faith into the future or business as usual. Either way it's a risk. Obviously the key is having enough evidence to support your approach—and even then, there are no guarantees.

Was Singur Too Much Risk?

When Ratan Tata chose to locate the Nano plant in Singur, he took an enormous risk. In retrospect, one could argue that it would have been a lot safer to build the plant in another state. One could also argue that the Nano project had taken enough risks already.

On the first day that Tata Motors' representatives went looking for land in Singur, there were demonstrations against them. Less than two months later, Mamata Banerjee threatened bloodshed if Tata proceeded with building a plant there.

Was Ratan naive to go into this?

No, because his dream for the Nano was bigger than the car itself. He took a calculated risk, supported by a solid business case, in the service of a greater cause. Officials in the new government of West Bengal courted him. Even though they were Communist, they knew they needed to build an industrial base there. In the service of his greater cause—to lift the Indian people out of poverty—Ratan pushed Team Nano to make the move to West Bengal.

He knew that India couldn't move forward if some states lagged so far behind. He knew the Bengali people had the highest literacy rate in India, and he knew they could see what had happened in places like Chennai and Bangalore where people had a chance to get out of subsistence farming and put their intelligence and energy into commerce, industry, and the global economy.

Tata Motors didn't need the land in Singur, and it didn't need the problems. The company already had thousands of acres of land owned by different entities in the Tata Group, and many more states offered enticing proposals of land and incentives. There is no evidence that Tata Motors had a significant financial or other advantage in building a plant there.

In concert with Ravi Kant and the other senior executives, Ratan

Tata made a leadership decision that was consistent with the Nano's cause. He felt the risk was mitigated by Tata's reputation. If anyone could make this work and bring the parties together for the greater good, it had to be Tata. And if they succeeded, the result would be like opening a fire hose of intelligence, skill, and entrepreneurial spirit within the Bengali people, as other companies jumped onboard to be part of the new West Bengal.

So was he naive and reckless to introduce these risks into the project? No, he was passionate in his belief that they could make a difference. He knew the government represented the wishes of the majority of the people when it called him to serve.

If the Hole You Are in Is Already Too Deep, Stop Digging

Two and a half years later, protesters led by Mamata Banerjee took over the business office in Singur on the day that 250-plus checks were to be delivered to the remaining unpaid landowners. They stopped the process of compensating the farmers and declared that the factory would never open. It was clear that the demonstrators would never cease, and as the violence escalated outside the gates of the Nano plant, it was clear that the political battle would no longer just risk delaying the project. As long as they continued to fight it out, there would be no Nano.

In the service of the Nano and the greater cause of providing safe, dignified mobility to the emerging Indian middle classes, Ratan Tata pulled the plug. The risk no longer served the cause. He couldn't let politics endanger his people or jeopardize the project any longer, and that's exactly what a tenacious, stay-the-course stance would have resulted in.

Our takeaway from the Singur experience is this: those who fail in the service of a great cause never really fail at all. Although the tangible losses at Singur were colossal, the intangible, immeasurable gains should not be overlooked. In going to Singur, Ratan Tata reinforced his commitment to the Tatas' legacy of nation building. In pulling out of Singur, he showed that he is willing to disadvantage the company for the well-being of his employees as well as the good of a nation. That this decision has endeared Ratan to the people of India and cemented yet another layer of brick on the wall of goodwill is beyond dispute.

FAIL FASTER

In many organizations the unwritten mantra is: "Avoid mistakes at all costs." The Nanovator's mantra? "If you're not standing on the edge, you're taking up too much space."

Nanovation is about pushing the edge of the envelope. Anytime you are trying to do something radically different and risky, you are bound to have some blowouts.

Nanovators accept the fact that innovation requires experimenting, and you can't experiment without making mistakes. The key is to quickly learn the lessons, move on, and do your best not to repeat them. The faster you put your ideas out there, the faster you learn about what works and doesn't work. This test it–learn–modify it cycle can expand your capacity for innovation and become a huge competitive advantage.

WHAT IF?

What if failure was an *intended* consequence?

In most organizations failure is an unintended consequence. Yes, places such as pharmaceutical labs and automobile crash test sites are the exception to this rule, but what if failure became an intended consequence in your business? In other words, what if every five years, each product in your portfolio had a mandatory retirement—regardless of how successful it is?

Would this create a burning platform that inspires you to focus on the future? Would it make innovation a priority and therefore a core capability?

*Adapted from Voyagers, 2007

As we have pointed out, Nano is as much a story of failure as it is success. First it was a 543 cc engine that failed to deliver the required power. Next it was a 586 cc engine—still not enough power. Finally after multiple experiments, Team Nano got it right with a 624 cc engine. Whether it was plastic molding, paper honeycomb, soya, or bamboo, Team Nano met with one failure after another while exploring new frontiers in materials manufacturing. But in Edison-like fashion, each experiment and failure moved the team closer to the ultimate result. And as one "failed" idea can lead to another successful idea, these experiments left the team with something to revisit as new versions of the Nano will be explored.

Celebrate Intelligent Failure

Remember the Dare to Try awards that the Tata Group Innovation Forum (TGIF) gives out each year? This is Tata's way of making risk taking acceptable and redefining what it means to fail. By celebrating intelligent failure the Group is essentially saying, "We can't grow if we don't push the limits, and we can't push the limits without screwing up. So let's not be embarrassed or intimidated by our failures; let's get them out into the open where we can learn from them."

Now, let's define *intelligent failure*. An intelligent failure is in keeping with the vision and the values driving the organization. It failed in spite of a solid business case, appropriate resources, and good execution.

Here is what one Group company learned from failing.

Tata AutoComp Systems' interiors and plastics division (TACO IPD) in Pune supplies plastic body panels for cars. When the Nano project was launched, Anil George, Srinivas Devareddy, and Gautam Pandit from TACO IPD decided to take a risk and develop a low-cost plastic door for the Nano. Now mind you, Team Nano hadn't asked for it, and there weren't any specifications because the car was still in the initial concept phase. The team from TACO IPD saw an opportunity—if there were no specs, perhaps they could help define them.

The guys at TACO IPD knew that weight and cost would be paramount, but beyond that it was a clean slate. No one waited for permission to act. Instead, they took the initiative to build a complete door, made of plastic, reinforced by a metal bar. If Team Nano accepted the door, annual gross revenues would be approximately $39 million. A worthy risk, given the development cost was less than $100,000.

Even though the door developed by TACO IPD was just outside the cost parameters established by Team Nano, Ratan Tata and the design team looked at it anyway. Ultimately the door wasn't accepted, and given the top-secret nature of the Nano project, the TACO IPD team got no explanation. Of course, team members were disappointed, but that didn't stop them from using the experience to learn.

In their postpartum debrief TACO IPD learned the following lessons:

- They could've done a better, more thorough job of capturing customer wants, needs, and insights.
- Better results might have been achieved if they had co-evolved and codeveloped the concept with the customer.
- A phased review depicting where they were on and off target could've steered the project better.
- By doing a better job of building a relationship with the customer at a strategic level, TACO IPD could be seen as a partner in the design process.

Perhaps the most important lesson was that in trying, TACO IPD gained the self-confidence to be a player in the design and development of car cockpits.

By highlighting this story and awarding the Dare to Try honor to TACO IPD, the Tata Group is sending a strong message that it welcomes risk takers. In doing so, it is breaking down the barriers of fear that prevent people from pursuing far-reaching ideas.

Bounce Back Stronger

If you are going to engage in Nanovation, get ready for a whole lot of really smart people telling you why you are nuts. These skeptics will come disguised as friends, family, colleagues, and industry experts. They may even show up as activists with a political agenda. But make no mistake, they will come—and they will be persuasive.

It happened to Ratan Tata. Why should you think you would be any different?

Nanovation requires a resilient spirit. Nanovators don't like to make mistakes and screw up any more than you do; but when they do mess things up, they aren't rocked by it as much, they don't give up easily, and they don't waste a lot of time looking in the rearview mirror. Looking back only causes them to focus on something they can't control and slows them down.

 "Man has never made any material as resilient as the human spirit."
Bern Williams

Resilience—the ability to bounce back—comes from emotional maturity. It's about celebrating success, but understanding that success is never final. It's about recognizing that failure isn't final as well. All of this comes from risking, failing, and trying again. It's a bit like lifting weights. The more times you go through this cycle, the more you expand your capacity to bounce back.

As we've seen, Team Nano was extremely resilient in the wake of pulling out of Singur. Despite extreme disappointment, its members continued to look toward the future. Unwilling to let a major setback derail their cause and their plans, they turned their gaze toward Sanand and never looked back. A truly resilient company has the ability to bounce back in the face of crisis. When it can't bounce back, it loses its relevance and ultimately dies an untimely death. That's what happened to Maytag.

Resilience also comes from not attaching yourself to the success or failure of a project too closely. Nanovators are certainly passionate about the projects they pursue, but they don't let the success or failure of those projects define them as human beings. In other words, they aren't weighed down by guilt and shame when they don't succeed. Instead, Nanovators draw meaning from failure by applying the lessons it teaches to grow and get better. That's what happened to TACO IPD.

 "Remember the two benefits of failure. First, if you do fail, you learn what doesn't work; and second, the failure gives you the opportunity to try a new approach."
Roger Von Oech

Even as we get ready to go to press in early 2011, Tata motors and Team Nano are being challenged with new opportunities to "learn on the fly" and bounce back stronger. For example, between the spring and summer of 2010, three cars caught fire due to different causes. But as one would expect from the Tatas, they didn't run from the issue; they jumped on it and immediately investigated it. Then they publicly reported what they found.

When the first car fire occurred in Mumbai, one of the most senior communications people in the company, Debasis Ray, was on-site before the fire was put out. He was there with other executives and engineers to try to figure out what went wrong, keep the public informed, and take care of the disappointed owner.

Tata Motors immediately assembled a twenty-member technical investigative team and an independent forensic expert from the U.K. to conduct an internal probe.

It turns out that one of the fire incidents was attributed to the remnants of a foreign object on the hot exhaust system, another was due to foreign electrical equipment installed on the exhaust, while the third incident was due to a ruptured fuel line. The investigation report said the three incidents were isolated and unrelated, and cleared the Nano of any manufacturing defects.

What is Tata Motors doing to bounce back after these sporadic incidents? First, the company has provided additional protection for the electrical and exhaust systems. It has installed a fuse to prevent a short circuit in the wiring and a noninflammable cover for the exhaust system. While the company's customer satisfaction studies show that 85 percent of current Tata Nano owners are very satisfied with the car, it has instituted a four-year or 37,000-mile manufacturer's warranty, at no extra cost. The warranty extends to existing Nano owners as well. Finally, the company has also launched a new comprehensive program that will help customers take care of the running maintenance of the car—for $2 per month.

Tata Motors has also been challenged with declining sales for four consecutive months in the last quarter of 2010. Some writers have speculated that the fire incidents have thrown a wet blanket on people's interest. While that may be a factor in why sales have dipped, there is a bigger issue at hand. We think the decline in sales might have more to do with a learning curve that comes with breakthrough innovation. When you are engaged in the untried, unproven, and unknown there is a lot of room for error.

Put yourself in the shoes of Tata Motors and think about all of the challenges revealed in this story: You are tapping into a new market with a radically new product, disrupted by political upheaval, disassembling a mother plant, moving it all the way across the country and reassembling it again, and trying to meet demand by ramping up production in two interim facilities—all at the same time. Is it really possible to account for everything?

"If things seem under control, you are just not going fast enough."
Mario Andretti

When you are doing something new and unprecedented, there are many things you would do differently in retrospect. For example, you might use different communication channels to appeal to various market segments. Social media is fertile ground for young students buying their first car. They are the most connected generation in the world. When something goes virtual with this target audience the masses know about it in a heartbeat. The world already knows about the Nano, but what if word spread that students are buying Nanos because it conveys a sense of being "hip" and a sense of Indian pride and ingenuity? That's only one communication channel. But what about the people at the bottom of the pyramid who aren't online and don't watch television or those who are intimidated by dealerships, financing, and negotiation? Buying a new car is a huge commitment for them.

Perhaps Team Nano didn't fully account for the complexity of marketing a passenger car to potential customers who never dreamed they could afford a car and who have never been through the car-buying process. Initially, 75 percent of the cars were sold in five major cities across India and 50 percent of those sales were to people who bought the Nano as a second car. And then there is the exclusivity factor. People still think the Nano is difficult to obtain given the media's widespread attention to relocating the mother plant and the Nano's limited production. What is Tata Motors doing to bounce back?

First, the company is redoubling its efforts to make financing the car easy. Tata Motors Finance offers a loan of up to 90 percent with a great interest rate—in just forty-eight hours—even for applicants with unclear documentation (a significant problem for people at the bottom of the pyramid). You might be asking, "What about the credit risk?" The company deployed a similar strategy when it launched the ACE truck and found that the default rate was negligible. It expects a similar response with the Nano. Tata Motors is also working with twenty-nine banks and nonbanking finance companies that aren't used to providing loans for people who don't have a regular salary slip. The goal here is to help these lenders become more comfortable casting a wider net by helping them deal with the risk profile of the Nano buyer.

Second, the company is increasing "hands-on" exposure to the Nano out in the rural areas where a massive percentage of its target market lives. These potential buyers need to see and feel and experience the car with people who can relate to them. What if you could go to the bazaar and learn about the Nano or talk to someone from an adjacent village who owns one? What if that person could tell you how Tata Motors helped them walk through the financing process step-by-step? Through five hundred new "Touch Points" (small sales outlets) and new training for salespeople Tata Motors is expanding its reach in city suburbs and remote villages uncovered by traditional dealer showrooms.

Third, Tata Motors has started a creative new television advertising campaign. One commercial shows a little girl in a small town, looking down the road through a pair of binoculars and asking her grandmother over and over again, "When will it arrive?" Finally, after navigating mountainous terrain, narrow roads, and compliments from admirers, the yellow Nano arrives. The little girl hugs the car as the neighbors file out of their homes and press in to get a closer look.

Tata Motors is aggressively working on all of these fronts. If the company showed us anything during the tumultuous move from Singur

(Tata Motors)

to Sanand, it was that Tata Motors knows how to learn quickly and then move with speed and agility. Remember, this was the company that dismantled, moved, and rebuilt an entire mother plant in fourteen months. And the aggressive moves appear to be paying off. Nano sales were up 60 percent in December 2010 and 68 percent in January 2011. In fact, more than two hundred Nanos were sold each day in January.

The Tatas, and particularly Tata Motors, have demonstrated the humility and tenacity to endure through tough times. Certainly, the Nano has hit some speed bumps. But Team Nano is digging deep and figuring out these issues. There is simply, and factually, too much historical evidence demonstrating this Group's ability to correct and bounce back. Success and failure are not end points. Success is something you earn again and again, and failure is an opportunity to begin again. If Tata Motors continues to learn from these things that have gone wrong and responds quickly, it will come back even stronger.

NANOBITE

Tata Motors created an environment where Team Nano never had to fear failure. It gave everyone the freedom to think openly, take risks, and leverage creativity.

Failure can become one of your company's strategic weapons when viewed as an opportunity to learn faster instead of a punishable offense.

The Tata Group has a Dare to Try award, and BMW has a "Creative Error of the Month" award. These high-profile awards are designed to redefine failure and remove the stigma from taking risks.

Here are a few suggestions for stepping through fear when you are faced with taking a risk:

- Stay focused on the bigger *yes*, the cause for which you fight.
- Remember that you will never know what you are capable of unless you push the boundaries and test the limits of what you think you can achieve.
- Don't wait for a guarantee—there are no guarantees.
- Rethink what it means to fail; failure builds resilience, exposes blind spots, broadens your perspective, and moves you closer to a solution.
- Stop getting ready, and make something happen—now.

QUESTIONS

- When was the last time you rewarded someone for an intelligent failure?
- When was the last time you challenged someone to think bigger?
- How many people in your organization are playing it safe right now and working on things that, five years from now, no one will really care about?

A WORD ABOUT THE RULES

"Civilization had too many rules for me, so I did my best to rewrite them."
Bill Cosby

If we are honest with ourselves, thousands of things drive Nanovation and make a project like the People's Car possible. These eight rules are certainly not comprehensive. Thankfully there are many books, written by thought leaders far more insightful and competent than we are, that you can add to your list. Nevertheless, we are absolutely convinced that if you ignore these eight ideas, your Nanovation is doomed.

Creating a culture that drives Nanovation is messy and multi-faceted. If the Nano project and the Tata Group have taught us anything, it is that you can't change culture by focusing on culture. It's not a program. You can't buy culture off the shelf. As we've said, personal change almost always precedes organizational change.

You create a culture of Nanovation by changing the way people think and by inviting them to join a conversation that changes the way they talk about things. Eventually a new language emerges within the organization, and people are inspired to reevaluate how they do things. The by-product of these changes is a culture where Nanovation becomes a way of life.

Part Four
The Nanovation Effect

Any intelligent fool can make things bigger, more complex, and more violent. It takes a touch of genius—and a lot of courage—to move in the opposite direction.

ALBERT EINSTEIN

The story of Nanovation doesn't end with the delivery of the Nano to the first buyers. That's just the beginning. Before the first fifty thousand Nanos hit the street, Team Nano was already making announcements of new developments: a Nano designed for Europe, a diesel Nano. There were rumors of a hybrid Nano. And then there were rumors of line extensions, like a Nano van or a Nano pickup. There was every possibility that a Nano—probably an entirely new design—would be headed for the North American market.

But Nanovation—and this book—is about much more than the

creation of safe, affordable transportation. It's about a diverse and far-reaching movement in business and design that we believe will radically change the way we think about products and the companies that make them.

We call it the Nanovation Effect.

THIRTY-ONE
The Nanovation Effect

The way to build a complex system that works is
to build it from very simple systems that work.

KEVIN KELLY

Imagine what you and your company could do if you could develop
one of the following breakthrough ideas.

- A water purifier an Asian or African villager can afford
- A $100 laptop computer
- A prosthetic knee for $20
- A modern apartment that costs just $8,000
- A handheld ultrasound device for rural clinics in China
- A $1,000 electrocardiogram for use in Indian villages
- A process that turns nonbiodegradable plastic trash into
  indestructible road surfaces

Do these seem like tough assignments? They're already on the market as the result of Nanovation. These are just a few of the stories we see on the first wave of Nanovation, and we'll explore some of them shortly. But again, they're just part of the story. The wave is even bigger than that.

When manufacturers and designers discover they can use Nanovation to reduce product costs by an order of magnitude and still deliver most of the original performance, how many ways will that disrupt the status quo?

When business leaders discover they can use Nanovation to deliver levels of customer-centric innovation that are literally off the scale; when they can use the Nanovation principles to realign their company, build customer loyalty and employee engagement, and dramatically disrupt their industry, how will that tilt the playing field to unimagined angles?

When manufacturers around the world discover they can not only build and assemble their products for less in Asia but also radically reimagine products and processes there; when they discover that they can take innovative cost-saving products designed for the bottom of the pyramid and repurpose them to serve the top of the pyramid, how will that change market fundamentals in the world's wealthiest countries?

To use a famous malapropism, Nanovation opens up a whole new box of Pandoras from which anything may emerge. It's that big a shift in thinking.

Some say that part of Albert Einstein's incredible genius was his ability to explain enormously complex ideas in simple terms. Maybe, but we suggest his secret was, well, simpler than that. We propose that genius is the ability to see the underlying principles of the complex and chaotic universe in simple terms and, having seen them, to synthesize them into the vernacular of a discipline that can be easily understood by others.

When Einstein says, "If you can't explain something simply, you don't understand it well enough," he's saying that most of us operate from an incomplete view of the situation and a partial set of facts. We make life complicated because we don't understand it. We make products that are overproduced and overpriced because we don't think we have any other option.

The competition said they couldn't build a Nano. Then, when the car was shown to the world, they said they didn't know how to make one. They said they couldn't make a car that inexpensive without sacrificing something. From their distant vantage point, a car was just a bag of parts and a zero-sum game. Parts cost what parts costs, and the only way to reduce costs was to reduce parts. They couldn't—and perhaps still can't—conceive of a world in which you can take 80 percent of the cost out of a critical subsystem and have it run as well or better than it did before.

But Ratan Tata and Team Nano *could* envision that. And their genius, in the case of the Nano and of Nanovation, was to see a problem clearly, to express it effectively, and to enroll others in a search for a solution.

The solution was simplicity itself.

Literally the innovative secret behind the Nano was the dramatic application of simplicity. In a world of chaotic complexity, radical simplicity can be a powerful force for change.

Southwest Airlines disrupted the whole airline industry with an extremely simple business model. It built a core competence where no one else was—the short-haul, frequent-flying, noninterlining (not connecting with other carriers) traveler.

Southwest flies only one type of aircraft. Cockpit configurations are similar, so pilots spend less time orienting themselves to a new cockpit and more time greeting customers in the Jetway or helping ground crews load bags. Maintenance crews use the same parts to service the same kind of aircraft, and flight crews are trained on the safety procedures of only one type of cabin. Flying the same aircraft lowers costs by promoting economies of scale, increases speed, improves service, and raises the level of safety.

It works because they keep it simple.

The problem is, as Team Nano demonstrated, simple isn't easy. But simple is worth the effort because the results of elegant, low-cost design are profound. After generations of making things bigger, heavier, hungrier, and more powerful—*because we could*—we're beginning to move the pendulum in the other direction—*because we don't have to.*

We don't have to have the biggest houses or the most humongous cars. We've moved from ostentatious boom boxes on our shoulders to simple and discreet iPods in our pockets. Sure, there will always be individuals who want to shout, "Look at me!" But we believe culture is passing them by. We believe a new culture is emerging that values quality more than luxury, practicality more than prestige, and efficiency more than extravagance.

In automotive terms, the horsepower wars are over. The smart wars are beginning.

In housing terms, the McMansion boom is over. The smart, sustainable, human-scale design movement is starting.

In technological disciplines of all kinds, the move is away from feature creep and supercomplexity and back to elegance.

That doesn't mean that our cars will be less comfortable or less fun to drive; that our homes will be less inviting and less family friendly; that the galaxy of electronic helpmates in which we orbit will be less interesting and useful. Not at all. But they will be greener, better thought out, and more effective.

It also does not mean that all humans will suddenly become smarter and make better decisions as leaders and managers. But it does mean that someone has moved the game forward and millions of the world's brightest minds have taken note.

> Nanovation opens up a whole new box of Pandoras from which anything may emerge. It's that big a shift in thinking.

Nanovation opens up a whole new box of Pandoras from which anything may emerge. It's that big a shift in thinking.

Just ask Jeffrey Immelt of General Electric. The company is in the process of disrupting its business model because GE's leaders see the wave coming. Writing in the *Harvard Business Review*, Immelt was blunt: if GE is to survive, it will need to become a master at developing low-cost innovations in India and China—innovations that knock current price-to-performance paradigms off their foundations—and then bring those innovations back to serve markets in developed countries. If it doesn't, the emerging giants in Asia—like the Tata Group—will pull the rug out from under GE's established market dominance. Not just in Asia, but back home, too.

Remember that Immelt was an honorary member of Team Nano as early as 2003, working with Ratan Tata on ideas of plastic construction. He's been thinking like a Nanovator ever since and working to bring his company along.

THE NEXT BIG THING: REVERSE INNOVATION

The way Immelt explains the change is this: for a couple of centuries, companies in the developed, industrialized nations took their products and adapted them for emerging markets. Immelt calls this process *glocalization*, adapting global products for local applications, and it was a nice business as long as the developed markets were the main show and the emerging markets provided incremental income.

But with the emergence of India and China in the last decade, that model can no longer stand alone. Now those markets are the growth opportunities while the developed markets are slowing down. And as those markets take existing technology and adapt it in innovative—*Nanovative*—ways, the balance of innovative power shifts.

As Jeffrey Immelt and GE see it, glocalization is being challenged by what they call *reverse innovation*: developing products in emerging markets—products that dramatically redefine the price-to-performance paradigm by delivering, say, 50 percent of the performance at 15 percent of the price—and then bringing those less-expensive but superuseful products back to the home market.

Case in point: GE's Healthcare group built a global business in ultrasound technology, selling premium products at premium prices to hospitals around the globe. In wealthy countries, performance mattered more than price, and so that's where GE Healthcare and its customers focused.

But the business failed to take off in Asia. The reason? Most of China's population relies on poorly funded local clinics in rural towns and villages, clinics that could never afford the $100,000-plus it costs to buy a large, immobile ultrasound appliance. And even if they could, most people who needed it would be too far away. For ultrasound to be relevant to most of the Chinese market, it needed to be inexpensive and portable.

> In the new price-to-performance paradigm, markets demand products that deliver 50 percent of the performance for 15 percent of the price.

In an earlier generation, GE leaders might have resisted investing in the development of a low-cost, low-margin device for China.

But in the new century, GE was learning to think small. The heads of the GE Healthcare team in China had the support of the global head of the ultrasound business; with his support, they got the go-ahead to develop a business around PC-based portable ultrasound and, by 2007, had the price down to just $15,000.

The resolution wasn't as fine as their top-of-the-line product, but it was plenty good enough for spotting problems with internal organs, such as enlargement or gallstones. And when sales started to take off, GE Healthcare had a nice little market in China.

But they soon discovered a bigger market. Suddenly emergency rooms, ambulance teams, and operating rooms in wealthy countries were clamoring for the portable ultrasounds, which they could use at the bedside or an accident site to check for ectopic pregnancies or fluid around the heart, or to place catheters. And the price? Compared to what was currently on the market, peanuts!

(General Electric)

Jeffrey Immelt shows off one of GE's newest Nanovations, the ultraportable ultrasound they call VScan.

In just six years, GE Healthcare built its portable ultrasound business from $4 million to more than $278 million as the market moved from China to the whole world.

Here's an interesting factoid: just as the Nano cost about 15 percent of a base model Volkswagen Golf, so the GE portable ultrasound costs about 15 percent of the company's standard nonportable model. And both deliver about half the performance of the big boys, but it's decent performance in the most usable zone and not the kind of performance one would miss the most.

"Innovation is invisible until it suddenly bursts into view."
Clive Thompson

And it just gets better: at the end of 2009, GE Healthcare announced an even more portable ultrasound device called the VScan. It looks like an iPod, it is battery operated, it includes voice recording for a doctor's notes, and it has presets for special uses such as cardiac testing. Even more portable and even less expensive, it sells for less than $10,000. By the time you read this, the cost may be down to $8,000!

Of course, you don't have to be Indian to create a breakthrough Nanovation. Anyone who's focused on a particular problem and committed to working through the cost constraints has the power to be a *Nanopreneur.*

Take the Jaipur Knee, invented by Stanford University engineering students Joel Sadler and Eric Thorsell. Sadler and Thorsell were challenged to design a low-cost artificial knee for the developing world. High-tech prosthetics, with their titanium joints, can cost $50,000 or more, but Sadler and his team produced one that's similar in design, but uses low-cost nylon polymer, for $20.

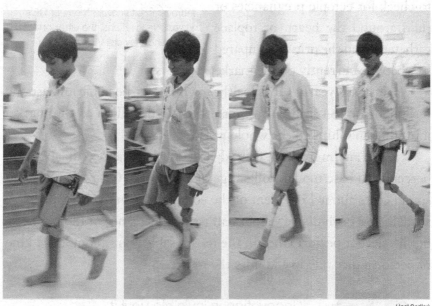

(Joel Sadler)

Now you can walk. For $20 (about Rs. 1,000) the Jaipur Knee got this boy going again. Nanovation is all about finding solutions to intractable problems, solutions that not only get the poorest people back on their feet but also pay big dividends in wealthy countries.

Stop for a moment and just think about that: $20 to put a kid back on his feet and get him on his way back to school, a child who might never have walked again if she had to rely on the current state of the art of Western technology. That's one small step for a kid in India, but it's one giant step for humankind when you consider, for instance, the millions of Americans who are uninsured and who would be unable to afford a $50,000 knee.

If you're a maker of titanium prostheses, this might be keeping you up at night. Or perhaps not. Even when we're looking for it, it's hard to see the future coming until it has actually passed us by.

Here's the big question: What product do you sell that someone could redesign to sell at 1/100th of what you sell it for?

Nothing? That's probably what the prosthetic knee makers said. Now they have three choices: ignore the Jaipur Knee and hope it doesn't come after them; hire lobbyists to support legislation to ban nylon polymer joints; or get into the game and become Nanovators. Our world depends on them choosing the third option. It's not just so that one company can be more successful; it's that the future of human evolution needs us to make this next step.

Here's an even bigger question: What if your company was the one to disrupt the price-to-performance paradigm? What if you were the Nanovators?

Reverse innovation is a paradigm shift of seismic proportions. As American companies remain obsessed with their stock valuations and quarterly earnings reports, they vacillate between being risk averse and trying anything they hope will work. But emerging giants in Asia are more willing to work toward breakthrough innovations, investing in the long run. And because their innovations tend to place a premium on cost-effectiveness—disrupting the price-to-performance status quo—they have the potential to blow away their global competition.

The $1,000 handheld electrocardiogram (ECG) that GE Healthcare developed in the Indian market is an example. The company used reverse innovation to develop a portable ECG device aimed at village clinics, the kind that Tata's CSR teams build everywhere they do business. It's great for a visiting nurse in India, but it's already finding global applications for emergency response teams and smaller clinics everywhere.

It's not that GE won't continue to adapt products sold in wealthy countries for sale in emerging markets. It will, where there's a good fit. At the same time, GE knows its future growth depends on its success at allowing innovation to rise in emerging markets so the company can adapt it for use in home markets. Because if it doesn't, someone else will. Remember what Tom Friedman said: "Whatever can be done will be done."

Tata is one emerging giant that GE is thinking about. With one hundred companies focused full-time on Nanovation, the Tata Group is rushing new ideas to market left and right, ideas that will be game changers.

Take the Tata Swach, a water purifier costing about Rs. 1,000 (about $21.50), which Tata launched at the end of 2009. Just two feet tall, the inexpensive blue-and-white Swach (the Hindi word for "clean") uses a combination of rice husk ash with nano particles of silver to clean up to eight hundred gallons of water, which is enough to last the average family for two hundred days. It uses no electricity and cost about half of the best-selling filter at the time of launch. Pour water from a river or pond in the top, and safely drink what comes out of the bottom. In a country where safe drinking water is in short supply—nearly 380,000 Indian children die each year from water-borne diseases—the Swach is one more lifesaver from Tata, and one more that was a personal project of the chairman.

"The quest is not to create the cheapest products," Ratan Tata told the press at the Swach launch. "Our focus is on reaching the largest number of people. That is what drove the Nano, that is what drove the low-cost housing project, and that is what is driving this, too."

Nanovation is focused on the needs of people and, through the application of technology to serve their needs, on the larger needs of society. In India, there is a profound need for simple and effective technology to improve the lives of the five hundred million people still living in subsistence or worse. Technology to give them access to education and information. Technology to allow them access to greater markets and opportunity. Technology to prolong the lives of children and enrich the lives of the elderly.

The low-cost housing that Ratan Tata mentioned above is one more example of Nanovation. In 2009, Tata Housing began offering apartment homes for sale in a suburban development outside Mumbai. They're new homes in a nicely landscaped park with good access to public transport (and plenty of room to park your Nano).

(Tata Housing)

At the Shubh Griha development in Boisar, a suburb of Mumbai, Tata Development offers affordable home ownership and plenty of Nano parking.

They have modern kitchens and bathrooms, and though they're small (from a 283-square-foot studio to a 465-square-foot one bedroom), they wouldn't be out of place in New York City. The price? Starting at $7,800.

Just as Indians emerging into the middle class need safe, dignified mobility, they also need safe, clean housing. Moving from shanties that lack the basic amenities of sanitation and indoor plumbing into a real apartment—and being able to buy the apartment and thus enter the real estate owning class—is a huge step for many Indian families. More than twelve hundred units are under construction in the first development, which, like the Nano, sold out so fast they had to hire security to manage the crowds lining up with down payments. And another three thousand units are planned.

(Tata Housing)

You'd pay a fortune for this floor plan in Manhattan or London, so for less than $10,000, no one is complaining about the size.

How do they get the apartments so cheap? Like the Nano, they simplify. Everything is good quality; it's durable and well designed. But it's simple and it's sound. Low-rise buildings cost less than high-rise buildings, the land is inexpensive, and the landowners agree to participate in postconstruction profits.

Tata is not the only Nanovator; there are Nanopreneurs everywhere in India.

ReaMetrix, in Bangalore, developed an HIV immune system monitoring test that cuts the cost by 80 percent. The company is exporting the product now to Africa and Latin America.

Tech-Nova Imaging developed a digital printing plate that takes 90 percent of the cost out of commercial printing.

Godrej, which builds popular kitchen appliances in India, has introduced a small refrigerator designed for village homes that sells at one-third the price of a standard fridge.

Videocon, another appliance maker, introduced a washing machine that sells for only $66. Its sells well because it understands the user experience: it's designed to pick up where it stopped when the power goes off, a common occurrence in India.

K. K. Plastic Waste Management, in Bangalore, is an offshoot of a company that manufactures plastic bags. Over the years the company began to worry about the ecological impact of its business and then hit upon a solution: if plastics take one thousand years to biodegrade and are thus indestructible, why not use them to build things that *need* to be indestructible, like roads? The company patented a process using plastic trash to make polymerized bitumen for roads. We love this story because it takes two seemingly intractable problems—what to do with plastic waste that doesn't degrade and what to do about roads that decompose with use—and uses them to solve each other.

This is a great example of looking for combinations and connecting dots.

Their roads last 50 to 65 percent longer than traditional roads and also solve the problem of what to do with plastic bags, which were creating a massive problem, clogging public drains, and even causing the deaths of hundreds of the sacred cows that roam the streets of Bangalore.

As we've said before, a key definer of Nanovation is the focus on the users and their habits. One great example of a company that gets this is India's leading maker of denim jeans. It understood that while city dwellers were happy to buy off-the-rack clothes items, rural families were used to having clothes made at the village tailor and often for less than store-bought. So Arvind created the brand Ruf 'n Tuf, marketing denim jean kits not to consumers but to tailors. The kits included sewing machine attachments for the heavier cloth, patterns, and plenty of denim.

Within two months, Arvind sold more than a million kits, much to the delight of village teenagers.

Innovation in process is as important as innovation in product. No one has done more than Walmart to reinvent the way we think about distribution and logistical efficiency. The company taught the world to take costs out of the supply chain. Can India teach us to take even more cost out of the system?

Cummins says yes. It is an example of an American company that, like GE, understands the potential of innovation in emerging markets. For the Indian market, Cummins decided to reinvent the way it thought about distribution. It designed an innovative range of modular generators aimed at the lower end of the market and then asked local distributors and users which combinations of product sets and components worked best in different situations. In essence, the company made users part of the design process and learned from them how to make both the products and the distribution system more responsive to customer needs and customer price points.

WHAT HAPPENS WHEN NANOVATION GOES VIRAL?

As all the vendors on the Nano project converted from innovation and design mode to production mode and ramped up their factories to feed parts to the temporary production facility in Uttarakhand and then to the Nano plant in Sanand, they realized they had something valuable on their hands, something potentially even more valuable than their original contract with Tata Motors to supply the Nano.

They had the knowledge of how to Nanovate. They had cracked the code on ultrafunctional, ultraelegant, ultra-low-cost design.

Renault/Nissan have said they'll partner with Indian motorcycle maker Bajaj to create a car that will sell for even less than the Nano. Can they do it? Why not? They'll start with a host of vendors eager to build on what they've learned from their journey with Team Nano.

"We cannot make a cheaper car. We don't know how to make a 1 lakh car unless we sacrifice something."
Shinzo Nakanishi, managing director, Maruti Suzuki India Ltd.

Maruti Suzuki says it doesn't know how to do it, but even without trying, how much could these vendors help the company reduce the cost of the Maruti 800? How much could they help Suzuki reduce costs on its entire product line, including vehicles sold around the world?

What happens when Bosch goes back to its clients in Germany, Japan, or the U.S. and says, "We know how to take hundreds of dollars out of the cost of your ECUs"? What happens when Delphi, Visteon, TRW, Saint Gobain, or any of the other vendors go to their clients and say, "Let us show you how to save money"?

What happens when they go to all their customers and say, "Our products now cost half of what they did last year"?

What happens when the idea of simplicity in design gets out there and becomes a competitive advantage?

The horsepower wars are over. The smart wars are beginning.

You can already see it happening: Porsche, Mercedes, BMW, and Audi are making their cars more powerful by making them smarter and lighter. And where they're actually increasing horsepower, they're doing it with engines that are lighter and 15 to 30 percent more fuel efficient, with lower emissions.

In the next few years, you'll see the best car companies start to make important breakthroughs in "adding lightness," as Lotus's Colin Chapman used to say. Jaguar (owned by Tata) and Audi are making significant breakthroughs in aluminum construction. Mercedes recently offered journalists a proof of concept by putting a modern, light turbo diesel engine in the body of a twenty-year-old Mercedes 190, the precursor of the current C-Class. The result was faster than today's car and a riot to drive. The reason? It weighed 850 pounds less than the current car.

Along with lightness, the next frontier will be cost. In 2009, Volkswagen introduced the CC, an attractive luxury sedan that's similar in style, performance, and quality to a Mercedes E-Class but costs $20,000 less. Even in a tight market, it has been a great sales success, with volume increase month after month.

So, good for Volkswagen. But what happens if Mercedes, drawing from the Nanovation experience, can cut $10,000 or even $15,000 off the price of the E-Class, without any reduction in performance or legendary Mercedes quality? Some might say that would dilute the prestige of the Mercedes-Benz brand, but would it really? Or would the company just add value to the long list of reasons to respect the brand? How would Jaguar, BMW, Audi, and Cadillac respond? How would Volkswagen race to take costs out of the CC?

Wishful thinking? You bet! Who wouldn't wish for any of the products we enjoy to cost less while also becoming lighter, greener, safer, and more enjoyable to drive? That's the power of Nanovation, and that's why you—whatever business you're in—can't afford to ignore it.

Nanovation doesn't just benefit the emerging middle class, rising out of poverty around the world. It may also be the force that saves the middle class in the West from sinking back into poverty.

What if American, European, and Japanese companies have increased productivity per person about as far as it can go? What if Walmart and the companies that supply it have taken all the cost out of the supply chain that they can wring? What if the only way the average, hardworking person in Akron, Birmingham, or Cologne can stay even is that a wave of Nanovation starts taking costs out of product design? What if the only way a working mom in Sakai or Sydney can plan on a better life for her children is that the company she works for starts to Nanovate?

If you lead a company, how can you rethink the products and services you provide? How can you disrupt your market and your industry so that you change the game forever? How can you turn your focus toward what's good for society as much as what's good for stockholders?

How can you Nanovate? The world is waiting to see.

THE NANOVATION EFFECT: a *movement* of innovators asking, How can we do in our industry what Tata and others have done in their industries? How can we reduce our product and service costs by an order of magnitude and still deliver most of the desired performance? Imagine . . .

- A prosthetic knee for $20
- A portable ultrasound device for less than $10,000
- A modern apartment that costs just $8,000

QUESTIONS

Pull your most creative thinkers together with those who really have their thumbs on the pulse of the industry. Then ask, "Among our competitors, who is most likely to create the next example of the Nanovation Effect? How will this change our business? What company is out there, lurking, ready to sell our product for 1/100th of what we sell it for?"

What are the opportunities in your business for reverse innovation—to deliver a product with 50 percent of the performance at 15 percent of the price in another market and then bring it back home (think GE's portable ultrasound device)?

How can you use simplicity to reduce costs, increase speed, and improve service?

What seemingly intractable problems (plastic that doesn't degrade and roads that decompose) exist in your industry? Outside your industry? Do you have the capability to connect the dots and use these two problems to solve each other?

What would happen if you engaged your suppliers in a stretch project that, in turn, enabled them to offer more value to their other customers?

THIRTY-TWO

Now *You* Can, Too

Ask not what your country can do for you—
ask what you can do for your country.

JOHN F. KENNEDY

Early in this book, we told the story of John F. Kennedy's inspiring call to put a man on the moon and how it inspired Ratan Tata, then a college student at Cornell. But there was another inspiring call to action made by President Kennedy, and it was in the first words he spoke as president when he called young Americans to public service with the words, "Ask not what your country can do for you—ask what you can do for your country."

He inspired a generation of Americans—and a generation all around the world—to get involved in making a better world. The best minds in America flocked to government, social work, and psychology to be part of solving the world's problems. They registered voters in places where votes were denied because of race and studied law so they could fight for equality. And because they did, they made a better world.

And so this book offers a call to action: ask not what your company can do for you—ask what your company can do for the world.

When this photo of President Kennedy and his daughter, Caroline, was taken, he had only eighty-nine days to live. He used them trying to stop a war, improve education, get voting rights for minorities, improve the economy, and go sailing with his daughter. What can you and your company do in the next ninety days to improve the world you live and work in?

Ask not what your company can do for you—ask what your company can do for the world.

Nanovation doesn't ask you to stop taking care of business as usual. It asks you to use your business skills and resources for more than profit. It asks you to make a profit *and* make a better world. Can you do it? Team Nano did.

> The world is waiting for you to disrupt it because out of disruption comes evolution. The Model T, the Volkswagen, and the Nano all disrupted the automotive industry of their times, and each made it better.

Southwest Airlines disrupted the airline industry and made it more democratic, more efficient, and more customer focused. And on the preceding pages, we've offered many examples of Nanovators in India and around the world who are making their work a cause, who are turning that cause into a movement, who are starting revolutions in their industries by creating products, processes, and services that are nothing short of elegant and do more with less. They refuse to make apology products, and they demand a return on innovation.

Team Nano did something everyone else thought was impossible. Team members did it because they were as focused on the social impact of their work as they were on the bottom line. They were constrained by a financial limitation—a seemingly absurd selling price coupled with a requirement to make a margin—which forced innovations that might not have been achieved otherwise.

And it wasn't innovation that was confined to the drawing board, not just innovation in big ideas, but innovation at the nano level. Innovation that got everyone at Tata and every vendor digging deep to find an inventive and elegant way to whittle a little more weight and cost out of each part while simultaneously looking for a performance advantage.

Think what it was like over those five years of long days, working late, missing family events; think what it was like to drive home and see a family of four go by on a scooter, the dad wearing a helmet because the law requires it, the mom and kids holding on without helmets because they couldn't afford a helmet for everyone.

Think what it meant to watch them go by, unstoppable in their desire to see their kids get educated, to build a better life; think what it felt like to members of Team Nano as they watched the families and thought, *Hold on; we've got the answer coming. We can fix this problem.*

Yes, we can.

If there's one thing we want you to take away from reading *Nanovation*, it's that things that look impossible today often turn out to be very possible tomorrow. Flying was once thought to be an impossible dream, as was going to the moon. Carrying a phone in your pocket was an impossible dream; a phone with more computer power than the ship that went to the moon was inconceivable. One day, in 1954, it was physically impossible for a human being to run a mile in less than four minutes. And then, the next day, Roger Bannister did it. Things that seem impossible today have a way of becoming possible as we learn new ways to do things. But only if someone refuses to be stopped by the impossible.

"Things are only impossible until they're not."
Captain Picard, *Star Trek*

Throughout much of the twentieth century, whenever adventurers traveled to Tahiti, one of the first things they were told was that

The future is defined by what we put off until tomorrow.

there was no surf. The truth is, on the reef surrounding the island there was plenty of surf. It was just unridable until one day when it wasn't. It was dangerous, crazy, sick, and scary, but it wasn't unridable.

So what unridable wave will you spend your future surfing? You'll never know until the day you dive in the water.

"Any sufficiently advanced technology is indistinguishable from magic."
Arthur C. Clarke

Ratan Tata knew how incredibly difficult it would be to bring the 1 lakh car to life. There were times he, too, believed it might be impossible. But he and the team kept going. As they'd done when they faced a financial crisis and had to cut costs by 10 percent. As they'd done when they brought the innovative little Tata Ace to market. They kept going until they learned how to win big by thinking small.

They made a difference with Nanovation. Many people said they'd fail. Many people said they couldn't do it.

But they did. And now you can, too.

(Aryind Jain/Flickr)

"In a revolution, as in a novel, the most difficult part to invent is the end."
Alexis de Tocqueville

(Jorge Silva, Reuters)

Epilogue

We began with this photograph, and we'll end with it because it reminds us of everything that made us fall in love with India, with the Nano, and with the incredible success story of the Tata team. We love this picture because it tells the story of families using motorbikes for transport (three generations, in this case!), but it also tells the story of India.

The traditional grandfather is maybe a little unsure of where they're heading, but the parents are supremely confident of their lives. Look at the dad smiling into the camera and the joy on the mother's face. And then look at the intelligence in the eyes of the two daughters. They're unstoppable, and we need them to stay that way.

This picture represents the mission of Ratan Tata and Team

Nano: not just to get this family a safer form of transport but to get them access to the education and financial security they'll need to change the world. Because the world needs these girls. It needs their intelligence. And it needs their full participation in the conversation of the twenty-first century.

In the two and a half years we spent exploring this case study of Tata Motors and the Nano, we came across many ironies that we've shared in this book. Here's the final one: at the end of 2009, as we began writing this book, Harley-Davidson announced that it had just cleared trade negotiations to begin importing Harleys into India. Maybe someday the dad here, having got his family educated and into Nanos of their own, can buy himself a Harley to cruise the countryside just for fun.

But right now, he's not riding that motorbike because he's born to be wild. He's riding it because it's the best he can do and because his family has places to go.

As we said earlier, the future is defined by what we put off until tomorrow. Harnessing the intelligence of these girls and a billion other young people like them can't wait. What can you and your company do to engage them, to involve them in making a better world, to put them to work in transforming life on earth?

That's *our* story. We can't wait to hear *yours*.

Acknowledgments

W hat do we have? What do we do? What do we accomplish that hasn't in some significant way been influenced by the contributions of others? We are so very grateful to the people who, directly and indirectly, made Nanovation possible.

To Ratan Tata for having the courage to tackle a huge problem that will literally change people's lives. Entrepreneur, statesman, visionary, and patriarch of Indian business, the venerable chairman of the Tata Group is as interested as he is interesting. He cares deeply about the people of India and the future of his country. Ratan was not only extremely gracious with his time; he was also willing to share the vulnerabilities, reservations, and regrets that come with doing something everyone deems impossible. This of course, added to the richness of the story. Few people we know think as big, and act as bold, as often as Ratan.

To Ravi Kant for believing in this project and for opening the doors to Tata Motors and giving us unlimited access to the people, facilities, and internal documents needed to get our arms around this story. If Ratan is the dreamer behind the Nano, Ravi is the doer. Underneath his quiet and humble demeanor is a generative leader who knows how to inspire flawless execution and get it done. Ravi is a formidable competitor who exemplifies the Tata philosophy of "Never Say Die."

To Prakash Telang, Managing Director, Tata Motors, who helped us understand the complexities of the Nano project and the challenges of rallying a geographically diverse team to pull it off. Prakash is one of those guys who exudes confidence and competence, yet is self-effacing with a wonderful sense of humor. To Rajiv Dube, former President, Passenger Cars, for showing us how stretch assignments and Ratan Tata's deep-seated belief in incredibly young people was a game-changer in and of itself.

In the midst of the crises we describe in the book, everyone associated with the Nano project was willing to collaborate enthusiastically. As we mentioned, Girish Wagh, team leader, seemed to be everywhere at once all over India. For a guy with an incredible amount of weight on his shoulders Girish still took the time to sit down with us on numerous occasions to share his insights. He also ensured that every one of his more than 500 team members were accessible to recount their experiences. Collectively, Team Nano invested hundreds of hours putting up with our endless questions and trying to help us better understand how they did it. We are especially grateful to each and every team member listed at the end of these acknowledgments. They inspired us with their creativity, challenged us with their sheer determination and perseverance, and entertained us with their stories. Mostly, they expanded our vision of what's possible.

To Debasis Ray who was our main point of contact for everything. Tata Motors has one of the best Corporate Communications groups in the business. After working with Debasis we know why. Debasis helped us strategize about who we needed to talk to and where we needed to go to capture the Nano story. Then, he ensured that we were connected to the right people. To Arup Mukherjee who set up our interviews, dug up materials, and escorted us from one Tata facility to the next. Arup devoted days and weeks to traveling with us from one end of India to another. Arup is the ultimate "can do" guy. He never tired of hearing us ask, "Hey, Arup, can we meet...? Can we get...? Can we go to...?" He always found a way to meet our needs. It's simply a fact; a research project of this magnitude could never have been undertaken unless these two go-getters were willing to do whatever it takes.

While the Nano is indeed a "Small Wonder," we have our own small wonder in India. First and foremost a friend, Prakash Idnani represents the San Diego Consulting Group in the Asia Region. In many ways this book is as much Prakash's vision as it is ours. Prakash introduced us to Ravi Kant and the rest is history. They say that there are only six degrees of separation between you and any other person on Earth. With Prakash that number is usually two. That's because his boundless energy, unwavering optimism and fearless approach to getting things done make him a magnet for the shakers and movers of the world. We are so fortunate to have him on our team.

In capturing the Nano story it was important to get some perspectives from business leaders outside of Tata Motors. Thanks to the following executives who gave us their tremendous insights on innovation and what the success of the Nano means for business. Anup Banerji, Managing Director & Group Executive at the State Bank of India, H.M. Bangur, Managing Director at Shree Cement and the person who bought 1,000 Nanos as incentives for his employees, Bernd Bohr, Chairman Automotive Group at Robert Bosch and a key player in helping Team Nano radically reduce the cost of parts, Mahesh Chauhan, Group CEO at Tata Motor's advertising agency, Rediffusion DY&R, who help produce the spectacular unveiling of the Nano and the "Now You Can" campaign, Dilip Chenoy, Director General, Society of Automobile Manufacturers who graciously made it possible for us to interview other auto executives at the annual SIAM conference, Hemant Contractor, Managing Director & Group Executive at the State Bank of India, Jamshyd Godrej, Chairman & Managing Director at Godrej & Boyce Mfg, Brijmohan Lall, Chairman at Hero Honda Motors, Arun Maira, Member of the Indian government's Planning Commission, and Sandra Pupatello, Minister of Economic Development and Trade in Ontario Canada.

To our publisher, Joel Miller, for giving us a chance to work with a superlative team at Thomas Nelson. Joel has a way of being encouraging and provocative all at the same time, while driving a project like this to a more elegant place. Good editors are the unsung heroes behind any book worth reading. In our case, Heather Skelton made this book eminently more readable without compromising the integrity of what we wanted to convey. Heather is a great collaborator with a cheerful "can do" spirit—we love that! Our designer, Walter Petrie, truly stepped up to the plate when it came to the layout and design of the book. Kristen Vasgaard, our packaging manager, was responsible for the book cover. She patiently listened to our ideas and then uncapped a wellhead of creativity. Way to go crew! And, to the Thomas Nelson sales and marketing team, Dave Schroeder, Jennifer Womble, and Jason Jones, for giving the book visibility and successfully bringing it to market. Thank you all for being so competent.

To Patti Cipro, the dynamo who takes charge of our office—and we do mean *take charge*. She handles a dizzying array of responsibilities with sheer competence and enthusiasm. Patti is the "rock" we lean on everyday and everyday she rises to the occasion with the kind of "can do" spirit that most people only dream of having. To Trish Derho, whose wise counsel and willingness to step into the breach whenever and wherever needed have been invaluable to us. Thanks for your unflagging faith in us over many, many years. To Adam Richardson our multi-media guru, artist, designer and talented go-to guy for everything creative and technical. Adam is sometimes our most ardent critic, but always with the intent to take us to the next level.

It was Pascal who cautioned writers, when referring to their work, to say, "our book" instead of "my book" because so much of what we say belongs to others. He's right. There are many intellectual giants whose work shaped our interpretations about what we learned from the making of the Nano. James MacGregor Burns, Gary Hamel, Tom Peters, Ken Blanchard, John Gardner, Roy Spence, C.K. Prahalad, Jeff Immelt, Vijay Govindarajan, Bill George, Peter Skarzynski and Rowan Gibson, Nirmalya Kumar, Tom Kelly, and of course, Clayton Christensen.

In addition, others helped us sharpen our storytelling skills. In particular, Malcolm Gladwell, whose ability to synthesize parallel streams of thought into new, original ways of looking at the world challenged us to look deeper into the story. And Albert Einstein, from whom we took this single quote as our touchstone for every sentence: "If you can't explain it simply, you don't understand it well enough." That challenging thought forced us to question everything we thought we knew and every paragraph we wrote. These gifted thinkers have stretched and challenged us, and hopefully, you, our readers are the beneficiaries of their influence.

JACKIE AND KEVIN WOULD ESPECIALLY LIKE TO EXPRESS THEIR GRATITUDE TO:

Taylor-Grace, Aubrey Hope and Dylan Freiberg

Our children are magnificent—they challenge us, stretch us, add texture and richness to our lives, and remind us that the future will belong to them sooner rather than later. As any writer will confess, they also make huge sacrifices when we disappear to write. After four books they know the drill, but that doesn't make up for lost time with them. Thanks guys for your unselfish support. You are the reason we work so hard to put a dent in the universe.

DAIN WOULD ESPECIALLY LIKE TO THANK:

Jean Compton

Jean is my most enthusiastic believer, supporter and creative critic and our work on this book would have been impossible without her. Writing *Nanovation* took two years of concentrated time: concentrated time meant turning down other projects; turning down projects meant putting some dreams on hold. But Jean never faulted in her support and belief in what Kevin, Jackie and I were undertaking. She believed, as we do, that *Nanovation* is more than a book, that it's a mission toward building better companies, where people can find meaning in their work and in their lives. Jeanie, you're my soul mate and partner and I'll always be grateful for everything you do to help me be a better man.

Kevin and Jackie

Like a farm team player being called up to the major leagues, like Ronnie Wood being asked to play with the Rolling Stones, like an F1 driver being called to drive for Ferrari, being asked by a pair of best-selling authors to join them on the journey of their next book was a once in a lifetime offer. Their grace and generosity in opening their winning partnership to me, their support and enthusiasm for my work and their vision as guides, teachers and spiritual warriors helped me step up to the task at hand and not embarrass myself unnecessarily. In the end, I got more than a book out of this: I got a life-long friendship for which I will always be grateful.

Dr. Frank Allen

It takes a great coach to help a player succeed far beyond his own expectations, and Frank Allen is that coach for me. Like the Aikido master that he is, he teaches me how to wave away trouble. Like a great Zen master, he keeps me focused on the present moment. And like a river guide, he teaches me to channel the flow of life and love.

INTERVIEWEES

These are the storytellers* who made
Nanovation possible. Thank you!

- Abhyankar, Umesh L, Project Manager, Vehicle Systems Engineering Automation, Engineering Research Center, Tata Motors
- Agrawal, Dr. Rakesh , Divisional Manager - Health & CSR Small Car, Tata Motors
- Ambardekar, S N, Plant Head, Comercial Vehicle Business Unit – Pune, Tata Motors
- Balasubramoniam, E, Head Sourcing Small Car Project, Passenger Car Business Unit, Tata Motors
- Banerjee, Surya, Asst. Manager - Administration Small Car Division, Tata Motors
- Banerji, Anup, Dy. Managing Director & Group Executive – State Bank of India
- Bangur, H.M., Managing Director, Shree Cement
- Bannur, Santosh Virupaxi , Divisional Manager (Planning) Small Car, Tata Motors
- Bhandari, Shailesh J, Jt. Managing Director - B.U. Bhardari Auto Pvt. LTD - Tata Motors FIAT
- Bhaskar, D. Vudaya , Manager, Small Car Project / Punc
- Bohr, Bernd Dr. Chairman Automotive Group / Member Board of Management, Robert Bosh GmbH
- Bolar, Jai, Division Manager (Product Development), Engineering Research Centre, Tata Motors
- C, Anil Kumar, Project Manager, Vehicle Safety Systems, Tata Motors
- Chauhan, Mahesh, Group CEO, Rediffusion DY&R (Advertising Agency)

- Chenoy, Dilip, Director General, Society of Indian Automobile Manufacturers (SIAM)
- Chobe, Prasann K, Plant Head, Commercial Vehicle Business Unit—Pantnagar, Tata Motors
- Contractor, Hemant , Managing Director & Group Executive (Corporate Banking Group) – State Bank of India
- D Vudaya Bhaskar, Executive Assistant, Head Small Car Project, Tata Motors
- Damami, Anand S., Project Manager,Drivetrain System Technologies, Tata Motors
- Desai, Jaydeep M,, Assistant General Manager, Manufacturing (TCF & Paint) Small Car, Tata Motors
- Deshpande, Abhay M , Deputy General Manager, (Development) Engineering Research Centre, Tata Motors
- Rajiv Dube. President, Passenger Cars Business Unit, Tata Motors
- D Dutt, Garima Ms, Manager, Corporate Human Resources, Tata Motors
- Godrej, Jamshyd, Chairman & Managing Director, Godrej &Boyce Mfg. Co. Ltd
- Goel, Adiya, Rama Motors—Tata Motors Dealer
- Goel, Jagdish, Rama Motors—Tata Motors Dealer
- Gosavi, Swapnil Satish, Sennior Manager (NPI), Small Car, Tata Motors
- Gupta, Dr. Surojit Mohan, Deputy Director, Society of Indian Automobile Manufacturers (SIAM)
- Hudson, David, Head NVH (Noise,Vibration,Analysis), Engineering Research Centre, Tata Motors
- Jadhav, Nikhil Atmaram, Industrial Designer (ERC Styling Studio), Tata Technologies
- Jain, Narendra Kumar, Deputy General Manager (Engines) Engineering Research Centre, Tata Motors

- Johny, Sam, Divisional Manager (Planning), Small Car, Tata Motors
- Joshi, Ravindra, Customer, Retired Water Works Engineer, Mumbai
- Kant, Ravi, Vice Chairman, Tata Motors
- Karyakarte, Sandeep, Project Manager, (ERC Styling Studio), Tata Technologies
- Katkar, V, Project Manager (Computer Aided Engineering), Tata Technologies
- Kulkarni, Vinod, Assistant General Manager, Corporate Sustainability, Tata Motors
- Kumar, Narendra, Deputy General Manager (Engines), Engineering Research Centre, Tata Motors
- Maira, Arun, Member of Planning Commission, Government of India
- Mankad, AM, Plant Head, Passenger Car Business Unit— Pune, Tata Motors
- Mirasdar, Keshav Krishna, Deputy General Manager (Proto Manufacturing) Engineering Research Centre, Tata Motors
- Mital, Rakesh, Assistant General Manager (Vendor Development), Small Car, Tata Motors
- Mukherjee, Arup, Assistant General Manager, Corporate Communications, Tata Motors
- Munjal, Brijmohan, Lall, Chairman, Hero Honda Motors LTD
- Nagbhushan, Gubbi Ramaswamiah, Head Engineering (Passenger Cars), Engineering Research Centre, Tata Motors
- Paralkar, M B, Consultant Advisor, Corporate Sustainability, Tata Motors
- Parekh, B.B., Chief Strategic Sourcing, Tata Motors

- Parikh, Jigar, Student, Among first Nano customers
- Patil, Sudhir, Senior Manager (NPI), Small Car, Tata Motors
- Phadke, Prasad Shridhar, Executive Officer, Head (Tata Motors Tech Centre), Engineering Research Centre, Tata Motors
- Pupatello, Sandra, Minister of Economic Development and Trade, Ontario Canada
- Rajhans, R G, Program Manager (Body Systems Engineering & Design), Tata Technologies
- Renavikar, Atul P, Deputy General Manager, (Auto Production) Engineering & Gear Aggregates, Tata Motors
- Seth, Nitin, Head - Car Product Group, Passenger Car Business Unit, Tata Motors
- Sinha, Sunil, Chief Executive Officer, Tata Quality Management Services
- Sorabjee, Hormazd, Editor, AUTOCAR India
- Tata, Ratan, Chairman, Tata Group Ltd
- Telang, Prakash, Managing Director, Tata Motors
- Vaidya, Rohit, Project Manager (Computer Aided Engineering), Tata Technologies
- Vichare, A.R. - First Nano Delivery Customer
- Vishwakarma, Ramesh, Head Manufacturing (Sanand Plant), Small Car, Tata Motors
- Wagh, Girish, Head Small Car Project, Tata Motors
- Wagh, Sachin, Senior Manager (Development) Engineering Research Centre, Tata Motors
- Wasan, Kasturilal, Managing Director, Wasan Motors Limited

About the Authors

DRS. JACKIE AND KEVIN FREIBERG speak, write, and consult on the unconventional practices of globally admired leaders who radically differentiate themselves. As authors of the international bestseller *NUTS! Southwest Airlines' Crazy Recipe for Business and Personal Success*, the Freibergs are ranked among the world's most influential speakers on innovation, culture, leadership, and service. They are the founders of San Diego Consulting Group, Inc. and freibergs.com, two global firms advising and equipping leaders for a world of change. Both PhDs, Jackie and Kevin speak globally as well as teach leadership seminars at the University of San Diego, School of Leadership and Education Sciences. They are the coauthors of *GUTS!* and *BOOM!* Jackie and Kevin can be reached at **freibergs.com**.

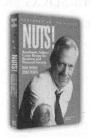  

DAIN DUNSTON helps some of the world's smartest companies build cultures of innovation. For more than twenty-five years, he's coached leaders on how to communicate with their people to build teams that are branded to the bone. Dain has worked with leaders in many of the world's top automotive, high-tech, health care, retail, and hospitality companies—IBM, Lilly, Bayer, Office Depot, Sherwin-Williams, Carlson, BMW, and Audi—helping them link purpose to performance, inspiring game-changing breakthroughs and building great brands. While Dain works closely with SDCG and freibergs. com, he can also be reached at **daindunston.com**.

THE SAN DIEGO CONSULTING
GROUP WORKS WITH CLIENTS
ALL OVER THE WORLD
TO CREATE.

BEST PLACES THAT ATTRACT
BEST PEOPLE WHO CAN DO
BEST WORK TO CREATE A
BETTER WORLD!

TO LEARN MORE ABOUT OUR:

- KEYNOTES, SEMINARS,
- EXECUTIVE COACHING AND
- INNOVATION BOOT CAMP

VISIT US AT:

WWW.NANOVATIONBOOK.COM

WANT TO START A
REVOLUTION
THAT DISRUPTS YOUR INDUSTRY?
LET'S GO!!

Index

523

education, 229–230, 246, 297
Einstein, Albert, 124, 457, 482–483
either-or thinking, avoiding, 431–432
electrocardiogram, handheld, 490
elegance, 149–164, 168, 218
    and simplicity, 165
emerging countries
    product development, 486
    road fatalities, 108
emissions, 169
emotional equity, return on, 196–199
employability, 230, 246, 298–299
employees
    creative potential, 383
    dignity, 68–69
    dreams of, 113
    empowerment, 290–291
    family moves, 283–284
    safety in Singur, 263–266, 268–269
    schedule flexibility, 381
empowerment, 290–291
energy sources, 191
engagement, 196–199
engine, 169, 409
engine shop in car factory, 252
entrepreneurial philanthropy, 19–20
entrepreneurs, 299, 387–390
environment, 228–229
    sustainability, 140–141
    tree plantation, 299
    in West Bengal, 246
equipment, transporting to Sanand, 289–290
experimentation, benefits of low-tech,
    166–168

F
failure, 468
    award for, 394–395
    meaning from, 472
    motivation and, 93–94
    as opportunity, 95, 476
    and success, 64
family on scooter, 6–8
farm productivity, 299

fear, facing, 462–463
feature creep, 174
Federal Aviation Administration (FAA), 171
Ferrari, 25
Fiat, 351
Ficosa, 54
Financial Times, 64, 126, 216
financing, 474–475
flooding, of West Bengal construction
    site, 249–251
focus, 155–159, 178, 344–345, 406
Ford
    Aspire, 178
    Model T, 103, 162, 214
    Mustang, 319
Fortune, 222
Frankl, Victor, 125
Friedman, Thomas, 34, 490
fuel economy, 169, 326, 328
fuel injection system, 154–155
future, focus on, 406

G
Galvin, Robert, 456
Gandhi, Mohandas, 18, 30, 144, 225
Gardner, Howard, *Leading Minds: An
    Anatomy of Leadership*, 359
gasoline. *See* fuel economy
GE Healthcare group, 486–488, 490
GE Plastics Technology Center, 52
Gell-Mann, Murray, 150
GEM (Chrysler), 48
Genentech, 380
General Motors, 141, 185, 450
generativity, 23–24
Geneva Motor Show, 29–30, 217
genius, 482
George, Anil, 469
George, Bill, *Authentic Leadership*, 428
getting wired
    authenticity, 336–337
    humility, 337–340
    integrity, 334–336
    positive disruption, 340–343